The First Letter of Peter

The First Letter of Peter

A Commentary on the Greek Text

Reinhard Feldmeier

Translated from the German by Peter H. Davids

BAYLOR UNIVERSITY PRESS

Front Cover Design by Hannah Feldmeier; Full Cover Design by David Alcorn
Book Design by Diane Smith

Translation of the original German edition by Reinhard Feldmeier: *Der erste Brief des Petrus*. Theologischer Handkommentar 15/I. © 2005 by Evangelische Verlagsanstalt GmbH, Leipzig. This translation is authorized by Evangelische Verlagsanstalt.

Library of Congress Cataloging-in-Publication Data

Feldmeier, Reinhard.
[Der erste Brief des Petrus. English]
The first letter of Peter : a commentary of the Greek text / Reinhard Feldmeier ; translated from German by Peter H. Davids.
p. cm.
Includes bibliographical references and index.
ISBN 978-1-60258-024-4 (pbk. : alk. paper)
1. Bible. N.T. Peter, 1st--Commentaries. 2. Bible. N.T. Peter, 1st--Criticism, interpretation, etc. I. Title.

BS2795.53.F4513 2008
227'.92077--dc22

2007046039

Printed in the United States of America on acid-free paper with a minimum of 30% pcw recycled content.

Dedication

Renate and Karlheinz Bierlein
Sigrid and Martin Wemmelund
amicis nobiscum peregrinantibus

Contents

Part II
Exegesis

Abbreviations

1. Canonical Scriptures: Old and New Testament

Gen	Genesis
Exod	Exodus
Lev	Leviticus
Num	Numbers
Deut	Deuteronomy
Josh	Joshua
Judg	Judges
Ruth	Ruth
1 Sam (1 Kgdms)	1 Samuel (LXX: 1 Kingdoms)
2 Sam (2 Kgdms)	2 Samuel (LXX: 2 Kingdoms)
1 Kgs (3 Kgdms)	1 Kings (LXX: 3 Kingdoms)
2 Kgs (4 Kgdms)	2 Kings (LXX: 4 Kingdoms)
1 Chr	1 Chronicles
2 Chr	2 Chronicles
Ezra	Ezra (LXX: 1 Ezra)
Neh	Nehemiah (LXX: 2 Ezra 11–23)
Esth	Esther
Job	Job
Pss	Psalms
Prov	Proverbs (Proverbs of Solomon)
Qoh	Ecclesiastes/Qoheleth (Preaching of Solomon)
Cant	Canticles (Song of Solomon)
Isa	Isaiah

Jer	Jeremiah
Lam	Lamentations (Lamentations of Jeremiah)
Ezek	Ezekiel
Dan	Daniel
Hos	Hosea
Joel	Joel
Amos	Amos
Obad	Obadiah
Jonah	Jonah
Mic	Micah
Nah	Nahum
Hab	Habakkuk
Zeph	Zephaniah
Hag	Haggai
Zech	Zechariah
Mal	Malachi
Matt	Matthew
Mark	Mark
Luke	Luke
John	John
Acts	Acts of the Apostles
Rom	Romans
1 Cor	1 Corinthians
2 Cor	2 Corinthians
Gal	Galatians
Eph	Ephesians
Phil	Philippians
Col	Colossians
1 Thess	1 Thessalonians
2 Thess	2 Thessalonians
1 Tim	1 Timothy
2 Tim	2 Timothy
Titus	Titus
Phlm	Philemon
Heb	Hebrews
Jas	James
1 Pet	1 Peter
2 Pet	2 Peter
1 John	1 John
2 John	2 John

3 John	3 John
Jude	Jude
Rev	Apocalypse/Revelation of John

2. Apocrypha (OT)

Bar	1 Baruch
Jdt	Judith
1 Macc	1 Maccabees
2 Macc	2 Maccabees
Sir	Jesus Sirach (Wisdom of Jesus ben Sirach)
Tob	Tobit
Wis	Wisdom of Solomon (Sapientia Solomonis)

3. Parabiblical Literature (so-called Pseudepigrapha)

Apoc. Mos.	*Apocalypse of Moses*, ed./trans. J. Dochhorn
Aris. Ep.	*Letter of Aristeas*, trans. N. Meisner
Ascen. Isa.	*Ascension of Isaiah*, ed. P. Bettiolo
2 Bar.	*2 Baruch (Syriac Apocalypse)*, trans. A. F. J. Klijn
3 Bar.	*3 Baruch (Greek Apocalypse)*, ed. J. C. Picard
4 Bar.	*4 Baruch (Paraleipomena Jeremiou)*, ed. R. A. Kraft/A. E. Purintun; trans. B. Schaller
Ep. Jer.	*Letter of Jeremiah LXX Bar 6 in Vulg/Luther*, ed. J. Ziegler
4 Ezra	*4 Ezra*, ed. R. Weber; trans. J. Schreiner
1 En.	*1 Enoch (Ethiopic Apocalypse)*, trans. S. Uhlig
2 En.	*2 Enoch (Slavonic Enoch)*, trans. Ch. Böttrich
3 En.	*3 Enoch (Hebrew Enoch)*, trans. H. Hoffmann
Jos. Asen.	*Joseph and Aseneth*, ed. Ch. Burchard, trans. Ch. Burchard

Jub.	*Jubilees*, trans. K. Berger
3 Macc.	*3 Maccabees*, ed. A. Rahlfs
4 Macc.	*4 Maccabees*, ed. A. Rahlfs, trans. H.-J. Klauck
Odes Sol.	*Odes of Solomon*, ed. H. Charlesworth
Pss. Sol.	*Psalms of Solomon*, trans. S. Holm-Nielsen
T. Job	*Testament of Job*, ed. S. P. Brock, trans. B. Schaller
T. 12 Patr.	*Testaments of the Twelve Patriarchs*, ed. M. de Jonge; trans. J. Becker
T. Benj.	*Testament of Benjamin*
T. Dan.	*Testament of Dan*
T. Gad	*Testament of Gad*
T. Iss.	*Testament of Issachar*
T. Lev.	*Testament of Levi*
T. Reu.	*Testament of Ruben*

4. Pseudo-Hellenistic Authors

Sib	Sibylline Oracles (Oracula Sibyllina), ed. J. Geffcken; trans. H. Merkel

5. Jewish-Hellenistic Authors

Philo	Philo
Abr.	*De Abrahamo*, ed. Cohn-Wendland IV; trans. J. Cohn
Agr.	*De Agricultura*, ed. Cohn-Wendland II; trans. I. Heinemann
Cher.	*De Cherubim*, ed. Cohn-Wendland I; trans. L. Cohn
Conf.	*De Confusione Linguarum*, ed. Cohn-Wendland II; trans. E. Stein
Congr.	*De Congressu Eruditionis Gratia*; ed. Cohn-Wendland III; trans. H. Lewy
Contempl.	*De Vita Contemplativa*, ed. Cohn-Wendland VI, trans. K. Bormann
Decal.	*De Decalogo*, ed. Cohn-Wendland IV; trans. L. Treitel

Det.	*Quod Deterius Potiori Insidiari Soleat*, ed. Cohn-Wendland I; trans. H. Leisegang
Deus	*Quod Deus sit Immutabilis*, ed. Cohn-Wendland II; trans. H. Leisegang
Ebr.	*De Ebrietate*, ed. Cohn-Wendland II; trans. M. Adler
Fug.	*De Fuga et Inventione*, ed. Cohn-Wendland III; trans. M. Adler
Her.	*Quis rerum divinarum heres sit*, ed. Cohn-Wendlaud I; trans. H. Leisegang
Gig.	*De Gigantibus*, ed. Cohn-Wendland II; trans. H. Leisegang
Ios.	*De Iosepho*, ed. Cohn-Wendland IV; trans. L. Cohn
Leg. 1, 2, 3	*Legum allegoriae I, II, III*, ed. Cohn-Wendland I; trans. I. Heinemann
Legat.	*Legatio ad Gaium*, ed. Cohn-Wendland VI; trans. F. W. Kohnke
Migr.	*De migratione Abrahami*, ed. Cohn-Wendland II; trans. R. Posner
Mut.	*De mutatione nominum*, ed. Cohn-Wendland III; trans. W. Theiler
Prob.	*Quod omnis probus liber sit* ed. Cohn-Wendland VI; trans. K. Bormann
Opif.	*De opificio mundi*, ed. Cohn-Wendland I; trans. J. Cohn
Plant.	*De plantatione*, ed. Cohn-Wendland II; trans. I. Heinemann
Post.	*De posteritate caini*, ed. Cohn-Wendland II; trans. H. Leisegang
QE 1,2	*Quaestiones et solutiones in Exodum I, II*, trans. R. Marcus: Exodus
QG 1, 2, 3, 4	*Quaestiones et solutiones in Genesin I, II, III, IV*, trans. R. Marcus: Genesis
Sacr.	*De sacrificiis Abelis et Caini*, ed. Cohn-Wendland I; trans. H. Leisegang
Somn.	*De somniis*, ed. Cohn-Wendland III; trans. M. Adler

Spec.	*De specialibus legibus*, ed. Cohn-Wendland V; trans. I. Heinemann
Jos	Flavius Josephus
A.J.	*Antiquitates Judaicae (Jewish Antiquities)*
C. Ap.	*Contra Apionem (Against Apion)*
B.J.	*Bellum Judaicum (Jewish War)*
Vita	*Vita (The Life of Josephus)*, ed. B. Niese

6. Qumran (Dead Sea Scrolls)

CD	Cairo Genizah copy of the *Damascus Document*, ed. F. García Martínez; trans. Maier I
1QapGen^{ar}	*Genesis Apocryphon*, Cave 1, ed. F. García Martínez; trans. Maier I
1QH^{a}	*Hodayot* (Thanksgiving Hymns), Cave 1, ed. F. García Martínez; trans. Maier I
1QM	*Milhamah* (War Scroll), Cave 1, ed. F. García Martínez; trans. Maier I
1QpHab	*Pesher Habakkuk*, Cave 1, ed. F. García Martínez; trans. Maier I
1QS	*Serek Hayahad*, Cave 1, ed. F. García Martínez; trans. Maier I
4QFlor	*Florilegium*, Cave 4 (4Q174), ed. F. García Martínez; trans. Maier II
4QJerApocr	*Jeremiah Apocyrphon*, Cave 4 (4Q385B), ed. F. García Martínez; trans. Maier II
6QD	Fragments, Cave 6 (6Q15), ed. F. García Martínez; trans. Maier I

7. Rabbinic Writings

18 Benedictions	18 Benedictions (Šemone Ezre), ed. W. Staerk
bBer	Talmud Babli, Tractate Berakhoth, trans. Goldschmidt I (Babylonian Talmud)
bSan	Talmud Babli, Tractate Sanhedrin, trans. Goldschmidt VIII—IX (Babylonian Talmud)

jMSh	Talmud Yerushalmi, Tractate Maaser Sheni, trans. R. Ulmer (Jerusalem Talmud)
jSan	Talmud Yerushalmi, Tractate Sanhedrin, trans. G. A. Wewers (Jerusalem Talmud)
mAv	Mishnah, Tractate Avot/Aboth, ed./trans. K. Marti/G. Beer
TJon	Targum Jonathan, on Jer: ed. A. Sperber; trans. R. Hayward
TN	Targum Neofyti 1, ed./trans. A. Díez Macho
TPsJon	Targum Pseudo-Jonathan, ed. M. Ginsburger
tSan	Tosefta, Tractate Sanhedrin, trans. B. Solomonsen

8. Apostolic Fathers

Barn.	*Epistle of Barnabas*, ed./trans. K. Wengst
1 Clem.	*1 Clement*, ed./trans. J. A. Fischer
2 Clem.	*2 Clement*, ed./trans. K. Wengst
Did.	*Didache*, ed./trans. K. Wengst
Herm.	*Shepherd of Hermas*, ed./trans. M. Leutzsch
Mand.	*Mandata* (Mandate)
Sim.	*Similitudines* (Similitude)
Vis.	*Visiones* (Vision)
Ign. Eph.	*Letter of Ignatius to the Ephesians*, ed./trans. J. A. Fischer
Ign. Magn.	*Letter of Ignatius to the Magnesians*, ed./trans. J. A. Fischer
Ign. Pol.	*Letter of Ignatius to Polycarp*, ed./trans. J. A. Fischer
Ign. Rom.	*Letter of Ignatius to the Romans*, ed./trans. J. A. Fischer
Pol. Phil.	*Polycarp to the Philippians*, ed./trans. J. A. Fischer

9. Apocrypha (NT)

Acts John	*Acts of John*, ed. M. Bonnet

10. Literature of the Ancient Church

ActScil	*Acta Scilitanorum (Acts of the Scilitanian Martyrs)*, ed. R. Knopf; trans. H. Rahner
Athenag, *Suppl*	*Athenagoras*, *Supplicatio*, ed. E. J. Goodspeed
Aug, *Pec*	*Aurelius Augustinus (Augustine)*, *De Peccato*, ed. K. F. Urba/J. Zycha
ClAl, *Strom*	*T. Flavius Clemens Alexandrinus*, *Stromata*, ed. O. Stählin (Clement of Alexandria)
Eus	Eusebius
HistEccl	*Historia Ecclesiastica (Church History)*, ed. E. Schwartz/Th. Mommsen
PraepEv	*Praeparatio Evangelica*, ed. K. Mras (Preparation for the Gospel)
Iren	Irenaeus
Haer	*Adversus Haereses*, ed. A. Rousseau
Epid	*Epideixis*, ed. A. Rousseau
Just, *Apol*	Justinus Martyr (Justin Martyr), *Apologia*, ed. E. J. Goodspeed
Lact, *MortPers*	Lactantius, *De Mortibus Persecutorum* ed. S. Brandt/G. v. Laubmann
MartPol	*Martyrium of Polycarp*, ed. R. Knopf
Min, *Oct*	*Minucius Felix*, *Octavius*, ed./trans. B. Kytzler: Octavius
Orig	Origen
Cels	*Contra Celsum*, ed. P. Koetschau
CommMatt	*Commentariorum in Matthaeum Series*, ed. E. Klostermann (Commentary on Matthew)
Princ	*De Principiis*, ed./trans. H.Görgemanns/ H. Karpp
Tert	Q. Septimius Florens Tertullianus (Tertullian)
Apol	*Apologeticum*, ed. E. Dekkers
Cor	*De Corona*, ed. E. Kroymann

Marc	*Adversus Marcionem*, ed. E. Kroymann
ResurCarn	*De Resurrectione Carnis*, ed. J. G .Ph. Borleffs
Scapul	*Ad Scapulam*, ed. E. Dekkers
Ux	*Ad Uxorem*, ed. E. Kroymann
Theophil, *Autol.*	Theophilus, *Ad Autolycum*, ed. J. C. Th. Otto

11. Pagan Authors

Apul	Apuleius
DeDeo	*De Deo Socratis*, ed./trans. M. Baltes
Met	*Metamorphoses*, ed./trans. E. Brandt/ W. Ehlers: Apuleius
Aristot	Aristoteles (Aristotle)
Cael	*De Caelo*, ed. D. J. Allan
Eth. Nic.	*Ethica Nicomachae*, ed. U. Wolf
Oec	*Oeconomica*, ed./trans. U. Victor
Cic	M. Tullius Cicero (Cicero)
NatDeor	*De Natura Deorum*, ed./trans. O. Gigon/L. Straume-Zimmermann
DeLeg	*De Legibus*, ed. C. Büchner
CorpHerm	*Corpus Hermeticum*, trans. J. Holzhausen
DiodS	*Diodorus Siculus*, ed./trans. C. H. Oldfather
Epic, *Men*	Epicurus, *Ad Menoeceum*, ed./trans. H. W. Krautz
Epict	Epictetus
Diss	*Dissertationes*, ed./trans. W. A. Oldfather
Ench	*Enchiridion*, ed. J. Schweighaeuser
Hes	Hesiodus (Hesiod)
Op	*Opera et Dies*, ed./trans. A. v. Schirnding
Theog	*Theogonia*, ed./trans. A. v. Schirnding
Hom, *Il*	Homerus, *Ilias* (Homer, *Iliad*), ed./trans. H. Rupé
Luc	Lucianus
Alex	*Alexander sive Pseudomantis*, ed./trans. Harmon I

PergrMort	*De Peregrini Morte*, ed./trans. Harmon II
MAnt	Marcus Aurelius Antoninus, ed /trans. Ch. R. Haines
Menand, *Frgm.*	Menander, ed. A. Thierfelder
Ovid, *Metam*	P. Ovidius Naso (Ovid), *Metamorphosen*, ed./trans. M. v. Albrecht
Plat	Plato, ed./trans. K. Hülser
Gorg	*Gorgias*
Leg	*Leges*
Phileb	*Philebus*
Polit	*Politicus*
Symp	*Symposion*
Plin, *Ep*	C. Plinius Caecilius Secundus, *Epistulae*, ed./trans. H. Kasten (Pliny, Letters)
Plut	Plutarchus (Plutarch)
Amat	*Amatorius*, ed./trans. H. Görgemanns
DeCap	*De Capienda Exodus Inimicis Utilitatate*, ed. Paton I et al.
EDelph	*De E apud Delphos*, ed. W. Sieveking/ H. Gärtner
FacLun	*De Facie in Orbe Lunae*, ed. C. Hubert et al.
GenSocr	*De Genio Socratis*, ed. Paton II et al.
IsEtOs	*De Iside et Osiride*, ed./trans. H. Görgemanns
Num	*Vitae Parallelae: Lycurgus et Numa Pompilius*, ed. K. Ziegler
PraecConiug	*Praecepta Coniugalia* ed. Paton I et al.
PythOr	*De Pythiae Oraculis* ed. W. Sieveking/H. Gärtner
SerNumVind	*De Sera Numinis Vindicta*, ed. Paton II et al./trans. H. Görgemanns
Superst	*De Superstitione*, ed. Paton I et al./ trans. H. Görgemanns
Polyb	Polybius, trans. H. Drexler: Polybios
Porphyr	Porphyrius
AdvChrist	*Adversus Christianos*, ed. A. v. Harnack
Marc	*Ad Marcellam*, ed. A. Nauck

PsPlat	Pseudo-Plato, ed./trans. K. Hülser
Alc	*Alcibiades*
Ax	*Axiochus*
Sallust, *DeDeis*	Sallustius, *De Deis et Mundo* ed./trans. A. D. Nock
Sen, *Ep*	L. Annaeus Seneca (Seneca), *Epistulae*, ed./trans. F. Loretto
Soph, *Ant*	Sophocles, *Antigone*, ed. A. C. Pearson/ trans. R. Woerner
Suet	C. Suetonius Tranquillus (Suetonius), ed./trans. H. Martinet: Suetonius
Caes (Claudius)	*De Vita Caesarum, on: Claudius*
Caes (Domitian)	*De Vita Caesarum, on: Domitian*
Caes (Nero)	*De Vita Caesarum, on: Nero*
Tac, *An*	Cornelius Tacitus, *Annales*, ed./trans. E. Heller
Theogn, *El*	Theognis, *Elegie*, ed. D. Young
Xenoph, *Mem*	Xenophon, *Memorabilia Socratis* ed./trans. P. Jaerisch

12. Inscriptions and Papyri

AP	*Aramaic Papyri*, ed./trans. A. Cowley
SIG	*Sylloge Inscriptionum Graecarum*, ed. W. Dittenberger
TAD I	*Textbook of Aramaic Documents*, Bd.1, ed./trans. B. Porten/A. Yardeni

13. Other Abbreviations

Aram.	Aramaic
B.C.E.	before the Common Era
C.E.	Common Era
ca.	circa
cf.	confer; compare
diff.	different
ed./eds.	edited by; editor/editors
Eg.	Egyptian
e.g.	*exempli gratia* (for example)
et al.	*et alii* (and others)

etc.	*et cetera* (and the rest)
f./ff.	following verse/page or verses/pages
fin.	finis (End)
fol.	folio
freq.	and frequently
frgm.	fragment
Heb.	Hebrew
ibid.	*ibidem* (the same author/work)
ill.	illustration/picture
inscr.	*inscriptio*/inscription
Lat.	Latin
LXX	Septuaginta/Septuagint
MPG	Patrologia ed. Migne, Series Graeca
MT	Masoretic Text
n.	footnote
no./nos.	number
NT	New Testament(al)
OT	Old Testament(al)
par./parr.	parallel/parallels
pers.	person
p./pp.	page/pages
ps-	pseudo-
s.	see
sc.	*scilicet* (thus in original)
sg.	singular
Syr.	Syriac
trans.	translation/translator (often into German)
v./vv.	verse/verses
v.l.	*varia lectio* (variant reading)
vs.	versus
Vg.	Vulgate
a	Aquila
q	Theodotion
S	Symmachus
WA	Weimarer Ausgabe; see Bibliography: M. Luther

Multiauthor works and journals are abbreviated according to the S. Schwertner, *Internationales Abkürzungsverzeichnis für Theologie und Grenzgebiete* (IATG^2), Berlin/New York, ^{2}1992.

Part I

Introduction

"Peter, Apostle of Jesus Christ, to the chosen foreigners in the dispersion [Diaspora] of Pontus, Galatia, Cappadocia, Asia, and Bithynia . . ."—this opening formula with information about the sender and addressees already points out the special character of the writing, the outward form of which is a letter and whose author is designated Peter, "Apostle of Jesus Christ." The recipients are Christians in an area that has about the same surface area as New York, Pennsylvania, and Ohio combined.[1] More unusual than this expansive address (which also appears elsewhere in early Christian literature)[2] is its addressing the addressees as "foreigners of the dispersion [Diaspora]." The doubled reference to the status of the recipients as minorities and outsiders, which is strengthened by the designation "foreigners," points to the special agenda of this writing *to interpret this foreignness as a mark of the essence of being Christian*. Accordingly, this introduction will now shed light on the situation of the early Christians insofar as that situation applies to the addressees of this letter according to this self-witness. Then the themes, perspective, and theological profile of 1 Peter will be sketched against this background. The final section of this introduction consists of questions concerning the literal character of the letter[3] and some pointers on the history of the impact of 1 Peter.

[1] Concerning the description of the addressees, see pp. 42f., 51–54.

[2] First Peter 1:1 reads like a combination of James 1:1 ("James . . . to the twelve tribes in the dispersion") and Rev 1:4 ("John, to the seven churches in Asia").

[3] Cf. with regard to this, R. Feldmeier, *Fremde*.

§1 The "Fiery Ordeal" (1 Peter 4:12)

The Situation of Suffering

"Beloved, do not be taken aback by the fiery ordeal . . . as though something strange was happening to you . . ." (1 Pet 4:12)—this statement is revealing in two respects: as a description of the situation and as an interpretation of the situation. First, concerning the description of the situation, the metaphor "fiery ordeal" allows one to guess how pressured this situation is. With the exception of Job, no biblical book deals so often and so extensively in relationship to its length with a situation of suffering as 1 Peter does. This suffering consists in the first place of the problems stemming from the hostility to the Christian community by pagan society. Dealing with this problem determines the whole letter. However, it is not government officials who in the first place promote this conflict; such officials are normally described positively in the context of 1 Peter (cf. 2:13f.). The Christians are first and foremost having problems with their immediate neighborhood, which has been taken aback by the behavior of their former fellow-citizens (4:4) and therefore excludes and defames the Christian community, is even hostile to it and denounces it (2:12, 23; 3:14-17; 4:4, 14-16). This situation is typical for early Christianity from its beginnings until the middle of the third century. Already in the oldest piece of Christian writing in existence, 1 Thessalonians 2:14, the author speaks respectfully to both Jewish and Gentile Christianity about "suffering through your fellow countrymen." According to the picture of Acts, official action against Paul began with incensed citizens.[1] The Neronic persecution as well, which appears to be a classic example of a state action against Christians, upon closer examination reveals itself to be a power-political move in which Nero redirected the anger of the people over the burning of Rome (which he may well have caused) against "those whom the people hated because of their outrageous deeds and designated with the name Christians."[2] The Caesar did not proceed against Christians

[1] Acts 14:4f.; 16:19-22; 17:8, 13; 19:23-40; 21:27-40.

[2] Tac, *An* 15.44.2: ". . . *quos per flagitia invisos vulgus Christianos appellabat.*" Even if we take into account that Tacitus wrote this report about fifty years

of his own accord, but instead used the existing hatred of Christians to shift the aggression from himself—and he did this effectively.[3] The persecution logia also witness to this hatred, which extended to one's closest relatives.[4] The narratives in Acts show how dangerous this could already be: societal discrimination meant a constant treat and included pogromlike attacks by the populace. While in the early period that Acts pictures, the government officials still often intervened to protect the Christians, from the second half of the first century on these conflicts increasingly ended at the cost of the Christians. When the governor Pliny at the beginning of the second century cited "the outrageous deeds that stick to the name [Christian]"[5] as sufficient grounds to put Christians on trial and execute them, the name "Christian" had already become a synonym for a criminal—a criminalization of Christianity, such as that which is intimated in 1 Peter 4:12ff. (especially 4:14, 16). On the basis of striking evidence, J. Molthagen[6] set forth the assumption

---

later and therefore his evaluation of Christians is colored by his time and the outlook of the circle around Trajan, there is still no reason to mistrust this statement in principle.

[3] The hatred was not limited to the "mob," as Tacitus's own evaluation shows, for although in his report about Nero's action he sees through Caesar's maneuver and therefore does not believe in the Christians' guilt, he nevertheless approves of their execution as taking place in the interest of the public good (Tac, *An* 15.44.5 end; on this translation and interpretation of *utilitate publica* see A. Wlosok, *Rom* 22.26): the Christians are guilty (*sontes*), and their cruel execution in a public spectacle is justified 15.44.5, "They were convicted less because of arson than because of hatred against the whole of humanity" (*An* 15.44.4: "*. . . haud proinde in crimine incendii quam odio humani generis convicti sunt*"). That Tacitus is not an exception in his condemnation of Christians is shown by Suetonius, who in his biography of Nero reckons among the useful deeds of the Caesar his action against this "type of people, who had surrendered themselves to a new and corrupting superstition" (*Nero* 16.2).

[4] See Mark 13:9-13; Matt 10:17f.; Luke 21:12-17. Even if these logia originally related to a Jewish Christian context, they were still easily transferable to a Gentile situation.

[5] See also the inquiry that Pliny sent to the Caesar Trajan in Plin, *Ep.* 10.96.2: "*an . . . nomen ipsum, si flagitiis careat, an flagitia cohaerentia nomini puniantur*" ("if . . . the name itself, if it remains without outrageous acts, or if the outrageous deeds that stick to the name should be punished").

[6] J. Molthagen, *Lage*, especially 451ff.; J. Molthagen, *Cognitionibus*, especially 128ff.

that, in view of both its nature and the high Roman culture of justice, Pliny's action is only understandable if there were some legal basis for it. Apparently Nero's action against the Christians had led to a first (local) criminalization of Christianity, which was then widened under Domitian to the whole empire "in order to create a solution for the many-sided unrest that frequently burst into flame over the existence of the Christian minority in this society."[7] This was especially the case when a charge brought by a private person made the official action against the Christians possible, as Pliny witnesses to. This official action, however, remained *reactive* until the third century; in his answer to Pliny, the Caesar Trajan makes it explicitly clear that he holds to the principle that officials are not to seek out Christians on their own.[8]

Therefore, the origin of the attacks against Christians lay in the remarkable massive rejection of the Christians by all social strata of the population. Indicators for this are the stereotypically repeated allegations of "outrageous deeds," which allegedly belong together with the name "Christian."[9] If social stigmatization expressed itself in such, for the most part totally unfounded, accusations, then the accusation of atheism[10] and hatred of humanity,[11]

[7] J. Molthagen, *Cognitionibus*, 129.

[8] Plin, *Ep* 10.97.1, "*conquirendi non sunt.*"

[9] Plin, *Ep* 10.96.2, "*flagitia cohaerentia nomini*," similarly Tacitus 15.44.2; one glimpse of these allegations appears in the speech of Caecilius in Minucius Felix, *Octavius* 8ff., which alleges against Christians virtually every imaginable atrocity—from ritual sacrifice of children to sexual promiscuity, including incest.

[10] This is found as a direct accusation, for example, in Luc, *PergrMort* 13; Orig, *Cels* 8.11; Min, *Oct* 8.1–9.2; in *MartPol* (Eus, *HistEccl.* 4.15.6) among others. On the whole issue, also see the research of A. v. Harnack, *Atheismus*; also W. Schäfke, *Widerstand*, especially 627–30.

[11] See first Tac, *An* 15.44.4; compare Tert, *Apol* 37.8, "*hostes . . . generis humani.*" A. Wlosok, *Rom* 21, demonstrates beautifully the context between this accusation and the (religiously conditioned) isolation of the Christians: the Christians ". . . were isolated from their pagan surroundings on the basis of their exclusive religion and their community organization. On the basis of their religious beliefs, they had to reject participation in public life, for otherwise they would be confronted at every turn by the pagan cultus. That was also true of such apparently apolitical events as plays, public games, and communal meals, totally apart from public celebrations, parades and solemnizations that had a direct connection with the cultus. In addition to this comes

of unbearable pride, and of rioting[12] already betray more about the underlying reasons of the conflict: it is in the end the incompatibility between the exclusive monotheism of Christianity[13] and the sacrally based ancient society. In the Roman Empire, the official religion was closely interwoven with every area of culture and society; and even more, it is nothing less than the spiritual foundation of Roman society and the idea of the state.[14] The state and its order are virtually sacral institutions.[15] This explains the apparent contradiction that the Romans were not in any way intolerant in religious things, even in Italy and all the more in the provinces,[16]

---

the fact that the Christians were organized as a community. They therefore appeared to their environment as members of an isolated fellowship that corporately rejected participation in public life on principle. And that necessarily led to the accusation on the Roman side of an offense against the state and society. *Odium humani generis* is thereby 'socially hostile mindset'; it is a moral and political accusation."

[12] For Celsus, the rioting is more or less the origin and essence of Christianity (Orig, *Cels* 3.5ff.; cf. 3.14; 8.2, etc.), which causes chaos (Orig, *Cels* 8.68). Christianity is "the theology of rebellion" (C. Andresen, *Polemik*, 221), it destroys "the world of divine order" (ibid. 222); cf. Tert, *Apol* 35.1, "*publici hostes*."

[13] Compare now to this the study of H.-J. Klauck, *Pantheisten*.

[14] Thus Polybius in the second century B.C.E. judged, "the greatest advantage of the Roman state . . . appears to me to lie in their view of the gods, and that which is a reproach for other people is precisely that which builds the foundation of the Roman state: a virtually superstitious piety. Their religion plays such a role in private as in public life and it is made so much the essence of both that one can hardly imagine it" (Polyb 6.56.6-8). Cicero judged similarly around a hundred years later (*NatDeor* 2.8), when he attributes the superiority of Rome over the other peoples exclusively to their specially faithful honoring of the gods, "and if we want to compare our situation with that of foreign peoples, then the following appears, that we in other areas are equal to or even inferior to them, but when it comes to religion, that is the honoring of the gods, we are far superior to them [*multo superiores*]." The speech of Caecilius in the *Octavius* of Minucius Felix (written at the beginning of the third century C.E.) shows the same picture: The stability of Rome is based on the conscientious practice of the religion (6.2)—a conviction that the philosophical skepticism advocated by Caecilius can in no way affect!

[15] Compare to this the arguments of A. Wlosok, *Rom*, 56ff.; similarly G. Alföldy, *The Social History of Rome*, 35: "The ideological basis of this conception of the state was religion."

[16] Compare A. N. Sherwin-White, *Pliny*, 776.

but that this broad-mindedness had its clear limits where proper respect was no longer shown for the religious legitimation of the state and the social institutions.[17] Irrespective of their particular religious or philosophical convictions in which the individual was generally free, loyalty was at least demanded with respect to the officially practiced religion, for it was not just a matter of religion in our meaning of personal faith persuasion; religion and politics were much more "both . . . parts of a web of power."[18] The Christians were caught in this "web of power," because, despite all their continually asserted loyalty to the state, they refused to recognize the cultus that legitimated the social order, which was necessarily understood as an attack on the foundation of this order.[19] From the perspective of their contemporary world, the disturbance of the social peace caused by the Christians confirmed this judgment. Christians were "enemies of humanity," because they joined together in their particular religion at the cost of the community, an exclusivity[20] that was not understandable for the ancients. This incompatibility could fade into the background for a shorter or longer time in daily life: "Many townships were apparently prepared and able to come to an arrangement with their outsiders and they with them."[21] But any crisis could quickly allow this incompatibility to again come to light.[22] That was even

[17] Compare the actions against the bacchanalic rites witnessed to by Livy 39.8-19.

[18] S. R. F. Price, *Rituals*, 11.

[19] Also the fact that Christians expected, even longed for, the soon downfall of this world did not contribute to their popularity; compare the polemic of Celsus against the notion in Orig, *Cels*, 4.6ff. 23; 5.14, etc; one encounters something similar in *Octavius* (Min, *Oct* 11.1ff.).

[20] The Jews had suffered under the same reproach for the same reasons, although they were far more tolerated, since they could cite an ancient tradition and also since, because of circumcision and food regulations, they were far less offensive in their penetration of pagan society than missional Christianity (on the equivalences and differences see R. Feldmeier, *Fremde*, 127–32). Actions against other religious groups were, in contrast, seldom, limited, and (as in the case of the bacchanal scandal) had a concrete cause. The prohibition of the Gallic Druids should not be traced back to just their practice of human sacrifice, but also to the political danger of this influential cast; on the prohibition of the Druids compare Suet, *Caes* (Claudius) 25.5 and Tac, *An* 14.30.

[21] F. Vittinghoff, *Christianus*, 333.

[22] Compare Tert, *Apol* 40.2, "*Si Tiberis ascendit in moenia, si Nilus non ascen-*

more true in that this incompatibility had social consequences[23] and, therefore, could repeatedly lead to tension in daily life: thus the Christian rejection of every form of honoring the gods made difficult, even prevented, participation in the celebrations of trade guilds and associations; the prohibition of eating meat from offerings made even sharing a meal together with pagans difficult,[24] which could arouse indignation, especially with respect to those festivals that were so important for a trade guild or similar community.[25] Deviation from funeral customs[26] and cemeteries also gave offense.[27] The situation became more pointed when economic interests were injured through the expansion of Christianity.[28] Last but not least, in the eyes of its contemporaries, Christianity produced social corruption in that this new "superstition" and the new

---

dit in arva, si caelum stetit, si terra movit, si fames, si lues, statim: Christianos ad leonem." ("If the Tiber floods the walls, if the Nile does not flood the fields, if the heaven does not move, if the earth moves, if famine, if plague, immediately [it is]: 'the Christians to the lions!'") According to W. Schäfke, *Widerstand*, 649, here ". . . a foundational structure of ancient religious thinking becomes visible: earthly misfortune is the consequence of human lapses with respect to the gods. The Christians, who neither honor the old gods nor make offerings to them, were therefore continually made responsible for earthquakes, famine, war and revolution, epidemics, floods and drought."

[23] This separation of Christians in daily life is clearly expressed by Caecilius in the *Octavius* of Minucius Felix, when he accuses, ". . . you keep yourselves far from every entertainment, even from the most respectable ones. You go to no plays, do not take part in parades, disdain the public meals; you abhor the games in honor of the gods, the meat and wine offered on the altars . . . you do not adorn your heads with flowers, groom your bodies with good smelling essences; spices are used by you only for the dead, and you don't even have a wreath left over for your graves" (Min, *Oct* 12.5).

[24] Cf. already 1 Cor 8.

[25] An example is the hatred of the Christians by the mother of the Caesar Galerius, which hatred had developed, according to Lact, *MortPers* 11, as a result of the Christians remaining away from the sacrificial meals that were celebrated virtually daily in her home town.

[26] Cf. Min,*Oct* 38.3, where Octavius denied that Christians put wreaths on the dead, and Min, *Oct* 38.4, where he points out that the Christians bury their dead just as secretly as they live.

[27] Tert, *Scapul* 3.

[28] The riot of the silversmiths in Acts 19:23ff. already shows this, and also the action of Pliny against the Christians appears to have been caused at least by the economic problems of the butchers (cf. A. N. Sherwin-White, *Pliny*, 709, on Plin, *Ep* 10.96.10).

community it produced penetrated the present social relationships and threatened to destroy them.[29]

The Christians were, by the way, fully aware of what they did by this behavior. Equally aggressive is the setting of commitment to Christ over family relationships in Matthew 10:34-37 at the end of the sending of the twelve: "Do not think that I have come to bring peace on the earth. I am not come to bring peace, but a sword. For I am come to turn a person against his father and a daughter against her mother and the daughter-in-law against her mother-in-law. And a person's enemies will be his own household. Whoever loves father or mother more than me is not worthy of me, and whoever loves son or daughter more than me is not worthy of me." First Peter also points out that when pepeole turn to Christianity, familial (cf. 3:1ff.) and neighborly bonds (4:3f.) would be endangered, even destroyed. Because the extended family with the inclusion of dependents, the οἶκος, was the basic building block of ancient society, the Christian mission was necessarily understood as an attack on the social foundations (cf. 1 Peter 2:18ff.). The accusations of "atheism" (ἀθεότης) or of "superstition" (δεισιδαιμονία/*superstitio*) on the one hand and "hatred of humanity" (μισανθρωπία/*odium humani generis*) on the other are, then, two sides of the same coin: from the pagan perspective, the first brings up the characteristics of the religious features,[30] the second the social outworking. Here people join together in their particular "superstition" in which they also isolate themselves and break away from other people; thus the accusation of Celsus, who in this exclusive monotheism heard the "the cry of rebellion."[31] In this context, it was certainly not a recommenda-

[29] This "sickness from rebellion" is a theme that Celsus returns to repeatedly in his argument when writing against the Christians. Cf. Orig, *Cels* 8.2 and 3.5.

[30] Cf. R. L. Wilken, *Christians*, 66, "To say, then, that Christianity is a superstition is not a matter of simple bias or the result of ignorance; it expresses a distinct religious sensibility. When Tacitus wrote that Christianity was the 'enemy of mankind,' he did not simply mean he did not like Christians and found them a nuisance (though this was surely true), but that they were an affront to his social and religious world."

[31] Orig, *Cels* 8, 2, στάσεως φωνή. If, according to Plutarch, the characteristic of a superstition is that it "does not have a common world with the rest of humanity" (Plut, *Superst* 166C), then that was true of the Christians to a special degree.

tion that the founder and patron whose name was taken by this religion had been executed on a cross by a Roman governor as a revolutionary.[32] Even when the attitude toward the Christians was somewhat undecided and during time of relative calm, the Christian faith and lifestyle expressed because of it could always be experienced again as a provocative injury to the foundation of the common life.[33] In a word, Christians had consciously placed themselves outside the religiously determined life context and had become "foreign" to it.[34] Correspondingly, they were in the end experienced as a foreign body despite their varied interactions with the ancient society and its institutions[35]—a foreign body that through its very existence jeopardized their societal foundations, that through its expansion disturbed peace and order and so was subversive.[36] Characteristic of this are the metaphors of sickness, plague, or epidemic that have, so to speak, struck the body of the

[32] F. Vittinghoff, *Christianus*, strongly advocates this aspect. His thesis that Christians "from the beginning were generally criminalized" (336) because of the person of their executed founder is not persuasive.

[33] The reason for the verdict against the Scilitian martyrs is revealing: They have fallen away from the *mos Romanorum* (*ActScil* 14).

[34] Tertullian in his *Apology* vehemently and aggressively asserted his opposition to large areas of life in general and in this context succinctly expresses the relationship of Christians to the public; cf. Tert, *Apol* 38.3, "*nobis . . . nec ulla magis res aliena quam publica*" ("to us . . . nothing is more foreign than the state").

[35] Ph. A. Harland, *Associations*, tried to demonstrate that ancient societies in general and the Jewish and Christian associations in particular interacted quite positively with the society and its institutions. As a criticism of the cliché of a widespread "sectarian or tension-centered approach" (A. Harland, 267), this qualification that refers to epigraphical witnesses is justified (but also cf. F. Vittinghoff, *Christianus*, especially 333ff.). Harland, however, in coming from the other direction tends to underestimate the tension between the Christians and the society, when the author of 1 Peter of all things becomes the chief witness of such "a positive interaction" (A. Harland). That 1 Peter more or less attempts that in certain situations will be shown in individual cases, but the whole letter assumes a basic alienation of the Christians from the society.

[36] In this context, it is revealing how Suetonius, *Caes (Nero)* 16.2 lists the action of the Caesar against the Christians between his measures to curtail luxury and his action against the infringement of the race drivers; it is therefore included in a context with other orders of the Caesar that Suetonius judges as useful.

Roman Empire.[37] Perhaps the masses were not able to express the idea so pithily as did the historians and philosophers, but they certainly experienced it similarly: in the slander, in the suspicion, and in the mockery, the distance that the pagans around them felt from the Christians is clear. It is simply the consequence of this distancing when, in the end, Christians are denied the right of existence, "You are not allowed to be."[38] From the Christian perspective, the Jesus of the apocalyptic speech formulated the same content, "You will be hated by everyone because of my name" (Mark 13:13 par.). If what has been said up to now was generally true for the Christians in the Roman Empire at the end of the first and the beginning of the second century, then the situation in Asia Minor where the addressees of 1 Peter lived appears to have come to a special crisis. For historical reasons, *Asia Minor* was especially closely tied to the Roman house of Caesar, and so it is no accident that early Christianity most clearly encountered resistance here.[39]

The Romans came to Asia Minor in 133 B.C.E. after Attalus III of Pergamum had willed his kingdom to them. After putting down a resistance movement during the years 129–126, they created the Province of Asia, which comprised the western costal region. This was again expanded eastward and southward in the year 116 to encompass the regions of Phrygia and Caria. The transformation of these regions into a Roman province also

[37] Paul is already described as a plague (λοιμός) in Acts 24:5. Plin, *Ep.* 10.96.9, speaks of the epidemic (*contagio*) of the Christian superstition, which spreads itself everywhere. Porphyrius charges that Rome is so infested by the sickness of Christianity that the gods are distant (Porphyr, *AdvChrist*, frgm. 80 = Eus, *PreapEv* 5.1.9f.). One meets this metaphor in Celsus' criticism of Christianity in the sense of the sickness (νόσος) of rebellion, which has infested the Christians and so by this means endangered the whole society (Orig, *Cels* 8.49).

[38] Tert, *Apol* 4.4, "*Non licet esse vos.*" Right at the beginning of his *Apology* (1.4) Tertullian speaks about a general *odi[um] erga nomen Christianorum* ("hatred against the name Christian"). The reference to hatred by the people already in Nero's reign (Tac, *An* 15.44.2) shows that it was not first in Tertullian's time that this was so. The right of existence is also denied to Christians in Orig, *Cels* 8.55, and in Just, *Apol*, appendix 4.1 the fierce order to die out is handed down, "The whole lot of you kill yourselves and get a move on to travel to God and make us no further trouble."

[39] Cf. also Acts, the Apocalypse of John, or the letter of Pliny.

strongly affected the economic life of Asia Minor. In 123 B.C.E. the members of the Roman order of knights were given the right to collect taxes there. They did this with such thoroughness that in the 90s, the Roman Propraetor Mucius Scaevola had to protect Asia from being totally plundered. Nevertheless, the high taxes resulted in ever more land having to be mortgaged or sold to the Romans. Therefore, it is only understandable that Mithridates IV of Pontus was greeted above all as a liberator in many parts of Asia in his fight against Rome and that his call to kill all Romans found many willing participants here. During his first war against Rome, in 89–84, he first lifted the tax burden that lay upon the cities of Asia Minor. After his crushing defeat in Greece, he, of course, needed money for a second army, which he squeezed out of Asia Minor. When resistance struck back, he cruelly smothered it. After Sulla defeated Mithridates the first time and drove him from Asia, it was again the Romans who in return laid a high fine on the disloyal cities. At the same time, the cities quartered the Roman troops, a demand that drove the cities bankrupt for the first time. Two further wars against Mithridates followed, which, however, affected Asia relatively little, but Bithynia and Pontus, which were the theater of war, suffered. In the civil war between Pompey and Caesar, in 49–48, Pompey demanded so much money that within two years the debt of the province doubled. The situation calmed down for a short time under Caesar, who tried to better the situation through relief and privileges and consequently garnered extraordinary thanks. For example, he is praised in an inscription in Ephesus in the year 48 B.C.E. as, "God manifest and common Savior of human life" (θεὸς ἐπιφανῆς καὶ κοινὸς τοῦ ἀνθρωπίνου βίου σωτήρ, *SIG* no. 760). An immediate worsening of the situation again took place under the murderers of Caesar, who had retreated to the East. Cassius ordered so high a tax that the representatives of the cities later said that they had not only had to hand over all their money, but their jewelry and cutlery as well. After the conquest of the Triumvirate, Mark Antony continued the plundering and demanded within two years the tax of nine years, but with Octavius (Augustus) came a final turn for the good. He involved himself in the well-being of the cities and even helped out with privileges and money. What impression that made upon the cities of Asia Minor is emphatically witnessed to by several preserved inscriptions that outbid one another in praise and glorification of the Caesar. The New Year itself was shifted to September 23, the birthday of Augustus, through a resolution of the Greek cities (presumably 9 B.C.E.). One can hardly say more clearly that now, with this ruler, a new age had dawned. As an example, an (incompletely preserved) inscription from Halicarnassos is cited. Despite all the flatteries that belong to such an inscription and behind which political calculation certainly stands, one cannot ignore that here true thankfulness and sincere glorification come to expression, since the situation had decidedly improved because of this Caesar:

> "Since the eternal and undying Nature of the Universe has granted the highest good to lavish good deeds to humanity in that it brought forth Caesar Augustus as a blessing to our life, the father of his fatherland, of the goddess Roma, the Father Zeus and Savior of humanity in general, whose providence not only fulfills the prayers of all, but even surpasses them—for peaceful are land and sea, the cities bloom in excellent just order, in harmony and prosperity, every good bears flower and fruit, people are full of good hope about the future, full of cheerful spirits for the present. . . ."[40]

When one looks over this outline of the history, the *relationship of Asia Minor to the Roman Empire clearly falls into two parts*: the first hundred years during the Republic was a time of constant oppression and plundering that drove to ruin the cities of Asia Minor; Asia had basically financed the Roman civil war. *Peace, prosperity, justice, and affluence, on the other hand, were inseparably tied to the following time of the emperors, beginning with Caesar*, in which period the culture also blossomed to a degree never before known, not the least of which is shown by the countless buildings erected during this time. In this, the spatial distance to Rome had a positive outworking in that negative impulses from Caesars such as Caligula and Nero were only noticeable in Asia Minor to a very toned-down degree (only Nero's art thefts were negatively perceived). And precisely for the time in which 1 Peter was probably written, Suetonius witnesses that although Domitian's rule was for his environs and for Rome, especially for the upper class

[40] The inscription is edited by G. Hirschfeld in C. T. Newton, *Inscriptions*, 63–65 (no. 894); for the translation cf. J. Leipold/W. Grundmann, *Umwelt*, 107 (no. 131).

in Rome, extremely burdensome, it caused no damage to the provinces. The truth is actually quite the opposite; the Caesar "also took particular care" (see Suetonius) "that the city officials and the provincial governors were set in order so that there had never been so reasonable or just civil servants."[41] The result of this was that precisely in the first Christian century, Asia blossomed into a center of the Caesar cult,[42] which was also grimly noted in Jewish tradition (cf. 4 Ezra 15:46-49). The Johannine Apocalypse reflects this dealing with the Caesar cult in various texts (2:13; 13:1ff.) and the tension right up to individual martyrs that stands in connection with it (cf. 2:13; 6:9f.; 17:6). But 1 Peter, despite its call to submission to the state authorities, also documents a massive rejection by the world around them.[43]

§2 The "Foreigners" (1 Peter 1:1; 2:11)

The Theological Interpretation of the Situation

"Beloved, do not let yourselves be surprised by the fiery ordeal that is taking place among you . . . as if something strange were happening to you . . ."—this statement from 1 Peter 4:12 is instructive: In provocative contrast to the temptation of the addressees, it contests the notion that this suffering that "surprises" the faithful is something "(in essence) foreign" to the Christians. Rather, such a fiery trial is only a consequence of who the Christians are, who are indeed "foreigners in the dispersion," as was stressed at the very beginning of the letter and repeated in 2:11 at the beginning of the second main section with the double predicate of "outsiders and foreigners" (cf. further 1:17). This somewhat unusual address expresses the situation of the Christians that has already been sketched: they are outsiders, marked, alien elements. Yet this address is, as we have said, also *interpretive of the situation*. For with that conceptualization 1 Peter purposefully reaches back to grasp a meager Old Testamental/Jewish tradition that understood the

[41] Suet, *Caes* (Domitian) 8; translation H. Martinet, *Suetonius*.

[42] Cf. S. R. F. Price, *Rituals*, 78–100.

[43] This is noticed too little in the research of Ph. A. Harland, *Associations*, especially 213ff.

existence as foreigners of the patriarchs and also that of the people as the flip side of election.[1] The uniqueness of 1 Peter consists, however, first in that the author makes this category, which is a more marginal category in the Old Testamental/Jewish tradition, the key concept for believing existence in the society. With a consistence that is unique in the Jewish/Christian tradition, the societal stigma becomes here a decisive factor of believing identity. With this, the letter has already set in motion an enormous historical influence.[2] Naturally, in the light of various world-fleeing false interpretations, one must carefully observe that in 1 Peter, the alienation from the world around them does not in the first place take its character from a negation of the world but is interpreted as the flip side of the belonging to God that is stressed in the whole letter, in 1:1f.; 2:4, 9f., by means of the concept of election as integration into the people of God, in 1:3f., 23; 2:2f., by means of the idea of rebirth as an eschatological renewal of existence. This shows that even though the address as "foreigners" is determined by the societal conflict situation, *the foreignness of the Christians is not in its essence derived from protests against society,*[3] *but from correspondence to God and belonging to his new society*. Thus, in this conception, the opposition to the surrounding world remains intact; its degeneration to death and triviality is continually stressed, and salvation means that the believers are called "out of darkness into his [i.e., God's] glorious light" (2:9). Nevertheless, this opposition is not absolute in the sense of dualism so that the negation itself would already be a stance. Rather, the foreignness is only the flip side of the overcoming of the alienation from God that has already taken place for the Christians. So, because Christ's death has opened access to God (3:18), the believers, in contradis-

[1] See below the exegesis of 1:1; this is presented in detail in R. Feldmeier, *Fremde*, especially 39–74.

[2] See below §7. Influence, pp. 43–45.

[3] Significantly, no "place" is stated where they are foreign—such as the (awful) world, the evil cosmos, and the like—although the category of foreignness appears to demand such a place. This sense of demand reveals itself in that not a few translations felt it necessary to insert a statement of place into the Petrine expressions of foreignness. One finds a revealing list of English translations in this respect in J. H. Elliott, *Home*, 39ff.—presumably a result of the "pilgrim theology" that is especially strongly advocated in the English-speaking world; cf. L. A. Barbieri, 34.

tinction to the "wandering sheep," have (already) "returned to the Shepherd and Bishop of your souls"—thus the point of the second christological confession (2:25). This explains why the pointed self-description of the Christians in 1 Peter as foreigners does not lead to a sectarian break with reality, but rather it opens up a new access to the surrounding world.

The Christians, so the message of 1 Peter has it, are foreigners in this society—and that is what they should be and through this foreignness correspond to their calling and at the same time give a witness to "the hope that is in you."[4] A further special feature of the address as foreigners, which 1 Peter shares with Hebrews 11–13,[5] is its eschatological pointedness: "Foreigners" are Christians, because they are reborn (so 1:3, 23; 2:2). This means, according to 1 Peter, that they have been redeemed from their ancestors' vain lifestyle and placed into a new life situation (cf. 1:18). Therefore, they have a future that is over and beyond[6] this world, which is passing away. Christian existence is being newly born (1:3, 23; 2:2), and it is life from a "living hope"[7] and from a self-understanding that is radically different from the surrounding world; the foreignness is finally based in the eschatological existence of the believers.[8]

If that is so, then the problems resulting from such a distance should no longer "surprise . . . as if something strange came upon you" (4:12), but one can even rejoice over them, for they are the

[4] Cf. on this R. Feldmeier, *Außenseiter*.

[5] Characteristic of Hebrews' understanding of existence is homelessness on earth resulting from an orientation on the future city of God. Compare 11:9f.; 11:13f.; 11:16 and 13:14.

[6] Cf. the three α-*privativa*, with which the beyond-this-world character of the Christian "inheritance in the heavens" is underlined in 1:4.

[7] Cf. 1:3, "procreated anew to a living hope"; 1:13 "τελείως ἐλπίσατε ἐπί . . ."; in 1:21 as a conclusion the result of the work of redemption is set forth so that the Christian faith and "hope in God" would be facilitated; the women who set their hope on God are examples that are praised (3:5); and according to 3:15 Christians are to give an account to others, not of their faith, but of the "hope which is in you." Hope in 1 Peter is an essential, if not in fact the constitutive element of Christian existence (see below Excursus 1: Hope, pp. 65–70).

[8] Cf. Goppelt, 155, "To be foreign is the sign of the Christian in society, for it is a sociological expression of the eschatological character of their existence."

other side of the coin of belonging to God.[9] The situation of societal exclusion and persecution can thus, insofar as it is understood as the result of belonging to God, be positively interpreted and thereby be accepted. The conclusion of the work, where the author in 5:12b establishes that he has written this letter "in order to encourage [you] and to testify that this is the true grace of God," confirms this. The suffering that results from conflict with society—so one could paraphrase this sentence—is not an expression of being abandoned by God, but, on the contrary, it confirms belonging to him. This is christologically established throughout the whole letter. Already in 1:11 a connection is established between the suffering of Christ and his consequent glorification. Then, 1:18-21 shows how those redeemed through Christ's giving of his life are placed in a critical relationship with respect to their previous life context. In 2:4-8, the simultaneous rejection by people and election by God are virtually the distinguishing marks of the "living stone" Christ (2:4, 6), in following whom[10] the believers for their part become such "living stones" (2:5). And 2:21-25 brings the suffering Christ before one's eyes, the Christ who precisely in taking on himself others' suffering on their behalf "left you an example, that you should follow in his steps" (2:21). In this conscious acceptance of foreignness and its consequences, societal exclusion is so integrated into the Christian identity that the previous experiences that test and threaten faith (cf. 1:6; 4:12) can now become virtually a moment of the assurance of faith. Thus the concept of foreignness that, in its original meaning was unequivocally negative, receives a positive, even an

[9] First Peter does not, of course, say that Christians must suffer. In contrast to so many sects, which seek the opposition of others and suffering as the confirmation of their specialness, this letter speaks very carefully about the tension and connects with the comment about suffering the characteristic limitation "if necessary" (1:6, "ἐι δέον ἐστίν"), "if it should be God's will" (3:17, "ἐι θέλοι τὸ θέλημα τοῦ θεοῦ"—here the rare-in-the-New-Testament *potentialis*/potential optative is used). The letter wants to say that the Christian life from hope can always lead to tension with a world that understands itself from what has already become, and that nothing is unusual about this. Suffering is therefore not instrumentalized into a means of self-confirmation. Rather it is about the new evaluation of experience from the perspective of God's future already opened through Christ.

[10] Cf. 2:4a, "report to him. . . ."

elite connotation,[11] as an expression of Christian uniqueness. But 1 Peter accomplishes still more with this: the author wants also to free the Christian from a fixation on suffering (cf. 4:12ff.) precisely through appropriately distinguishing them as "foreigners" from the world around them, and he thereby opens to them a freedom that stems from faith, a freedom for open, responsible behavior in the arena of social conflict. This is the purpose of 1 Peter's frequently misunderstood admonitions. The following exegesis will show how, through this interpretation of the situation of the addressees in relation to their hostile environment and the suffering that results from it, a different orientation toward existence and action is made possible. The statements about the foreignness in 1 Peter have, therefore, an ethical dimension besides an ecclesiological and eschatological one.

§3 "In Order to Encourage and to Testify" (1 Peter 5:12)

The Arrangement of the Letter

The attempt to find a clear arrangement in 1 Peter—as also in comparable early Christian writings (James, 1 John, *Barnabas*, *2 Clement*)—meets with problems. Frequently foundational theological statements mix with paraenetic instructions. Things that he has already said are again taken up in a different way, no theme is definitively closed, a convincing progress of thought is not recognizable.[1] Corresponding to this, one can hardly find a

[11] This is underlined by the adjective ἐκλεκτός in 1 Peter 1:1, which underlines the positive other side of "foreignness" in the sense intended in 1 Peter (cf. Calloud/Genuyt, 33).

[1] The individual paragraphs are, on the one hand, relatively independent and yet, on the other—in part only loosely—connected with each other. One does indeed find continuing attempts in the literature—significantly very different from one another—to find an overall structure for 1 Peter, but when one examines these more closely they are hardly more than a table of contents. While, as the following exegesis will show, one can at times state quite precisely for subparagraphs what the logical relationship of the individual parts is to what goes before and what follows and what meaning they have in their respective contexts, it is far more difficult to do so for the work as a whole.

single formal division in this writing. The individual paragraphs are related to one another by conjunctions and particles; clear demarcations are rare.[2] Despite these difficulties, one can discern focal points in this writing that allow one to divide it into two main parts. The first part (1:3–2:10) and the letter opening that leads to it (1:1-2) concern the new being of the Christians, their hope, and the interconnected concepts of salvation, holiness, and sanctification. It concerns the theological foundation of Christian existence.[3] Accordingly, a conceptualization dominates that presents the inaugurated salvation and the new being and status of the Christian that result from it.[4] The defining themes of the rest of the letter, the oppressed situation of the believers, and the paraenesis, are indeed addressed in a general and foundational manner, but they are still subordinated to the main themes of hope and election (especially 1:3-12; 2:4-10).[5] Therefore, 1:3–2:10 forms the first main part, the foundation in that there is not so much a

[2] Cf. on this R. Feldmeier, *Fremde*, 134.

[3] Compare the titles given to the first part, "Basis and essence of the Christian existence in society" (Goppelt, 89) and "The theological foundation in the salvific action of Jesus Christ and in baptism" (Frankemölle, 32).

[4] In the following overview, the first number indicates how often the respective idea appears in the paragraph; afterward comes the total number of appearances in 1 Peter for comparison: σωτηρία 4 (4); κληρονομία 1 (1); ἐλπίς 2 (3); πίστις 4 (5); so also the picture of rebirth 3 (3); ἱεράτευμα 2 (2); λαός and ἔθνος for the Christians as the new people of God 4 (4); ἅγιος as an attribute of the Christians 5 (5); ἁγιασμός 1 (1); ἐκλεκτός for the Christians 2 (2; also twice more for Christ himself; as a designation for the Christian church it is included one more time in the *hapax legomenon* συνεκλεκτός in the letter closing 5:13).

[5] Thus the suffering of Christians is touched on only briefly in 1:6f. as "various temptations" in which faith proves its worth and in defiance of which the believers rejoice. In tone this clearly contrasts with the second part, which discusses suffering at some length and reflects on it theologically in relation to the suffering of Christ; thus especially 4:12ff.; cf. 2:18-24; 3:13-18. Likewise, in 1:13-17 and 2:1f., the text points only generally and foundationally to the obligation, included in the salvation that has been given, to a lifestyle that corresponds to it; here it deals, so to speak, with the relationship of indicative and imperative, with the new being itself and not with the concrete paraenesis itself as in the second part. Accordingly, here ἅγιος is the decisive main term, which comes up seven times in a short paragraph (so also ἁγιασμός once), while in the rest of the letter it only occurs once, as an attribute of Old Testament women (so also ἁγιάζειν occurs once).

treatment of a first theme as the foundational interpretation of the Christian life in the light of one's relationship with God[6] so that in this way, the theological foundation is laid for the following paraenetic and pastoral exposition. In other words, it concerns the transformation of the perspective of the addressees, who are presently being tested, through a reference to God's already inbreaking salvation.[7]

In 1 Peter 2:11, the author starts anew. With the address "beloved" (ἀγαπητοί), he again makes direct contact with his addressees and designates them anew with a double expression as "foreigners." Here he addresses them personally for the first time (παρακαλῶ) and thereby at the same time sets forth a further theme—exhortation. With it, he deals in detail with the Christians' threatening situation and gives detailed directions for the behavior of individual groups and also for the whole community. One does indeed find foundational theological discussions in this section, especially in the hymnic passages that praise the work of Christ in redemption (2:21-25; 3:18f.); in this part of the work, these have without exception an explanatory function, so they are therefore formally subordinate[8]—even though they (with respect to the less systematic than more reader-oriented pastoral nature of 1 Peter) could stand alone with a certain dynamic of their own over the context. Thus, 1 Peter 2:11–5:11 forms the second main part of the work.

[6] Cf. G. Delling, *Existenz*, 109; similarly M. Clévenot, *Versuch*, 49, ". . . here [that is, in 1:13–2:10] the people are called . . . The letter itself has not yet begun." Despite interesting individual aspects, however, the overall division that Clévenot develops is not convincing.

[7] The introductory and foundational character of this paragraph also reveals itself formally in that this whole foundation is itself the continuation of the eulogy that is begun in 1:3. It is true that the eulogy ends in 1:12, yet through the causal διό it is tied to what follows. Only in 2:10 does one come to a final conclusion, with which the clear new beginning in 2:11 accords with the double address to the addressees and the first usage of the first person singular. The section between can be, as shown later, divided into subparagraphs, yet it lacks a clear division. The individual statements are joined through conjunctions or especially through coordinating participles (cf. especially 1:22; 2:1, 4). That is normally typical for sections that in the author's thought belong closely together and that he interweaves through an appropriate simultaneousness (cf. the same form of connection in 2:18; 3:1, 7, 9 for the long paraenesis 2:13–3:12).

[8] Cf. on this E. Lohse, *Paränese*, 85ff.; C. H. Talbert, *Plan*, 149f.

That 2:11 presents an important transition is not disputed by the exegetes. What is disputed is the extent of this section. Most of the exegetes divide this work into three main sections, whereby the demarcation is uncertain. For most, a new section begins in 4:12 with the clear transition from 4:11 to 4:12, but others let the section continue until 4:19.[9] Still others let it go until 3:12.[10] Now the second part from 2:11 can be divided into further subsections, most clearly at 4:12 (see next). However, there also remains a clear connection between the individual parts through the repetition of similar parts and also through the two central themes of lifestyle and suffering. The theme of suffering is focused on ever more strongly toward the end of the letter seen as a whole; yet the note has already been clearly souned earlier and is sounded right up to the blessing on the suffering (3:14; 4:14) and the expression of the central thought that to be oppressed is to participate in the suffering of Christ. Conversly, the parenesis that demoniates in 2:11-4:11 recurs in 5:1-5 (or 5:1-9).[12] Because of this, it does not appear proper to start in 4:12 a new main section analogous to 2:11.[13] Since, however, a transition is clearly indicated, one can start the second section of the second main section with 4:12, a section in which no new theme is brought up but rather the focus of the discussion is shifted from paraenesis to dealing with suffering. Consequently the first section of the second main part is titled "exhortation and comfort" and the second "comfort and exhortation"—each according to its focus. This decision is also indirectly confirmed by those exegetes who divide the letter into three main parts but who in doing so relate parts two and three

[9] Selwyn, 227; C. Spicq, *Pierre*, 131; Frankemölle, 21.

[10] W. J. Dalton, *Proclamation*, 72ff.; H. J. B. Combrink, *Structure*, 43, 53ff.

[11] 4:13f., prepared for in 2:21 and 3:14-18; cf. also the blessing on the suffering in 3:14 and 4:14 and also the referring of suffering to the will of God in 3:17 and 4:19.

[12] In part, introduced by the term ὑποτάσσεσθαι (2:13, 18; 3:1; 5:5).

[13] The assumption that from 4:12 on a totally different situation is addressed, that therefore in 4:12–5:14 comprises an addition that turns from addressing the newly baptized to addressing the whole church (so R. Perdelwitz, *Mysterienreligion*, 26; Ph. Vielhauer, *Einleitung*, 584f.; contra W. G. Kümmel, *Einleitung*, 369ff.; Schelkle, 5; Balz/Schrage, 62; Brox, 33f.; Frankemölle, 64f.), is not persuasive. See below for further discussion.

to each other in terms of content and therefore document their belonging closely together.[14]

Thus if in the opening part the relationship of God to humanity[15] and its consequence for the being of the believers[16] is in view (therefore the *self-understanding* of the Christian community), then the second main part now concerns their *outward relationship*; that is, both what the *active* side of Christian *behavior in the world* and what the *passive* side of Christian *suffering from the world* require. Consequently here in this second main part, on the one hand, words and conceptual fields dominate that address the oppressed situation of the addressees,[17] and, on the other, the conceptualization of paraenesis occurs.[18] The two main parts can be subdivided as follows:

[14] When Goppelt, 42, designates his closing part (4:12–5:11) as a concrete bringing to a point of the discussion of 2:11–4:11, when Frankemölle, 45, speaks with respect to parts two and three of the "two paraenetic main parts of the letter," or when Ph. Vielhauer, *Einleitung*, 581, entitles his second part "paraenesis" and his third "updating repetition of the paraenesis," they demonstrate that their parts two and three belong closely together over against part one. (Cf. also Achtemeier, 301f).

[15] Characteristic for this is the very beginning, 1 Peter 1:3-5, which in hymnic style and passive participles praises the deeds of God to and on behalf of the believers.

[16] This becomes clear especially at the end of this section, in 2:5, 9f.

[17] In the following, the first number gives the frequency of words in the section of 1 Peter 2:11–5:11 designated the "second main part." The second number in parentheses shows how frequently the respective term appears in the whole of 1 Peter: πάσχω 12 (12), πάθημα 3(4), λύπη 1(1), πύρωσις 1(1); so also βλασφημέω 1(1), ὀνειδίζομαι 1(1), and καταλαλέω 2(2) for the hostility of the environment.

[18] Παρακαλέω 3[3], ὑποτάσσω 6[6], ταπεινός, ταπεινοφροσύνη, ταπεινόφρων, ταπεινόω 4[4] (as the attitude Christians strive for), ἐπιθυμία 3[4] (as the counter-force that alienates one from God and must be fought), and the contrast of good and evil behavior and conduct ἀγαθοποιέω 4[4], ἀγαθοποιΐα 1[1], ἀγαθοποιός 1[1], ἀγαθός 7[7], κακοποιέω 1[1], κακοποιός 3[3], κακός 5[5]). The two main themes of the second part are connected especially by the latter insofar as the Christians, in spite of their good lifestyle—in part even because of it (cf. 4:4)—are slandered and denigrated (cf. 2:12, 20; 3:13, 16f.; 4:19), and on the other hand precisely with respect to this situation they are held to a life that will put the lie to these slanders (2:12, 15; 3:1, 15f.).

1:1-2	Prescript: The Addressees as Foreigners and People of God
1:3–2:10	The Reason for the Foreignness: Rebirth and the People of God
	1:3–2:3 Rebirth
	1:3-12 Introductory Eulogy: Rebirth and Joy in Suffering
	1:13–2:3 Rebirth and the New Way of Life
	2:4-10 The Regenerate as God's People
2:11–5:11	Freedom and Obedience: Foreigners in the Society
	2:11–4:11 Exhortation and Comfort
	2:11-12 Living as Foreigners
	2:13–4:6 New Way of Life within the Society
	2:13–3:12 Subordination under Authority as Witness
	3:13–4:6 Hostility of the Environment as Challenge
	4:7-11 Exhortation to Love One Another
	4:12–5:11 Comfort and Exhortation
	4:12-19 Suffering as Fellowship with Christ
	5:1-5 Leadership and Service within the Community
	5:6-11 Closing Exhortation and Comfort
5:12-14	Letter Closing

The structure intimates that the letter takes up the main themes from various sides in a way that could be described as more counseling/pastoral in order to make its comfort and directives understandable. It is not the theological discourse, the strict and clear treatise about certain themes, that stands in the foreground, but rather the attempt to facilitate for the addressees a new orientation in the perception of themselves and their world and so to influence their behavior. "1 Peter is 'planned' only by his pastoral intention to establish theologically and to practice paraeneticly the mode of Christian existence in certain difficult situations."[19] That does not in any way mean that the author of the writing did not have a plan, that there are no steps forward in the progress of the letter. It is only that this is not demonstrable in a formal arrangement; it reveals itself in the progressive illumination and reframing of the situation. First Peter is an offer of identification to oppressed and persecuted Christians. It is perhaps precisely this pastoral and less discursive approach, which is more oriented on free speech, that is the reason for the significant importance of this letter in community life up to today.[20]

§4 "Rebirth" and "People of God"

The Crossing of the Vertical and Horizontal Dimensions of Soteriology

As is clear from the discussion up to now, 1 Peter is a pastoral writing in which intensive and theologically original reflection exists precisely in the interest of praxis. The exegesis will demonstrate this with many examples. Here, for the purpose of orientation, we will point out the theological guidelines that mold the foundations of the first main part.

1. One of these is the reference to rebirth, which is gradually unfolded in the section 1:3–2:3. This metaphor and its daring unfolding from siring from immortal sperm through birth to nursing with "the milk of the word" (1:3f., 23-25; 2:2f.) document 1 Peter's endeavor *to make plausible the eschatological existence of the Christians in a new context.* 1 Peter indeed no longer speaks about the kingdom of God, also no longer about the new creation, but the author personalizes the Christian message of salvation about the inbreaking of the eschaton with the metaphor of new birth in the sense of a transformation of earthly existence, a metaphor that one finds neither in the Old Testament nor in Jesus or Paul, but

[19] Brox, 37; cf. W. G. Kümmel, *Einleitung*, 368ff.; W. C. van Unnik, *Christianity*, 81f.; V. P. Furnish, *Sojourners*, 11, among others.

[20] See below §7. Influence, pp. 43–45.

that since the time of the Principiate spread ever more widely in both Judaism and pagan religiosity and then in early Christianity.[1] Generally with this somewhat drastic picture, redemption is interpreted as the overcoming of the circumstances of existence put in place with the first birth. Consequently, 1 Peter describes its message of salvation as a ransom from the vain life context (1:18f.) and as an overcoming of transience (1:23-25). Participation in the indestructible, divine fullness of life is granted to the elect through divine regeneration and the new birth.[2]

2. This exposition in 1:3–2:3 is framed by 1:1f. and 2:4-10,[3] which in dependence upon Old Testamental/Jewish traditions points out that the "regenerate" are at the same time God's chosen people.[4] The address as "elect foreigners in the dispersion" already has with all three motifs (foreignness, election, dispersion) spoken to the addressees as members of the people of God, and the extension of the address in verse 2 intensifies this reference to the people of God theme with the obedience and blood-sprinkling motif, which alludes to the covenant-forming act at Sinai (Exod 24:7f.). This theme recedes in 1:3–2:3[5] in order to return to the foreground ever more clearly in the final section of the first main part (2:4-10).[6]

[1] See below Excursus 7: Rebirth, pp. 127–30.

[2] See below on 1:23-25 together with Excursus 2: "Imperishable, Undefiled, Unfading," pp. 73–77. The unique (in the New Testament) formulation of 2 Pet 1:4, which interprets the redemption given in the calling as participation in the divine nature, brings more or less adequately to expression that which 1 Peter expresses with rebirth.

[3] As Boring, 90f., rightly observed, the thematic division between 2:3 and 2:4 cuts across the actual syntax, but that is quite typical for 1 Peter (cf. 3:13–4:6).

[4] For, "Israel" as "controlling metaphor" for the understanding of the new community of faith in 1 Peter cf. Achtemeier, 69–73.

[5] It is sounded yet again in the metaphor of heirs (1:4), in the reference to the prophetic prophecies (1:10-12; cf. 1:24f.), so also in the exhortation to holiness that corresponds to God's (1:15f.), where Leviticus 11:44 is cited (the rest of the chapter is about food commands that separate the people of God from the world around them).

[6] That takes place in 2:4f. with the allusions to the community as God's spiritual house and his priesthood and in 2:6-8 with the reference to the founding of the building on Zion, Above all this is the case in 2:9f., where next to the "chosen generation" and the "royal priesthood" the salvation-historical term λαός that is employed in the LXX virtually without exception as a synonym for Israel is used fully three times for the Christian community.

The theme of God's people thus plays a dominant role in the letter opening and in the closing part of the first main part and thereby frames the block 1:3–2:3, which is delineated by the expression concerning rebirth. This interlocking of the two motifs, which moreover are both explicitly referred back to divine mercy as the motive for God's initiative (1:3; 2:10), makes it clear that in 1 Peter they are *complimentarily related to one another*—if the reference to rebirth lays the accent on the heavenly—thus the "vertical" dimension of soteriology as the overcoming of the misery of the *conditio humana* through God's "regenerating" action on the believers, just so the reference back on the Old Testamental/Jewish theme of the people of God underlines that those discredited and criminalized foreigners in the society are members of a fellowship. Those who are born again to "a living hope" are at the same time "living stones" in God's "spiritual house" (2:5). Moreover this fellowship is rooted in the traditions of the old covenant and relates itself to the prophetic promises; it is therefore located in the history of salvation. And finally the "elect foreigners" also receive a visible social form and an assignment in society that are then explained in the second main part of the letter. This framing stands at the same time against an individualistic, history-less or world-fleeing misunderstanding of salvation. This is the salvation whose (freeing!) "beyond-this-world-ness" through rebirth and corresponding theological ideas ("salvation of the soul") are so strongly stressed.

§5 **"For It Is Written"** (1 Peter 1:16)

1 Peter and Tradition

First Peter can therefore in the interest of communicating the author's theology also tread these relatively daring paths of translating his message of salvation into the situation and culture of his addressees because he takes over Old Testamental, early Jewish,

---

So also ἔθνος ἅγιον (the expression that in the context of God's theophany on Sinai is used for the people of God who are normally λαός [Exod 19:6]) is used once. Also the formula that God "has *called* you out of darkness into his wonderful light" (2:9) alludes to their election.

and early Christian traditions in a frequency that is without parallel in the New Testament and weaves them together—apparently without effort—into a new whole.

The writings of the Old Testament are to be mentioned in this respect in the first place. Only in Hebrews and the Apocalypse do we find a comparable density of Old Testament citations and allusions. In 1 Peter, in contrast with Hebrews, the citations with two exceptions (1:16; 2:6) are not specially designated; the language of the biblical Scriptures merges as it were organically into the exposition of the letter and proves to be a decisive reference point and foundation for this argumentation. As with Paul, the author of 1 Peter has in this use of Scripture a clear preference for the prophet Isaiah;[1] then follows—at a clear distance—Psalms[2] and Proverbs.[3] The latter is unusual, and, because the Psalms cited have in part a wisdom character (cf. 1 Pet 3:10-12, where Ps 34:13-17 is cited), this choice of scriptural words reveals something about the bias of the letter, for example, to make life from the promise plausible by developing a corresponding experience of the world. A number of further Old Testamental citations and allusions are added to this,[4] in which it is significant that in 1 Peter only in 1:16 (Lev 11:44f.; 19:2) does one find a direct citation of the Torah that was central for contemporary Judaism.

The mediator of this tradition is *early Judaism*, above all Hellenistic Judaism. That fact already reveals itself in that the biblical writings are cited in the Septuagint version, or also—as with Daniel—in the version of (Proto-)Theodotion.[5] Besides this, one finds in 1 Peter allusions to further writings of early Judaism

[1] Isa 40:6f. in 1:24; Isa 40:8f. in 1:25; Isa 28:16 in 2:6; Isa 8:14 in 2:8; Isa 43:21 in 2:9; Isa 10:3 in 2:12; Isa 53:9 in 2:22; Isa 53:4, 12 in 2:24; Isa 53:5 in 2:24; Isa 53:6 in 2:25; Isa 8:12f. in 3:14f.; Isa 11:2 in 4:14; cf. further allusions to Isa 52:3 in 1:18; Isa 28:16 in 2:4.

[2] Ps 33:9 in 2:3; Ps 118[117]:22 in 2:7; Ps 34:13-17 in 3:10-12; Ps 22:14 in 5:8; cf. the allusions to Ps 118:22 in 2:4; Ps 39:13 in 2:11; Ps 89[88]:51 in 4:14; Ps 55:23 in 5:7.

[3] Prov 10:12 in 4:8; Prov 11:31 in 4:18; Prov 3:34 LXX in 5:5; cf. further allusions to Prov 17:3 in 1:7; Prov 31:17 in 1;13; Prov 24:21 in 2:17; Prov 3:25 in 3:6.

[4] Gen 23:4 in 2:11; Gen 18:12 in 3:6; Gen 7:13ff. in 3:20; Exod 24:7f. in 1:2; Exod 19:6; 23:22 LXX in 2:9; Lev 11:44f.; 19:2 in 1:16; Hos 1:6, 9; 2:25 in 2:10; Ezek 22:25 in 5:8; Job 1:7 in 5:8.

[5] Dan 4:1 θ; 6:26 θ in 1:2; 6:27 θ in 1:23.

such as *1 Enoch*[6] and the Wisdom of Solomon.[7] This influence of Diaspora Judaism is decisive in the theological concepts that play a central role in 1 Peter, first of all the self-designation as foreigners[8] and the motif of rebirth,[9] but immortality as a soteriological attribute[10] and talk about the soul[11] also have their closest equivalents in Hellenistic Judaism.

Besides this, 1 Peter has also picked up a great deal of early Christian tradition. The author has repeated recourse to confessional formulas (cf. 1:18-21; 2:21-25; 3:18f.) and the *Haustafel* tradition (2:18–3:7; cf. 5:1-5). An "apostolic theology" that in part leads directly to the apostolic fathers[12] comes to formulation in 1 Peter. The integrating character of the "Catholic" Epistles shows itself also in that 1 Peter is the only New Testament writing that, to an extent worth mentioning, takes up the two foundational streams of tradition in the New Testament canon, the Jesus tradition of the gospels[13] and the Pauline tradition,[14] and combines them

[6] *1 En.* 1:2 and 16:3 in 1 Pet 1:12; perhaps *1 En.* 9:10; 10:11-15 in 1 Pet 3:19.

[7] Allusion to Wis 1:6 in 2:25; Wis 12:13 in 5:7.

[8] See above and also R. Feldmeier, *Fremde*, 39–74, 95–104.

[9] See below Excursus 7: Rebirth, pp. 127–30.

[10] See below Excursus 2: "Imperishable, Undefiled, Unfading," pp. 73–77.

[11] See below Excursus 4: Soul and Salvation of the Soul, pp. 87–92 and also R. Feldmeier, "Seelenheil."

[12] See below §7. Influence, pp. 43–45.

[13] The literary and theological influence of Matthew on 1 Peter is extensively described in R. Metzner, *Rezeption*.

[14] The "Paulinisms" in 1 Peter show themselves, for example, in the common'Εν-Χριστῷ formula; cf. the agreements between 1 Pet 1:14 and Rom 12:2, 1 Pet 2:13-17 and Rom 13:1-7 and also 1 Pet 3:9 and Rom 12:17. For virtually the last century and a half it has been and continues to be pointed out in scholarly research, "If the prescript were lacking the name, one would view this writing as more likely belonging to the Pauline school . . ." (F. Schröger, *Verfassung*, 239, n. 1). Schelkle, 5–7 (who believes that a knowledge of Romans by 1 Peter is possible), Achtemeier, 15–19, and N. Brox, *Tradition*, 183, give a good overview of the relationship of 1 Peter to the Pauline letters; cf. the judgment of Brox in his commentary, page 45f.: First Peter "is namely in many aspects so clearly Pauline that, as has often been said, without the datum of the name in 1:1 one would certainly suspect a student of Paul, but not the apostle Peter, to be the author." That is, to be sure, constantly disputed, but the arguments against it are not persuasive. The problem with the law that is typical for Paul is also absent in 2 Corinthians,

in an independent manner and adapts them.[15] First Peter turns out to be a writing that combines innovative theological statements and metaphors (such as "foreignness," "rebirth," "salvation of the soul," "living stones," etc.) with an intensive reference back to the biblical, early Jewish, and early Christian tradition. Such a reference back to trusted language and traditions creates approval and serves the supplemental legitimation of what is said.

§6 "Peter, Apostle of Jesus Christ" (1 Peter 1:1)

Questions of Introduction

Unity

In its less systematic manner of presentation, 1 Peter is a rewarding object of literary methodologies. That does not need to be presented here in detail.[1] Two arguments continually recur in the various solutions. One is that because of 1 Peter's impersonal and general discussion and its lack of letter characteristics, its nature as a letter is disputed, and therefore the framework—1 Peter 1:1f. and 5:12-14—is judged to be secondary. At the most, it is asserted in this connection, baptism plays a special role, in this writing and

---

as well as in the deuteropauline Colossians. K. Aland, *Verhältnis*, 201, has again effectively underlined this Pauline character of the writing against the background of the writings of the Apostolic Fathers and the theological development of the literature of the second century, ". . . the varying opinions of some New Testament scholars can be explained by their not having the writings of the Apostolic Fathers and the lines of theological development outside of the New Testament in the literature of the second century sufficiently in their field of vision" (K. Arland, 201). However, the view of H. M. Schenke/K. M. Fischer, *Einleitung*, 203, that 1 Peter was originally a (pseudepigraphical) Pauline letter, appears to me pure speculation.

[15] J. Herzer, *Petrus*, has recently undertaken a thorough revision of this thesis of the Paulinism of 1 Peter. Even if the independence of 1 Peter from the Pauline tradition with respect to the wealth of terminological references that is stressed by Herzer strikes one as somewhat forced, yet it is still his contribution to have shown by direct comparison with the Pauline tradition the frequently noted theological independence of this letter.

[1] One can find an extensive discussion in Brox, 19ff.

because of this there is the attempt to determine that specifically 1:3–4:11 is a baptismal address or something similar. The other argument is one that views 4:11 as a conclusion and finds that from 4:12 onward a totally different situation is assumed than in the previous part of the letter; if 1:3–4:11 deals with the possibility of suffering, then now its reality is assumed.

When it comes to the letter characteristics, Paul's letters may not be taken as the sole standard for the genre "letter." In comparison with other ancient letters, 1 Peter absolutely can be considered to count as one (see next). There is absolutely no valid literary-critical argument for the removal of the framework; the framework is clearly interlocked with what follows,[2] whereby the references are again so independent that the assumption of a conscious adaptation is not persuasive. To this is added a blessing that is also typical for other letters, which blessing begins with 1 Peter 1:3ff. (cf. especially 2 Cor 1:3ff.; Eph 1:3ff.), so that also in terms of form, 1 Peter 1:3ff. connects directly to 1:1f. The references to baptism are imported from other letters in that what is in fact the central notion of rebirth in 1 Peter (1:3, 23-25; 2:2f.) is identified with baptism on the basis of John 3:5 and Titus 3:5. This overlooks that 1 Peter does not make this connection; speaking about rebirth without reference to baptism and about baptism (3:20f.) without reference to rebirth. Even if the author's discourse on rebirth were to allude to baptism, which can in no way be considered to be demonstrated, then it would not be about baptism in itself but about the eschatological renewal of believing existence, with the result that the assumption of a type of baptismal address is in no way persuasive.

When it comes to the transition between 4:11 and 4:12, one also encounters similar doxologies elsewhere within letters.[3] The

[2] 1:1 with 1:17 and 2:11 through the theme foreigner; 1:1f. with 1:15; 2:4, 6, 9, 21; 3:9; and 5:10 through the thought of election; 1:2 with 1:14, 22 through the key word "obedience," and with 1:12, 15, 16; 2:5, 9; 3:5, 15 through the word field "holy/sanctification"; in the same way 5:12 relates itself back to 2:19f. through the purposeful statement about grace; 5:13 again mentions election and possibly with "Babylon" also foreignness.

[3] Cf. Rom 1:25; 11:36; Eph 3:20f. In *1 Clement* one even encounters such a doxology a total of nine times (20:12; 32:4; 38:4; 45:7; 50:7; 58:2; 61:3; 64; 65:2); cf. Achtemeier, 292: ". . . such a doxology is used far more often within the body of a letter than as its conclusion, and it is so used here."

assertion that in the first part only the possibility of suffering is allowed for contradicts statements such as 1:6; 2:12; 3:16, and 4:4 that proceed from the already present oppression. On the other hand, the evident correspondences between the two parts that allegedly are separate speak clearly against such literary-critical division, for these correspondences do not confine themselves to only theological concepts such as election/calling, grace, or glory, but extend themselves to the evaluation of suffering and how one deals with it: in both parts, discrimination and denunciation by those around them are the cause of suffering (2:12; 3:16; 4:4, 14). This suffering, however, takes place according to God's will (3:17; 4:19; cf. 1:6) and is understood as a test to be passed (1:6; 4:12). On the basis of their belonging to God, the believers are expected to rejoice already in the present suffering (1:6, 8; 4:13); those who suffer because of their faith are blessed (3:14; 4:14; cf. 2:19f.). Christians should also meet through good behavior the charge that they are evildoers (2:12, 15, 19f.; 4:15f.; 19; cf. 3:10f.; 16) and so sanctify Christ/glorify God in the suffering (3:15; 4:16). The statements in 4:1ff. thus fit totally organically into the context up to this point; differences in the intensity of the description of suffering can be explained from the intensification of the dealing with the problem of suffering toward the end of the letter, as was shown earlier. Thus, there is no reason to doubt the unity of 1 Peter.

Form

With the rejection of the literary-critical hypotheses of division, all the definitions of form based upon them are also invalidated, those definitions of form that, disputing the character of 1 Peter as a letter, want to find in it or in its core material that it was made of a "homiletic composition,"[4] an "edifying homily,"[5] a "baptismal address,"[6] even datable in Easter week,[7] a "circular letter for the Passover Festival,"[8] the order of a baptismal service in

[4] A. v. Harnack, *Chronologie*, 451–65.
[5] W. Soltau, *Einheitlichkeit*, 304–33.
[6] R. Perdelwitz, *Mysterienreligion*, 5–28.
[7] J. Danielou, *Sacramentum*, 141.
[8] F. A. Strobel, *Verständnis*.

the Church in Rome,[9] or similar definitions.[10] First Peter contains the essential characteristics of a letter from prescript (1:1f.) and blessing (1:3ff.) to its letter closing with personal news, greetings, and a wish for peace (5:12-14) and thus should be formally viewed as such.[11] Certainly, as has already been indicated, this writing nowhere deals directly with the individual situation of a certain community, but speaks only very generally about the Christians' problems and duties. Therefore, in a certain way, it already has the "church" in view. In the same way, in the whole work one discovers nothing about the relationship of the sender to the recipients. The reason for this is that, as the address already shows, the letter is conceptualized as an open letter, as is also elsewhere customary in Old Testament and Jewish[12] and also in New Testament literature.[13] A certain closeness of 1 Peter to the letters to the exiles in

[9] Windisch, 156ff.

[10] Brox, 20, and Frankemölle, 19, present further proposals; in those works, there is also more extensive criticism of these proposals of genre.

[11] Cf. Frankemölle, 17f., "In ancient times, including in Judaism, every communication was actually formulated as a letter so that it is not the private letter (as was common in the Pauline literature) that sets the alleged standard by which all other letters are to be measured. The relationship of the Pauline letters (apart from Romans) with private letters is altogether an exception determined by the personal acquaintance of Paul with the addressees. Various types of letters were the result of various communication situations. An overview over Hellenistic letters (. . . for a form and genre overview cf. K. Berger, *Gattungen*, especially 1326–63) and also over Jewish letters (Jer 29; Bar 6; 1 Macc 5:10-13; 12:6-12; 2 Macc 1:1–2:19) shows that antiquity did not know any binding rules for the composition of letters. The variety of content and the pragmatic intention (private letter, business letter, political or philosophical letter, among others) determine its form. Also the integration of smaller genre and forms (proverbs, examples from nature or history, thanks or praise of the gods, among others) is common and are even recommended in reflections on letter writing (so, for example, Demetrius, Philostratus, Cicero, Quintilian). First Peter does not in any way breach the ancient practice when the author adapts *Haustafeln*, songs and confessional formula, proverbs and standardized exhortations. Also when the addressees are not continually directly addressed in the body of the letter, the tradition was selected according to the concrete life situation of the addressees. To this extent the variegated prosaic and poetic forms of speech in the letter are to be interpreted as pragmatic with reference to the addressees."

[12] Cf. 2 Macc 1:19; 1:10–2:19.

[13] Cf. the apostolic decree in Acts 15:23-29, but also James and Hebrews.

Babylon (Jer 29:4-23; 2 *Bar.* 78–87) frequently is pointed out.[14] L. Doering has made this definition of form plausible through a number of further pieces of evidence.[15] In doing this, he distinguishes two traditions: one is connected with the *topos* "Jeremiah as letter writer" in connection with Jeremiah 29[36],[16] and the other consists of the administrative letters to the Diaspora.[17] The abundance of evidence supports the idea that there was in reality in early Judaism a distinct genre of "Diaspora letter." The explicit reference to "Diaspora" in the address already makes it likely that 1 Peter is an authoritative early Christian writing and consciously models itself on this early Jewish form of Diaspora letters. It is possible that the reference to Babylon as the place the letter was sent from (see next) also supports this, as does its closeness to James. In James, as in 1 Peter, major apostolic figures of Palestinian Jewish-Christianity express themselves in the form of episcopal circular letters to communities existing in widely scattered locations. This letter form possibly may imply a distinction over the Pauline tradition: while one knew letters in the genre private letters to individual communities from this missionary to the peoples, one associates the form "official" Jewish circular letter with the great Jerusalem apostles. In relation to this, one can certainly dispute whether 1 Peter really was sent as a letter or whether it was literarily clothed only in this form.

Author

Despite the clear identification of the sender, the authorship of 1 Peter has been disputed since the beginning of the nineteenth

[14] Goppelt, 45; K. Berger, *Formgeschichte*, 366; cf. already C. Andresen, *Formular*, 236 n. 12; 243. Extensively on James as a letter to the Diaspora, W. Popkes, *Jakobus*, 61–64.

[15] L. Doering, "Der Erste Petrusbrief als frühchristlicher Diasporabrief," unpublished paper for the seminar "Catholic Epistles and Apostolic Tradition" of the SNTS, Bonn, 2003.

[16] *Ep. Jer.*; TJon 10:11; *2 Bar.* 78-87; *4 Bar.* 6:17-23; 4QJerApocr.

[17] The oldest evidence is the so-called Passover Papyrus from Elephantine (*AP* no. 21/*TAD* I, 54f.); to this one adds the two introductory letters in 2 Maccabees (1:1-9; 1:10–2:19) and also letters in the rabbinic literature, among them three Aramaic letters of Rabbi Gamaliel (tSan 2.6; jSan 1.2; jMSh 5.6; bSan fol. 11b), which clearly establish the existence of authoritative letters with halakhic and calendric content in both more distant areas of the land of Israel and in the Diaspora.

century. The reasons given for this are weighty, even if they are not as unequivocal as most assert.

Against the Petrine authorship, the following are brought forward:

1. The letter is written in elevated Greek. This appears unusual for a Galilean fisherman who according to the biblical testimony is ἀγράμματος (Acts 4:13).[18]

2. The Old Testament is cited exclusively in the Septuagintal translation, while in a Palestinian Jew one would expect at least the influence of his knowledge of the Hebrew Bible.[19]

3. If the statement of location as Babylon at the end of the letter refers to Rome (see pp. 40–42), this speaks for a dating after 70, because only after this date is there evidence for the equation Rome/Babylon on the basis of the parallel of the destruction of the Temple.[20] But then the authoring of the letter clearly lies after the probable death of Peter (64 C.E.).[21]

4. The address in 1 Peter 1:1 assumes that Christianity has spread over the whole of Asia Minor. But that is first "conceivable after the middle of the 60s and certain about 80"[22] and therefore also refers to the time after Peter's death.

[18] Cf. Achtemeier, 4f.: "While one may surely presume some facility in Greek even among Palestinian fishermen in the first century who lacked formal education, the kind of Greek found in this epistle was probably beyond such a person, and hence the language was in all likelihood not given its present form by Simon Peter."

[19] There were indeed other Christian writers who were originally bilingual (or trilingual if you include Hebrew), such as Paul and Matthew, who often cite the Septuagint; however, there are frequently places precisely in their writings in which they independently refer to the Hebrew biblical text. Strangely enough, this is totally lacking in 1 Peter, although nevertheless its author, if it were Peter, as a Galilean had Aramaic as his mother tongue, and therefore he would be more capable of falling back on the Hebrew Old Testament than the bilingual Paul.

[20] Cf. C. H. Hunziger, *Babylon*, 71.

[21] On the sojourn of Peter in Rome and his death, probably in the context of the Neronic persecution, see K. Aland, *Tod*; H. Lietzmann, *Petrus*.

[22] Goppelt, 29; there is also more detailed evidence; similar are H. Gunkel, *Petrus*, 27; Brox, 27.

5. The letter assumes that an extremely tense relationship between the Christian communities and their fellow citizens has become a lasting situation and that it continues for all believers in the Roman Empire (cf. 5:9) who are now known by the new designation "Christian" (4:16). That fits better in the period of the last two or three decades of the first century, when the Christians had become so widespread and numerous that others were to a large extent aware of them and that they were, especially on the part of the general population and through them increasingly on the part of the officials, put under more pressure empirewide.

6. If 4:12ff. should refer to official actions against Christians that took place against the believers just because of their belonging to Christianity,[23] then this is difficult to conceive of before the Neronic persecution, particularly because only at this time did the distinction from Jews begin to become increasingly conscious to those outside the faith.[24]

Besides these main objections, a series of further indications speak more against the authoring of this letter by the Apostle Peter than otherwise: it is remarkable that the letter does not reveal anything about the close relationship of its author to Jesus,[25] a relationship that we know about from the gospels.[26] In his writing, the author takes up various traditions of the Hellenistic-influenced church,[27] which makes it quite probable that no person from the

[23] Cf. Plin, *Ep* 10.96.2, which refers to the action against Christians simply on the basis of *nomen ipsum*; see above p. 3 n. 5.

[24] Cf. Goppelt, 62.

[25] First Peter 5:1 does not refer at all to being an eyewitness (totally apart from the fact that the historical Peter could hardly be designated an eyewitness of the suffering of Jesus). A reference to being such an eyewitness would make no sense in this context. It would be quite different, however, if the author participated in Christ's suffering in the form of what he himself suffered as a "martyr," which is what his choice of words indicates (cf. κοινωνός in 5:1 with κοινωνεῖν in 4:13). In this way remains ". . . the clearly soteriologically intended equivalence of suffering and glory (cf. 4:13f.), and besides this the author is shown to be authorized with respect to this matter to give his 'exhortations' in the situation of persecution because he is no outsider but a 'participant' himself in the misery of suffering." (Brox, 229).

[26] According to Brox, 45, 1 Peter is ". . . insofar devoid of any originality in respect to this that it counts."

[27] Goppelt, 67; cf. Brox, 45, "Instead of some type of primary knowledge that the author has due to being a historical witness, the letter reveals his dependence upon various church traditions. . . ."

first period of the church is speaking here.[28] This is even more true as 1 Peter reflects Pauline tradition (see earlier), which also speaks more against Petrine authorship than otherwise.[29] We also know nothing about the relationship of the Apostle Peter to the communities addressed in 1 Peter. It is also questionable whether Peter—particularly after the conflict in Galatians—could authoritatively address communities that lay in Paul's area of mission and do so without dealing with Paul in any way.[30] This appears to point more to a later time in which Peter has become the apostolic authority *par excellence* (Matt 16:18f.).

It is worth mentioning in this context the total lack of the Jewish-Christian/Gentile-Christian problem that stands in the foreground in Galatians 2. In reality, the question of the law and of the mission to the Gentiles, the critical issues of the early period, appear to (no longer) play a role here. Even Jewish traditions, especially the idea of the people of God, which is central for 1 Peter, are applied to Christian communities that consist for the most part of Gentile Christians in an astonishingly unquestioning manner without this application being specifically justified (cf. by contrast Eph 2:11ff.).[31] The warning in 1 Peter 5:2 about not assuming leadership for material gain implies paid leadership

[28] This is especially true in view of the sayings of Jesus, which the author draws from the tradition; cf. N. Brox, *Tradition*.

[29] Cf. Brox, 46, ". . . according to the information that we can gain from Galatians 2 and Acts we cannot assume that Peter had thought and spoken as Pauline as 1 Peter does." In this context, Brox points out that one should not raise a deep division between Paul and Peter and one should not say that a rapprochement of Peter to Pauline theology is impossible. But it is strange that 1 Peter does not contain precisely the Pauline theological ideas of the conflict between Paul and Peter and thus offers "a Pauline tradition without this conflict" (Brox, 46). That corresponds in general to the developmental stage of the Deuteropaulines.

[30] One should simply compare with this the manner with which Paul writes on a community that is foreign to him (see Rom 15:14ff.).

[31] Cf. 1 Pet 2:4f., 9f., with Rom 9–11—Achtemeier, 69: "In a way virtually unique among Christian canonical writings, 1 Peter has appropriated the language of Israel for the church in such a way that Israel as a totality has become for this letter the controlling metaphor in terms of which its theology is expressed. Unlike Paul, who finds a continuing place for Israel in God's plan of salvation, 1 Peter has no references at all to Israel as an independent entity, either before or after the advent of Christ."

and points to a more advanced, and hence later, state of church order.[32] This speaks more for composition after 70 C.E., when especially the authority of Palestinian Jewish Christianity was broken. Furthermore, the communities that are addressed in 1 Peter display a developmental level that points to a later time. Thus, they lack the special problems of young emergent communities such as these that we encounter in Paul's letters. In a sense, those addressed already have become "church."[33] Likewise, the references to the constitution of the community point to a memory of the old charismatic ministries (4:10f.), which is, however, already clearly overlaid with an early form of a presbyterial constitution (5:1-5), just as in some post-Pauline writings (with the exception of Acts, which, however, does this as a retrospect).[34] Also, while 1 Peter 2:13ff. does indeed clearly echo Romans 13:1ff. in its attitude toward the state authorities, it is formulated in a significantly more restrained way, particularly in view of the religious dignity of the officials.[35] Conversely one notices the catechetical character of the writing, its pastoral practice. "It is at least most unlikely that Peter, a man of the first generation and in the situation of the first experiences of church would have composed a circular letter with this type of formality and content in which 'the' condition of Christian existence as such would be discussed that early (not the present situation of a concrete church, as in the Paulines)."[36] Finally, to this is added the conceptuality that is strongly influenced by Hellenistic thought.[37]

As has been stated already, none of these arguments is in itself as compelling as is usually claimed. When one examines the situation of the Christians, Tacitus (*An* 15.44.2) testifies that at least with respect to Rome, there was a relatively large Christian community[38] during the lifetime of Peter, and correspondingly massive

[32] Cf. Achtemeier, 37.

[33] Cf. M. A. Chevallier, *Condition*, 388.

[34] Cf. Goppelt, 64.

[35] Cf. ἀνθρωπίνη κτίσις in 1 Pet 2:13 with θεοῦ διάκονος in Rom 13:4.

[36] Brox, 46.

[37] Cf. the "negative theology" in the description of the "inheritance" in 1:4 and the talking about the "foreknowledge" of God in 1:2, etc.

[38] According to Tac, *An* 15.44.4 (which, of course, he wrote at the beginning of the second century) under Nero "*multitudo ingens*" of Christians were executed.

rejection of the Christian community existed on the part of the population (see earlier). Still earlier, 1 Thessalonians 2:14 assumes that suffering because of one's own fellow citizens was already a widespread phenomenon. The very good command of a foreign language—and that without the possibility of special training—is indeed surprising, but still not so impossible as is often claimed,[39] particularly since one must take into account the bilingual nature of Palestine[40] at this time.[41] The author's exclusive use of the LXX could be consideration for the traditions of his addressees; one observes a similar phenomenon with Paul, who was apparently trained in Jerusalem[42] and therefore probably could speak Hebrew. The argument about Babylon assumes that this term does indeed refer to Rome and that it is not used as something of a symbol (which would be quite fitting for the theme of being foreigners) for exile.[43] And even if Rome is intended and its identification with Babylon is indeed first documented after 70, in view of the many writings that have been lost, this *argumentum e silentio* cannot exclude with certainty that this tradition is not older, particularly because in Daniel the conflict with the Seleucid Empire is clothed in the historical clothing of a conflict with Babylon.

[39] On the other hand, in ancient times there were indeed writers with a Semitic background, such as Lucian of Samosata, who were some of the best Greek stylists. From a more recent time one can name the example of Pole Joseph Conrad (apparently his name was Josef Teodor Nalecz Korzeniowsky), who only learned English as an adult (and that as a sailor!) and yet became one of the greatest stylistic masters of English literature; cf. F. Neugebauer, *Deutung*, 72, "How can a simple fisherman from the Sea of Galilee write in this way? Whoever asks, thinks, of course, that he knows a lot; for example, that a fisherman from the Sea of Galilee must necessarily have a low IQ and deficient gift for language, disregarding the possible coauthorship of Silas. Arguments such as these base themselves on deceptive academic images and often result from a lack of contact with so-called simple people."

[40] Cf. M. Hengel, *Hellenization*, 7ff.

[41] The historical Peter could also possibly have learned the basics of Greek in Beth-Saida (= Julias!) in his youth. Jobes, 325–38, even tries to prove that there are syntactical indications that 1 Peter was written by "an author whose first language was not Greek" (337).

[42] Cf. Acts 22:3; the Pharisaic training that he himself testifies to (Phil 3:5) also indicates this.

[43] See below pp. 40f., 254f.

This is aggravated by the fact that in contrast to the Pauline letters, we do not possess an original writing that is certainly from Peter with which a comparison would be possible. Other open questions are why of all things the Pauline coworker Silvanus is named or how one should think of the distribution of the pseudepigraphical writing in just the area to which it is addressed.[44]

Despite these critical counter-questions, which should lead to somewhat more modesty with respect to apodictic judgments,[45] the totality of the objections nevertheless speaks with a greater likelihood against the apostle Peter as the author of this work, particularly since pseudepigrapha were also otherwise disseminated in early Christianity. What is uncertain in the case of a pseudepigraphon is the intention behind the information about the author, particularly the connection with the naming of Paul's companion Silas. A classical answer is the so-called secretary hypothesis, according to which Silas wrote the letter as instructed by Peter.[46] That allows one to more easily explain the closeness to the Pauline tradition. This of course assumes that the letter originated during Peter's lifetime and that the letter has at least an indirect authenticity, which, as shown earlier, is less likely. Another interpretive possibility of the expression γράφειν διά τινος that is widely documented is a reference to the bearer of the letter.[47] One should not exclude totally the possibility that after Peter's death some of his disciples continued to work according to his intent.[48] Eusebius'

[44] According to N. Brox, *Verfasserangaben*, 62, this problem belongs "to the most unclear questions in the whole pseudepigrapha." Brox points out (Brox, 65f.) that in early Christianity forgery was by no means simply an accepted matter of course, as would be claimed by modern apologetes, but that it would also not have been evaluated as a moral outrage. Brox grants, of course, "It certainly appears to me in the light of this background that no truly plausible description of the 'start' of a pseudepigraphical (for example, pseudapostolic) writing is possible." (Brox, 66). F. Neugebauer, *Deutung*, 67f., has pointed out this problem forcefully. In the end, he does therefore consider it more likely that the letter was written by the apostle himself (Neugebauer, 72).

[45] Cf. Davids, 7: "But neither can one demonstrate that Peter could *not* have written the letter."

[46] Th. Zahn, *Einleitung*, 16f.; L. Radermacher, *Petrusbrief*, 293; Davids, 198f.

[47] Cf. W. G. Kümmel, *Einleitung*, 374; Brox, 242f.

[48] Cf. Achtemeier, 42; Boring, 25–30.

(*HistEccl* 3.39.15) reference to Papias (which is, of course, disputed) designates Mark, to whom 1 Peter 5:13 appears to refer, as Peter's interpreter, and so, it is alleged, a connection between these two figures of early Christianity is not absurd (see next on 5:13). In that case, the widely held assumption that the references to Mark and Silvanus have no contact with historical reality is no more than an assertion. It is quite possible to ask whether traditions, perhaps transmitted by former coworkers of Peter, have not played a role here,[49] even if this cannot be proved. The reason for the collection of "apostolic" traditions could have been a reaction to the collection of Pauline letters.[50] This continued in the collection of "catholic epistles," which came forth as their own body of literature beside the gospels and the *Corpus Paulinum*.

Date of Composition

The question of authorship is not least meaningful in relation to the problem of dating, on which the contemporary situation that can be assumed as background for 1 Peter is in turn dependent. If one starts with the assumption that the author of this work was not Peter himself, then one will think on the basis of the information just presented that a date of composition after 70 is likely.[51] When one tackles the *terminus ad quem*, the reference to 1 Peter in the *Epistle of Polycarp* (about 120) gives every indication that 1 Peter could hardly have been composed after the end of the first century. The use of 1 Peter by Papias[52] points in the same direction, as does that by 2 Peter, which assumes that 1 Peter is already an authoritative writing (2 Pet 3:1). Furthermore, 1 Peter is the only post-Pauline writing that still knows about the charismatic constitution of the community (4:10f.; cf. Rom 12:6ff.), even if this is already clearly overlaid by an early form of a presbyterial constitution. Now beginning around 110 in Asia Minor, Ignatius had

[49] Cf. Goppelt, 348, who suggests as a likely possibility that "in the letter representatives of the Roman community transmit a tradition that is influenced by Peter and Silvanus."

[50] This suggestions stems from a conversation with Martin Hengel.

[51] This is especially true on account of the identification of Rome and Babylon and speaks against Goppelt, 64f., who suggests a period of composition between 65 and 80.

[52] According to Eus, *HistEccl* 3.39.15.

begun advocating the monarchial episcopate as at least the most appropriate form of constitution for the Christian community;[53] 1 Peter, which shows a decidedly earlier stage in the development of the community constitution, could well have come into being before the turn of the century.[54] Clues are lacking for a more exact dating, although the lack of references to martyrs in contrast to the Apocalypse of John (cf. Rev 6:9; 17:5f.), which was also sent to Asia Minor, points rather to the early period of Domitian (between 81 and 90).

Place of Composition

The letter gives no direct clues about its composition; only the greeting from the "the co-elect [community] in Babylon" (5:13) can be understood as an indication. Because nothing is known about a relationship of Peter to the Mesopotamian Babylon and the oldest remains of the walls of the Egyptian Babylon go back to Trajan,[55] it is more reasonable to view this name as a cipher. Two possible meanings for this stand out. The first sees in this a codename for Rome. That is quite possible, because after the destruction of Jerusalem by the Romans there is evidence for Babylon as a cryptogram for Rome in both Christian[56] and Jewish tradition. With this fits the fact that after the end of the first century, Peter is, according to unanimous church tradition, brought into relationship with Rome (*1 Clem.* 5:3f.; *Ign. Rom.* 4:3). The other possibility would be to see in the reference to Babylon at the end of the letter an equivalent to the Diaspora that is referenced in 1:1; "Babylon" as the place of exile would be a symbol for the

[53] Already in the Pastoral Epistles active presbyters emerge from the presbyterate as *episkopoi* (1 Tim 3:1f.; Titus 1:5-9). *First Clement* (54:2; 57:1) assumes similar conditions in Rome as in the Pastoral Epistles; on the place of 1 Peter is the history of church offices cf. Goppelt, 64f.

[54] The apparently unproblematic relationship to the governmental authorities could also speak in favor of this (1 Pet 2:13-17), since this appears to point to the time before the final years of Domitian's reign. At that time there was persecution of various groups, which could also have affected the Christians (so Goppelt, 63), although with respect to this, when it comes to the Christians we have no clear evidence of widespread persecution in the time of Domitian.

[55] Cf. K. Aland, *Verhältnis*, 204.

[56] Cf. Rev 14:8; 16:19; 17:5; 18:2, 10, 21.

existence of the people of God (cf. 2:9f.) away from home in the dispersion.[57] What speaks for this is that this Diaspora situation in 5:13, as in 1:1f., is connected with thought of election and thereby with the tradition of the people of God.

The two interpretations—cryptogram for Rome and symbol for the dispersion—do not need to be mutually exclusive. It is worth serious consideration that 1 Peter has taken over the traditionally fixed possibility of using Babylon as a codeword for Rome, although in doing this—in contrast to the clearly anti-Rome Apocalypse of John—he has not (primarily) chosen this designation in order to underline the anti-God nature of Rome as the "Whore Babylon" (and at the same time to encode this dangerous criticism from non-Christians), but as a cipher for the Diaspora existence of the Roman community. This interpretation will be accepted here as the most likely. Thus in the case that in 1 Peter 5:13 Rome is at least also meant by "Babylon," as Eusebius already assumed (*HistEccl* 2.15.2), there remains the question of why this place of composition would be given in this presumably pseudepigraphical writing. Does this information about location only serve the fiction about the author, because Peter's martyrdom is thought to have taken place in Rome,[58] or does the writing actually come from Rome? Because the linguistic closeness of 1 Peter to other works written in Rome (above all to *1 Clement*[59]and through some unusual concepts also the *Shepherd of Hermas*[60])

[57] K. Berger supposes something like this in his reference to "the Jewish tradition of the Diaspora letters, especially testified to in the prophets Jeremiah and Baruch"; there Babylon is ". . . not negatively evaluated as in the apocalyptic writings and therefore stands for the assumed middle of the Diaspora, as in the letters of Jeremiah and Baruch" (*Formgeschichte*, 366). Similarly the Dead Sea Scrolls appear to use Damascus as a symbol for their existence as foreigners (cf. J. Maier, *Texte*, 49f.; Th. W. Gaster, *Scriptures*, 5). Herzer (*Petrus*, 264–66) also views the identification of Babylon with Rome as problematic and wants to view the former at least mainly as a symbol for the Diaspora situation that sets the tone for the letter.

[58] Peter's martyrdom in Rome is already in general suggested in the indirect information in *1 Clement* 5:3f. and Ignatius, Romans 4:3; it is clearly witnessed to from the second half of the second century (cf. Goppelt, 33f.).

[59] Cf. on this H. E. Lona, *Clemensbrief*, 56; see further the lists in Elliott, 138–48.

[60] Thus one finds ἀγαθοποιέω four times each in 1 Peter and Hermas, ἀδελφότης twice in 1 Peter and once in Hermas, ταπεινόφρων only in 1 Peter in the New Testament but also in Hermas 43.8 *Mand.* 11.8.

speaks for Rome as the place of composition and because on top of this, its closest contact with the Pauline tradition is with Romans, this place of composition will be accepted here as the most probable. In that case (if the place name then means Rome), 1 Peter is the first writing of early Christianity that—fictive or real—now goes from west to east. That is the opposite direction to the way which both the mission and the first early Christian literature (cf. Romans) had gone.[61] However, one should not on this basis come to the far-reaching conclusion about the place of priority of the Christian community in Rome.[62]

Addressees

One clearly can see from the letter that the community predominately, although not necessarily exclusively, consists of Gentile Christians: the religious disqualification of the community members' past as a futile way of life (1:18) and idolatrous impulses (4:3; cf. further 1 Pet 1:14; 2:25; 3:6) or statements such as 2:10, that those addressees were once not the people of God, can hardly refer to a Jewish past. Whatever may be the case about the place of composition (see earlier), there is little doubt that 1 Peter, as its address says (1:1) was sent to Asia Minor and arrived there: in the

[61] Cf. Goppelt, 353, "Through the greeting in 5:13 our letter becomes the first explicit Christian writing known to us that builds the arch of church contact from Rome to Asia Minor that in the second century would become the basis for the Catholic Church."

[62] This is true for the supposition that, because of the connection with the capital city of the world (in the case the information is to be taken historically), one is also to see here the first stirrings of a farther-reaching claim of Rome; so W. Bauer, *Rechtgläubigkeit*, 106. Goppelt, 66, also intimates this possibility: "Behind this letter stands the Christian community of the capital city of the world, which had become for the whole church the first community of martyrs because of the action of Nero and, through the martyrdom of the two most important apostles, the agent of their legacy. The letter discloses to all a sign of the series of ecumenical writings that would go out from the Christian community in Rome to the East." Less persuasive is Vielhauer's suggestion that here Paul is "forcefully [subordinated] to Peter"; the bias of the sender Peter/Silvanus is therefore ". . . also the establishment of the authority of Peter over the area of the Pauline mission" (Ph. Vielhauer, *Einleitung*, 589).

second century, it was cited by Polycarp there.[63] Without giving further details, Eusebius[64] transmits the tradition that Papias from Hierapolis in Phrygia "cited testimony from 1 John and 1 Peter." The situation of the addressees assumed in this letter also fits this address; that is, this situation was in essence characterized by suffering, which, as already shown, was indeed especially acute in Asia Minor in the early period.[65]

§7 The Influence of First Peter

First Peter offers theology as *scientia eminens practica*, as an intellectual argumentation concerning the faith, which floods the reality of his addressees with a new light and so opens up the perspective of hope in a situation of suffering. So it is not without reason that 1 Peter is more extensively used as a text for preaching than any other biblical document. This writing was especially influential, then, in an area which often is taken notice of only on the edges of exegesis, that is, in the *praxis pietatis* in its various aspects, upon which 1 Peter has developed an unusually broad influence because of the marked accent that the author has placed in his description of Christian existence on its horizontal and vertical referents. See for example the central importance of the category of foreignness for the existence of Christians in the world, which stretches from the early Christian communities[1] through monasticism in its various forms,[2] revival movements and edifying Christian literature,[3] Christian hymnology,[4] and up to personages of our day such as

[63] *Pol. Phil.* 1:3 (1 Pet 1:8); 2:1 (1 Pet 1:13); 2:2 (1 Pet 3:9) and 8:1 (1 Pet 2:24); cf. further the allusions to 1 Peter in *Pol. Phil.* 5:3; 7:2; 10:2.

[64] Eus, *HistEccl* 3.39.17.

[65] Cf. the Apocalypse of John and the Letter of Pliny (*Ep* 10.96).

[1] Παροικία or ἐκκλησία παροικοῦσα, that is, "being away from home" or "the church that is away from home," becomes a self-designation there, and from this the English word "parish" is derived.

[2] This reaches from ancient up to modern times, from which we also find reflections in Protestantism; cf. R. Feldmeier, *Fremde*, 214f.

[3] Cf. J. Bunyan, *Pilgrim's Progress* and Its Followers (cf. R. Feldmeier, *Fremde*, 216 note 38).

[4] Cf. on this R. Feldmeier, *Fremde*, 211–18.

D. Bonhoeffer[5] or John XXIII.[6] Hardly less influential were his statements about rebirth as a metaphor for the eschatological existence of believers. There are also easily remembered metaphors influenced by 1 Peter such as those referring to believers as "living stones," to Christ as the "chief shepherd," or to Satan as a "roaring lion" going after prey.

What is surprising is the influence of this primarily pastoral writing on the formation of dogma: nowhere in the New Testament are so many components of the later creeds, above all of the second article in the creeds, brought together in so close a space as here. Only at this point in the New Testament is God named not only "Father" but also "Creator" (4:19); in doing this his power (omnipotence) is stressed.[7] From the second article we find, besides the passion (3:18), also Christ's descent into the realm of the dead (3:19; 4:6), his resurrection (3:18, 21), his ascent into heaven (3:22), his sitting at the right hand of God (3:22), his return (ἀποκάλυψις 1:7, 13; 4:13), and his judgment of the living and the dead (4:5). Of these, the descent to the realm of the dead is only found in 1 Peter. Also, the expression κρῖναι ζῶντας καὶ νεκρούς has been taken over from 1 Peter 4:5.[8] From the third article, we add to this the Spirit as the divine power of life (3:18) with which are connected the resurrection of the dead (3:21) and

[5] Cf. D. Bonhoeffer, "While the world keeps holiday, they stand aside, and while the world sings, "Gather ye rose-buds while ye may," they mourn. They see that for all the jollity on board, the ship is beginning to sink. The world dreams of progress, of power and of the future, but the disciples mediate on the end, the last judgement, and the coming of the kingdom. To such heights the world cannot rise. . . . They stand as strangers in the world in the power of him who was such a stranger to the world that it crucified him." (D. Bonhoeffer, *The Cost of Discipleship*, 61f.)

[6] Over the one-sided emphasis on the being of the church in *Lumen Gentium* John XXIII, taking up the Augustinian category of *ecclesia peregrinans*, the church away from home, has stressed the church's being on the move.

[7] It is true that 1 Peter does not contain the term παντοκράτωρ—this appears with a single exception (2 Cor 6:18 in a citation of the Old Testament) only in the Apocalypse of John—but in both of his doxologies the work does indeed praise God's eternal power (4:11; 5:11; cf. 5:6), which comes out to be virtually the same thing.

[8] Similar expressions are also found in Acts 10:42 and 2 Tim 4:1, but it should be noted that the creed uses the terminology of 1 Peter.

the forgiveness of sin (2:24; 3:18, 21). With his division of the functions of Father, Son, and Spirit, 1 Peter has also laid the basis of what would later develop into a Trinitarian concept.[9]

The connection of original theological reflection and pastoral care always has drawn theologians in its path, among which Martin Luther is not the least, for whom "this Epistle of Saint Peter . . . [is] the most noble book in the New Testament and the purest Gospel"; the letter was, for Luther, the standard for that which could be considered gospel, "from this you can judge all other books and teachings, whether they speak Gospel or not."[10] The high valuation of this letter in Lutheran theology is also witnessed to by the greatest theologian of old Protestant orthodoxy, Johann Gerhard, to whose exegesis of almost a thousand pages this commentary is more than a little indebted.

[9] Cf. Davids, 22f.

[10] From Luther's Preface to 1 Peter, WA 12.260.

Part II

Exegesis

I. Prescript: The Addressees as Foreigners and People of God 1:1-2

Literature on 1 Peter 1:1-2: **O. Bocher**, "Jüdische und christliche Diaspora im neutestamentlichen Zeitalter," *EvDia* 38 (1967), 147–76; **N. Brox**, "Tendenz und Pseudepigraphie im ersten Petrusbrief," *Kairos* NF 20 (1978), 110–20; **M. A. Chevallier**, "1 Pierre 1/1 à 2/10. Structure littéraire et conséquences exégétiques,"RHPhR 51 (1971), 129–42; **M. A. Chevallier**, "Condition et vocation des chrétiens en diaspora. Remarques exégétiques sure la 1re épître de Pierre," *RevSR* 48 (1974), 387–98; **W. Dalton**, "The Church in 1 Peter," in *Tantur Yearbook* (Jerusalem, 1981–82), 79–91; **G. Delling**, "Der Bezug der christlichen Existenz auf das Heilshandeln Gottes nach dem ersten Petrusbrief," in H. D. Betz and L. Schottroff, eds., *Neues Testament und christliche Existenz* (*Festschrift* H. Braun) (Tübingen, 1973), 95–113, especially 105–7; **E. Fascher**, "Fremder," in RAC VIII (Stuttgart, 1972), 306–47; **R. Feldmeier**, *Die Christen als Fremde* (WUNT 64; Tübingen, 1992); **V. P. Furnish**, "Elect Sojourners in Christ: An Approach to the Theology of I Peter," *PerkJ* 28 (1975), 1–11, especially 2–6; **P. Gauthier**, "Meteques, Perieques et Paroikoi: Bilan et points d'interrogation," in R. Lonis (ed.), *l'Etranger dans le monde grec* (Travaux et mémoires: Études anciennes 4; Nancy, 1988), 23–46; **P. Lampe**, "'Fremdsein' als urchristlicher Lebensaspekt," *Ref.* 34 (1985), 58–62; **J. R. Mantey**, "Unusual Meanings for Prepositions in the Greek New Testament," *Exp* 25 (1923), 453–60; **J. R. Mantey**, "The Causal Use of Eis in the New Testament," *JBL* 70 (1951), 45–48; **J. R. Mantey**, "On Causal Eis Again," *JBL* 70 (1951), 309–11; **R. Marcus**, "On Causal Eis," *JBL* 70 (1951), 129–30; **R. Marcus**, "The Elusive Causal Eis," *JBL* 71 (1952), 43–44; **D. J. McCarthy**, "The Symbolism of Blood and Sacrifice," *JBL* 88 (1969), 166–76; **D. J. McCarthy**, "Further Notes on the Symbolism of Blood and Sacrifice," *JBL* 92 (1973), 205–10; **D. Sänger**, "Überlegungen zum Stichwort 'Diaspora' im Neuen Testament," *EvDia* 52 (1982), 76–88; **W. C. van Unnik**, "'Diaspora' en 'Kerk' in de eerste eeuwen van het Christendom," in W. H. Beekenkamp (ed.), *Ecclesia. Een bundel opstellen* (*Festschrift* J. N. B. van den Brink) (Nijhoff, 1959), 33–45; **G. Walser**, "Flüchtlinge und Exil im klassischen Altertum, vor allem in griechischer Zeit," in A. Mercier (ed.), *Der Flüchtling in der Weltgeschichte. Ein ungelöstes Problem der Menschheit* (Bern, 1974), 67–93; **Ch. Wolff**, "Christ und Welt im 1. Petrusbrief," *ThLZ* 100 (1975), 333–42.

(1:1) Peter, Apostle of Jesus Christ, to the elect foreigners in the dispersion who are from Pontus, Galatia, Cappadocia, Asia and Bithynia, (2) [chosen] according to the predetermination[1] of Father God[2] in sanctification through[3] the Spirit to obedience and to sprinkling with the blood of Jesus Christ. Grace [be with] you and peace in abundance.[4]

On the text: **1** Instead of Ἀσίας καὶ Βιθυνίας B* reads Ἀσίας, ℵ * 048 and a few other manuscripts have καὶ Βιθυνίας. The leaving out of καὶ Βιθυνίας in B* could be determined by content: Pontus and Bithynia formed a single province.

This beginning corresponds to the normal letter formula of that time, with its designation of the sender and addressees followed by a greeting. This formula was used both in pagan correspondence and also in the New Testament.[5] In filling out this formula, the author indeed uses Christian diction in highly compressed speech—there is no finite verb and 75 percent of the words are substantives[6]—already ringing the changes on his central theological concepts.

1:1

The author first introduces himself as Peter. This is the Greek translation of the honorary name that Jesus gave to Simon (i.e.,

[1] For the justification of this translation of πρόγνωσις see below pp. 55–57.

[2] The double expression θεὸς πατήρ "is often virtually a name of God" (Blass-Debrunner-Rehkopf §254, n. 2) and is therefore translated here with "Father God." In 1 Peter, this implies both fatherhood with respect to Christ and with respect to the believers (see below on 1:3).

[3] Πνεύματος is a *genitivus auctoris*, cf. Goppelt, 86; Brox, 57; Schelke, 21.

[4] The optative used to designate a wish that can be fulfilled is conjugated in the aorist in the New Testament except in Acts 8:20 (cf. Blass-Debrunner-Rehkopf §384).

[5] Especially in the Pauline letters, but also in other early Christian letters such as 2 Peter, 2 John, Jude, Revelation, *1 Clement*, *Polycarp*, *Martyrdom of Polycarp*.

[6] Twenty-four of thirty-two words; the impression of compression is strengthened through the total absence of articles.

"rock"),[7] which soon became a fixed epithet and finally totally replaced his old name in Greek-speaking early Christianity. This name had a ring of importance in the early church (cf. Matt 16:8), and it secured attention for any writing that cited this Peter. As in most of Paul's letters,[8] this name is filled out through a reference to the apostolate.

The title of honor "Apostle," through which a person was designated a "delegate" of Christ and which person could then also claim for himself a special authority,[9] is seldom used in the gospels. Where this happens, it designates the followers of the earthly Jesus and especially those followers that made up the circle of the Twelve (Mark 3:14; 6:30; Matt 10:2; Luke 6:13; 9:10; 17:15; 22:14; 24:10).[10] Paul's encounter with the Resurrected One and his commissioning by him is the basis for his self-understanding as an apostle, although with the metaphor of "untimely born" (1 Cor 15:8f.) and his self-designation as "the least of the apostles" (1 Cor 15:9) he himself grants that this self-designation is very much disputed.[11] Exactly who held this title in early Christianity is no longer able to be clearly discerned. Besides the Twelve, the Lord's brother James (1 Cor 15:7; Gal 1:19), Barnabas (1 Cor 9:6; Gal 2:9) and also Andronicus and Junia (Rom 16:7) are designated apostles.[12] This shows that the circle was in any case larger than the Twelve.

Therefore, the title "apostle" can on the one hand designate followers of the earthly Jesus and on the other those called by the Resurrected One. Both fit Peter; indeed, each to a special degree. According to the testimony of the gospels, he along with his

[7] Κηφᾶς, Aramaic כיפא, meaning rock or stone. The Aramaic form is still used by Paul alone (and once by John, John 1:42); the synoptic gospels use only the Greek form Πέτρος.

[8] The exceptions are Philippians and 1 and 2 Thessalonians (which identify the sender together with others who are not apostles).

[9] Cf. K. H. Rengstorf, "ἀποστέλλω," 432.

[10] In line with this Luke in Acts limits the concept of apostle strictly to the Twelve and with one exception (Acts 14:4, 14—a pre-Lucan source?) does not name Paul an apostle. The attempt to derive the circle of the Twelve from the Easter experience is discussed by G. Theißen and A. Merz, *Jesus*, 200f. and for good reasons rejected.

[11] Cf. 1 Cor 9:2; Paul also has to struggle continually (most clearly in 2 Cor) for the recognition of his apostolate.

[12] On Junia as a woman and on the evidence for female apostles in general see U. E. Eisen, *Women Officeholders*, 47–62.

brother Andrew were the first followers of Jesus (Mark 1:16-18 par.), and he had a special place in the circle of the Twelve, which is also shown in the conferment of the honorary name "Peter." After Jesus, the protagonist of the gospels, he is the one who is named the most, who stands in the first place in the lists of the apostles, and who acts most independently in the circle of the followers of Jesus.[13] According to the witness of all of the gospels, Jesus repeatedly turned to him with special words of commissioning in which the meaning of Peter for early Christianity is also reflected.[14] But Peter also appears to have played a special role in the resurrection, to which not only the gospels (Mark 16:7; Luke 24:12; John 20:2ff.) but also Paul testify in that Peter alone was the addressee of the first appearance of the Resurrected One (1 Cor 15:5). Peter is one of the three "pillar apostles" who led the early Christian community in Jerusalem (Gal 2:9), and not by chance he is also the first in Jerusalem whom Paul sought out after his call experience (Gal 1:18). Finally, Peter was also active as a missionary,[15] indeed, increasingly also in the Diaspora;[16] according to Acts 10, he was (despite Gal 2:9) even a decisive person in preparing the way for the mission to the Gentiles. Peter is, so to speak, the classic apostle. Unlike Paul, he does not have to defend his apostolic status.[17] However the authorship of 1 Peter is evaluated, for its hearers/readers it is always attributed to the follower of Jesus and apostle because of this identification of the author. They hear the voice of a decisive figure in early Christianity. That must always be taken into account as one reads this work.

[13] Cf. especially his confession of Jesus as Messiah in Mark 8:29 and his conflict with Jesus in 8:32f. that follows this; further see Mark 9:5; 10:28; 11:21; 14:29, 54, 66-72. His failure is then specifically pointed out by Jesus (cf. Mark 14:30, 37). The synoptic side references underline this special place of Peter through scenes in which he appears as an independent actor (cf. Matt 14:28-31; Luke 5:1-11; John 21:15-19); cf. R. Feldmeier, *Petrus*.

[14] Other than Mark 1:17 par., see Matt 16:17-19; Luke 22:31f.; John 21:15-17; cf. on this Ch. Böttrich, *Petrus*, 91–96.

[15] Acts 8:14ff.; 9:32ff.

[16] Peter's stay in Antioch is witnessed to by Gal 2:11-14. 1 Cor 9:5 testifies to Peter's travels; 1 Cor 1:12 could point to a mission in Corinth (cf. on this Ch. Böttrich, *Petrus*, 189ff.).

[17] Cf. Davids, 46.

[18] Cf. Deut 28:25; 30:4; Neh 1:9; Jdt 5:19; Isa 49:6; Jer 13:14 v.l.; 2 Macc 1:27; cf. W. C. van Unnik, *Selbstverständnis*, especially 69–88.

The letter is addressed to Christians "in the dispersion." The term διασπορά goes back to the LXX and describes the situation of the scattered people of God in exile among foreign populations.[18] In 1 Peter, the place where they are scattered is the five (or four)[19] large provinces in Asia Minor in which the addressees live.

The exact understanding of the place names in 1 Peter is disputed. Usually one assumes that provinces of the Roman Empire and not geographic regions are intended. But even then a lot remains baffling: the west part of Pontus had formed the Roman province of Bithynia and Pontus since the time of Pompey; the east part (Pontos Plemoniakos) came under direct Roman rule again after the death of Polemon II (63 C.E.) and was at first unified with Galatia (later, under Trajan, with Bithynia) into a single province. A mystery in the letter's address is the divided naming of Pontus and Bithynia at the beginning and end of the enumeration. There are a variety of conjectures about this: the conscious emphasis on these provinces because of a special urgency,[20] the route of the letter carrier's travel,[21] or the inadequate geographical knowledge of the author.[22]

However, it will become clear in what follows that this dispersion (just as the addressing of the addressees as "foreigners") is not solely intended geographically.[23] Independent from the question of whether 1 Peter was really sent as a circular letter, this sweeping "catholic" address shows that it is not dealing with correspondence in the narrower meaning but that it is dealing more with a circular letter written by an authoritative person "concerning the situation."[24] The reference to the situation, which doubtless plays a decisive role in 1 Peter, is, then, a general reference: It concerns not an individual Christian community but the situation of the communities in Asia Minor altogether and even beyond this, the situations of all "brothers and sisters in the world" (5:9).

[19] See below.

[20] Goppelt, 28f.

[21] E. G. Selwyn, *Peter*, 119.

[22] W. Schrage, *Staat*, 63.

[23] The reference to the inheritance of the Christians in heaven in 1:4 already makes it clear that although the foreignness is indeed concretely experienced in society, this foreignness in the end refers to a difference between the believers and the present form of the world.

[24] See the Introduction, (c) Author.

The recipients are addressed as "elect foreigners." This double expression sums up the central theme of the letter: Christian existence between God's election and society's rejection. The latter is underlined through the use of the relatively rare term παρεπί δημος, which designates a person who is staying (usually short-term) in a place where he or she is not at home and where he or she also does not intend to take up permanent residence.[25] At the same time, this self-designation "foreigner" picks up a slender Old Testamental/early Jewish tradition that understands distance from and conflict with the world around them as a result of election by God and membership in his people.

The semi-nomadic existence of the Patriarchs could in the Old Testament already be interpreted as a qualified foreignness due to God's election (cf. Gen 17:8; 23:4; 28:4; 35:27; 36:7; 37:1). Insofar as this foreignness therefore implied a special relationship to God right from the start, the legally and socially negative designation could be religiously "reversed in valence" and interpreted positively as an expression for continuing dependence on God. Therefore, one can have here the unusual occurrence that the socially excluding category of foreigner, through which one group signals to another that it does not belong, becomes the very self-designation of a people (1 Chr 29:10ff.; cf. Lev 25:23) or of pious individuals (cf. Ps 39:13; 119:19, 54). This tradition is, as we noted, slender; it appears that it was especially remembered (with reference to the Patriarchs) in times of crisis (such as the Babylonian exile).

The picture is similar in early Judaism: While the mainstream of early Jewish theology focused on national existence and virtually suppressed the remembrance of the existence of the Patriarchs as foreigners,[26] the motif of being a foreigner typically played a role in those places where loyalty to the tradition brought about conflict with the rest of society. This is intimated in Qumran in their comments concerning opposition to a people who had become impure[27] and is taken up in expanded form by Philo of Alexandria, who developed his philosophy of religion in the context of a pagan society that was becoming ever more hostile, which would finally

[25] Cf. R. Feldmeier, *Fremde*, 8–12.

[26] One need only read the relevant historical overview in Judith 5:5-21 or Josephus, *A.J.* 1.154ff.

[27] Cf. CD 5.5f.; further 1QM 1.2f.

destroy the centuries-long hope of the Jews for integration in Egypt.[28] Here one finds the connection of foreignness and election that can give the conceptualization virtually an elite tone.

Through the conscious use of this tradition, 1 Peter makes it possible for the believers to place their own experience of being foreigners into a relationship with earlier pious persons and thereby to set themselves into the context of the history of salvation and by this means to interpret it theologically. This referent of the address to the tradition of the people of God is intensified by means of the attribute ἐκλεκτός, "elect," which is found only in 1 Peter as a predicate of the addressees and is central to the first part of the work.

The word is found at least four times in 1 Peter out of the total of twenty-two occurrences in the whole New Testament; to this we add συνεκλεκτός in 5:13. According to Schrenk, 1 Peter is ". . . the only writing in the New Testament in which ἐκλεκτός received a thematic meaning right from the beginning. . . ."[29] At the same time, the statement about election refers in the first place totally to Christ: he is the "(corner)stone" chosen by God (1 Pet 2:4, 6)—significantly as an antithesis to his rejection by human beings (1 Pet 2:4). Because it is constituted through Christ as cornerstone (2:5), the Christian community is then also a "spiritual house" built from "living stones." Therefore, through Christ the predicate of election is passed on to Christians in 1 Peter 2:9 as the "elect race" (γένος ἐκλεκτόν) and now stands in parallel to the attribute "God's people." In 5:13 (συν)εκλεκτή is virtually a synonym for the Christian community.

Therefore, election and foreignness correlate: "Election" designates separation by God, which finds its social form in integration into the people of God. On the other hand, societal exclusion as a "foreign body" results from this. On this basis, then, in a type reverse conclusion 1 Peter can assure the oppressed Christians of their belonging to the people of God and his race, house, priest-

[28] In many writings, Philo designates the "sage" as a foreigner on earth, which the context clearly shows virtually always means obedience to the Jewish Torah that trains one in the highest virtues (cf. Philo, *Conf.* 75-82, further Philo, *Her.* 267, 274; *Agr.* 63ff.; *Somn.* 1.45; *Congr.* 22ff. among others). Especially instructive for the context of societal exclusion is Philo, *QG* 4.39.

[29] G. Schrenk, "ἐκλέγομαι," 195.

hood, etc. *The address "elect foreigners of the dispersion" makes it clear that the foreignness of the Christians in society and their special connection to God and also their integration into the community that he founded reciprocally entail each other.*[30]

1:2

In the second part of the address, the election[31] is based on God the Father's "foreknowledge," that is, however, immediately supplemented though sanctification through the Spirit and also the obedience and sprinkling by the blood of Christ; God's action on the believers is, therefore, right from the beginning explicitly Trinitarian.

At the head of the list stands the "foreknowledge [i.e., πρόγνωσις literally translated] of God the Father." This motif of divine predestination becomes explicit in 1:20 by means of the corresponding verb προγινώσκω. It is also expressed in 2:8 through another verb. The toned-down translation of the term πρόγνωσις with "purpose"[32] does not do justice to the theological weight of the expression.

The other uses of this relatively uncommon word confirm this. The verb προγινώσκω does not occur at all in the LXX with God as the subject; in the New Testament it occurs only three times, twice in Romans (Rom 8:29 and 11:2) and the other time in 1 Peter 1:20. The findings are similar for πρόγνωσις. In the LXX, it is used only twice (i.e., in the Greek Judith, and there it stands for the divine predestination of the future).[33] In the New Testament, the Peter of Acts uses it yet again in his Pentecost sermon (Acts 2:23). There, as a hendiadys with the parallel idea

[30] On the context of election and foreignness cf. also V. P. Furnish, *Sojourners*.

[31] The other possibility would be a reference of the Trinitarian formula to the apostle (cf. J. A. Cramer, *Catena*, 42, "Ἰδοὺ κατὰ πρόγνωσιν Θεοῦ Πατρὸς ἑαυτὸν Ἀπόστολον ὠνόμασε"; this interpretation is also found in some other Church Fathers, cf. Wohlenberg, 5). However, such a referent is unlikely because of the clear reference in v. 2 to the tradition of the people of God, which is already clearly alluded to in the address as ἐκλεκτοὶ παρεπίδημοι διασπορᾶς in 1:1.

[32] Brox, 57; cf. V. P. Furnish, *Sojourners*, 5.

[33] In Jdt 9:6 πρόγνωσις describes God's predestination of his judgment as a comfort in the oppression by the enemy; similarly also in Jdt 11:19.

of "fixed plan," it makes it clear that the death of Jesus corresponded to a divine plan. Therefore, this concept occurs in the Greek writings of ancient Judaism only after the second/first pre-Christian century in order to describe divine predestination; early Christianity took over this terminology. Presumably this represents the Jewish/Christian transformation of the widespread (originally Stoic)[34] notion in the Hellenistic world of a divine steering of the world through providence (Greek πρόνοια/Latin *providentia*). This concept became current (again) precisely in the New Testament period, and it had a relatively great importance not only in the Stoa of the period of the Caesars and in Middle Platonism,[35] but also in the contemporary Hellenistic Judaism.[36] However, this concept is lacking in the New Testament.[37] That certainly has to do with the fact that in the whole of the biblical Scriptures the classical idea of fate[38] is avoided, as is the concept of providence that became significant in ancient as well as in modern religiosity.[39] But this has also equally to do with the increasing need for theological systemization in the context of enculturation in the Hellenistic culture. Nevertheless, προγινώσκειν takes the place of

[34] In the Stoic interpretation of the world the concept of providence "has become a dogma . . . even virtually the core of their theology" (J. Behm, "προνοέω," 1007).

[35] In the first century C.E., two philosophical apologies for the concept of providence were written: *De providentia* by the Stoic Seneca and *De sera numinis vindicta* by the Middle Platonist and Delphic priest Plutarch (cf. on this R. Feldmeier, *De Sera*).

[36] Philo's conflict with his doubting nephew Tiberius Alexander, who probably later apostatized from Judaism, consists of two books "About Providence"; cf. further Philo, *Ebr*. 199; *Legat.* 336; *Her*. 58; in other early Jewish literature Wis 14:3; 17:2; *Aris. Ep*. 201; *3 Macc.* 4:21; 5:30; *4 Macc.* 13:19; 17.22 and Josephus (*A.J.* 4.47; 18.309; *B.J.* 3.391). With respect to this topic, the concept of divine predestination is also found in Qumran (1 QS 3.13–4.26), just as Josephus also emphasizes in view of Essenes (*A.J.* 13.172—there by the use of the term εἱμαρμένη).

[37] This notion was first taken up later in early Christian literature (cf. *1 Clem.* 24:5; *Herm.* 3.4 vis 1.3).

[38] Mythologically in the form of Moirae, i.e., the Fates, philosophically in the idea of *factum* or of *fortuna* (*caeca*) that is the εἱμαρμένη or the τύχη.

[39] There are even churches that are dedicated to providence (such as the Providence Church in Heidelberg). The meaning of this concept, however, reaches beyond Christianity (especially in its Enlightenment variant). Hitler himself loved to speak about providence!

προνοεῖν, probably as a conscious allusion to the Old Testamental concept of God's "recognition" as the deliberate affirmation and election of his chosen ones.[40] Accordingly then, the New Testament use of the concept (of the substantive πρόγνωσις in Acts 2:23 and 1 Peter 1:2, and also in the verb προγινώσκειν in Romans 8:29; 11:2 and 1 Peter 1:20) is not concerned with the philosophical postulate of a divine steering of the world (πρό νοια) that is accessible to reason (νοῦς), but with the theological conviction that the election and redemption that have so to speak recently taken place in Jesus Christ correspond to a consistent divine willing of salvation that was already determinative in the prophecies of the Old Testament (1 Pet 1:10f.) was even already fixed before the creation (1 Pet 1:20).

Πρόγνωσις means here—thus in connection with the concept of election in 1:1—the gracious will of God that is effective in the election, his predestination to salvation.[41] Admittedly 1 Peter does not show any interest at all in a speculative filling out of a predestination *teaching* with all its implications, but the first signs of such a teaching are present,[42] and without doubt in 1:2 and 1:20 is the need to recognize that the election to salvation that recently has taken place in Jesus Christ is to be understood as something that was already at work in God's previous dealings in creation and history and therefore corresponds to a divine self-determination before time. The more accessible designation of God in this text with the personal metaphor "Father" underlines that this predestination is not the determination of a fate.

The specification ἐν ἁγιασμῷ πνεύματος follows right after divine predestination. This expression can be variously translated "in the holiness [or sanctity] of the Spirit" or "in the sanctification through the Spirit." If the Trinitarian formula justifies the election

[40] Hos 5:3 LXX; ἐγὼ ἔγνων τὸν Ἐφραίμ; cf. also Amos 3:2.

[41] Cf. Gerhard, 32, "Πρόγνωσις ergo . . . *significat non solum praevisionem aeternam certorum individuorum & personarum salvandarum, sed etiam ordinationem mediorum, quibus DEUS homines salvare decrevit.*" It goes still further in the Reformed tradition; Th. Beza, *Novum Testamentum*, translated κατὰ πρόγνωσιν with "*ex praenotione Dei*" and in his commentary offers the alternative translation "*Ex antegresso decreto seu proposito Dei*," adding the reason, "*Omnia enim ista sunt synonyma*" (Tu. Beza, 2.424; cf. also the commentary on οὓς προέγνω in Rom 8:29, Tu. Beza, 57).

[42] Cf. 1 Pet 2:8 (end), where being scandalized by Christ is also referred back to divine determination.

through the (indirect) action of God on the addressees, then in reality only the second translation is possible. This interpretation is also supported by 2 Thessalonians 2:13, in which the divine action of "election to salvation" is further defined through this same expression. Finally, 1 Peter does indeed recognize (as is also otherwise common in biblical context)[43] holiness as an attribute of God (1:15) or his Spirit (1:12), but these statements are always made in soteriological contexts; that is, they point to the holiness of the Christian community that results from a relationship to the holy God (especially 1:15f.; cf. further 2:5, 9; 3:5). The genitive πνεύματος is consequently to be interpreted as *genitivus auctoris* (see earlier); the Spirit is the logical subject of the expression.[44] As such, it designates the power that seizes people and connects them with God, so that as God's possession they become holy themselves.

The third adverbial specification extends both of the previous ones. After God the Father's willing salvation and the sanctifying action of the Spirit, this specification now turns to the work of Jesus Christ in redemption, which is the logical subject of this third part. The preposition εἰς states the goal of the election: "consecration into the community of salvation based upon Christ's blood."[45] There is clearly an allusion to Exodus 24:7f., which concerns God's forming of the covenant with his people. Exodus 24:7 first describes the self-commitment of the people to obedience; then there follows in Exodus 24:8 the sprinkling with the "blood of the covenant." This scene, in which the new relationship with God, founded through blood, is connected with a self-commitment of the people of God, is clearly, in the view of 1 Peter, especially well suited as a type for the new reality of the believers that has been opened through Christ's suffering and death—believers who exactly through Christ's redemptive giving of his life (cf. 1 Peter 1:19; 2:24; 3:18) are integrated into the people of God (2:9f.; cf. 2:4f.) and are thereby heirs of the promise (1:10-12; cf. 1:4). The

[43] Originally, it did indeed designate simply the dynamic-magical religiosity, that which is endowed with power, whether it be as object or occurrence; it also referred to devoted people or offerings (cf. H.-P. Müller, קדש, 594–97). The attribute was then, however, focused on YHWH; cf. the Trishagion in Isa 6:3 or Ps 99:3, 5, 9 (H.-P. Müller, 597ff.).

[44] Elliott, 307, 318, correspondingly translates "through the sanctifying action of the Spirit."

[45] Windisch, 52.

sprinkling with the blood of Christ is, so to speak, *the new covenant*, and 1 Peter is then totally free to reclaim the honorable attributes of the Old Testament people of God for the Christian community (cf. especially 2:4f.; 2:9f.). First Peter has also retained the duty of obedience (that he has placed in front.).[46] Thereby he has in the prescript already underlined the relationship between the salvation opened through the death of Christ and the duty that it puts in place to a corresponding way of life. This will then be further explicated in the first main part of the letter (1:13–2:3),[47] in part by taking up the same terms, and the rest of the letter also continually returns to this relationship.

The letter opening, which evokes the themes of the following writing, closes with a wish of peace that is also a promise of

[46] Since a Trinitarian formula appears in verse 2 and the "obedience" does not fit in with this so well, it is continually discussed whether the genitive Ἰησοῦ Χριστοῦ should be referred to not only the sprinkling with the blood but also precisely to this obedience. However, every attempt to interpret this along these lines meets with the difficulty that then Ἰησοῦ Χριστοῦ must be a *genitivus objectivus* in view of ὑπακοή, while with reference to the blood it can only be understood as a *genitivus subjectivus*. Also the attempt to give a causal interpretation to εἰς is not convincing. The question of the extent to which there exists a causal εἰς in the New Testament and other contemporary writings was the subject of a controversy between J. R. Mantey ("Eis"; "Eis Again") and R. Marcus ("Eis"; "Elusive Eis"). However, 1 Pet 1:2 was still not yet understood as causal. The attempt of F. H. Agnew, "Translation," to justify a causal interpretation here on the basis of the alleged meaning of Jesus' obedience in 1 Peter (cf. also Elliott, 319) is not persuasive. The author of 1 Peter never speaks of Jesus' obedience, but rather relatively often of the obedience of the believers (1:14, 22; cf. 3:6); Agnew therefore also speaks extremely vaguely about the "obediential attitude of Jesus" (F. H. Agnew, 72). Because of this, the philologically closest meaning of the obedience of the elect with respect to God is preferred, which meaning corresponds both to the sense of the Exod 24:7f. tradition that is taken over here (in which it unmistakably concerns the obedience of the people to God's direction) and also to 1 Peter's concern to closely connect the promise of salvation and the demands that result from it.

[47] Thus at the beginning and also toward the end of the discussion (1:14, 22), the term ὑπακοή is again taken up (which term does not appear anywhere else in 1 Peter and also in the New Testament is only used a total of fifteen times). Between the two stands, a christological section composed in rhythmic prose, which praises redemption as a ransom through the αἷμα Χριστοῦ; cf. also the designation of the believers as "obedient children" in 1:14 (cf. further 1:22).

grace. Only the wish for peace "in abundance" (πληθυνθείη), formulated in the optative, drops out from the traditional schema.[48] This schema is a traditional expression for a letter opening[49] and perhaps is at the same time an allusion to less peaceful external circumstances of the "foreigners in the dispersion."[50]

II. The Reason for the Foreignness

Rebirth and the People of God 1:3–2:10

The section comprising 1:3 to 2:10 forms the first main part of 1 Peter. As shown in the introduction (p. 23–25), here the author foundationally establishes the positive other side of the existence of Christians as foreigners. In doing this, he weaves together and complementarily relates to one another two motifs, a salvation-historical/ecclesiological motif and an eschatological motif. The *belonging to the people of God* that is so massively stressed in 1:1f. is taken up again and further developed in 2:4-10. This frames the block 1:3–2:3, the explication of the renewal of life in the end times, by means of the metaphor of rebirth.

A. Rebirth 1:3–2:3

In this section, with its drastic picture of a new birth, which will moreover be further developed in a daring way—from new siring out of imperishable sperm through birth to nursing with "logos-milk" (1:3f., 23-25; 2:2f.)—1 Peter presents in a clear outline his message of salvation as life from hope (1:3, 13, 21) on the basis of

[48] The same formula appears in 2 Pet 1:2; similarly Judges 2. The putting together of grace and peace in this place appears in all genuine and apocryphal Pauline letters; cf. Rom 1:7; 1 Cor 1:3f.; 2 Cor 1:2; Gal 1:3; Eph 1:2; Phil 1:2; Col 1:2; 1 Thess 1:1f.; 2 Thess 1:2; 1 Tim 1:2; 2 Tim 1:2; Titus 1:4; Phlm 1:3,—but nowhere else in Greek literature independent of Paul. Therefore, "its presence in 1 Peter 1:2 is an indication of direct influence from the Pauline letters" (Boring, 51).

[49] Dan 4:1q; Dan 6:26q and also Dan 4:37c LXX; cf. also Dan 3:31 MT; 6:26 MT; tSan 2.6.

[50] See above Introduction, pp. 1–13.

being ransomed from a vain life-context (1:18f.) and the overcoming of transience (1:23-25). In the process, this section is again divided into two parts: 1:3-12 forms the (unusually extensive) introductory eulogy, and, in three paragraphs, 1:13–2:3 establishes the foundational context of salvation and sanctification, of promise and obligation.

1. Introductory Eulogy: Rebirth and Joy in Suffering 1:3-12

The letter begins in 1:3-12 with a eulogy, with praise to God for the future salvation that he has inaugurated.[1] The form is traditional, similar to the eulogies that one finds in the Old Testament and in ancient Jewish texts.[2] The view of those addressed is thus directed first of all on God and the salvation that is inaugurated by him that has radically transformed their lives. They are "procreated anew to a living hope" (1:3). From this perspective of hope that which oppresses them also appears in a new light: the present sadness is relativized in view of the coming salvation, indeed eclipsed by joy. Thus praise of God, promise and comfort affect each other. "This section therefore functions as the *prooemium* for the discussion to follow, showing how the triune God has established the church as a community of hope by reason of the resurrection of Jesus."[3]

(i) Praise over God's Salvific Action 1:3-5

Literature on 1 Peter 1:3-5: **J. Coutts**, "Ephesians I. 3-14 and I Peter I. 3-13," *NTS* 3 (1956–1957), 115–27; **G. Delling**, "Der Bezug der christlichen Existenz auf das Heilshandeln Gottes nach dem ersten Petrusbrief," in H. D. Betz/L. Schottroff, *Neues Testament und christliche Existenz* (*Festschrift* H. Braun) (Tübingen, 1973), 95–113; **V. P. Furnish**, "Elect Sojourners in Christ: An Approach to the Theology of I Peter," *PerkJ* 28 (1975), 1–11, especially 6–10.

[1] On the genre of eulogy cf. P. Schäfer, "Benediktionen"; R. Deichgräber, "Benediktionen."

[2] Gen 14:20; Exod 18:10; 2 Chron 2:11; 6:4; Ezra 8:25; Ps 65 (66):20; 71 (72):18; 123 (124):6; 134 (135):21; Dan 3:26; Tob 11:17; 13:1; *Ps. Sol.* 2:33, 37 (cf. Elliott, 330 n. 10).

[3] Achtemeier, 91.

(3) Praised [be] the God and Father of our Lord Jesus Christ who, according to his rich[4] compassion, has procreated us anew to a living hope through the resurrection of Jesus Christ from the dead, (4) to an imperishable, undefiled, and unfading inheritance that is kept in heaven for you, (5) who are being protected in the power of God through faith to salvation, [which stands] ready to be revealed at the end of time.

On the text: **3** instead of εἰς ἐλπίδα ζῶσαν some witnesses such as the minuscules 1505 and 1852, the Syriac and Bohairic translations, and also some church fathers read εἰς ἐλπίδα ζωῆς. This clearly secondary reading is an attempt to interpret the attribute "living" (see next).

As the prescript has already done, this start of the eulogy also offers theology in a linguistically extremely compressed form. That appears in the syntax: verses 3-5 form a single coherent nominal sentence in which not a single copula is used. Since the classical period, the nominal sentence was used above all in refined and emphatic speech, in hymns to a degree, but also in proverbs or official decrees.[5] From the stylistic point of view alone, an impression of festive, uplifted, but also established validity is communicated. This can hardly be reproduced in English, and thus the verbal adjectives and participles are here translated through finite verbs. In verse 4, one notes the change to the second person: While previously the discussion was about the fact that God had procreated *us* anew, after v. 4 the inheritance in heaven is kept *for you*. This serves to intensify the address.

1:3

"Praised be God"—such a start with praise to God (or thanks to him) is more than simply convention: in such a beginning with praise, it becomes clear that believing existence is not based in itself, but is indebted to God's provenient affection. Believing existence is therefore essentially a responding state of being

[4] Cf. Huther, 53, "Through πολύ the wealth of the divine compassion is emphasized."

[5] Cf. Schwyzer, II, 623, the pure nominal sentence became "gradually a poetic archaism or a form of expression of special stylistic value or finally to a short form of official speech."

that corresponds to God's personally addressing the believers in Christ (and only as a result of this is Christian existence then also a responsible state of being). Yet one of the central acts of true equivalence is praise and thanks, for precisely there one's own interests (individual or collective) do not stand in the first place, but those of the other who is praised.[6]

This God who is praised is further defined as "the Father of our Lord Jesus Christ." The designation of Christ as "our Lord" underlines the connection of the believers with Christ. The picture of new siring (1:3; cf. 1:23; 2:2f.) makes it clear that those who belong to this Lord also enter his Father/Son relationship. The participle ἀναγεννήσας used here for the metaphor of divine fatherhood is an aorist participle; the punctiliar *Aktionsart* means that with respect to this "new siring," we are not dealing with a universal "nature" of God (as the Homeric Zeus who is more or less defined as the "father" of gods and human beings), but that the new siring is founded in a single historical event. This event is the resurrection of Jesus Christ, which is named in the text that follows. It is through the resurrection that God has conquered the world's separation from himself, a world that is subjected to transience and thereby sin and death, and has made a new beginning possible. One finds similar statements in Paul as well;[7] in 1 Peter, this divine life-power that is imparted through the resurrection of Christ is brought to a head with respect to the existence of the believers in the concept of rebirth: God, as "the one who has procreated us anew," is the origin and defining power of their new

[6] First Peter continually emphasizes the meaning of speech—better, of dialogue with God—for the constitution of the existence of the "newly procreated." Thus in 1:14ff. ἐπικαλεῖν of the τέκνα ὑπακοῆς corresponds to the divine καλεῖν, the believers are born again through the divine word (1:23-25), they are nourished with "word-milk" (2:2), and they can accordingly give an apology (i.e., answering word) to the unbelievers who ask about their *logos* (i.e., reason or word) for the "hope that is in you" (3:15), just as, on the other hand, the non-Christians are defined by the fact that they do not trust the word (cf 2:8; 3:1).

[7] The apostle can make this explicit in various ways—as God's justifying (cf. Rom 3:26; 4:5; etc.) and reconciling action (cf. Rom 5:10; 2 Cor 5:18), but also in this way, that through the resurrection of Christ God had revealed himself as the one who "makes alive" (Rom 4:17; 1 Cor 15:22, 45) so that in Christ the "new creation" has already become a reality (2 Cor 5:17; Gal 6:15).

life, so-to-speak their life principle, and accordingly is then called upon as father by them (1:17; cf. 1:2).

This action of God in rebirth is further defined in three ways. First, the basis in God himself is indicated; it is, so to speak, the divine motivation: God's great compassion. This reference to God's compassion as the motivation for his action corresponds to biblical modes of thinking and speaking.[8]

In the pagan world, at least among the educated, such speech about divine compassion is by no means self-evident, because generally affect was viewed as outside control and therefore as something inferior that is incompatible with true divinity.[9] In his *Symposium*, Plato had adjudged Eros only the status of a daemon, because love, as evidence of a lack, cannot be compatible with divinity; Eros is therefore ". . . between the mortal and immortal . . . a great daemon" (Plato, *Symp* 202d).[10] Then the Middle Platonist Apuleius stressed with reference to Plato that the highest God "is free from every shackle of suffering or action and is not obligated to any type of task by some form of return service."[11] Even if this "axiom of *apatheia*"[12] was not always dealt with consistently in lived religiosity,[13] yet emotions were at most something that the divinities could have, but not that in which their being consisted. In contrast to this, the being of the

[8] One finds similar formulations in the LXX in Num 14:19; Neh 13:22; Ps 24:7; 50:3; 105:45; 108:26; 118:88, 149; Sir 16:12; 50:22; Lam 3:32; Dan 3:42; 1 Macc 13:46; in the New Testament Titus 3:5. On the relationship of the introductory eulogy to the Pauline eulogies cf. J. Herzer, *Petrus*, 49–54.

[9] On the axiomatic nature of *apatheia* cf. the discussion of W. Elert, *Christologie*, 71–132.

[10] One could, on the other hand, attribute affects to daemons—but precisely this confirmed their lesser divinity.

[11] Apul, *DeDeo* 1.124. Celsus later attacks Christianity with similar arguments.

[12] This formulation comes from W. Elert, *Christologie*, 74ff.

[13] Apuleius himself in the eleventh book of his "Golden Ass" lets Isis appear as ruler of the world and announce redemption to the transformed Lucius with the reason that she was "moved" by his requests (*tuis commota . . . precibus*) and "gripped with pity" (*miserata*), and because of his fate she helps him (Apul, *Met* 11.5.1.4). The most marked deviation is Plutarch's definition of Eros as God in his *Amatorius* (756Bff.).

[14] H. Spieckermann, *Liebeserklärung*, has shown not only that this is true for the New Testament testimony to God but that "God's self-determination to love" can be seen already as a constitutive part of the Old Testament statements about God.

biblical God consisted in this, that he committed himself to a counterpart as a free grant, that he—according to the famous formulation in 1 John 4:8, 16—*is* love.[14]

The expression "according to his great compassion" makes it clear that "rebirth" is caused by God alone. It therefore is not so much about a reaction of God to his dependents coming to him, but it is based in the essence of God, who of his own accord turns to his counterpart, communicates himself to that one, and so transforms them.[15]

How important precisely this motif of the divine compassion is is shown in that the letter returns to it again at the end of the first main part in 2:10, where in a *parallelismus membrorum* he equates the constitution of the believers as the people of God with God's compassion toward them. Both rebirth to a living hope and also calling as the people of God are based upon God's compassion. *God's compassion thereby connects the two key soteriological ideas of 1 Peter.*

The second further definition of the "new siring" specifies the goal or the result of this "new procreating" with εἰς: the "living hope." The high theological valuation of hope is a characteristic of 1 Peter[16] and stands in marked contrast to the evaluation of hope in the Hellenistic culture as an ambivalent human behavior.

Excursus 1: Hope

"We are full of hope throughout our whole life," says Plato (*Phileb* 39e). In reality, it is indeed one of the defining characteristics of human beings that they hope. Human beings anticipate their future. They are ahead of their time. On the one hand, hope is human's strength—the whole of human development and culture is only explicable because humans have the ability to loose themselves from the immediate stimulus-response context, and

[15] Cf. Luther's twenty-eighth thesis in the Heidelberg Disputation, "*Amor Dei non invenit sed creat suum diligibile*." This creative love stands in contrast to human love, which is dependent upon an object worthy of love, "*Amor hominis fit a suo diligibili*" (WA 1.365).

[16] The Christian life is distinguished by the fact that it is determined by hope (1 Pet 1:13, 21; 3:5), and Christians are obligated to give information about and account for this "hope in you" (ἐν ὑμῖν ἐλπίς) to unbelievers (3:15).

thereby from the more or less unconscious integration into the present, and to imagine the future and so to plan. But that is only the positive side of the coin; the other side is the Latin proverb "*Spes saepe fallit*," "Hope often deceives." Hope is therefore at least two-sided. Sophocles (497–406/5) thus discovers in his *Antigone* (Soph, *Ant* 615–19), "See how that hope whose wanderings are so wide / truly is a benefit to many men, / but to an equal number it is a false lure of light-headed desires. / The deception comes to one who is wholly unawares / until he burns his foot / on a hot fire" (Sophocles, *The Antigone of Sophocles*, trans. Sir Richard Jebb [Cambridge, Cambridge University Press, 1891]). This ambivalence of hope becomes narrative in the traditional Pandora myth[17] developed by Hesiod (ca. 700 B.C.E.), when beside the evils sent to punish humanity only hope remains in Pandora's jug.[18] Those who interpret this passage continually speculate about whether this hope that remains for human beings is likewise an evil or—because it is separated from the evils—a good. The ancient authors already interpreted this in contradictory ways: for some, hope is the holy goddess remaining for human beings, while for others it is a nasty daemon (*Theog* 1135ff.; 637f.). Today both interpretations have firm supporters.[19] The myth and its understanding of hope remain

[17] Hes, *Op* 57–105; according to the parallel tradition in his *Theogonia* (Hes, *Theog* 570–613) the woman herself is the divine punishment.

[18] With respect to the unclear metaphor in this text cf. the commentary by E. G. Schmidt, "Einführung," 199, "If the story were conceptually of a piece, it would state that hope (*elpis*) was withheld from humanity by Zeus' intention, that their life is therefore hopeless. But Hesiod intends instead to express the opposite: however badly it may go with humanity, at least hope remains for them. The two details of the tale require therefore different interpretations: Evils have come upon humanity because they *escaped* from Pandora's jug; hope is among humanity because it *remained* in the jug."

[19] The Marxist philosopher Ernst Bloch sings the love song of hope as "a remaining good"—thus the heading of the chapter in his main work about the Pandora myth with the descriptive title of "The Principle of *Hope*." Hope is, for him, the necessary subjective correlate to the persuasion that human history is developing towards a classless society; hope is then at the same time the "already" in the "not yet." As an anticipation of the future being-at-home hope therefore helps to cope with a present not yet released (E. Bloch, *Hoffnung*, 389). By way of contrast, for Friedrich Nietzsche hope is nothing other than empty illusion and, like every lie, in the end only contributes to the exponentiation of evil. Nietzsche's interpretation of the myth is, then, consequently pessimistic: "Zeus wished precisely that humanity, which is already

ambiguous—and that is perhaps not accidental, for it fits the nature of hope that *shifts between (harmful) deception*[20] *and (alleviating) comfort*. In his tragedy "Prometheus Bound" Aeschylus (525–456 B.C.E.) expresses hope's tragic ambiguity when he has the Titan, whom the gods have punished in forged shackles, say that because of suffering he no longer allows human beings to see the future. Instead of this, he has planted "blind hope" in their hearts.

The biblical statements about hope are conspicuously different. It is true that even in the Old Testament, hope can have a negative ring about it, but this does not depend upon the human attitude of hope itself but upon the object upon which this hope is set. Insofar as people depend upon worthless things, they miss their existence. Against this stands an unqualified positive evaluation of hope insofar as it directs its trust toward God.[21] Such a hope is not founded upon the unstable foundation of human expectation and fears but on the certainty of the trustworthiness of God; it bases itself *not on something* that one wishes to obtain or avoid but *on God, the basis and content of hope*. Right in the prayers of the Old Testament, the Psalms, one continually comes across confessions such as "the Lord is my hope" or something similar (Ps 13 [12]: 6a; 40 [39]:4; 61 [60]:3; 62 [61]:7f.; 71 [70]:5; 91 [90]:9; 142 [141]:6; 146 [145]:5) or confessional addresses such as "I hope/have hoped in you" (Ps 7:2; 16 [15]:1; 25 [24]:20; 31 [30]:7, among others). The one who bases his or her trust on God will not be put to shame (Ps 22 [21]:6; 25 [24]:20; cf. Rom 5:5), but will be blessed (Ps 34 [33]:9; 84 [83]:13). For this reason, hope is something other than the anticipation of what is desired; rather it becomes in a certain respect a synonym for the relationship to God.[22] Insofar

---

so very much tormented by the other evils, would yet not throw away its life, but move forward, continuing to allow itself to be tormented anew. Thus he gave hope to humanity; it is in reality the evilest of evils, since it lengthens the torment of human beings" (F. Nietzsche, "Menschliches," I, 71).

[20] Again, Hesiod, "The idle man who waits on empty hope, lacking a livelihood, lays to heart mischief-making; it is not a wholesome hope that accompanies a needy man . . ." (Hesiod, "*Works and Days*," in *The Homeric Hymns and Homerica with an English Translation*; trans. Hugh G. Evelyn-White [Cambridge, Mass.: Harvard University Press/London: William Heinemann, 1914], 500–2).

[21] Cf. A. Jepsen, בטח.

[22] R. Bultmann, "ἐλπίς," 520, "The difference between hope and trust disappears."

as the one who hopes does not hope in something, but hopes in God and trusts in him, hope as such already can become the substance of salvation. *Spes* and *res sperata* come together—to the extent that through hope the conquest of death becomes one's own. According to Wisdom the hope of the righteous—in contrast to the "empty hope" of the foolish and godless (3:11, ἡ κενὴ ἐλπίς)—is as a hope based in God already itself "full of immortality" (3:4, ἡ ἐλπὶς αὐτῶν ἀθανασίας πλήρης).

The New Testament builds on this Old Testamental/early Jewish understanding of hope to the extent that, here as well, the element of stable trust determines the idea of hope. At the same time, this hope becomes more specific in the New Testament—that which is hoped for in the future has already come to pass in Jesus Christ. The Christian hope is thus based upon *God's act* in the resurrection of Jesus Christ from the dead, through which he has defined himself as creator out of nothing and thereby as the death-conquering life force,[23] who thus through the cross has saved from sin, death, and decay. The future is already decided in Christ and, with reference to the gospel, believers are then also certain of their future, without the "suffering of the present age" and the groaning and sighing of the creation (Rom 8:18f.) thereby being covered up. "We have been saved in hope" (Rom 8:24, ἐσώθημεν). Such a hope is the pledge of the confidence of faith; it "will not disappoint" (Rom 5:5; cf. Rom 5; 2-4; 8:23-25). With reference to Abraham, Paul can even designate faith as hope against hope (Rom 4:18), as a trust that is stronger than the apparently incontrovertible evidence of our world such as nothingness and death (Rom 4:17). The having or not having of such hope thus forms virtually the *differentia specifica* between Christians and non-Christians (1 Thess 4:13; Eph 2:12); the Christian God is a "God of hope" (Rom 15:13); the Christian faith is "nothing less than . . . a *religion of hope*."[24]

Together with other New Testament writings that mediate Christianity to the Hellenistic world,[25] 1 Peter has the emphasis

[23] Rom 4:17, "ζῳοποιῶν τοὺς νεκροὺς καὶ καλῶν τὰ μὴ ὄντα ὡς ὄντα," cf. 1 Cor 15:22, 45; see also Davids, 19.

[24] H.-J. Eckstein, *Hoffnung*, 18.

[25] Besides the letters of Paul (and here especially Romans and 1 Thessalonians) and Acts, one can name the Deutero-Pauline Ephesians, Colossians, Titus, and also Hebrews.

on the hope of life as the center of Christian existence. Yet, probably as a result of the massive present oppression, in 1 Peter more decisively than in the other writings an "anchor [is laid] in the future."[26] This is probably also connected to the religious context that has been sketched in that Christianity increasingly presented itself as the antithesis to a world characterized by "emptiness" and "transience" and thereby as a religion of redemption. As a trusting anticipation of the renewed reality, hope becomes here virtually the life principle of the regenerate Christian humanity.[27] Precisely this underlines the description of hope as "living." The same attribute qualifies the "divine word" in 1:23, Christ as the "living stone" in 2:4. All three occurrences of this type of attribution have a commonality in the way they are connected (in the closest way) with the new life of the believers. The living hope is the goal of rebirth (1:3), the "living word of God" as "immortal sperm" establishes the new existence of the regenerate (1:23-25), and the "living stone" is that stone that awakes the believers to life so that those who have connected themselves to him have now themselves become "living stones" in order to be built together with him into a "spiritual house" (2:4f.). The description of hope, word and stone as "living" may in all three cases be understood as inclusive, such that the item that one so describes is thereby qualified as a form of the appearance of the divine life-power that communicates itself through this to the believers. *"Living" also specifies with the substance of salvation the recipients of this substance*, recipients who through hope, the divine word and the "living stone" Christ take part in God's life and therefore are regenerate. *The living hope is a hope that makes alive.*[28]

[26] E. Schweizer, *Christology*, 372.

[27] Gerhard, 48, defines hope in this way as "*regenerationis nostrae causa formalis*," as the cause of rebirth, which it at the same time "forms," therefore defining its essence.

[28] With his own precision, Johann Gerhard has put into a nutshell the various aspects of this talk in 1 Peter of living hope as an invigorating power of God that already fills the present existence with joy and at the same time gives a participation in God's eternal life and as such not only stands in contrast to the emptiness of human hope but also produces the faith that becomes active in love (Gerhard, 55, "Quo sensu spes illa, ad quam DEUS nos regenerasse dicitur, vocetur viva? *Resp. 1. Ratione objecti, quia fertur in DEUM vivum & in Christum, qui est* vita aeterna. *1 Joh. 5. v. 20. 2. Ratione effecti, quia spes illa cor vivificat, h.e. spirituali gaudio perfundit, ac fides Christum*

"Living hope" therefore is not simply an enallage (an exchange of an attributive genitive and an adjective), as the *varia lectio* on this text make obvious (ἐλπὶς ζωῆς). Rather it is indeed a metonymy, as Beza already suggested for the understanding of ἐλπὶς ζῶσα, when he understood the expression "μετωνυμικῶς *pro re sperata, ut in Rom. 8.24, & alibi saepe.*"[29] Admittedly, by this it is not sufficiently shown that all three items that are specified in the first main part of 1 Peter as "living"—hope, word, and the stone Christ—show their livingness precisely in that they communicate (divine) life to the believers.[30] With a comparable meaning, the Psalmist says that with God is the source of life (Ps 36:10), or the Gospel of John yet more clearly identifies Christ himself as "the life" (John 11:25; 14:6; cf. John 1:4; Acts 3:15) and thereby means just this, that through him (eternal) life is communicated (John 5:26; 6:33-35, etc.; similarly 2 Cor 4:10f.). Thus, analogous to 1 Peter, one also finds in John a use of the specification "living" when the Johannine Christ designates himself as "living water" (John 4:10f.), or as "living bread" by means of which those who eat of it "will live eternally" (John 6:51). The common specification of the biblical God as the "living God" also not only stands in opposition to the "dead" idols, but bases itself in the end on the resurrection (1 Thess 1:9f.) and so relates to the power of God through which he communicates (eternal) life (John 6:57). In the resurrection, the living God has shown himself to be the God who makes alive (Rom 4:17; 8:11; 1 Cor 15:22, 36, 45; John 5:21; cf. 1 Pet 3:18), he is the "God of the living" (Mark 12:27 par.).

1:4

If the focus of verse 3 lay in action of God that is praised, then now in verse 4 the hope to which the believers are regenerated will be more specifically described: they are regenerated to an "imperishable, undefiled, and unfading inheritance that is kept in

---

veram vitam apprehendens vitae spiritulis participes nos facit. Hab. 2. v. 4. Rom. 1. v. 17. Gal 3. v. 11. 3. Ratione adjuncti. Spes humana est σκιᾶς ὄναρ, *est* κενή inanis & vacua, *Sap. 3. v. 1. cum sit de rebus vanis ac transitoriis, sed spes, in quam DEUS nos regenerat, est viva & solida, firmo innixa fundamento, quae proinde non confundit, Rom 5. v. 5. 4. Ratione contrarii. Fides, per quam regeneramur, non est mortuum quid & inefficax, sed viva & efficax per caritatem. Gal 5. v. 6 Jacob. 2. v. ult.*").

[29] Th. Beza, *Novum Testamentum*, 425.

[30] The closest parallel to this with a view to hope is the already cited text in Wis 3:4, where it is said about ἐλπίς that she is ἀθανασίας πλήρης.

heaven for you." Various theological ideas of 1 Peter intersect in the metaphor of inheritance (κληρονομία): (1) κληρονομία (Heb. נחלה) originally designated the land promised to the fathers (Deut 12:9; 19:14; Josh 11:23; 15:20 etc.); thus it stems from the Old Testamental/Jewish *people of God tradition*.[31] Thereby a connection to the reception of this tradition in the framework of the first main part (1 Pet 1:1f.; 2:9f.) is established. (2) This "inheritance" became in ancient Judaism,[32] as also in early Christianity,[33] a metaphor for the eschatological substance of salvation consisting of (eternal) life. The specification of the inheritance here through the three attributes formed with an α-*privativum* and also its formation of a parallel with the "living hope" are consistent with this. (3) At the same time, in the context of 1 Peter, the metaphor of inheritance relates to rebirth; as also in Paul (cf. Rom 8:14-17; Gal 4:6f.), being a child of God is the basis for a claim to the inheritance. (4) The crossing of present and future that is characteristic of Christian existence "between the times" is also contained in the metaphor of inheritance—as they are "heirs," their salvation is indeed still future, but as regenerate children of God the Christians already have the right of inheritance. Thus the reference to "inheritance" also fits with the foreignness of Christians that is stressed in 1:1.

[31] Tradition-historically the Old Testamental conception of Israel's "inheritance" which in the Old Testament relates to the Promised Land, stands in the background here. This conception, however, was already eschatologized in early Judaism, when the earth is promised as an inheritance to the elect (cf. especially *1 En.* 5.6-8). 1 QS 11.7f. states that the elect will have their portion (inheritance) "in the lot of the saints."

[32] *Pss. Sol.* 14.10 says that the pious will inherit "life in joy."

[33] The New Testament speaks about the "heirs" of eternal life (Mark 10:17 par.), of God's rule (Matt 25:34; 1 Cor 6:9f.; 15:50; Gal 5:21), of salvation (Heb 1:14) or of an "(eternal) inheritance" as the gift of eschatological salvation promised to the Christians (cf. Acts 20:32; Gal 3:18; Eph 1:14, 18; 5:5; Col 3:24; Heb 9:15). According to Matt 5:5 the meek inherit the γῆ, which is time and again interpreted as the land of Israel; most recently J. Laaksonen, *Jesus*, 353–72, holds Matthew 5:5 to stem from Jesus and sees here a promise of taking possession of the Promised Land. In my opinion, such an interpretation is at most only true for a preliminary stage of this Beatitude, in the case that such a preliminary stage ever existed (in the parallel tradition of the Beatitudes in Luke 6:20f., it is lacking). The parallel promise of heaven in Beatitudes 1 and 8 (Matt 5:3, 10) makes it more likely that this should be understood in the sense of the common Matthean putting together of "heaven and earth," therefore that γῆ designates the whole world.

The eternal being at home with God[34] because of election and rebirth implies being foreign. "For it is precisely the promised home that makes homeless" (D. Sölle).

This inheritance is further defined through the three attributes "imperishable, undefiled, and unfading." Such a placing together in a row of adjectives of denial built with the α-*privativum* is characteristic of the negative theology of the ancient metaphysic.[35] All three attributes define the divine through its difference from that which is viewed as the essence of this world, namely the undertow of transience that shows itself in destruction, defilement, and aging, whose undertow destroys all that is beautiful and living. First Peter probably picks up these attributes from ancient metaphysics through the mediation of Diaspora Judaism,[36] but that which in ancient metaphysics expresses the independence of the divine from the earthly-human he grants to the "regenerate." *These attributes, which define the divine through the negation of the earthly-human reality, become in 1 Peter soteriological attributes*. This means in view of 1:4 that the attributes make clear what it means to have a "living hope": participation in the indestructible fullness of divine life is guaranteed to the elect through the divine new siring.[37]

[34] Cf. also 2:25, where the returning of wandering sheep "to the shepherd and bishop of your souls" is praised as the point of the hymn to Christ.

[35] Cf. Aristot, *Cael* 1.270a; 1.277b; 1.282ab; Plut, *EDelph* 19.392E; 20.393A, etc. The non-biblical origin of the attributes has already come to the attention of R. Perdelwitz, *Mysterienreligion*, 45–50; nevertheless, he interprets them thus, that through them Christian baptism is distinguished as the antithesis to the mysteries.

[36] In Philo, one finds the attributes used here, ἀμάραντος and especially ἄφθαρτος, as attributes of the heavenly reality. This does not mean that 1 Peter is directly dependent upon Philo. Too many witnesses of Diaspora Judaism have been lost for such a conclusion. It could also well be that the same milieu of the Diaspora synagogue influenced both Philo and Peter. Particularly in view of 1 Peter 1:4, a relationship to Wisdom of Solomon catches one's attention, since in Wisdom one encounters all three ideas as attributes of heavenly things: ἄφθαρτος in 12:1 of the divine spirit, in 18:4 of the light of the divine law; ἀμίαντος in 4:2 in the context of the picture of a competition as a metaphor for a virtuous life ("unfading prize" for the victory) and ἀμάραντος in 6:12 of wisdom.

[37] See below on 1:23-25.

Excursus 2: "Imperishable, Undefiled, Unfading"—The Reception and Transformation of Metaphysical Attributes of God in 1 Peter

The first attribute, which later in the work will play a still larger role in the context of rebirth (1:23; cf. 1:18), is *imperishability*. The conceptual field of ἄφθαρτος and ἀφθαρσία has no equivalence in the Hebrew Bible,[38] but on the other hand, it is characteristic for pagan religious philosophy. Epicurus virtually has a preference for this attribute.[39] Through it (together with a second attribute μακάριος), he expresses the total independence of the gods from the world: because they do not allow themselves to be affected by the world in any way, they are happy and imperishable. One is therefore dealing with an exclusively divine attribute that expresses the contrast of transcendence and immanence. Even where, in contrast to Epicurus, the communication between the divine and the human is central, the negation of the human-earthly reality remains the defining quality of this attribute, as is shown in the furious conclusion to Plutarch's *De E apud Delphos*, which presents the light God of being, in contrast to the dark Daemon of transience,[40] as a being separated from all becoming and passing away, who is therefore also ἄφθαρτος, imperishable and unchanging, as is stressed a full three times in this context. On the other hand, this attribute is seldom used for human beings, and when this happens (such as in Middle Platonism), it is only for the divine in the human being in which, precisely in contrast to their otherwise earthly existence, they participate through the mediation of the soul.[41] Philo witnesses to the attractiveness of

[38] It appears in the LXX only in two relatively late Hellenistic writings, Wisdom and *4 Maccabees* (ἀφθαρσία in *4 Macc.* 9:22; 17:12; Wis 2:23; 6:18f.; ἄφθαρτος in Wis 12:1; 18:4).

[39] It does not yet appear in Plato. Aristotle uses it in his metaphysic to describe the total difference of the heavenly bodies and their movement from the earth.

[40] 393A–394A; in *De Iside et Osiride* Plutarch will even designate him a κακὸς δαίμων.

[41] Only very seldom can an imperishability of the soul sometimes be suggested (cf. Plut, *SerNumVind* 17.560B), and this assumes a process of radical separation from the world that Plutarch can describe as virtually a second death: the body must die first, then the soul, before the divine νοῦς, purified from everything earthly, again enters the divine being (cf. Plut, *FacLun* 28.943 A–E; thus the human being again becomes a unity out of trinity and duality).

such a negative theology for Diaspora Judaism as well when he names God simply ὁ ἄφθαρτος;[42] thus he understands the negation of finiteness as a synonym for God. Admittedly, Philo then also applies this attribute to God's νοῦς (Philo, *Leg.* 3.31), to his λόγος (Philo, *Her.* 79; *Conf.* 41) and to divine powers in general (*Cher.* 51), thus to the aspects of the divine being that are turned toward and work in the world. From this, it is not a large further step to making this imperishableness a property of human beings. That step is based on the creation of human beings in the image of God, through which the human as a thought of God was "imperishable by nature" (*Opif.* 134, ἄφθαρτος φύσει). Though the turning toward the bodily—thus Philo understands the "Fall"—this imperishability of the species, namely that furnished by creation, was lost (*Opif.* 152), but it is retained as the destiny of individual people, who should strive "to obtain from the One who has not become and is imperishable [that is, from God] the bodiless and imperishable life."[43] In a synergism between human efforts for the "virtues"—meaning following the Torah[44]—and the supporting action of God imperishability becomes a soteriological attribute: "without divine grace," so Philo, *Ebr.* 145, "it is neither possible to escape from the sphere of influence of the mortal nor to continually remain in the sphere of influence of imperishable."[45] This *"biblicization" of the Hellenistic concept of imperishability* is less reflected upon in other Hellenistic Jewish writings but is therefore all the more clear. According to Wisdom, the human being as God's image is designed for imperishability (2:23) and, despite its intermediate loss on the basis of the Fall,[46] can again be confirmed through "following the Law" (6:18). For *4 Maccabees*' legends of the martyrs, holding fast to the Torah and the God of Israel in

[42] Philo, *Leg.* 3.31.36; *Sacr.* 63, 95; *Deus.* 26; *Her.* 15, 118, 205; cf. further Philo, *Gig.* 15, 45, 61; *Ebr.* 110. With this, he expressly stresses that God himself stands beyond time. This means that the limits of time are subject to him, i.e., that he is equally immediate to every time (Philo, *Deus.* 32).

[43] Philo, *Gig.* 15; cf. Philo, *Her.* 35; *Post.* 135; *Plant.* 44; *Ebr.* 136, etc.

[44] Cf. Philo, *Her.* 205; *Migr.* 18f.; *Abr.* 55; *Plant.* 114, etc.

[45] Similarly in Philo, *Congr.* 107f., God "out of grace" protects the imperishable inheritance and receives into the imperishable race (cf. Philo, *Mut.* 79, etc.).

[46] This is how one should understand the statement in 2:23f., "God has created human beings for imperishability and has made them the image of his own eternity. But through the Devil's envy death came into the world."

the midst of a corrupt world ruled by death means indestructible, eternal life; indeed, the one who truly holds firm to God's commandments is already in death transformed into imperishability.[47] In the Jewish/Hellenistic conversion novel *Joseph and Aseneth*,[48] the Jew as a true honorer of God participates in the divine blessing and thereby in immortality and imperishability (8:5; 15:5; 16:16).[49] Accordingly, the pagan woman who converts is also as a member of the people of God gifted with imperishable youth and beauty (16:16; cf. also 18:9).[50] One sees suggested here what 1 Peter will logically develop, that *the attribute of imperishability in the context of a biblically influenced theology does not have its point in the ontological contrast of God and human, but in the inclusion of the human in the sphere of the divine life and the resulting creative transformation of the human that results from this*. According to Wisdom of Solomon 4:10-13, the righteous person will be carried away, transformed, and perfected by God. *Joseph and Aseneth* describes a renewal by God that transforms the whole person (*Jos. Asen.* 16:16; 18:9). *Fourth Maccabees* 9:22 directly speaks about transformation. In this sense, Paul (especially in 1 Corinthians 15 in the context of his great conflict with the deniers of the resurrection) then highlights

[47] In *4 Maccabees*, an overhaul of the Jewish martyr legends of the Seleucid period on the basis of popular philosophy, comes from the first or second century C.E. and was created in Antioch (cf. A.-M. Denis/J.-C. Haelewyck, *Introduction*, 561–73, especially 571f.; cf. also H.-J. Klauck, *4. Makkabäerbuch*, 665–69). Through their steadfastness the martyrs have become participants in ἀφθαρσία (*4 Macc.* 17:12; as a comparison 9:22). The reasoning is a mixture from Hellenistic and Jewish thought: the victory in the martyrdom interpreted as a competition is won through the virtue and prowess (ἀρετή) of the "athletes of the divine legislation" (τῆς θείας νομοθεσίας ἀθληταί, 17:16; cf. 17:15), which is nothing other than their piety (θεοσέ βεια). According to *4 Macc.* 9:22, the youth who is tortured to death because of his piety is even in death "*transformed* in fire *to imperishability*" (ἐν πυρὶ μετασχηματιζόμενος εἰς ἀφθαρσίαν).

[48] Also here the dating is uncertain; it ranges between the first century B.C.E. and the beginning of the second century C.E.

[49] The daily occurrences of eating, drinking, and anointing received their special features through the blessing. Cf. Ch. Burchard, *Joseph und Aseneth*, 604f.

[50] According to Ch. Burchard, *Joseph und Aseneth*, 604ff., this transformation into a perfect creature is due only to the fact that now as a Jewess she belongs to the community of the true honorers of God and participates in the blessing through her life in this sphere.

the transformation of the perishable into imperishability as a soteriological point of the theology of the cross.[51]

The attribute "undefiled" also comes from a Hellenistic background and describes cultic purity,[52] but, in view of the divine, it also has an ontological dimension to the degree that it belongs to the essence of the divine not to contaminate itself through contact with the human sphere.[53] One encounters ἀμίαντος as an attribute of God in Philo as well; but "undefiled" is, according to the Jewish philosopher of religion, also everything that belongs to God—from his name to his wisdom to the souls that associate with him and the virtues.[54] Because of this, the concept ἀμίαντος far more than ἄφθαρτος[55] gains an ethical meaning: in Jewish tradition, ἀμίαντος designates cultic purity, but also sexual virginity,[56] just as, on the other hand, sexual offense[57] and idolatry[58] or any passion[59] defiles the person or his or her soul.

"Unfading" (ἀμάραντος) is a rare word that does not appear to establish its horizon of associations through a definite tradition.[60] It occurs only one more time in the New Testament,

[51] Cf. R. Feldmeier, "Θεὸς ζῳοποιῶν."

[52] Plut, *IsEtOs* 79.383B; *PythOr* 3.395E; *Num* 9.66B; cf. further Philo, *Spec.* 1.113.250; *Fug.* 118.

[53] Cf. Plut, *EDelph* 20.393C; *IsEtOs* 78.382F; for the Middle Platonist Apuleius, living two generations later, the grandeur of the gods consisted in ". . . that they are not defiled by any contact from our side" (Apul, *DeDeo* 1.128).

[54] Cf. Philo, *Leg.* 1.50; *Cher.* 50; *Det.* 169; *Migr.* 31; *Fug.* 50, 114; *Somn.* 2.185; *Spec.* 4.40.

[55] Φθορά and its derivatives can also mean "vice," "degeneration," or "seduction" (cf. Wis 14:25f.; Philo, *Det.* 102; *Spec.* 4:89; *Decal.* 168; *Ios.* 84; *Conf.* 48).

[56] There is a lack of a Hebrew equivalent in the LXX; cultic purity is expressed by this in 2 Macc 14:36 and 15:34, and sexual virginity in Wis 3:13; 8:19f.; cf. Heb 13:4 in the New Testament.

[57] *T. Reu.* 1.6; *T. Lev.* 7.3; 9.9; 14.6; 16.1; *T. Benj.* 8.2f.; cf. *T. Iss.* 4.4; Wis 14:26.

[58] Sib 5.392; *4 Macc.* 5:36; 7:6; *Pss. Sol.* 2:3; 8:22.

[59] Cf. Philo, *Cher.* 51.

[60] In the biblical writings, one finds ἀμάραντος elsewhere only in Wis 6:12, where it is an attribute of wisdom (parallel to "magnificent"). First Peter 5:4 uses a derivative for the crown of honor that the leader of the community will obtain through proper behavior.

also in 1 Peter; in 5:4 the "crown of glory" is distinguished from the fading crowns of the military or athletic victor by means of ἀμαράντινος. First Peter has presumably consciously chosen this attribute with its metaphor of vegetation as an antithesis to the withering of all human flesh described in 1:24, which is explained there through a *dictum probans* from Scripture[61] about grass and flowers.[62] Besides ontological indestructibility and freedom from earthly contamination, the aspect of freedom from the inherent tendency to self-destruction *qua* aging found in (virtually) all living things is also stressed by this term, and thereby the continuing vitality of the inheritance.

As the three negative attributes already have stressed that the divine eternity bursts open the context of our reality that is determined by becoming and passing away, so this point is now also further strengthened through a spatial metaphor: this "inheritance" is "in heaven." This means above all that it is not about an earthly home, as it was for the Jewish people of God in the dispersion, but about one in the beyond.[63] But the point here also is not the separation of heaven and earth, but the perspective of hope opened in the present by it: salvation does not need to be created first, but it already exists as an inheritance in heaven; it is "kept" there and indeed "for you." The following verse underscores this again when it says about this salvation that it already lies ready to be revealed, thus to a certain degree pushes for its realization here on earth. The "under" aspect of the present, which is defined by suffering and death, as will be explained in the following verses, is thus right from the start embraced and transcended by God's dimension, in which dimension believers *qua* "living hope" already participate. That which other New Testament letters express with the (political) picture of heavenly citizenship or the heavenly city (Phil 3:20; Gal 4:26; Heb 12:22; 13:14) 1 Peter describes with the metaphor of rebirth and the heirship that is connected to it.

[61] Isaiah 40:6-9 is selectively cited in this regard and placed in a new context (see below on 1:24).

[62] The verb μαραίνειν is used in Job 15:30; 24:24 LXX for the frailty and passing away of the person who turns away from God.

[63] K. Niederwimmer, "Kirche," 106, speaks about a spiritualized conceptuality.

1:5

After the view of the heavenly inheritance, verse 5 stresses the present effectiveness of God as a power that "protects" or "guards" the believers.[64] Before he goes into the oppression and trials of the addressees in the next verse, our author assures them of divine support as a power that preserves them. This preservation takes place "through faith," a preservation to the salvation that already lies ready for its final revelation. Faith is therefore here, as also normally elsewhere in the New Testament, not simply the human being's holding something to be true,[65] but the acceptance of the message of salvation, by means of which the human is at once placed into a new relationship to God, into an attitude of trust that embraces and determines his or her whole existence, of commitment, of hope (cf. 1:21).[66] Through such faith, then, which does not make one ashamed (2:6), the power of God can also become effective in the believers so that through it they are preserved in God's power to salvation (1:5) and accordingly can also stand against Evil (cf. 5:9); πίστις here virtually designates an authority that mediates between God and the believers.[67]

From this experience of divine power, one views the καιρὸς ἔσχατος, not as an indefinite "sometime," but thus: that the eschatological salvation as the ultimate rescue from the current suffering (cf. 1:9f.), which already determines the life of the regenerate as that which is believed and hoped and with respect to God, "stands ready to be revealed," already pushes its way into this world.

[64] The word φρουρέω "guard" can have either negative (Gal 3:23; cf. 2 Cor 11:32, watch over, hold in prison) or positive connotations (Phil 4:7, preserve, protect).

[65] James represents an exception where the demons themselves "believe" that "God is one" (Jas 2:19).

[66] Cf. R. Bultmann, "πιστεύω," 217; Bultmann speaks of an "attitude that constitutes the existence"; as such "πίστις absolutely governs the life."

[67] Precisely, Gerhard, 60, "*. . . quia virtus divina non immediate nec ex absoluto quodam DEI decreto, sed mediate per fidem nos in salutem conservat.*"

(ii) Rejoicing and Trial 1:6-7

Literature on 1 Peter 1:6-7: **P. R. Fink**, "The Use and Significance of En Hoi in I Peter," *Grace Journal* 8 (1967), 33–39, especially 35. **T. Martin**, "The Present Indicative in the Eschatological Statements of 1 Peter 1:6, 8," *JBL* 111 (1992), 307–12.

(6) You rejoice then, now for a short time—if necessary—saddened by various trials (7) in order that the genuineness of your faith may come to light, which [genuineness] is more valuable than gold that, although it passes away, [likewise] proves itself to be genuine by means of fire—resulting in praise, glory, and honor at the revelation of Jesus Christ.

1:6

Starting from the preserving divine power along with a simultaneous view of the coming salvation, now for the first time the oppressive present of the addressees is brought into view from the new perspective. With it initially stands in the foreground—an apparent paradox—rejoicing. In the exegesis, it is debated whether that present ἀγαλλιᾶσθε in 1:6, 8 should also be translated as a present or if one is dealing with a futuristic present, what in actuality amounts to the alternatives, whether joy is already something present or whether this is a reference to future rejoicing.

The representatives of a futuristic interpretation of ἀγαλλιᾶσθε refer to the fact that the relative phrase joining the sentences, ἐν ᾧ in 1:6, refers back to ἐν καιρῷ ἐσχάτῳ in 1:5 and ἀγαλλιᾶσθε as the predicate of the relative sentence can therefore only be understood in a future sense.[68] Furthermore, effusive joy, as it is described here, is characteristic of the salvation-filled future, as 4:13 shows. However, one must now observe that 4:13 also speaks about a present joy in suffering that will then be fully released in future rejoicing. Concerning the various "tempering" of present joy in this passage and that one should not overvalue this—in 4:12ff. a suffering is spoken about that has become yet much more intensive that that in 1:6, 8! The representatives of a present interpretation, on the other

[68] Cf. T. Martin, "Indicative," especially 310.

hand, point to the fact that ἐν ᾧ is used elsewhere in 1 Peter "as a conjunction and not strictly as a relative pronoun."[69] The referent of the relative is therefore here a generally causal reference to the whole previous paragraph,[70] and thus ἐν ᾧ should be translated here by "therefore."[71] Thus the obvious conclusion is that ἀγαλλιᾶσθε in 1:6, 8 is to be understood in a present sense, particularly because the discussion in 1:10–12 has as its total goal to qualify the present as the fulfillment of prophecy.

The matter is difficult to decide, for the author of 1 Peter, who generally writes a thoroughly refined Greek, has now used the present once (and he does this once again in 1:8, where the present meaning is yet clearer because of the parallel with ἀγαπᾶτε). On the other hand, it seems artificial if here (as also in other places) a rather unequivocal relative phrase joining the sentences is reinterpreted. Possibly the answer is so difficult because the wrong question is being asked. In the progress of the letter, it will be shown repeatedly that a sharp differentiation between present and future is not appropriate for 1 Peter, because it is his concern to interpret the present totally in the light of the future that has been opened for the believers. Thus the verse does indeed view future rejoicing, but this cannot be totally separated from the present.[72] In what follows, 1 Peter again and again makes it clear how the eschatological joy is anticipated in the present joy and thus pushes back the shadows of trial and temptation.

In order to make this "superiority" of joy over suffering still more plausible, the suffering is relativized here at the beginning in that its temporal limitations are referred to.[73] The oppression is qualified as "various trials." The term used here, πειρασμός (temptation/trial), is influenced by Diaspora Judaism in its religious connotation and widely taken up in the New Testament. The understanding of πειρασμός in 1 Peter is especially close to the wisdom tradition and James: the sorrow resulting from temptation on the basis of alienation by the world around them

[69] P. R. Fink, "Use," 33.
[70] P. R. Fink, "Use," 38.
[71] P. R. Fink, "Use," 35.
[72] Cf. Elliott, 339, "As with many concepts presented in this letter . . . , so in the case of rejoicing, present and future realities tend to intersect and overlap."
[73] ὀλίγον refers to the duration of time; cf. Schelkle, 35.

(cf. 1 Pet 4:12) is interpreted in 1 Peter 1:6f. with virtually the same words as in James 1:2f. as an opportunity for the testing of faith, which is almost to be welcomed as such, particularly because it "[is] a paradoxical privilege to belong to those who are being tempted just because of faith."[74] However, in a stronger way than James, 1 Peter also underlines dependence on divine preservation (1 Pet 1:5; cf. 5:10), which is close to the Lucan writings or also 1 Corinthians 10:13. The question of who causes the temptation is not discussed in 1 Peter.[75]

Excursus 3: Temptation/πειρασμός

The substantive πειρασμός is a derivative of the verb πειράζειν. In profane Greek, the verb means "test" or "try." It can also be used in the New Testament in this sense (Acts 9:26; 16:7; 24:6). Far more commonly, however, it is used to express a test in the religious sense, a meaning that in the New Testament the substantive πειρασμός takes without exception. This one is dealing with a widening of profane Greek through the linguistic usage of the Septuagint, which translates the Hebrew נסה piel with πειράζειν (the substantive נסיון, which is first found in later Hebrew, corresponds then to πειρασμός).[76] In this way, a term for the endangering of the relationship with God was formed. As such, temptation *per definitionem* only concerns believers. "The unbelievers . . . Satan truly has under his control anyway."[77] To the degree that temptation is not being spoken about only as a danger in general (1 Thess 3:5; Gal 6:1; Jas 1:12), "temptation" can be caused by the tempting of people through their desires (1 Tim 6:9; Jas 1:13f.; cf. 1 Cor 7:5); more commonly, however, it is persecution and suffering that cause one to take exception to God (Luke 8:13; 1 Pet 1:6f.; 4:12; 2 Pet 2:9; Heb 2:18; Jas 1:2; Rev 2:10). In the first case,

[74] W. Popkes, *Jakobus*, 82.

[75] At least the people around them are mentioned as the cause of suffering (2:12; 4:12f., etc.), and at the end, the Devil makes his entrance (5:8); a text like 1 Pet 4:17 ("For the time has arrived that judgment begins with the house of God"), however, makes it not appear impossible that in 1 Peter's mind God is also the (co-)causation of suffering and the "temptation" that is caused by suffering.

[76] Cf. Jastrow, 916.

[77] K. G. Kuhn, "πειρασμός," 202.

πειρασμός corresponds more to the English word "temptation" and in the second more to "test" or "trial."

Temptation can be understood *exclusively negatively as an overpowering threat to faith* that the person is unable to withstand unless divine preservation protects him (1 Cor 10:13). Jesus' exhortation in Gethsemane, "Watch and pray so that you do not fall into temptation, for the Spirit is willing but the flesh is weak" (Mark 14:38), makes coming into temptation virtually identical to apostasy[78] (as can be seen in the next scene in which the disciples, in contrast to Jesus, are not praying but sleeping; they run away and leave their master alone). Prayer should prevent one from falling into (the power of) temptation at all. In contrast to Jesus, who has just proved himself as God's son in the conflict with the tempter,[79] the threatened believer can only ask God for protection, who "knows how to save the pious from temptation" (2 Pet 2:9; cf. Rev 3:10, there with reference to the great affliction of the end time). Accordingly, what was originally the last request of the Lord's Prayer also reads, "And lead us not into temptation" (Luke 11:4c), which is made more specific by Matthew by means of its expansion, "but deliver us from the Evil One" (Matt 6:13).

On the other hand, temptation is virtually greeted in James, who understands it in the wisdom tradition[80] as a test belonging to Christian life, a test that gives *an opportunity for proving oneself, even a reason for joy* (1:2). Accordingly, anyone who stands firm in temptation is declared blessed (Jas 1:12).[81] Hebrews 11:17 can similarly praise Abraham's faith, who—being tempted by God (πειραζόμενος)—offered his son Isaac.

The Lucan writings, for one, take a mediating position in which temptation is indeed a danger that can lead to apostasy (cf. also Luke 8:13) but does not inevitably do so. Here, it is

[78] There are similar formulations in early Jewish prayers; cf. bBer fol. 60b, where the one praying to God makes the request not to come under the power (לידי) of sin, guilt, temptation, (נסיון) and shame. Sin, guilt, temptation, and shame are paralleled to one another here.

[79] Mark 1:12f.; Matt 4:1-11; Luke 4:1-13. Heb 4:15 can then refer to this and say about God's son that he "was tempted in all ways as we [are], but without sin."

[80] Cf. W. Popkes, *Jakobus*.

[81] Cf. on this Ch. Burchard, *Jakobus*, 52f.

prayer with the help of which temptation can be withstood.[82] In Paul, the mediation is different; in 1 Corinthians 10:13, he distinguishes between a human temptation, which apparently up to then had been withstood by the Corinthians, and a temptation that goes "beyond your ability" and from which God himself must defend them.

1:7

By means of a conclusion, *a minore ad maius* from gold that passes away[83] to the so very much more valuable faith, a comparison—introduced by the final conjunction ἵνα—now follows, a comparison that contains a *first interpretation of the "temptations" as testing and purification*. If even the genuineness of gold must be tested through fire, then how much more the exceedingly more valuable faith. Yet there is more: as all the dross is separated by the melting of metal so that in the end only the pure precious metal remains, so suffering is understood as a process of separation in which faith is proven in that it is purified.

The comparison of suffering to the melting of metal is influenced by wisdom and can be found in similar contexts in the Old Testament and early Judaism: "For you, God, have tested us and purified us as silver is purified . . .," the Psalmist confesses and yet thanks God.[84] "See, I have purified you, but not as silver, but instead I have tested you in the glowing oven of misery," says God to Israel in Isaiah 48:10. Jewish wisdom then made this into a principle: "As

[82] Luke has thus reshaped his Gethsemane narrative accordingly so that the doubled command, "pray that you do not come into temptation" (Luke 22:40, 46), frames Jesus' prayer. Thereby the praying Master becomes an example for the disciples, an example from whom one can learn how one gets out of temptation (cf. also Heb 2:18). Here, temptation is a synonym for affliction; holding firm is evidence of being true to one's faith. Therefore, Luke in his version of the Gethsemane scene has left out the reason, "the spirit is willing but the flesh is weak" (Mark 14:38b); instead Jesus in Luke has already earlier attested to his disciples that they have held out with him in his trials. Similarly, Paul says in his farewell speech in Ephesus in Acts 20:19 that he has served his Lord "with all humility and tears and trials [πειρασμοί] that befell me through the attacks of the Jews" (cf. also Acts 15:26 v. l).

[83] From an eschatological perspective gold belongs to the perishing world—therefore its description as transient.

[84] Ps 66:10; vv. 11f. describe this testing.

the crucible silver and the oven gold, so the Lord tests the hearts" (Prov 17:3). *Suffering is thereby not a sign of being abandoned by God, but, quite the opposite, as a test sent by God it is evidence of election*: "Gold is tested in the fire with respect to its genuineness and people who are accepted [δεκτοί] in the melting furnace of humiliation" (Sir 2:5). First Peter touches surprising close yet again to the Wisdom of Solomon.[85] In Wisdom of Solomon 3:5f. (directly following to the "hope of complete immortality" 3:4b; cf. 1 Pet 1:4) testing and the being honored by God that follows from it are similarly connected: ". . . and after they [i.e., the righteous] are disciplined just a little they will be brought to mind with great benefaction, for God tested[86] them and he found them worthy, he tested[87] them as gold in the melting crucible."

The first (wisdom) interpretations of suffering as testing and proving in which it is necessary to stand the test are followed by further ones which reach deeper theologically. Yet this first interpretation is also important, for it helps to bring the apparently meaningless alienation into connection with God's will and so to win for it a first meaning. Such an interpretation of the situation frees the addressees from the depressing role of simply being victims of slander and persecution. Interpreted as test and refining, suffering now becomes a challenge and requires the highest level of activity in order to come through the situation. Thereby 'testing' receives a competitive undertone. This is further stressed through the reference to reward that will be won through standing against the trials; at the revelation of Jesus Christ those who are now slandered and libeled will receive "praise, glory and honor"; for example, God's revelation in the end of time will turn the hierarchies of this reality upside down (cf. Luke 1:49-53).

One should observe in this context that πίστις is not only the entity through which God protects the believers (thus 1:5) but that here the word contains an active aspect; as fidelity, this faith can also be tested, and in passing the test it can be rewarded through God's recognition. The chronological specification of this divine recognition—"at the revelation of Christ" (1 Pet 1:13; cf. 4:13)

[85] Cf. Introduction, pp. 26f. See further on the attributes in 1:4; here is further evidence for the closeness of 1 Peter to Hellenistic Judaism and more specifically to its wisdom tradition.

[86] Ἐπείρασεν—cf. πειρασμοί in 1 Pet 1:6.

[87] Ἐδοκίμασεν—cf. τὸ δοκίμιον in 1 Pet 1:7.

—makes it clear that the reality of this world moves toward a goal determined through Christ and that it is according to this goal that the question of success or failure in life is to be judged.

Here at the beginning both—hope and suffering—are simply placed against one another; therefore 1 Peter summons them here to joy despite suffering (whereby suffering is still relativized as something temporary). That will change in what follows: the oppression increasingly will be focused on in its full severity, and thereby will both—suffering and joy—then be so placed in relationship that the inner relationship between suffering and grace will come to the fore in an ever clearer form so that then joy in suffering, in the end even joy because of suffering, can be expected of the addressees. The next verses, which come back to the motif of joy, already point in this direction.

(iii) Faith without Sight 1:8-9

Literature on 1 Peter 1:8-9: **G. Dautzenberg**, "Σωτηρία ψυχῶν (1 Petr 1, 9)," *BZ* NF 8 (1964), 262–76; **R. Feldmeier**, "Seelenheil. Überlegungen zur Soteriologie und Anthropologie des 1. Petrusbriefes," in J. Schlosser (ed.), *The Catholic Epistles and the Tradition* (BEThL 176; Leuven, 2004), 291–306; **P. R. Fink**, "The Use and Significance of En Hoi in I Peter," *Grace Journal* 8:2 (1967), 33–39; **T. Martin**, "The Present Indicative in the Eschatological Statements of 1 Peter 1:6,8," *JBL* 111 (1992), 307–12.

(8) You love him [i.e., Jesus Christ], although you have not seen him; believing in him, you rejoice with unspeakable and beatific joy, although you do not yet see him before your eyes, (9) [and] you [thus] receive the goal of your faith, the salvation of your souls.

On the text: **8** Instead of ὃν οὐκ ἰδόντες ἀγαπᾶτε ("You love him, although you have not seen him.") A P Ψ 33, the majority text, the Bohairic translation, Clement of Alexandria, and, with slight deviation, also Augustine read[88] ὃν οὐκ εἰδότες ἀγαπᾶτε ("whom you love without knowing about him"). On the formation of this variant cf. Wohlenberg 17f., who, among other evidence, cites *Pol. Phil.* (lat.) 1.3 as evidence for the main textual variant: "*quem cum non videritis, nunc diligitis, in quem nunc non aspicientes creditis, credentes autem gaudebitis gaudio inenarrabili et gloroficato*" ("whom you, although you

[88] Aug, *Pec* 27 refers οὐκ εἰδότες to the time before conversion.

have not seen him, now love; in whom you believe, without now gazing on him; but as believers you rejoice with an inexpressible and glorious joy"). Not only do the weighty external witnesses speak against οὐκ εἰδότες, but also according to 1 Peter 1:18f. those who believe are with respect to Christ εἰδότες.

1:8

The theme of joy in contrast to the present is again developed, now, of course, not against the "trials that make one sad," but in dealing with the hiddenness of Christ in the present and thus the concealment of everything on which faith hopes and depends.[89] For this reason—fitting the pastoral-comforting intention of the letter—this challenge of the grant of salvation is enveloped and thereby robbed of its destructive ability to act on its own. This takes place in that the author takes as his starting point the present love of the community to the invisible Christ;[90] in doing so the first statement with the aorist οὐκ ἰδόντες possibly refers to the fact that they had not known the historical Jesus[91] and the second with the present μὴ ὁρῶντες to the present invisibility of Christ. In this believing trust in the concealed Christ, the contrast between presence and absence is surpassed by the personal relationship to him. This is immediately taken up into the self-understanding of the believers, because their faith and their love are now interpreted as fellowship with the Christ who is withdrawn from their eyes. In faith and love, the (yet) absent one is (already) present to them—and therefore their present is filled with joy. Yet more: because this presently expressed joy is in turn described as "inexpressible" and "beatific," then these are eschatological attributes. Through faith and love, the Christians live already now "between

[89] In Heb 11:1-3, this trust in that which is not seen is virtually the definition of faith; the blessing of the one who has not seen but nevertheless believes in John 20:29 also says something similar (cf. also 2 Cor 5:7; Rom 8:24f.).

[90] Jesus Christ is seldom the object of love in the New Testament; outside of the Gospel of John (8:42; 14:15, 21, 24; 21:15-17) it is found only once, in Eph 6:24 (cf. also Just, *Apol* 2.13).

[91] Cf. Elliott, 342. The οὐκ ἰδόντες is "appropriate for believers of the postapostolical period who had learned of Jesus only through the proclamation of the good news (1:12, 25; 4:17)."

the times"; they already presently participate in the rejoicing of the end time.[92]

1:9

The following verse, which speaks about the attainment of salvation, also uses the present participle in order to make clear that the "regenerate" already now take part in the future salvation that as the "goal of faith" determines the present[93] and gives a perspective to it. The concept σωτηρία ψυχῶν, "salvation of souls" is remarkable, for in 1 Peter (1:9) it appears for the first time in ancient literature in this form. Ψυχή in 1 Peter appears to designate *the anthropological correlate to God's turning toward the world*, the "soul," namely, on the one hand, as the receptor of the saving salvific action (1:9; 2:25; 4:19), on the other, as that self which is purified through obedience (1:22), to be made subject to God (4:19) and to be preserved in the fight against the "fleshly desires" (2:11).

Excursus 4: The Soul and Salvation of the Soul in 1 Peter

In most commentaries, despite all indications that point in another direction, any relationship between 1 Peter and a Greek-influenced conception of the soul is almost categorically rejected (and thereby also the assumption that σωτηρία ψυχῶν is about the salvation of the soul). Thus that which is meant in 1 Peter by ψυχή is not primarily taken from the letter itself; rather a tradition-historical derivation of the interpretation is set forth and from this it is deduced that in 1 Peter the "soul" can only be the equivalent for life or for the personal pronoun. The research of Dautzenberg on the concept σωτηρία ψυχῶν demonstrates this in a virtually exemplary way;[94] it is continually cited with agreement right up

[92] Cf. Davids, 59.

[93] κομιζόμενοι is a present participle and cannot be translated simply as a future (cf. Brox, 66f.; Frankemölle, 34). The following reference to the prophets (vv. 10-12) also clearly aims at the present time as the already beginning time of salvation.

[94] G. Dautzenberg, "Σωτηρία." In his latest publication on the topic (G. Dautzenberg, "Seele") Dautzenberg no longer formulates his conclusions with respect to 1 Pet 2:11 in such an apodictic manner, without, however, looking more carefully into the question of what could be meant by ψυχή in

to the newest commentaries.[95] There, Dautzenberg comes to the conclusion, "The Jewish-Christian tradition that lies behind 1 Peter 1:9 offers no evidence at all for valuing the soul as the higher essence in the human being and likewise none for a contrast to the body."[96] Yet closer examination shows that the argumentation is shaky because Dautzenberg right from the start only examines the "Jewish-Christian tradition" with respect to which "Jewish" means for him especially the writings from Qumran (written in Hebrew and Aramaic) but not the writings of Greek-speaking Judaism, especially the work of Philo of Alexandria, in which one after all finds a developed teaching about the soul.[97] Dautzenberg's argumentation is therefore based on a *petitio principii*, because the conclusion is already predetermined by the limitation of the materials selected for comparison. To this one adds still further inaccuracy.[98] In contrast, a more careful analysis of the places in which 1 Peter speaks about the ψυχή shows a decidedly different picture. Already in 1:9, the talk about the σωτηρία ψυχῶν is reminiscent of other New Testament texts such as Mark 8:35—but this at first

---

the New Testament. Nevertheless, the old work of Dautzenberg is cited up to today, and it is also with this that the following argues.

[95] This reaches from the commentaries of Goppelt, Spicq, Davids, Boring, Brox, and Achtemeier right up to the newest commentary of Elliott, 344. When Brox gives as a reason "the conception of an immortal soul in contrast to the body, which [soul] represents the better and remaining part of the human, is unknown there [i.e., in early Judaism and early Christianity]" (Brox, 67), this claim is at any rate false in light of Hellenistic Judaism (cf. Philo) and also questionable in view of early Christianity. Here as well the question is too limited: naturally one does not find in 1 Peter the same concept of the soul as that in Middle Platonism, but it is worth considering why he so often speaks of the soul with respect to the relationship to God (see below).

[96] G. Dautzenberg, "Σωτηρία," 274.

[97] On the concept of the soul in Judaism in the time of the Second Temple cf. G. Stemberger, "Seele," 740f., who shows that "the teaching about the soul in Hellenistic popular philosophy" was taken over in Diaspora Judaism and was increasingly accepted in Palestinian Judaism as well; Stemberger counts contemporaries of 1 Peter such as the Pharisees and Josephus among those who were accepting this teaching. On the Philonic concept of the soul, also see the further discussion in this excursus.

[98] On the conflict with Dautzenberg, cf. R. Feldmeier, "Seelenheil," 291–306, especially 292f.

disregards the question whether in the gospels as well more is not meant by the term ψυχή than only "life" (cf. Matt 10:28). For any Greek reader or hearer, it would be highly likely he or she would interpret this expression of the notion of the "salvation of the soul" against the background of the ancient concept of the soul (which was also common in Diaspora Judaism), especially since, as is the case in 1 Peter, it is the summary of the message of salvation about rebirth to an everlasting inheritance (1:3f.), which is set against the transience of all flesh (1:23f.). That confirms exactly the view of the Jewish-Hellenistic literature that Dautzenberg has bracketed out, although they (especially Philo)[99] stand far closer to 1 Peter than the writings from Qumran that Dautzenberg cites. Admittedly, the Jewish religious philosopher does not use the pithy expression σωτηρία ψυχῶν, but he does indeed speak in various places of the salvation of the soul. Thus he interprets Exodus 15:1 (the destruction of the Egyptians by God) that God stands with the soul in the fight against the passions and irrational drives and so graces it with σωτηρία (Philo, *Ebr.* 111). Philo's exegesis of the history of Abraham's departure (Gen 12:1-3) begins with the notable observation, "God, who wants to cleanse [καθῆραι] the soul of the human being, gives her first the opportunity for salvation [σωτηρία] through resettlement from three places: the body, sense perception, and the spoken word." (Philo, *Migr.* 2).

These two references are therefore especially revealing because they not only speak about the salvation of souls, but they also explain it in a way that immediately reminds one of the next two texts in which 1 Peter speaks about the soul: 1 Peter 1:22 exhorts that the "souls" should be purified in the service to the truth. And the fight in the soul against passion and lack of restraint, about which Philo repeatedly speaks (cf. outside of Philo, *Ebr.* 111, also Philo, *QG* 4.74 and especially Philo, *Opif.* 79–81) has a correspondence to 1 Peter 2:11, where the fight of the fleshly passions against the "soul" is spoken about. Salvation of the soul, purification of the soul, the fight between the passions and the soul—these relatively unequivocal correspondences between Philo and 1 Peter show that 1 Peter—here as well influenced by Hellenistic

[99] This is, however, not only true of Philo; cf. *T. Job* 3:5, where the prayer of Job, who has turned from idols to the God of Israel, begins with the words, "My Lord, who comes to the salvation of my soul" (κύριέ μου ὁ ἐπὶ τῇ σωτηρίᾳ τῆς ἐμῆς ψυχῆς ἐλθών).

Judaism—in reality thinks of something similar to a "soul" as the innermost center and "higher self" of the human being,[100] perhaps similar to "the hidden person of the heart" (3:4). One also finds such a taking over of the idea of the soul, incidentally, in other writings of early Judaism. When the Wisdom of Solomon says that God has breathed a ψυχή into humanity (15:1) that is weighed down here by the transient body (9:15), which soul the unrighteous soil (14:26), while the souls of the righteous are in God's hand (3:1) and therefore have hope and immortality (3:4), then it witnesses to the dissemination of the Jewish concept of the soul in the same way as *4 Maccabees* (written in Syria about the same time as 1 Peter), which clearly distinguishes the God-given soul from the body (13:13), and it is then in that work also the souls that receive divine punishment (13:15) or divine reward (18:23) after death.[101] This also fits well with the other places in which 1 Peter uses the term ψυχή, even if these, taken by themselves, are less unequivocal. Thus Christ—this is the final point of the hymn in chapter 2—is described as shepherd and bishop of the "souls," to whom the believers have returned from the wandering of their earlier life (2:25). In 4:19, it states that the persecuted Christians should entrust their "souls" to the righteous creator—here as well the "soul" appears to be differentiated from the whole earthly-bodily existence. The one exception appears to be the expression in 3:20 that eight "souls" had been saved from the flood in Noah's ark. But here as well a closer look shows that in this scene (consciously set out as an "antitype" to the salvation through baptism

[100] One cannot demonstrate that the author of 1 Peter knew Philo, but the familiarity of the letter with Hellenistic-Jewish traditions, which we encounter above all in Philo, is indisputable, as, for example, I have shown in the metaphor of being a foreigner (R. Feldmeier, *Fremde*, 60–72). It reveals itself again on this topic, both with respect to the salvation of the soul and also with respect to rebirth (see below Excursus 7: Rebirth, pp. 127–30).

[101] The body is indeed not devalued in *4 Maccabees*, but it is the soul through which the person stands in relationship to God (cf. H.-J. Klauck, *4. Makkabäerbuch*, 672f.). On the wider dissemination of a dichotomist anthropology see also Apocalypse of Moses 13:6; 31:1, 4; 32:4. According to J. Dochhorn, *Apokalypse des Mose*, these are texts that belong to the final redaction of the *Apocalypse of Moses*. In its older layers the *Apocalypse* is not yet dichotomist. This is an example for how such concepts gained in influence in ancient Judaism.

referred to in the following verse) deals with considerably more than physical life alone (see on pp. 206ff.).

With the reference to the concept of the soul, one can also gain a better insight into the concept of salvation (which is central for 1 Peter) as an *"everlasting" life* that transcends this transient reality. It is indeed true that the overcoming of finiteness is not based on the metaphysical quality of the indestructible reasoning being, as in the Platonism of that period,[102] but eschatologically on God's saving action in Christ, which already determines the present of the believers as "living hope"; nevertheless, one also finds in 1 Peter resemblances to a dualistic anthropology: the soul as addressee of salvation participates in the divine glory and thereby also in God's immortality (see earlier), while the flesh is decidedly the sphere of transience (1:24), of suffering (4:1) and of death (3:18; 4:6). Most remarkable is the foundational statement in 2:11, which introduces the second main part. Here it is stated that the *fleshly* desires are engaged in a war, however not, as Paul would say (cf. Gal 5:16f.), a fight against the (divine) spirit, also not, as Philo would say, a fight within the soul,[103] but a fight against the soul (2:11). A clearly Hellenized anthropology is presented here[104] that, however, is not developed by 1 Peter in the sense of an anthropological dichotomy even if one can also find indications of such a concept in other places (cf. 3:4; 4:2). It is sufficient for 1 Peter to have found in the term ψυχή a category for the human self vis-à-vis God with which he can couple the horizon of associations that this term has for his addressees, who are at home in the sphere of the Greek culture and language. These associations are namely (1) the affinity of ψυχή with the divine, which therefore (2) is to be kept free from all passion and desire as tethering it to the world,

[102] Cf. just the Pseudo-Platonic Tractate Axiochus, whose theme is the substantiation of the immortality of the soul in dealing with human anxiety in the face of death. There θεῖον πνεῦμα is talked about, which is in the soul and is the basis of its immortality (PsPlat, *Ax* 370C). In Plutarch cf. Plut, *SerNumVind* 560B–C.

[103] According to Philo, *Opif.* 81, one is dealing with a fight that the παθῶν ὁρμαί fight against the ἀρεταί, a war within the soul (πόλεμος κατὰ ψυχήν).

[104] The soul is something like the mediating authority between the bodily world and the sector of the divine; cf. more or less Plut, *GenSocr* 22.591Dff.

is to be "purified," but so also (3) is able to survive death.[105] The author of 1 Peter may thus be one of those who prepared the way for the Christian concept of the soul, and one asks whether the concept of the soul, which for at least two millennia has contributed to the plausibility of Christian anthropology and soteriology, might not nevertheless be worth further theological reflection.

(iv) The Prophets 1:10-12

Literature on 1 Peter 1:10-12: **S. Cipriani**, "Lo 'spirito di Cristo' come 'spirito di profezia' in 1 Pt 1, 10-12," in G. Lorizio/V. Scippa (eds.), *Ecclesiae Sacramentum* (*Festschrift* A. Marranzini) (Neapel, 1986), 157–67; **J. Herzer**, "Alttestamentliche Prophetie und die Verkündigung des Evangeliums. Beobachtungen zur Stellung und zur hermeneutischen Funktion von I Petr 1, 10-12," *BThZ* 14/1 (1997), 14–22.

(10) The prophets, who have prophesied about the grace that was destined for you, have searched for and investigated this salvation, (11) in that they investigated at what point in time or rather under what prevailing circumstances the Spirit of Christ, who prophesied in them the suffering [determined] for Christ and the glory [awarded] to him, had indicated. (12) It was revealed to them that they did not serve themselves but you, [and namely] in view of that which is now preached to you through those who have announced to you the gospel in the Holy Spirit sent from heaven, into which [even] the angels would wish to look.

On the text: **11** Numerous manuscripts (L 33, etc.) have ἐδηλοῦτο instead of ἐδήλου τό. Because the oldest tradition had neither accents nor word separation, this is a purely interpretive variant, which in theory could also have been intended by the author. With the reading ἐδηλοῦτο the meaning appears that the prophets investigated about when the Spirit, who was working in them and prophesying Christ's suffering, had revealed himself, and with the reading ἐδήλου τό the prophets investigated what point in time the Spirit that was working in them pointed to when he prophesied the suffering of Christ.

[105] On the concept of the purification of the soul that was widespread in Platonism cf. the discussion of H. Dörrie/M. Baltes, *Platonismus* 2:271–76.

1:10

The salvation opened through Christ is immediately tied back to the Old Testamental history of salvation. This is typical for the whole of the early Christian theology,[106] in doing what they especially gladly referred to the prophets (cf. Luke 24:25-27; Acts 3:18 and many others). The main focus is therefore—in marked contrast to the mainstream of contemporary Judaism—not on the Torah, but on the prophetic aspect of the biblical tradition. The Old Testament is read as prophecy of the Christ-event,[107] with respect to which 1 Peter above all cites Isaiah (the principle witness of the biblical promises, as it were).[108] The idea that the prophets only had a preparatory function in view of the situation of the community is also found in Qumran[109] and in *1 Enoch* 1:2. Because the prophets only have that in view in their prophecy that is fulfilled in the Christian community (1 Peter 1:12 then speaks explicitly of "serving") the situation of the societally marginalized followers of Christ is theologically all the more highly valued.

1:11

The activity of the prophets is described as an ἐκζητεῖν and ἐραυνειν, a "seeking" and "investigating." By this is meant a subordinate level of knowledge in contrast to the present situation. And not only that: insofar as the present point in time is one to which the prophets related in anticipation, that they aspired to

[106] It is either flatly stated that the salvific action had taken place "according to the scriptures" (cf. the old piece of tradition 1 Cor 15:3-5) or the selected texts are cited (cf. Mark 12:10f.; 14:27; 15:24, 29, 34; in Matthew these become reflective citations).

[107] Cf. Rom 1:2; Heb 1:1; Matt 26:56; Luke 1:70; 18:31; Rev 10:7; Moses himself was viewed in terms of prophecy, cf. Luke 24:25-27; Acts 3:21ff.

[108] Cf. 1 Peter 1:24f.; 2:6, 8, 9, 12, 22-25; 3:14f.; 4:14; otherwise, of the other prophets only Hosea is cited (once in 1 Pet 2:10).

[109] Cf. 1QpHab 7.1-5, where the prophecies of the prophets are interpreted with respect to the present of the community; "And God spoke to Habakkuk that he should write down what will come upon the final generation. But God did not inform him about the completion of the time. And when it says, 'So that the one can hurry who reads,' the interpretation of this relates to the teacher of righteousness, whom God has informed about all the secrets of the words of his servants the prophets"; similarly 1QpHab 2.5-10.

comprehend, this present time is indeed[110] to be understood as a point in time in which what was prophesied begins to be realized. The actual subject of the prophesying is not, however, the various prophetic figures, but the one "Spirit of Christ." This Spirit was active in the prophets "testifying beforehand." This highlights that the prophesying in the past and the salvation proclaimed in the present, about which the following verse will speak again by means of an appeal to the Spirit, is indebted to the same divine activity, that a unitary divine will is at work in both to accomplish his salvation.

The content of this prophesying about Jesus Christ is, as usual, the passion and resurrection, although in the version that 1 Peter chooses, because it is open to application to the oppression of the persecuted believers (not least through the unusual plural of suffering and glory) it is "the suffering [determined] for Christ and the glory [awarded] to him afterwards." Christ's fate was made transparent for the interpretation of the present situation: "Indeed, his passion, death, and subsequent resurrection show the way present suffering is related to future glory, and thus provide Christians with a model for the way they are to live a faithful life in the midst of a hostile society."[111]

1:12

It is again expressly stressed that the great men of God of the past had only a *serving function* in view of the persecuted and not-so-large Christian community. Their announcements related to exactly that (αὐτά) which is now proclaimed to the community as gospel. The angels themselves,[112] who are already "in heaven," wish to see what the believers have already (νῦν) received through

[110] Against J. Herzer, "Prophetie," 18f., who sees the continuity to the Old Testamental prophecy in that for the Christians as well salvation still lies in the future. That is indeed correct, but it overlooks the difference between the two situations insofar as that which the prophets have investigated is realized now in the proclamation of the gospel (cf. the marked νῦν in v. 12, the relativization of which by Herzer is not plausible).

[111] Achtemeier, 65.

[112] It is possible that this argument received additional weight due to the rivalry between human beings and angels (on this topic cf. P. Schäfer, *Rivalität*).

the proclamation that has taken place among them,[113] which—this is especially stressed—is caused and determined by the Holy Spirit sent from heaven. From this also comes yet new impetus into the contrasts of verse 8: the distance of the "not yet seen" is beaten by the "already now" real Spirit-produced relationship to salvation.

Here, for the first time, both glory and suffering are connected together with each other in Christ's fate, if also for the present only in the sense of one after the other. Thereby our author has already made it clear that the present suffering has another side in the reality that is defined through Christ, this other side being the future glorification that has already become a reality in Christ and therefore defines the self-understanding of his followers.

(v) Summary 1 Peter 1:3-12

"Hope" is a central category for the whole letter,[114] a category that one encounters a number of times in the first part of this letter as the starting point or end point of the argumentation.[115] This is precisely not only about that which is still pending. When 1 Peter stresses that the future is already kept by God and stands prepared (1:4f.), when the believers rejoice because salvation, the "goal of faith," is already present, then this shows that it is the author's point to present the content of the Christian hope as something that is already a reality in God's actuality (1:4, "in heaven") and thus also defines the present of those who belong to him. Through this new interpretive framework the experiences of those addressed are given a new quality; the present receives a new perspective. As those "regenerated to a living hope," the Christians participate in the epochal change that took place in Christ (cf. especially 1:3f.); their life is thereby defined as "eschatological" existence. The conquest of death that has taken place through the resurrection is

[113] Διηκόνουν is imperfect; i.e., it expresses the duration of the action, while ἀνηγγέλη is aorist, therefore describes punctiliarly the proclamation of the gospel that had begun at a particular point in time. It is not possible to place the two *Aktionsarten* imperfect and aorist into one as "events of the *past*" (J. Herzer, "Prophetie," 21).

[114] Cf. 3:15, where it is expected of Christians to answer for the "hope that is in you."

[115] First Peter speaks directly about hope or hoping at the beginning of the eulogy (1:3), in the beginning of the paraenesis (1:13) and at the end of its explanation (1:21).

interpreted in 1 Peter as a participation in the everlasting divine life (cf. especially 1:3f. in connection with 1:23-25). Suffering is thereby not only robbed of its destructive high-handedness and relativized, but it also even receives a positive interpretation. The tension that nevertheless still remains between two so contradictory conditions is bridged through the anticipatory joy of the believers, who on the basis of the fate of Christ know salvation already to be present with God. At the same time, the addressees are assured of the power of God that already keeps and preserves them (cf. 1:5).

The apparently paradoxical togetherness of suffering and joy is thus based in a double reference of the believers on the one hand to the God who calls them and on the other to the world around them that rejects them. *In Christian existence*, one could say, *a power struggle takes place between the present and oppressive experience of suffering on one side and the anticipated joy of hope on the other*. In this situation, it is the central concern of 1 Peter[116] to strengthen the anticipated joy of hope, to bring about an orientation on the promised and in hope anticipated salvation of God as the middle and center of the self-understanding and life goal of his addressees. Accordingly, the hymnic eulogy aims with their praise of God's deed (1:3-5) at the present human reaction described in 1:6-9, which reaction consists in rejoicing and "inexpressible and beatific joy" (1:8; cf. 1:6).

2. Rebirth and the New Way of Life 1:13–2:3

Using the conjunction διό, which does not appear anywhere else in the letter, in 1:13–2:3 the letter draws a conclusion from the praise of the divine action of salvation: the "living hope" (1:3ff.) that is opened up in rebirth is now through the imperative "set your total hope upon" also claimed as an active orientation of existence and behavior on the part of those who are addressed (1:13), which orientation proves its worth in a lifestyle different from the surrounding world (1:14–2:3). Here also, as already in the eulogy, highly compressed speech and unique, even in part overloaded, metaphors (cf. 1:13; 2:2) are used to express basic

[116] On the early Jewish (especially *2 Baruch*) and early Christian traditions (especially Matt 5:11f. par.; Luke 6:22f.; Jas 1:12) used in this cf. W. Nauck, "Freude."

concepts about Christian existence, in which process *the connection of gift and duty, of salvation and sanctification, now stands in the center.* This takes place in three sets of arguments that make clear in their respective specific ways that the obligation to "obedience," which is repeatedly stresseed in 1 Peter (1:14, 22; cf. 1:2), together with a corresponding "way of life,"[1] arise, as it were, on their own from the promise of salvation.

(a) In the first paragraph (1:14-21), the necessity of differentiation from the former way of life is deduced: conformity to the former standards[2] can not determine the life of the ones who "totally hope" (v. 13); orientation on God and his grace therefore makes the regenerate at the same time "children of obedience" (1:14). This is positively described with the concept of sanctification in the sense of a lifestyle that corresponds to the holy God (1:15f.). This relationship to God that constitutes the believing existence is further defined in two ways: Believers live "in fear" before God the judge (1:17), and they live in faith and hope before God as the savior (1:18-21).

(b) In the second paragraph (1:22-25), the Old Testament theme of holiness and sanctification is again taken up in Hellenistic form as "purification of the soul" and is newly connected with the emphasis on obedience. Thereby, this obedience is now for the first time defined in terms of content in the form of the (doubly stressed) obligation to mutual love (1:22). This is also based on the salvation perspective that has been opened by the gospel, whereby the metaphor of the divine "new siring" that was used in 1:3 is now taken up in the picture of (accomplished) rebirth and is interpreted as the overcoming of human life's slavery to death through the "imperishable sperm" of the divine word (1:23-25).

(c) The positive definition of obedience in 1:22—as an obligation to mutual love—is augmented in 2:1 through the negation of a vice catalogue that lists the behaviors that should be avoided by the believers. This is based on a renewed taking up of the theme of rebirth, which now (after siring and birth) goes further in the striking, daring picture of "newly born nursing infants," who grow up by means of the "milk of the word" (λογικὸν γάλα) into salvation.

[1] First Peter uses the term ἀναστροφή (1:15, 17, 18) for this.

[2] In the usage μὴ συσχηματιζόμενοι (1:14) stands the term σχῆμα = form, shape, attitude, then also condition (cf. Rom 12:2).

The three paragraphs reveal a common structure: They are dominated by a paraenetic demand expressed through a finite imperative verb (1:13, 17, 22; 2:1f.), which is made more specific through participles that should be interpreted imperativally. As clearly as the imperative dominates here, it is also equally indefinite: hope, be prepared, live holy, live in fear, purify the soul, love, set aside evil, and the like—these are fundamental but at the same time totally open and general demands. Therefore, this text is still less about concrete behavioral directives; one finds these in the second main part of the letter. Here in the "theological" opening part the inner connection between promise and demand initially is foundationally developed, whereby the negative delimitations of 1:14 and 2:1 enclose the positive demands of sanctification (1:15f.) and love (1:22). The first main part leads into the portrayal of the new being as community, whereby here as well the imperative initially is again used, when the description of the "spiritual house" (2:5) that joins to the "living stone" Christ (2:4), who is at the same time the "chosen cornerstone" (2:6), is connected to the summons to let themselves be built as "living stones"(2:5), before the paragraph then transitions to the second main part through a summarizing statement about the new status of the believers as God's people (2:9f.).

With respect to the noticeable closeness of 1 Peter to Pauline theology even on the level of individual formulations,[3] this pointed stress on a way of life corresponding to the faith, the intersection of indicative and imperative already within the theological foundation of the letter, marks a shift in accent over the Pauline tradition. "Here unlike Paul the imperative does not follow from the previously developed indicative, but the paraenesis stands at the head and is justified by means of the attached reference to the will and deeds of God."[4] First Peter and Paul do indeed agree in the theological principle that the divine gift goes before all Christian self-definition and makes this possible—the three times repeated picture of new siring or rebirth (1:3, 23-25; 2:2) leaves no doubt about that;[5] yet 1 Peter's concern (already noticeable in

[3] See Introduction, pp. 27f. n. 14.

[4] E. Lohse, "Paränese," 86.

[5] The "*prae*" of the divine action reveals itself also in the meaning of the divine calling/election (1:1, 15; cf. 2:4, 9).

1:2 in the letter opening) to weave right from the beginning into the consolation of divine grace a corresponding way of life as a second constitutive element of Christian existence appears to be a characteristic of many theologians of the third generation[6]—perhaps as a reaction to a misunderstanding of the proclamation of grace, with which Paul already had to fight as well.[7] This also forms a remarkable commonality between 1 Peter and the other "Catholic Epistles," which are different in so many ways. It is also worth noting that the shaping of the Christian lifestyle is not dealt with within the sections concerning the people of God but within the sections concerning rebirth. This underlines the theocentric orientation of 1 Peter's ethical teaching.

(i) "Obligating Hope" 1:13

(13) Therefore—the hips of your minds girded up, in a sober condition—hope completely on the grace that will be granted you at the revelation of Christ.[8]

1:13

The initial statement draws upon the central note of hope with, however, a different accent. "Hope entirely" is the first imperative in this letter. If the hope in 1:3ff. was already the total substance of salvation that the believers are granted as a consequence of their "new siring due to grace" through God, then now the hoping is also a duty: verse 13 now demands from the addressees an unlimited directing of their whole existence on the salvation promised by God.

This paraenetic accentuation is underlined by means of two *participia coniuncta* that complete and strengthen the imperative in that they set out the behavior resulting from the hope as quasi-self-evident. At the same time, the not totally clear command to

[6] An impressive example is the framework of the directives in the Sermon on the Mount; Matt 5:17-20; 7:15ff.; especially 21-23.

[7] Cf. Rom 3:8; 6:1f.

[8] Bauer-Aland 1706 interprets φερομένην as "which will be announced to you." That, however, fits poorly with the statement that is connected to it, "at the revelation of Christ." What is intended is far more the grace which will then be "brought."

hope completely is thereby made more specific. The semantic unit dominated by the first participle speaks—at the visual level rather clumsily—about the "girding of the hips of the mind." In the ancient world, one shortened the long garment that hindered walking with the belt of the hips. This can become a metaphor for readiness for action in a general sense[9] and then in a special religious sense.[10] The latter is the case here, in which the picture is strained by the addition of τῆς διανοίας. Through this unconventional combination of metaphorical and non-metaphorical speech—evidently a stylistic method valued by 1 Peter[11]—the author arrives at a penetrating precision: The picture of the gathered up garment as an expression of immediate readiness for action is connected to intelligence and mind; that means the readiness for action concerns the person in their personal center described through thinking and willing. The aorist participles used here make it clear: the believers should make themselves ready now; a "jolt" as it were should go through their thinking. In the second semantic unit, the supplemental motif of soberness appears and stands in the present: apparently soberness is an attitude worth taking up and preserving. The metaphor of soberness valued in 1 Peter[12] gains its contour from the opposition to drunkenness. Because this is an expression for lack of restraint and unconsciousness and therefore for loss of self, "soberness" thus describes the alert consciousness that does not fall victim to blurring because of one's own fault and undignified foreign control. This exhortation to soberness (as the parallel exhortation to vigilance)[13] finds its home in the New Testament mainly in eschatological contexts[14]

[9] Cf. Prov 31:17 in praise of the capable housewife.

[10] In Ephesians 6:14, the picture describes the readiness of the *miles Christianus*. In part, Exod 12:11 is also interpreted allegorically, where the belt of the hips of the Israelites becomes an expression of their readiness for departure. Philo (*Sacr.* 63) interprets this as the readiness to carry out the transition from passion to virtue in thankfulness and respectfulness towards God. Luke 12:35 interprets this as the readiness to expect the (returning) Lord.

[11] Cf. the "wordy milk" in 2:2.

[12] Νήφειν is a preferred term for 1 Peter—on the six occurrences in the NT three are in 1 Pet (1:13; 4:7; 5:8), the other three in the *Corpus Paulinum* (1 Thess 5:6, 8; 2 Tim 4:5); cf. further 1 Cor 15:34, and also *CorpHerm* 1.27.

[13] Both are used in parallel in 1 Pet 5:8 and 1 Thess 5:6.

[14] Especially clear is 1 Thess 5:6, 8.

and warns about allowing one to be deceived and dazed by the reality that lies before one's eyes.

The reference to the grace that will be given to them at the Parousia then also fits with the eschatological connotation of soberness as with that of a garment's belt (Luke 12:35). Normally the stress in 1 Peter is on the present dimension of this grace (cf. 2:19f.; 5:12), which also resonates here in the present φερομένην; yet with the references to the ἀποκάλυψις Ἰησοῦ Χριστοῦ, which here—just as in 1:7 and 4:13—must mean the emerging of Jesus at his Parousia,[15] emphasis is placed on its futuristic character, whereby—just as already in 1:3ff.—the future substance of salvation becomes a power that determines the present through "hope." The sentence structure explained earlier underlines this eschatological qualifying of the paraenesis: the dominating finite verb is the imperative of hoping, to which the behaviors described by the participles are subordinated. In this way, the author once more refers back to the reception of salvation, but also introduces the transition to the demand.

(ii) Obedience as a Counterpart to God's Holiness 1:14-16

(14) As obedient children do not adapt [any more] to your desires that previously [ruled] you due to your ignorance, (15) but, as a counterpart to the one who has called you, you also become holy in your whole way of life, (16) for it is written, "Be holy, for I am holy."

On the text: **16** Instead of ἅγιοι ἔσεσθε ("you should be holy") K P 049 and other witnesses read ἅγιοι γένεσθε ("[now] become holy"); the Majority Text reads ἅγιοι γίνεσθε ("become [in principle] holy"). The change is not caused by the biblical model in Lev 11:44 LXX, which goes with the main reading, but is presumably theologically motivated. Holiness is no longer understood as a state in which one should live, but as a goal toward which one should immediately (γένεσθε) or in principle (γίνεσθε) strive.

[15] This fits with the meaning of this expression in the rest of the New Testament (1 Cor 1:7; 2 Thess 1:7; cf. on this A. Oepke, "καλύπτω," 586). Therefore, in my opinion, one cannot leave the question of whether ἀποκάλυψις here refers to the historical Jesus or the Parousia undecided as Elliott, 356f., does.

1:14

The recipients are addressed as "obedient children." The child metaphor corresponds to the father metaphor and refers to rebirth; at the same time, the obligation of a child to obedience is now connected to it. In contrast to the negative associations with respect to the word "obedience" that predominate today, one must keep in mind that those associated with hearkening to someone, in a falling in line with or submission to someone carried out in obedience (ὑπ-ακούω), is not understood in the New Testament context as a negation of freedom but as an attachment to God through which the believers for the first time become free. First Peter 2:16 makes this more pointed in the apparently paradoxical formulation that the Christians as "God's slaves" are free. This freedom proves itself here in the turning away from the dependencies of the previous life, which 1 Peter—in the typical black-white schema of the language of repentance (Eph 4:17-19; cf. 1 Pet 2:9)—characterizes by means of the catchwords "ignorance" and "desires" as corrupt with respect to consciousness and will.

Excursus 5: The Desires

One generally especially associates turning from sensual pleasures (from gluttony to sexuality) with the fight against the (fleshly) desires. That is not totally false: The control of the instinctual life is for the whole ancient ethic a prerequisite for successfully being human. That is not only true for the "Socratic" lines of Platonism, Cynicism, and the Stoa,[16] but also for the hedonistic counter proposal, for Epicurus. The philosopher of Kepos himself "demanded asceticism";[17] his concept of pleasure is restrictive and serves reason more than the stomach.[18] All ancient philosophies, then, are united in this, that the unfiltered animalistic impulses abolish the freedom of people for a self-determined life. By means of their

[16] Epictetus (50–120 C.E.) counseled to abstain from all feelings of desire (ἡδονή) (Epict, *Ench* 34).

[17] M. Erler, "Socrates," 216, "Epicurus demanded asceticism, but he meant thereby, not radical abstention, but judicious weighing."

[18] Epicurus is most concerned with peace of mind through contentedness, therefore the reasonable rule and integration of the drives; his highest value is *ataraxia* (freedom from mental disturbance), by no means excess.

desires, people make themselves slaves of that which does not fit their nature, as Epictetus repeatedly stressed in his diatribe on freedom. "True freedom is not reached by the satisfaction of every wish, but through the extermination of the appetites [ἀνασκευὴ τῆς ἐπιθυμίας]."[19] Despite all their differences, the hedonism of Epicurus is connected with the moralist Epictetus by the persuasion that only through the control of the drives is it possible for the human being to reach the true happiness.[20] For the critic of the desires, it is not about compulsive repression of sensuality, but the integration of the animal impulses as a prerequisite for a successful life. This conviction was also owned by Hellenistic Judaism:[21] Philo repeatedly stresses that the Jew as the truly wise person abstain from sensual passions (cf. Philo, *Conf.* 75–82), which he not infrequently explicitly and polemically contrasts with the non-Jewish orientation with respect to being and acting, whose "land is desire and whose law is sensual pleasure" (Philo, *QG* 4.39). In Josephus' *Apologia* as well, it is precisely sexual morality by which he exemplifies the superiority of the Jewish Law.[22] It may also play a part that one saw in this a chance to commend oneself as a—not infrequently also ethically discredited—religious minority with an especially austere ethic, a strategy that early Christianity then also appropriated. However, this pressure for legitimization

[19] Epict, *Diss* 4.1.175; similarly Epict, *Ench* 34.

[20] At the same time, Epicurus argues using differentiation in the concept of desire, "Therefore if we say that pleasure is the goal, we do not mean by this the pleasures of the unrestrained and those which consist in consumption, as some assume, who are ignorant of this . . . or interpret perversely, but to feel neither pain in body nor disturbance of soul. For it is not drinking orgies and continual revels, also not the enjoyment of boys and women, of fish and everything else that a extravagant table offers that produce a pleasurable life, but a sober mind that tracks down the reasons for each choice or avoidance . . ." (Epic, *Men* 131f.). On the other hand, Epictetus required μέγας ἀγών, the "great fight of the soul" against the passions (Epict, *Diss* 2.18) with the goal of complete freedom from them, "But for the time being totally remove desire. For if you desire something that is not under your control, you will of necessity be unfortunate . . ." (Epict, *Ench* 2).

[21] In the Old Testament, the fight against the desires has no part; only in late writings as in *4 Maccabees* does the control of the passions then become a dominating theme.

[22] Cf. Jos, *C. Ap.* 2.199–203, 215. In Jos, *C. Ap.* 2.244f. in his critical evaluation of the Greek gods he castigates their unrestrained sexual life as "the most shameless of all" (πάντων ἀσελγέστερον).

only strengthened that which was also generally recognized independently of the issue: The fight against the desires was about life success, a life that for Jews and Christians was synonymous with fellowship with God and obedience to his will. However, pleasures and desires, desires that seized the believers and influenced them in a foreign way, stood against just this alignment of one's being with God's will. Therefore, they also needed their own efforts in order to take from the passions their destructive characteristics, whereby the "destructive" is seen in a good Jewish way as the obstruction of divine righteousness (*4 Macc.* 2:6ff.). Through their power of judgment[23] oriented on God's will, the believers control "not only the rage of sensuality, but also every desire (ἐπιθυμία)" (*4 Macc.* 2:4)—and can thus integrate sensuality meaningfully into their personality: "The power of judgment as a masterful gardener takes all these [i.e., the passions], thoroughly cleans them, prunes them, ties them up, puts a net on them, pours water of each type all around them and thus refines the undergrowth of the habits and passions. For reason is the guide of the virtues and the supreme master of the passions" (*4 Macc.* 1:29f.). But one is only capable of this if one has tamed the desires, and for this one requires a certain degree of "practice" in bringing oneself under control, even "asceticism."

What is problematic about the desires is, therefore, not their sensuality as such, but their power over people that hinders their level-headed self-determination—so goes the philosophical variant—or the orientation of life on God (this being the Jewish-Christian reception and transformation of this thought). The latter is what is meant in 1 Peter 1:14 by the warning about συσχηματίζεσθαι, thus the exhortation not to allow the form of one's life, the σχῆμα, to be determined by the passions.[24] This power-encounter in people between the relationship to God and the (fleshly) passions is yet more intensified in 1 Peter 2:11 in the drastic picture of a war by the passions against the soul (as the

[23] *Fourth Maccabees* speaks of "the power of judgment," but, as his discussion shows, means orientation on the Torah.

[24] In Rom 12:2, where one also encounters συσχηματίζεσθαι, it is explicitly contrasted with "renewal of the mind," the one who orients themselves by God's will; on the differences between Rom 12:2 and 1 Pet 1:14 cf. J. Herzer, *Petrus*, 245–48.

aspect of the person directed toward God). The metaphor of a war clearly reflects the consciousness that there a hostile power assaults the inner person and seeks to conquer it in order to stop the orientation of "the obedient children" (1 Pet 1:14) on God as their father (1:17; cf. 1:2).

These passions were earlier effective on the basis of ἐν τῇ ἀγνοίᾳ, that is "on the basis of ignorance" (ἐν should be interpreted causally here, as also frequently in 1 Peter[25]). With ἄγνοια, 1 Peter takes up a term that in Hellenistic Judaism already described the ignorance of God on the part of the "gentiles."[26] In the New Testament as well, ἄγνοια characterizes the person before his or her conversion (Acts 3:17; 17:30; Eph 4:18). And as the knowledge of God in the New Testament means "primarily recognition, obedient or thankful bowing under the one known,"[27] so correspondingly the ignorance of God does not primarily describe a noetic deficiency, but an existential reserve—and thereby also a perverted orientation of being and behaving. Therefore, this ἄγνοια leads to the state that something else in the form of lust wins power over the person,[28] as the author of 1 Peter explains in looking back over the earlier life of the called.[29] *Therefore, ignorance and desire only describe two sides of the alienation of people from God.*

[25] Cf. 1 Pet 1:2, 5, 12, 17, 22, etc.

[26] Wis 14:22; Philo, *Decal.* 8; Jos, *A.J.* 10:142, etc. To this extent it means a "*lack of the necessary knowledge for the salvation of the soul*" (R. Bultmann, "ἀγνοέω," 119), even if Bultmann's attempt to interpret the term as Gnostic is not persuasive.

[27] R. Bultmann, "γινώσκω," 704.

[28] Notable is 1 Corinthians 15:34, where the exhortation to soberness (1 Pet 1:13!) and to avoidance of sin is connected with the warning that "some are ignorant of God [ἀγνωσία θεοῦ]." *CorpHerm* 1.27 also unites all of the motifs (sleep, drunkenness, ignorance of God and soberness).

[29] This concise expression of the notional complex that forms its basis is developed more fully in Ephesians 4:17ff.: in connection with ἄγνοια (which virtually as its own hypostasis "is in them") the nullity of their minds (4:17) and the hardening of their hearts (4:18) are spoken about, through which their understanding was darkened and the (not yet believing) are "alienated from the life that is from God" (4:18). Accordingly the "old self" was then also basically directed by the "deceitful [ἀπάτη] desires" (4:22).

1:15-16

The positive other side of the differentiation, which note was already sounded in verse 14 in the expression "obedient children," is introduced with the adversative ἀλλά, and in verses 15 and following discussed under the catchword "holy." This word also contains a clear element of differentiation: "Holy" is *per definitionem* that which is separated from the sphere of the profane.[30] Such separation is nevertheless only the other side of belongingness to the God (cf. 2:5, 9) who is holiness itself.

In the Old Testament, the attribute of holiness is thought of most closely joined with God—"holy" is first God himself in his transcendence and greatness. Thus, the one on the throne in the calling vision of Isaiah is praised with the *Trishagion*, "Holy, holy, holy is YHWH Sabaoth . . ." (Isa 6:3; cf. Rev 4:8). The power of this holiness can be communicated to places (for example the temple), but also to people who belong to God. This is in the first place an accolade, but it can then also contain an obligation. This is especially clear in Leviticus, where in the context of the provisions of the law holiness becomes a mandate of the members of the people of God, "For I am the Lord, your God. Therefore you shall make yourselves holy, so that you will be holy, for I am holy; and you shall not make yourselves impure through any kind of creature that creeps on the earth. For I am the Lord, who led you out of the land of Egypt so that I might be your God. Therefore you shall be holy, for I am holy." (Lev 11:44f.). Holiness has here become a task of the called insofar as this "make holy" means a constant alignment with God's commands implemented in life, especially in the separation from other orientations of existence in the environment. This separation has its reason in belongingness to the electing God, "who has led you out of the land of Egypt, so that I might be your God. Therefore you shall be holy, for I am holy." The turning of the "holy" God toward his chosen ones and the becoming holy of those belonging to this God therefore interlock. The introduction of the Holiness Code (Lev 19:2) exhibits this same structure. It is cited here by 1 Peter, "You shall be holy, for I, the Lord, your God, am holy." Because this summons to holiness in Leviticus 19 is then followed by numerous concrete directions on how one should shape one's life, among them

[30] In that case that the Hebrew קדשׁ is derived from קד (cf. O. Proksch, "ἅγιος," 88; W. Kornfeld, "קדשׁ," 1181), then separation is already in the term in Hebrew.

> also the famous commands to love of the neighbor and love of the foreigner, then it underlines the fact that holiness takes shape in this world in obedience to God's command.

The interpretation of the command as making oneself holy corresponding to God's holiness, as one finds in Leviticus 11 and then programmatically in Leviticus 19:2, played a central role in Hellenistic Diaspora Judaism precisely as the theological foundation for the Jewish way of life in a pagan environment. "Leviticus 19 was probably considered by the Jews in antiquity as a kind of summary of the Torah. . . ."[31] The author of 1 Peter also here again shows his closeness to the traditions of Diaspora Judaism in that his is the only New Testament writing to cite Leviticus 11 or 19 explicitly and to name correspondence to the holiness of God as the real motive for the lifestyle of the "elect foreigners in the dispersion."[32] Thereby, *the ethic is based directly in the relationship to God*. But in doing so here as well the precursory activity of God in calling is firmly held onto: As ὁ καλέσας ἅγιος God has set the believers in a relationship to himself and thus has made them holy (cf. 1 Pet 1:2), so sanctification is the answer to it.

(iii) God, the Father and Savior 1:17-21

> *Literature on 1 Peter 1:17-21*: **W. C. van Unnik**, "The Critique of Paganism in 1 Peter 1:18," in E. E. Ellis/M. Wilcox (eds.), *Neotestamentica et Semitica* (*Festschrift* M. Black) (Edinburgh, 1969), 129–42.

(17) And if you call upon as father the one who judges each person without partiality according to his deeds, then spend the time of your being a foreigner in fear, (18) in the knowledge that you were not redeemed with transient things, with silver or gold, from your vain way of life that was handed down to you by your ancestors, (19) but through the expensive blood of Christ, as of an impeccable and unblemished lamb, (20) chosen indeed before the founding of the world, but revealed at the end of the ages for your benefit, (21) you

[31] P. W. van der Horst, "Pseudo-Phocylides," 191.

[32] One finds a parallel in terms of content in 1 Thess 4:3-8, where the calling of Christians to holiness is stressed, also in distinction to a behavior described as that of "the pagans, who do not know God."

who became those who through him trust in God, who resurrected him from the dead and has given him glory so that your faith and your hope are focused on God.

1:17

God is defined here in two ways; he is, on the one hand, the father who is called upon. That points back to previous statements: As father of Jesus Christ (1:2), he has procreated the believers anew (1:3) and is therefore also called upon as father by them.[33] But they are thereby also, as 1:14 says, obedient children. Insofar as the concept of God as father also implies that of God as judge, which is why one is to live before this one "in fear." This reference to God as judge appears relatively frequently in 1 Peter.[34] In the context of dealing with unjust suffering, this reference serves several times as the comfort and the relief of those affected (1 Pet 2:23; 4:5, 19). On the other hand, the comment here in 1:17 about God, who "judges each person without partiality according to his deeds" underlines the responsibility of each person for his or her actions.[35] Both aspects of the divine judgment—the comforting and the admonishing, indeed, the warning—are traditional.

Excursus 6: God as Judge

In terms of the history of religion, this concept that the divinity calls people to account in a post-mortem judgment is widespread. In the Mediterranean area, it is first already demonstrable in Egypt[36] before 2000 B.C.E. (*Instruction for King Meri-ka-Re*)[37] and

[33] 1 Pet 1:17; cf. Gal 4:6; Rom 8:15; and especially the Lord's Prayer, Matt 6:9-13 par.; Luke 11:2-4.

[34] In contrast to the majority of other New Testament statements about judgment, in 1 Peter it is not Christ but exclusively God who is the judge—an indication of the "theocentric orientation of 1 Peter" (Boring, 85).

[35] ἔργον "stands singularly here for the total behavior, the way of life" (Goppelt, 120, with reference to Isa 40:10; 62:11; 1 Cor 3:13ff.; Gal 6:4; Rev 22:12).

[36] H. Brunner, *Religion*, 130, "It appears that every concept in other religions of such a judgment, at least in the Mediterranean and the areas dependent upon it, are determined by Egypt."

[37] This work is a Pharaoh's instruction of his son and successor, Meri-ka-Re. "The court of justice which judges the wretched, you know that they

the Egyptian *Book of the Dead* (about 1500) assumes without exception the concept of recompense in the hereafter according to one's deeds.[38] The awareness is expressed in these texts that the gods as the embodiment of the good and as the guarantors of truth and righteousness (Egyptian *ma'at*) cannot be indifferent about evil; accordingly, ethical criteria become the standard for entrance into the hereafter. That then has also found its way into impressive descriptive pictures in which the weighing of the souls is depicted. This concept became popular in Western thought especially through Plato. This man—the concluding myths in *Gorgias* and the *Politeia* are above all to be cited—adopts this concept *in the context of a final evidence for his ethic*. In contrast to an interpretation of reality that claims values are only arbitrarily established, the arguing reason is indeed able to bring out counterarguments; it is able to do defend the philosopher's certainty of a comprehensive just world order, but it is not able to verify this empirically. At this point, it is the place of the final mythic narratives, which make it clear by means of a parable that this world is in reality formed and determined by a just order. This reaches beyond the sensually ascertainable world and thereby likewise beyond the individual

---

are not lenient on that day because the unlucky are condemned. . . . It is bad if the accuser is all knowing. . . . After death the person remains alone, and their deeds are laid in a pile beside them. There one remains eternally and whoever complains about it is a fool. But whoever arrives (on the other side) without having done injustice will be there as a god, striding free as the lords of eternity." (H. Brunner, *Religion*, 131); cf. further R. Grieshammer, *Jenseitsgericht*.

[38] Cf. the negative confession of sin before the judge of the dead in saying 125.10ff., which assumes a recompense in the hereafter (125.9, "Day of Accounting") and indeed will be delivered in a court session before the gods (cf. E. Hornung, *Totenbuch*, 28f.): "The . . . 'Lord of Complete Truth' is your name. I have come to you; I have brought you justice and have driven injustice from you. . . . I have done no injustice against people and I have not maltreated any animal. . . . I have offended no god. I have damaged no orphan with respect to their property. . . . I have not added pain and not have left (anyone) hungry; I have caused no tears. I have not killed and I have (also) not ordered to kill; I have not harmed anyone." (E. Hornung, *Totenbuch*, 233f. This is only the beginning—the whole passage is more than ten times as long!).

bodily existence,[39] but precisely thus it points again to the unconditional responsibility for life in the world.

The concept of God as judge is also common in the Old Testament[40]—nevertheless in a very specific way. For one, we do not experience a judgment of the dead in which the deeds of the individual are weighed. When, for example, the prophets speak about judgment, they are describing a punishment that takes place within history, either a punishment on the arrogant foreign peoples or a punishment on disobedient Israel. *Apparently in the Old Testament one does not come to the thought of judgment through general reflection about justice, but through faith in God as the (clearly just) Lord.* God's judgment is thus an intervention by the creator and

[39] Cf. J. Annas, "Plato," 124, "The whole point of the myth is the contrast between what seems, now, to be the end [death, possibly an unjust death like Socrates'] and what really is the case on a deeper level (the mythical events which will take place after death)."

[40] Very early in Israel the functions of the creation of justice and the setting to rights were connected with God. This is already shown in the personal names (in part, theophoric) built from the verbs for judgment (especially with דין and שׁפט, thus the tribe Dan, David's chancellor Jehoshaphat, 2 Sam 8:16; David's son Shephatiah, 2 Sam 3:4, etc.), which are in part relatively old, but especially since the time of David are more commonly in evidence (K. Seybold, "Gericht," 460). As in other culture circles in the ancient orient, one also finds in Israel the institutions of the ordeal or God's judgment (cf. Exod 22:6ff.; 1 Kgs 8:31f.) as a court of last resort in especially difficult legal cases: in the appeal of the accused (1 Sam 24:13; Judg 11:27) as of the accuser (Gen 16:5; Exod 5:21) for the first time the verb שׁפט is then used with YHWH as subject (cf. H. Niehr, "שׁפט," 426). "Create justice for me, Lord, according to my righteousness and innocence!"; as this prayer has done in Ps 7:9 so do all prayers of the accused call upon the judgment of God (cf. Ps 7:7, 9, 12; 17:1f.; 35:24; also Job 16:18ff.; 19:25ff.; 29-31; 38:1ff., etc.). The punishing intervention of God in the case of the offense of an individual is repeatedly narratively presented in the Pentateuch and also in the history books: It is worth mentioning Miriam, who became leprous as punishment for her rebellion against Moses (Num 12); Moses and Aaron, who were not allowed to enter the promised land due to their doubt (Num 20:1-13); Achan, due to whom (after his theft) the whole people had to suffer at first (Josh 7); Saul, whom God rejected after his disobedience and abandoned to his enemies (1 Sam 15ff.), or David, who was punished with the death of his child after his murder of Uriah and his adultery with Bathsheba (2 Sam 11f.). However, the concept of the judgment of God as a history-forming intervention had first developed in the period of the kings and assumes indeed the concept of the kingdom of God.

sustainer of the world who does not allow his will and the order he put in place to be disregarded without consequences.[41] In both the Psalms and the Prophets, one can see a process of development toward universal judgment as a new putting in order of reality, a judgment that despite the horror that is connected to it is virtually longed for, as Psalms 94 shows, which in view of oppressive injustice begins with the cry, "God of repayment, YHWH, God of repayment, appear! Arise, judge of the world. Pay back the proud for their deeds." (Ps 94:1f.).

Naturally, it is especially the suffering, the victim, for whom the announcement of judgment is gospel. Nevertheless, one must guard oneself from a far too single-line derivation from the simple need for retaliation; in not a few prophetic texts (cf. also Isa 26:8f.) or prayers in the Psalms judgment and salvation belong most closely together as good news: God himself comes and sets up his kingdom in judging. Thus in the Psalms, the judgment of God becomes a matter of almost effusive joy and praise (cf. Ps 96; 98). That continues in early Judaism. There the horror of judgment can indeed be depicted, yet "the word judgment" remains there as well "for the most part a *cheerful word*."[42] The Targum Neofyti also stresses this close relationship between God's goodness and his judgment in a striking way.[43] In the narrative about Cain's murder of his brother, the Targum inserts a final debate between the brothers. Cain, angry about the preference given to Abel, disputes an ethical foundational structure of reality: "The world was not created with love and it is not ruled according to the fruit of good works. . . . There is no judgment and there is no judge." But there is thus also no longer any responsibility, and the result of such autonomy is the murder of a brother. Yet the murderer

[41] The word choice shows this as well; while the Greek term for "judge" is oriented on the process of differentiation (κρίνω from "separate, sort out, divide") and consequently right from the beginning describes a forensic act in which an individual comes to judgment, the Hebrew שׁפט orients itself on the process of the exercise of rule. It originally meant "lead, rule," then "decide" and finally "judge, secure justice"; cf. H. Niehr, "שׁפט," especially 412–17.

[42] P. Volz, *Eschatologie*, 92.

[43] TN, Gen 4:1-8. The tradition is also evidenced in TPsJon and in the *Fragment Targum* (cf. M. Ginsburger, *Fragmententhargum*) on Gen 4:8. Thus it is widespread in the paraphrasing Palestinian Targum.

does not have the last word. A confession of the righteousness and goodness of God—in the mouth of the victim Abel—is set against the cynicism of the triumphal violence of the murderer: "I see that the world was created with love. . . . [And just because of this] there is a judgment and a judge." The judgment here is the evidence itself of this, such that the world was created with love/mercy (ברחמים); God's judgment is the result of his mercy.

This announcement of judgment contains a warning, even threatening undertone, that concerns the human being as doer of injustice. Especially in paraenetic texts, responsibility before God is stressed. If this is thought of as primarily collective in the Old Testament, then in early Judaism as in early Christianity increasingly the responsibility of the individual shifts into the center. In connection with this individualization, there is then also the fusing of the Old Testamental and Hellenistic conceptions of judgment: The hope of the setting up of a divine kingdom is connected with the individualization of eschatology and a corresponding judgment of the individual according to his or her deeds. Thus there comes into being the conceptual conglomeration that comes from a final judgment with individual assessment of the respective deeds and corresponding recompense and thereby combines various circles of conceptualization with one another.[44] This forms the

[44] The degree to which the two circles of conceptualization could fuse is shown in 4 Ezra. In this early Jewish apocalypse, which may have come into being towards the end of the first century C.E. and wrestles with God about the question of his faithfulness and righteousness in view of the destruction of Jerusalem, in one and the same vision there is promised the coming of the Messiah, his 400-year kingdom, and also the resurrection and the final judgment, but without further ado this is supplemented with the concept of a judgment of the soul of the deceased following death—which is widespread in the Hellenistic sphere—which souls must suffer or be blessed according to their behavior during their lifetime: "When the verdict goes out from the Most High that a person should die, when the spirit separates itself from the body so that it may again be sent to the one who had given it, then it first worships the glory of the Most High. Now if it was one who was a despiser who has not followed the way of the Most High, has despised his law and hated those who feared God—these souls do not go into the chambers, but must immediately wander around in great pain, always lamenting and sorrowful in seven ways . . . [The description of the seven sufferings follows, the last and greatest of which consisting of passing away in shame, disgrace and fear in confrontation with God's glory.] . . . But for those who have followed

background for the early Jewish (and then also the early Christian) eschatology with consequences for the picture of humanity and the establishment of the ethic. An example of this is the *Mishnah* tractate Aboth, the only tractate in the *Mishnah* that has been used in liturgy.[45] There, human existence is frequently interpreted as a loan[46] for which the person some day must give account before his or her judge.[47] That God is the judge is, in the first place, the *good* news that world history is not already world judgment. At the

---

the way of the Most High this is the decree, if they should have separated themselves from this transient vessel . . .: first, with great joy they look on the glory of the one who receives them. Then they will come to rest in seven steps. . . . [Then follows the listing of six steps.] . . . the seventh, which is greater than all those previously named, that they rejoice with confidence, trust without confusion, and rejoice without fear. For they make haste to look on the face of the one whom they served during their life and from whom they will receive a reward in glory" (4 Ezra 7:78b-98).

[45] On the liturgical use of mAv cf. K. Marti/G. Beer, *Abot*, XV.

[46] Cf. mAv 3.16, "Everything is given on surety, and the net is spread over all the living." In the picture of God as the monger to the borrowers and writing down everything in his debt register, this is parabolically discussed in order then to sum up, "For the judgment is a judgment of truth and everything is prepared for the meal [of the righteous]."

[47] Cf. mAv 4.22, "Those born are destined to die and the dead to come to live again, and those who have come to life again to be judged in order to experience, to make known and to become aware that he is God, he the sculptor, he the creator, he the observer, he the judge, he the witness, he the Lord of judgment, and he who will judge at one time, praised be he! For before him there is no injustice, not forgetting, no favoritism, and no acceptance of bribes; for everything belongs to him. . . . For without your will you are created, without your will born, without your will you live, without your will you die, and without your will you will answer and give account before the king of the kings of the kings, the Holy One, praised be he!" The sentence initially outlines in three concise statements the fate and purpose of humanity: death, resurrection and judgment. Clearly life is here also totally determined by its reference to the future world, in which this typically culminates in judgment. The goal is "knowledge, proclamation and experience," as it says, therefore recognition. The object of recognition is God, as is virtually hammered in in the sevenfold listing in that it is said, "that he is God, he is the sculptor, he the creator. . . ." The list is divided in two: The first half of the statements relates to God as the author and Lord of the world. The three attributes of the second half—judge, witness, and Lord of judgment = accuser—make it clear that with the exception of the accused all the roles in the court are filled by God himself.

same time, *the responsibility of the person before God* is underlined by this. One finds similar statements in the New Testament as well, for the redemption that Christ brought does not in any way exclude the responsibility of the individual for his deeds, as Paul also stresses when in 2 Corinthians 5:10 he says that "we must all appear before the judgment seat of Christ so that each receives according to that which he has done in his earthly existence, be it good or evil." So it is also precisely the returning Christ in that great picture of the judgment at the end of the apocalyptic discourse in Matthew 25:31-46 who assesses and condemns people according to the measure of love practiced or denied.

It is explicitly added that this life is to be spent "in fear" before God. "The fear of God" does not mean an obsessive religious dread of God; rather in early Jewish literature it can be paralleled with love of God;[48] as such, it does not diminish life, but as the "beginning of wisdom" (Ps 111:10; Prov 9:10; Sir 1:16) virtually heightens it: "The fear of the Lord gives honor and fame and grandeur and then crown of joy. The fear of the Lord will refresh the heart and give cheerfulness and joy and length of days" (Sir 1:11f.). That does not exclude that—particularly in connection with the thought about judgment—in this is mirrored a consciousness of the majestic holiness of this God, which in all the joy over God's closeness yet also brings horrifyingly to consciousness the experience of one's own lack of holiness (cf. Isa 6:5; Luke 5:8). Nevertheless, the fear of God does not stand in contrast to a trustful turning toward God as father—just as it was also indeed part of Paul's secret of his relationship to God that he totally entrusted himself to this heavenly father as a child (Phil 2:15; cf. Rom 8:14ff., 31ff.), can exultantly rejoice about this closeness in Christ (Phil 2:17f.; 3:1; 4:4)—and at the same time stand before him in fear and trembling and try to obtain his salvation (Phil 2:12). Precisely the special closeness of God then also intensifies the consciousness of one's own distance from God resulting in a fright—and a special obligation to a new orientation. The formulaic ἐν φόβῳ stresses both; really φόβος is a constitutive element of πίστις (Rom 11:20; 2 Cor 5:11).[49] This is underlined again by means of the reference to God's lack of partiality, who precisely "without looking on the

[48] Sir 2:15f.; cf. also Luther's exegesis of the Ten Commandments in the *Small Catechism*, "We should *fear and love* God."

[49] Cf. R. Bultmann, *Theologie*, 321–24.

person"[50] judges each according to his or her deeds.[51] In a way that is typical for him,[52] 1 Peter at the same time speaks about one's way of life, ἀναστροφή. The time of one's life is described as the time of being a foreigner. That reminds one of the central motif of the letter, "foreignness" (in the address, 1:1, and at the beginning of the second main part in 2:11). In 1:17, the reference to the "time of being a foreigner" underlines the temporary nature of this present life and connects this with the prospect of the return to God, father and judge.

1:18

Now, alongside establishing the obligation to a new way of life because of God's judgment, comes the establishing of the obligation through the remembrance[53] (εἰδότες) of redemption. In doing this, the first verse is formulated negatively: The redemption took place "not with transient things" (οὐ φθαρτοῖς). That makes clear in the first place that the freeing from this life characterized by transience did not take place by means of something that itself came from this transient world. That is again stressed through the explicit negation "not with silver or gold." Gold and silver stand for the most valuable things that a person can accumulate in this world, because by means of them one can procure virtually anything on earth. But precisely because of this these

[50] The word ἀπροσωπολήμπτως is only found here in the whole Greek Old and New Testament; nevertheless it is known in early Jewish (cf. also *T. Job* 4:8) and early Christian literature (cf. *Barn.* 4:12). In the New Testament, the same content can be expressed through the negation of προσωπολημψία (Rom 2:11) or προσωπολήμπτης (Acts 10:34). The motif of a divine judgment without consideration of the deceiving external is already developed by Plato in the myth of the hereafter in his *Gorgias* (Plat, *Gorg* 523a–524a).

[51] Judgment according to works connects authors as different from one another as Matthew (16:27) and Paul (2 Cor 5:10; cf. Rom 14:10b, 12).

[52] The term ἀναστροφή is one of 1 Peter's preferred terms: Six of thirteen occurrences in the New Testament. Περιπατεῖν, which is close in meaning, is scattered over the whole New Testament. The motif of way for way of life is found in both the Greek (cf. Xenoph, *Mem* 2.1; Epict, *Ench* 19; *Diss* 2.23) and the Hebrew world (cf. Ps 1:6; 119:9, 105; Prov 2:8ff.; 3:6, 23; Isa 26:7ff., etc.).

[53] Paul can likewise refer to the knowledge of the community with εἰδότες (Rom 6:9; 1 Cor 15:58; 2 Cor 4:14; cf. Eph 6:8, 9).

goods potentiate "avarice"; as a fixation on the transient, they are not at all able to free one from the emptiness of this existence.[54] For this a totally different substance is required—the offering of the life of another.

The provocative antithesis to the pagan self-understanding is conspicuous. For this self-understanding was that which was transmitted from the ancestors, the *mos maiorum*, highest norm. In that it is cast in doubt here with the adjective μάταιος, the contrast to the society around them and thereby the "foreignness" of the Christians is once again strongly stressed. The Septuagint and, following it, early Judaism, as also early Christianity, described with the attribute μάταιος ("vain," "futile," "without truth," "without perspective") that orientation of existence and behavior by means of which the person denied his or her dependence upon God and thereby is given over to transience and futility.[55] It is at the same time a synonym for the gods of the world around them and thereby for a perverted religious orientation.[56] It is from this "futile" existence that Christians are "redeemed." The concept of redemption refers to a number of roots: For one, it reminds one, especially in connection with a "purchase price," of the redemption of slaves.[57] "The purchase [for freedom] by God marks a change of ownership and frees from the pre-Christian life relationships, understood as [freeing] from slavery."[58] But at the same time a relatively clear allusion to Isaiah 52:3 LXX also appears

[54] There is also possibly at the same time an allusion to the statements of the Old Testament prophecies of judgment (Zeph 1:18 and Ezek 7:19 stress that gold and silver can not save one on the day of wrath).

[55] Cf. Ps 94[93]:11 (cited in 1 Cor 3:20); concerning idolatry *Aris. Ep.* 134; 137; Sib 3.29, 547, 555; 5.83; concerning wealth *Aris. Ep.* 321; concerning the violence of wrath *T. Dan.* 4.1; in the New Testament cf. further 1 Cor 15:17; Rom 8:20; Eph 4:17.

[56] Cf. Lev 17:7 LXX, "And shall no longer offer your offerings to the spirits of the field [τοῖς ματαίοις] . . ."; in the New Testament cf. Acts 14:15, where Paul and Barnabas summarize the content of their missionary preaching in the face of the inhabitants of Lycaonia, who hold them to be gods, with the words, "We preach the gospel to you so that you will turn from these idols [ἀπὸ τούτων τῶν ματαίων] to the living God."

[57] Jos, *A.J.* 12.28, 33, 46; 14.107, 371; 15.156; *B.J.* 1.274, 384 witnesses to the redemption of slaves through gold and silver; cf. H. M. F. Büchsel, "λύω," 341; A. Deissmann, *Licht*, 275ff.

[58] J. Herzer, *Petrus*, 124

here, an allusion to God's promise to the prisoners in Babylon that he will not redeem them through silver (οὐ μετὰ ἀργυρίου λυτρωθήσεσθε), therefore to the freeing actions of God in the history of the people of God. Finally, the Greek term λυτρόω also reminds one of Mark 10:45, where Jesus interprets his offering of his life as a λύτρον ἀντὶ πολλῶν, as "redemption money for many." This final reference is made yet stronger by means of the following verse, which makes an explicit reference to Jesus' death as an offering. The decision is not clear whether all three motifs—redemption of slaves, freeing from exile, and atonement through Jesus' death—were present to the author of 1 Peter when he wrote these lines, and we know still less just what the addressees associated with them. But this multiplicity of allusions that does not exclude one another can well be intended; nevertheless, all the motifs that one encounters here indeed have in common the aspect of freeing from dependence and lostness and so strengthen each other in their declarative effect.

1:19

The redemption took place through the blood of Jesus, which in its redemptive effect is compared to the Old Testament (unblemished) lamb for an offering. The offering is thereby far more than a human substitutionary work precisely where it deals with God's reconciliation; on the great Day of Atonement, it is the substitutionary gift of life made possible by God (from grace) so that God can again come into the middle of his people who had forfeited his life.[59] Jesus' sacrifice of his life is also understood in this sense in the New Testament: by this, human beings have not reconciled God, but God has reconciled human beings, indeed, the whole cosmos with himself (2 Cor 5:19; Col 1:20; further Rom 5:1-11).[60] Even if 1 Peter does not discuss this concept further but in a

[59] H. Gese, "Sühne," especially 100: "The person as such in their distance from God has become in view of the revelation of the divine glory a slave of death. But God opened a way to himself in the symbolic atonement that took place in the cultus that he revealed." Gese's thesis was confirmed by his pupil Janowski (cf. B. Janowski, *Sühne*).

[60] H.-J. Eckstein, *Glaube*, 26, ". . . the human being does not grasp the initiative here in order to bring God around and to reconcile him again, but God gives to the human being, who is in a damaged condition through their own fault, the possibility of a new life with the new community. . . ."

formulaic manner takes the common conviction of reconciliation through the blood of Jesus for granted, it is still also clear for him through the image of the purchase price that by this an event is meant in which God has created the possibility of reconciliation. First Peter places his own accent on the contrast of the blood of Christ to worldly goods. This appears to be superfluous, but through the explicit contrast of "transient" precious metals with the blood of Christ as an "impeccable and unblemished sacrificial lamb" the whole event of redemption is set into an explicit contrast to the earthly sphere, and thereby its difference with respect to its essence is clarified anew. This is not about an ontological contrast between transient and eternal (which in the light of the contrast of precious metal with the very much more perishable blood would also not make sense); the contrast between precious metal and blood marks rather a contrast between two ways of life and their opposite theological valuation. For gold and silver are the means of the violent procurement of life at the cost of others: its procurement already costs life;[61] whoever gathers it, exploits others (Jas 5:1-6; cf. Rev 17:4); as "lure of evil" and the fuel of wars[62] precious metal is *ferro nocentius*, more damaging than iron that is used to make deadly weapons.[63] In contrast to this, here redemption takes place through the offering of life. This motif is strengthened yet more through the use of the image for Christ of a flawless (and thus appropriate for an offering in the Temple) lamb. First Peter 1:19 alludes to the power of an offering to bring about salvation.[64] The metaphor of a sacrificial lamb has, however, a semantic surplus that reveals itself precisely in the contrast to the lion in the end of the letter (1 Pet 5:8): while the predator that "walks around seeks someone to devour" lives from the blood of another, the lamb is the sacrifice *par excellence* from which others

[61] This began in prospecting for the precious metals: ancient mines were for the most part notorious as places of the agonizing death of those who were condemned to work in them (cf. on this B. M. Rebrik, *Geologie*, 125ff.).

[62] Cf. on this the discussion of the role of gold in the "Iron Age" by Ovid, *Metam* 1.140ff.; cf. also *Pss. Sol.* 17:33.

[63] So Ovid in his description of the Iron Age, "*iamque nocens ferrum ferroque nocentius aurum prodierat*" (Ovid, *Metam* 1.141f.).

[64] Cf. J. Jeremias, *Abendmahlsworte*, 216f., who on page 217 presents the rabbinical evidence for a concept of atonement connected with the blood of the Passover lamb (Exod Rabba 15.13 on Exod 12:2; Exod Rabba 15.13 on Exod 12:8).

live. The lamb also symbolizes Christ as the one who did not live from others, but offered himself up for them.[65]

1:20

God himself stands behind this death, the God to whose forknowledge (which already has been referred to in 1:2) the salvation event is ascribed. The sending of the Son is now ascribed to the divine self-determination before all time that precedes all created being, which self-determination is placed in the adversative position to its realization at the end of time. This contrast of a pretemporal divine plan and its historical actualization in the Christ-event occurs frequently in the New Testament[66] and early Christian[67] (epistolary) literature. The plan makes it clear that in the redemption through the blood of the lamb the change of the ages has come to pass (and this purchase price is everlasting insofar as it refers to a divine decision before the origin of this transient world and so can also lead out beyond it). At the same time, this reference to time is again aimed at the Christian community: the afterthought "on your behalf" places the believers, who are on the margins of the world around them and shoved to the side, into the center of salvation history—God's plan before time and his end-time actualization of this plan aims at them.[68]

1:21

Before the letter returns again to the imperative in verse 22, the intimated reference in the end of verse 20 to the divine actions on the believers is further discussed: Their trust in God is based on Christ's saving act. This God has, as it were, committed himself in

[65] In Revelation 5 this is expressed through a break in the metaphor: The lion from Judah who can open the book with the seven seals is announced—but a slaughtered lamb enters; cf. on this R. Feldmeier, "Lamm."

[66] Probably the oldest evidence is the (not totally certain) conclusion of Rom 16:25; cf. further Col 1:26; 2 Tim 1:9f.; Titus 1:2f. and also Eph 3:5, 9; John 17:24.

[67] Cf. *Ign. Magn.* 6:1; *2 Clem.* 14:2; *Herm.* 89:2f. *Sim.* 9:12.

[68] Cf. Brox, 83, "These few words fling open universal and world-historical dimensions, which lead directly to the fate of the addressees: The dramatic, pre-cosmic and end time event is willed by God 'δι' ὑμᾶς/on your behalf.'"

the resurrection; he is "defined" as the one who raised Christ from the dead and endowed him with glory. This is the basis of "faith and hope on God." The situational development of Christology is here again clearly recognizable: According to 1 Peter, God has revealed himself in the fate of Christ as the one who can and will transform the lowness, suffering, and death of those who belong to him into triumph, glory, and eternal life.

For yet a further time (1:3, 15, 17; cf. further 2:9, 23), God is described here, not with adjectives, but with participles. First Peter shares this characteristic with Paul;[69] and it is revealing for speech about God, because adjectives describe the being, but participles, on the other hand, describe the effect and action. More precisely, the New Testament epistolary literature deals with an action of God aimed at his counterpart. Even in that exceptional case, in 1 Peter where an adjective is used (for the holiness of God in 1:14f.), this is connected with the participle καλέσας, which makes it clear that this holiness does not have its point in a demarcation against human beings, but in their inclusion, indeed in the self-communication of God to his counterpart.

(iv) Love as the Proof of New Life 1:22-25

Literature on 1 Peter 1:22-25: **M. Evang**, "Ἐκ καρδίας ἀλλήλους ἀγαπήσατε ἐκτενῶς. Zum Verständnis der Aufforderung und ihrer Begründungen in 1 Petr 1,22f.," *ZNW* 80 (1989), 111–23; **E. A. La Verdiere**, "A Grammatical Ambiguity in First Peter 1:23," *CBQ* 36 (1974), 89–94.

(22) With souls that in obedience to the truth have been purified to unfeigned love of the brothers and sisters love one another steadfastly out of pure hearts (23) as those born anew—not from perishable sperm, but from imperishable, [that is] by means of the living and remaining word of God. (24) For "all flesh [is] as grass, and all its glory as the grass' flower. The grass has withered and its flower has fallen to the ground, (25) but the word from the Lord remains eternally." But this is the word that was proclaimed to you as gospel.

[69] Cf. R. Feldmeier, "Paulus."

On the text: **23** The expression that is certain in the witnesses, δια λόγου ζῶντος θεοῦ, can be translated either as "through the word of the living God" or as "through the living word of God" (see the exegesis at that point). A number of readings attempt to remove the uncertainty of the text by means of rearrangement, additions, or omissions and thus document that this question was already then a point of conflict: διὰ λόγου θεοῦ ζῶντος ("through the word of the living God" Ψ, 2), διὰ λόγου ζῶντος τοῦ θεοῦ ("through the living word of God"),[70] διὰ λόγου ζῶντος ("through the living word" miniscule 36).

The sequence is determined by the imperative "love one another steadfastly." This imperative is framed by two perfect participles. The first is active and speaks of the purification of the soul in obedience to the truth and therefore stresses the renewal of existence through one's own endeavors, while the second is passive, calling to remembrance once again the action of God in rebirth that goes before all self-determination and is the foundation for the mutual love. Both participles are clarified through two prepositional definitions, whereby the first definition gives the ground and goal of the purification ("in obedience . . . to love of the brothers and sisters") and the second the origin of rebirth ("not from perishable sperm . . . through the word").

1:22

The sanctification as "obedient children" called for in the previous section (1:14) is now taken up in the charge to purify their souls in "obedience to the truth." In the Old Testament, the verb ἁγνίζειν is a *terminus technicus* for cultic purification[71] and is still used in the same way in the New Testament,[72] but already in early Judaism and early Christianity, especially in the "Catholic epistles" (Jas 4:8; 1 John 3:3). It was then also used for purification of thought and action.[73] Here as well, 1 Peter takes up a concept that is at home in the biblical context but clothes it in a typical Hellenistic garment as purification of the soul.[74] However, while

[70] In *Nestle-Aland* the witnesses are not listed; in the *Editio critica maior* the variant is not documented.

[71] Cf. Exod 19:10; Num 11:18; Josh 3:5, etc.

[72] John 11:55; Acts 21:24, 26; 24:18.

[73] Cf. Ps 19[18]:10; Prov 20:9; *4 Macc.* 18:23; 1QS 3.4-9; 4.20f.; *1 Clem.* 21:8; 48:5.

[74] See above Excursus 4: Soul and Salvation of the Soul in 1 Peter, pp. 87–91.

in contemporary philosophy by purification of the soul is meant above all its freeing from every form of passion,[75] 1 Peter now for the first time specifies the behavior that is demanded as *love*. As this love was related initially (1:8) to Christ, so it is now love toward fellow human beings, which, as a result of faith in salvation, should determine the way of life for the believers. With respect to this, both the further definition "love *one another*" (ἀλλήλους) and the term φιλαδελφία show that here (as also in other places)[76] love within the Christian community is meant. This in no way implies contempt or even hatred toward those who do not belong to one's own community;[77] arguably, however, in the light of the external pressure that the Christians can only meet through holding together, the relationships within the community are above all on the author's heart (similarly Gal 6:10). The demand of φιλαδελφία appears more frequently in the New Testament (cf. Rom 12:10; 1 Thess 4:9; Heb 13:1; 2 Pet 1:7).

One should notice that the command to love is defined in a number of ways: Souls should be *purified* resulting in *unfeigned* sibling love, and this love should come from a *pure heart*. Similar commands also appear in other places in the New Testament,[78] and they bring to a head in view of social intercourse with one another that which up to this point has been called "sanctification" (1:15f.; cf. 1:2); lying and hypocrisy are the greatest dangers to such a community founded upon mutual love. In this context, one should also notice the further definition according to which the purification of the soul resulting in sibling love should take place "in obedience to the truth." The term "truth" (ἀλήθεια), which only occurs here in 1 Peter, is certainly here also "a shorthand expression for the many ways of describing the salvation that has been given";[79] but the author of 1 Peter probably does not use

[75] Virtually as a principle Epictetus in *Diss* 2.18.19 formulates, "Have the wish to become pure in fellowship [i.e., community] with yourself and with God." Such a thing takes place in "the great fight" of the soul against fear and desire (Epict. *Diss* 2.; cf 1 Pet 2:11).

[76] Cf. 2:17; 4:8f.; further 5:14.

[77] This is made clear in 2:17, where in parallel to love toward the brothers and sisters the Christians are urged to "honor" all people.

[78] On the command to love or believe without hypocrisy see Rom 12:9; 2 Cor 6:6; 1 Tim 1:5; 2 Tim 1:5; Jas 3:17.

[79] Brox, 86.

this term accidentally in distinction to hypocrisy: in accordance with divine truth, the soul becomes pure, which makes possible unfeigned love. The adverb ἐκτενῶς can describe the duration *and* the intensity of the love; both are represented in the literature.[80] On the basis of the affinity to ἄφθαρτος/μένων in the second participial construction in verse 23,[81] the temporal interpretation is preferable here; the author of 1 Peter concerns himself above all with fidelity and trustworthiness. However, the translation with "steadfast" attempts to take into consideration the aspect of intensification in the sense of an undivided commitment[82] that resonates in the Greek.

1:23

The basis is laid for the command to love through a renewed reference to the "new siring,"[83] which 1 Peter now refers to with a perfect passive participle of result in order to characterize rebirth as something already completed. Despite all of one's own effort that is necessary for renewed behavior, the new existence is still not founded upon one's own action but in the divine grant that preceded it and that produces the renewal of the person. As was already the case in the image of redemption in the previous paragraph, here again the "non-worldly" source of the redeeming means of salvation is stressed—here through the antithesis between "perishable" sperm (as a prerequisite for the first siring) and the "living and remaining word of God"[84] as the "imperishable" sperm.[85] This as well is again a relatively daring image: The

[80] Cf. Goppelt, 127, "with total commitment"; Schelkle, 52, "fervent"; Brox, 85, "enduring."

[81] Cf. M. Evang, "Verständnis," 116.

[82] Goppelt, 130.

[83] Cf. Spicq, 72: ". . . actualisez la grâce de votre régénération, qui est d'abord et avant tout une capacité d'amour."

[84] Grammatically both participles, "remaining" and "living," could refer to God; thus the Vulgate translates, "*per verbum Dei vivi et permanentis*." Both the reference of word to the imperishable sperm and the statement in 1:25 in which "remain" is explicitly said about the word make it more likely that both of these participles refer to λόγος (cf. already A. Bengel, *Gnomon*, 628). On the grammatical justification of this reference cf. also E. A. LaVerdiere, "Ambiguity," especially 91–93.

[85] On the image of seed for the word of God cf. Luke 8:11.

divine word is described in its action in analogy to human sperm. Just as this makes possible biological life, so the word—which itself is "living and remaining"[86]—communicates its livingness and imperishability so that those newly born by it are removed from the general transience, the word of the gospel as the word of the creator (1:20) possesses "birth-giving power."[87]

1:24

The livingness of the word of God is presented yet again in verses 24-25 with the help of a citation from Isaiah 40:6-8 LXX. The biblical word stands in a comforting oracle at the beginning of Deutero-Isaiah; however, it is interpreted in a new way by means of the changed context: In Isaiah, the glory of God as the basis of hope and confidence is contrasted with human frailty thereby to stress God's superiority over the peoples and thus to justify his promise to Israel. In 1 Peter, a *dictum probans* comes into being for the antithesis between human transience and divine eternity from the contrast of the withering grass and fading flower on the one side and the enduring word of God on the other.

1:25

This "enduring"[88] word is at the same time the word that—as the something of an afterthought explanation stresses—was proclaimed "to you" as gospel. What was said in 1:3f. about the "living hope" and the "imperishable inheritance" is also true of the "living word" and the "imperishable sperm": It is the divine life that the elect share in through hope, through faith, and through the proclamation of the gospel.

(v) New Birth and New Beginning 2:1-3

(2:1) Since you have now laid aside all badness and all deception, hypocrisy and resentfulness and all slander, (2) as newly

[86] The two participles could grammatically refer to God. That is, however, less meaningful. That God is living is self-evident, and the character of the word as "remaining" will be repeated again at the end in 1:25.

[87] Ch. Wolff, "Christ," 335.

[88] One should note the repetition in v. 25 of the verb μένω used in v. 23.

born nursing infants desire the unadulterated milk of the word [of God] so that through it you grow into salvation, (3) if "you have tasted that the Lord is delightful";

On the text: **2:3** Instead of χρηστὸς ὁ κύριος ("the Lord is kind") P[72] K L 049 and other witnesses read χριστὸς ὁ κύριος ("Christ is the Lord"). The variant is based on a confusion of η and ι; see the exegesis of 2:3 next.

The text of 2:1-3 is also dominated by an imperative, the command to desire the λογικὸν γάλα, the "word-milk." A short vice catalogue is associated with this by means of a present participle, the vice catalogue describing what those Christians who keep their souls pure in obedience (cf. 1:22) should put aside. A first subordinate clause introduced by a final ἵνα gives the purpose of the imperative, a second its reason.

2:1

The new birth leads to new behavior, as is now yet again underlined through the negation of a vice catalogue in which the demand is intensified yet more through the triple addition of the attribute "all." In terms of content, the behaviors stigmatized here (deceit, hypocrisy, resentment, and defamation) are, above all, those that poison the climate between people and therefore contradict the mutual love that was commanded previously, just as they contradict the central thought of the following section (2:4-10), the new community.

2:2

This vice catalogue, however, is not now carried forward by means of a corresponding virtue catalogue, but flows into the demand, "As newborn nursing infants desire the unadulterated milk of the word [of God]." We are dealing again with the mixing of metaphor and "real" discourse[89] that is typical of 1 Peter. In the context of the letter, this expression takes up the theological con-

[89] The *nomen proprium* is designated "real discourse" only with reservations, for the description of metaphor as "unreal discourse" that results from this is problematic (cf. E. Jüngel, "Wahrheit," 74–77). Precisely the successful metaphor can grasp the facts in a more accurate, "more real" way than the so-called real discourse.

cept of rebirth and develops it further: On top of new siring and birth through the divine word, there now follows the "nursing" of the newborn[90] with the "logos-milk" and also the corresponding growth. The comparison of Christians with nursing infants is only found here in the New Testament. Precisely there, where the responsibility of the believers to comply with the new birth through a new ethical orientation is emphasized, their dependence upon God is underlined at the same time with this (in the ancient context a quite provocative metaphor); it stresses that becoming new can only take place when the believers are continually "nourished" by God,[91] and that is indeed with that "word-milk."

This concept also has precursors in the Judaism of the period: According to Philo, the divine logos is the "imperishable food" for those souls that, not being fixated on sensuality, "love to look on heaven."[92] Thus God and his Logos become not only the sole author of the origin of new life, but also here the whole growth "to salvation" about which the letter is speaking comes exclusively from him; the regenerate exist and grow only in constant "spiritual metabolism."[93] It is toward this very thing that the believers should direct their desire, as the only imperative in this sequence demands. They should desire with the unrestrained intensity of a hungry nursing baby. As has already happened with the images of siring and of birth, so here again, it is stressed that the regenerate are in the first place only receivers, and precisely that is the condition for their becoming new.

[90] It is possible that the concept of the sinlessness of small children stands in the background (so Windisch, 58, with reference to contemporary early Jewish texts such as 2 Macc 8:4 and Philo, *Her*. 38).

[91] Boring, 93: "For 1 Peter, the divine 'milk' of the word of God is something Christians must never outgrow."

[92] Philo, *Her*. 79, cf. *Det*. 85; cf. further *Jos. Asen*. 12.2, where the divine word is described as the life of the creature.

[93] A similar metaphor is also found in the early Christian *Epistle of Barnabas*, which, in its allegorical interpretation of the biblical statement about the "Promised Land," relates the milk and honey to faith in the promise and the word, which—as milk and honey the child—"make alive" the believers (*Barn*. 6:17). The most far-reaching interpretation of this picture with respect to God is found in the *Odes of Solomon*, where God's breasts are milked by the Holy Spirit (*Odes Sol.* [syr] 19.1ff.; cf. J. H. Charlesworth, *Odes*, 81f.).

Excursus 7: Rebirth

Literature on the excursus: **R. Feldmeier** (ed.), *Wiedergeburt* (BThS 25; Göttingen, 2005).

Insofar as we can allow a judgment on the basis of the scanty condition of the sources, one meets the metaphor of rebirth from the first century C.E. onward, in the sense of a religiously conditioned transformation of the human being of whatever nature, in various texts of Jewish, Christian, and pagan origin.[94]

In the Jewish sphere, Philo's *QE* 2.46 constitutes the most striking parallels. It is about the interpretation of Exodus 24:16b, in which the Jewish philosopher of religion allegorically interprets the tradition that on the seventh day, Moses was called upward to God as an indication of a "second birth" through God himself, which is contrasted to the first birth through "perishable parents." Through this second birth, the soul is freed from the body and participates in "the most holy nature of the *hebdomas* [week]." The further use of this metaphor in Hellenistic Diaspora Judaism is also witnessed to by Ps-Philo, *De Jonah*, in which the prophet who turned to both God in the belly of the fish (25f., §95.99) and the repentant inhabitants of the city of Nineveh (46, §184) is described as born again.[95] The statement in the novel about repentance that was written in Egypt, *Joseph and Aseneth*, is also related; there the daughter of the priest uses in the context of her conversion to Judaism the verbs ἀναζωοποιεῖν (8.9; 15.5; 27.10), ἀνακαινίζειν (8.9; 15.5, 7) and ἀναπλάσσειν (8.9; 15.5) as an expression of the divine action upon her.

The pagan evidence is from a somewhat later date, coming from the circles of the mysteries. The most striking evidence is the eleventh book of the *Metamorphosis* of Apuleius. The redemption through Isis of a certain Lucius from his donkey form prefigures rebirth through induction into the mysteries. Freed from blind fate through this induction and placed under the protection of a "seeing fate,"[96] Isis as *numen invictum* (Apul., *Met* 11.7) and *omnipotens dea* (Apul, *Met* 11.16) through a type of client relationship, protects her

[94] Cf. F. Back, "Wiedergeburt."

[95] Cf. on this F. Siegert, *Predigten*, 163f., 166f., 207.

[96] Apul, *Met* 11.15; this seeing of the deity is the conscious antithesis to *caecitas fortunae*.

disciple in both this life and in the realm of the dead. The disciple is therefore *renatus quodam modo* (Apul, *Met* 11.16). The spread of the rebirth metaphor in the context of an induction into the mysteries is also witnessed to by an inscription in the Mithraeum of Santa Prisca in Rome that describes the day of initiation as the new birthday; likewise, some taurobolium inscriptions refer to the birthday of the mystery initiate.[97] The terminology of rebirth is also evidenced—in the fourth century—by Sallustius.[98]

In the New Testament, apart from 1 Peter, the notion is found above all in conversation at night between Jesus and Nicodemus in John 3; here (especially 3:5), as in Titus 3:5, baptism is interpreted by this notion (cf. further John 1:13). In contrast to these texts that relate rebirth and baptism to each other, James 1:18 (just as 1 Peter) through the metaphor of rebirth, stresses the effectiveness of the divine word. Rebirth in the Hermetic texts is a special case.[99]

The notions described through the metaphor of rebirth are, however, so disparate that they likely cannot be ascribed to a unitary type.[100] Yet more hypothetical are all the attempts to demonstrate dependence among the heterogeneous witnesses.[101] To that degree, the majority of contemporary interpreters are right when they reject the direct derivation of the concept of rebirth from these parallels. However, just as unpersuasive is the rejection of any consideration of the religion-historical sources, say on the basis of the equation of rebirth with baptism.[102] Rather, precisely the simultaneous observation of contact and differentiation, of reception and transformation, show how 1 Peter through the taking up and creative combination of various concepts has translated

[97] Cf. on this W. Burkert, *Mysterien*, 84.

[98] Sallust, *DeDeis* 4 = 8.24 ed. Nock—there the reborn (ἀναγεννώμενοι) receive milk after the fast; cf. 1 Pet 2:2f. (cf. K. Wyß, *Milch*).

[99] On *CorpHerm* 13 cf. F. Back, "Wiedergeburt," 64–69.

[100] Cf. the statements of W. Burkert, *Mysterien*, especially 83–86. The witnesses for the ritual of rebirth are, according to Burkert, "partially too vague, partially to variform to encourage a simple and at the same time comprehensive theory" (W. Burkert, 84).

[101] In view of the contexts and dependencies of the New Testament texts, Burkert warns "that the conception of the New Testament is directly dependent upon pagan mystery teaching is philological—historically so far indemonstrable . . ." (Burkert, *Mysterien*, 86).

[102] Cf. R. Feldmeier, "Wiedergeburt," 77–81.

the truth of the gospel into a new language in order to allow it to also become effective in a differently influenced life-context. For that purpose one should also far more intensively than before consider rebirth as an independent religious metaphor rather than fading it out through hasty "interpretations." What follows gives in thesis form a summary of the meaning of the image of rebirth in 1 Peter:

The metaphor of rebirth personalizes eschatological salvation. As birth so is rebirth an event related to the individual human being. If birth determines one's earthly existence, then rebirth stands for the correction or overcoming of the conditions set up with the first birth (cf. especially 1 Pet 1:23f.). The focus on "soul salvation" means a not insignificant shift of accent with respect to early Christian eschatology that was characterized by apocalyptic, such as that articulated in Jesus' sermon on the coming kingdom of God or the expectation of a new creation (from Paul[103] to Revelation).

Rebirth underlines the renewal of the existence of the believers that has already taken place and with this the presence of salvation. The personalization allows one, even in an unredeemed world—and the suffering continually addressed in 1 Peter strongly underlines this lack of redemption—to name a place where eschatological renewal has already taken place, namely in the believers.[104] In the repeated motif of joy in suffering (1:6; 4:13f.; cf. 3:14; 5:12), this renewal can already be experienced as the overcoming and transformation of the negative experience of the world and thereby a foretaste of the coming glory.

This salvation, however, is only present insofar as God's future in the form of hope already conditions the present of the believers. In that rebirth is defined as rebirth "to a living hope" the author of 1 Peter makes it clear that the reference to the future remains constitutive of this rebirth. The life of the elect is new on the basis of the "inheritance in heaven" (1:4) that is indeed already dedicated to them in the resurrection of Jesus Christ (1:3), but only "at the end of time" will it be

[103] Cf. especially Rom 8:18ff.; also the new creation in 2 Cor 5:17 admittedly refers to the individual believer, but is at the same time open to being referred to the divine salvific action on the whole creation (cf. 2 Cor 5:19).

[104] By this not only the starting point in baptism is indicated, but also the new state.

revealed (1:5). This future salvation for the earth is only present in the form of faith and love (cf. 1:8); in the "living hope" the yet absent salvation of the believers becomes present—without the loss of its futurity—as an enlivening and thus joy-producing perspective.

The regenerate live in this world as "foreigners"; at the same time they are integrated into the new community of God's people. Thereby, the condition of salvation receives a social and historical form.

At the same time with rebirth, God and the human being are defined in their relationship to one another: God as the power of life that overcomes human existence's slavery to death, human beings as "children." As such, they are no longer only creatures, but then participate quasi-genetically in God as "father."[105] Expressed differently, through the new siring God grants participation in his own livingness and eternity. Accordingly, through the process of rebirth exclusive attributes of the divine such as imperishability, unfadingness, and unpollutedness become attributes of the new life (especially 1 Pet 1:4, 23; cf. further 3:4; 5:4).

Rebirth stresses that the new existence is thanks to the God who in his word gives us participation in himself. As people can contribute absolutely nothing to their siring and birth, so also the metaphor of new siring or the renewed birth underlines that salvation is something that happens to someone, that the regenerate is simply a receiver.

Through the reference to God as "father," the regenerate are at the same time "obedient children" (1:14). The word of God that transforms people is not only the transforming and promised word, but at the same time the commanding word insofar as it, in contrast to the previous orientation of being that is defined by "desires," expects correspondence to God's holiness (1:14ff.).

2:3

This paragraph also closes with an Old Testament citation from Psalm 34[33]:9, which continues the sensuality of the previous metaphor when it speaks of "tasting" the goodness and kindness

[105] Cf. γεννηθέντα οὐ ποιηθέντα (*genitum, non factum*) in the Nicene Creed, which has precisely this point, that Jesus' sonship goes beyond the more external relationship of producer and product and implies a participation in the being of God. Second Peter 1:4 also probably means this by participation in the divine nature.

of God or, here, Christ.[106] A wordplay lies behind this: on the basis of itacism[107] χρηστός and χριστός were at that time pronounced the same; therefore the sentence could be heard at the same time as "Christ is Lord" and "the Lord is delightful [kind]," and not a few textual witnesses, among them such important ones as P[72] and the miniscule 33, also read χριστός. Other than in two Old Testament citations (1 Pet 1:25; 3:12), in which the person referred to is not clear,[108] in 1 Peter the title κύριος then without exception refers to Christ (1:3; 2:13; 3:15). It is he who is enjoyed in the "word-milk" and produces the growth to salvation. Precisely through its recourse to sensuality the "taste" of the divine goodness[109] implies—along with the metaphor of nursing in verse 2—an immediate connection of the regenerate to that "imperishable" reality (cf. 1:23).

B. The Regenerate as God's People 2:4-10

The previous section, 1 Peter 1:3–2:3, explained how the existence of believers in their self-understanding and their relationship to the world is renewed through their calling. Despite the thick network of concepts from biblical and early Jewish tradition[1] and Old Testament citations and allusions,[2] the soteriology is clearly Hellenized. Even the metaphor of rebirth that is used three times and characterizes this first part shows this, which metaphor presents the earliest Christian soteriology as the overcoming of the perishability of earthly existence through participation in God's livingness and seeks to make Christian eschatology plausible in the context of late ancient religiosity. The Hellenizing of the

[106] This becomes clear through 1 Pet 2:4 where the "Lord" from 2:3 is taken up in the image of the "living stone," by which Christ is meant unequivocally.

[107] Cf. on this Blass-Debrunner-Rehkopf §24.

[108] The question, however, is to whom 1 Peter relates these citations. At the very least in 1:25, on the basis of the parallel statement in 1:23, God himself could be meant (Elliot, 391, differs).

[109] The adjective χρηστός is encountered repeatedly as an accolade for sensory goodness (cf. Luke 5:39; further Jer 24:3ff.).

[1] God's mercy, inheritance, prophets, lamb, resurrection, faith, hope, foundation of the world, end of time, and so on.

[2] These come from both the Torah (Exod 24:7f.; Lev 11:44f.) and the Prophets (Isa 40:6-8), as well as the Writings (Ps 34[33]:9).

soteriology has consequences: in "salvation of the soul" (1:9), the coming kingdom of God or the new creation no longer stands in the foreground, but the salvation of the believers. However, this salvation—and here, despite all the Hellenizing the biblical-Jewish inheritance indeed shows itself to be influential—is no purely individual event but integrates the "regenerate" into a new community. That note already sounded in the prescript in 1 Peter 1:1f., in which with the terms "election," "Diaspora," and "foreigners" in verse 1 and also through the allusion to the covenant formation at Sinai in verse 2 the people of God tradition is immediately multiply alluded to. Precisely this is further developed now in 2:4-10, the final section of the first main part. Directly connected to the previous verses (relative conjunction and participial construction), once more an explicit reference is made to the divine livingness that has become theirs in the act of rebirth; those who are newly sired to a *living* hope (1:3), the regenerate through the imperishable sperm of the *living* word (1:23) through their coming to the *living* stone Jesus Christ (2:4) are now themselves built into a spiritual house as *living* stones (2:5). The image of a stone for Jesus Christ allows a twofold aim. The statements in 2:4, which summarize in anticipation the florilegium of biblical texts on the stone (2:6-8), initially make the double character of election clear in Christ: Election connects with God, but at the same time separates one from the world around and so creates a distance, indeed, a tension with fellow human beings. At the same time, the image of the stone in combination with that of the house, which was possibly developed from the former,[3] allows the transference of this double aspect of the chosen and rejected "living stone" Christ to the Christians as the "living stones" of God's spiritual house (2:5). Thereby the salvation-historical or election-theological interpretation of the "foreignness" of the Christians in society is christologically based for the first time. That is further deepened in the citations and allusions of verses 6-8: Christ is a firm foundation for the believers, while the downfall of unbelievers is brought about through him. The paragraph comes to a climax in 2:9f. in a unique burst of collective titles of dignity that stresses belonging to a new, God-elected community, the "Christians."[4]

[3] So Ph. Vielhauer, *Oikodome*, 145, ". . . an allegory extracted from the evidence of scripture, a new witty application of the evidence of scripture. . . ."

[4] First Peter assumes the self-designation "Christian" (4:16; cf. Acts 11:26)

1. The Building Up into a Spiritual House 2:4-8

Literature on 1 Peter 2:4-8: **O. Kuss**, "Der Begriff des Gehorsams im Neuen Testament," *ThGl* 27 (1935), 695–702; **W. Pesch**, "Zu Texten des Neuen Testaments über das Priestertum der Getauften," in O. Böcher/K. Haacker (eds.), *Verborum Veritas* (Festschrift G. Stählin) (Wuppertal, 1970), 303–15, especially 306ff.; **P. Prigent**, "I Pierre 2,4-10," *RHPhR* 72 (1992), 53–60; H. Schlier, "Die Kirche nach dem 1. Petrusbrief" in J. Feiner/M. Löhrer, *Mysterium Salutis: Grundriss heilsgeschichtlicher Dogmatik, das Heilsgeschehen in der Gemeinde*, vol. IV/I (Einsiedeln et al., 1972), 195–200; **E. Schüssler Fiorenza**, Priester für Gott: Studien zum Herrschafts- und Priestermotiv in der Apocalypse (NTA7; Münster, 1972), 51–59; **Ph. Vielhauer**, *Oikodome: Das Bild vom Bau in der christlichen Literatur vom Neuen Testament bis Clemens Alexandrinus* (Diss. theol. Heidelberg, 1939), 144–51; **R. Metzner**, *Die Rezeption des Matthäusevangeliums im 1. Petrusbrief: Studien zum traditionsgeschichtlichen und theologischen Einfluß des 1. Evangeliums auf den 1. Petrusbrief* (WUNT II/74; Tübingen, 1995), 176–81.

(4) Come to him, the living stone—rejected indeed by human beings, but by God chosen, precious—(5) also allow yourself as living stones to be built as a spiritual house into a holy priesthood to present spiritual offerings, pleasing to God through Jesus Christ. (6) For the Scripture contains [the statement], "Look, I am placing a stone in Zion, laying it on the outmost corner, chosen and precious; and whoever believes in him will not be put to shame." (7) For you now, you who believe, honor, but for those who do not believe, "the stone that the builders have rejected, this one became the cornerstone" (8) and "stone of scandal and rock of offense." Those who do not obey the word stumble against [him], to which they were also destined.

On the text: **7** Instead of ἀπιστοῦσιν ("the unbelievers") that is witnessed to by, among others, P^{72} ℵ B C Ψ and the Coptic translations, A P, the majority text and the Peshitta read ἀπειθοῦσιν ("the

---

as one of the first New Testament writings to do so. This consciousness of a distinct identity also probably explains the phenomenon that is so noticeable precisely in the transference of the epithets of the people of God in 2:4-10, i.e., 1 Peter's "forgetfulness of Israel."

disobedient"). On ἀπειθεῖν cf. 1 Pet 3:1; 3:20; 4:17; in 1 Peter, this verb exclusively describes refusal of the proclamation of salvation (cf. 4:17: τί τὸ τέλος τῶν ἀπειθούντων τῷ τοῦ θεοῦ εὐαγγελίῳ—"What will the end of those be who do not believe God's gospel?"). The word ἀπιστεῖν only occurs in this place in 1 Peter.

The introductory verses 4-5, which are directly tied to the previous verses through the relative conjunction, are again dominated by an imperative: οἰκοδομεῖσθε. This passive imperative stresses anew dependence upon the divine action; the moment of active action is not excluded by this, but by means of the participle προσερχόμενοι it is nevertheless correlated and subordinated.

2:4

Through the relative conjunction, reference is made to the preceding; however, when this happens, a totally new image is begun—that of building with living stones. At first, Christ is presented as "a living stone."[1] The unusual metaphor apparently goes back to an early Christian florilegium about the image of a stone for Christ that 1 Peter cites here (see following vv. 6-8). The participle προσερχόμενοι summons one to come to this living stone, to join oneself to him, in order then to form one building with him; insofar as the addressees of this summons are compared to "living stones" in 2:5, the image is also here again strained in the interest of catechesis. The situationally oriented interpretation of the image of stone is typical: in anticipation of the combination of Old Testament citations about the catchword "stone" cited in the following verses, this image is interpreted in two contrasting directions ("it is true . . . but") in which the contrast is based upon the respective person of reference. There, on the one hand, are "the people" (2:5), the ἀπιστοῦντες (2:7) who reject the stone, but on the other hand, it is God who has chosen this stone, to whom the stone is "precious." Just as the author of 1 Peter in his address about his recipients as "elect foreigners" already looked at social exclusion and selection by God together, so now this double aspect also becomes a characteristic of Christ himself: As a stone rejected by people he is in God's view "chosen, precious"—and and such he is the cornerstone of the new building (1 Pet 2:7). This definition of the character of

[1] Jobes (144) emphasizes that the author of 1 Peter, who applies the stone metaphor first to Jesus, does not refer to Peter as the "rock."

the Christian community between selection by God and exclusion from society thus contains a christological basis (vv. 7f.).

2:5

Before the letter further pursues the juncture of divine election and social exclusion, it speaks for the first time about the central thought of the paragraph, the Christian community. Two things are made clear about this: The first is the promise that through connection with the living stone Christ, Christians will themselves become living stones[2] and therefore come to share in the livingness of Christ.[3] On the other hand, paraenesis is again immediately joined with it: as the summons "come [to him]" already intimated, Christians should let themselves be built into a "spiritual house" (cf. 1 Cor 3:9-11). Therewith, it is stated explicitly for the first time that the new life of the regenerate has the form of a new community. Only as a "building," as a collective, can the "living stones" fulfill their intended purpose to be a "spiritual house." With the metaphor, 1 Peter indeed alludes to the concept of the Christians as God's temple[4] that is also evidenced in other places in the New Testament, "not in the sense of a building, but as a collective designation from the standpoint of sanctification."[5] This metaphor is revealing for the understanding of the community in 1 Peter:

[2] The unusual image of "living stones" is also found in *Jos. Asen.* 12:2 (with another meaning).

[3] Gerhard, 168, "*Diversa tamen ratione CHRISTUM vocat lapidem vivum ac fideles lapides vivos. Christum vocat vivum in significatione activa, quia vitam lapidibus super se extructis communicat. Fideles vocat vivos in significatione passiva, quia vitam a lapide fundamentali Christo, cui superstructi sunt, accipiunt.*"

[4] Cf. Eph 2:20-22; 1 Cor 3:16; 6:19; This idea, that the true temple was spiritual, formed not by a physical building but by the community of worshipers themselves, was fairly widespread in Qumran (1QS 8.4-10; 1QH 6.25-28; 4QFlor 1.1-7; 1QpHab 12; and others). Elliott's contesting of the connection between the spiritual house and the motif of the temple and his interpretation as "house(hold)" (J. H. Elliott, *Home*, 165–266, repeated in his commentary, 414–18) is not persuasive. Elliott needs the independent house metaphor for his theory of the correspondence between οἶκος and πάροικος (on the criticism of Elliott's theory cf. R. Feldmeier, *Fremde*, 204–10).

[5] Ph. Vielhauer, *Oikodome*, 146.

(1) Thereby, it becomes clear that a Christian fellowship does not constitute itself as a religious society. The summons with the passive imperative to *let* oneself be built makes it clear that this fellowship does not live from its own relationships, but that it is founded and preserved by means of the action of the Spirit in it (cf. 1:2; 4:14).

(2) The community as a "spiritual house" is not only the work of the divine Spirit, but also his possession and the place of his presence.

(3) This includes at the same time the obligation to evidence this presence, as is shown by the extension of the metaphor of "spiritual house" through the sacral collective designation "royal priesthood" that through its way of life should bring "spiritual offerings."[6]

Immediately next to the encouragement that the Christian community is the place of the presence of God in this world comes the demand to bear witness to God in this world. The adjective ἅγιος speaks for this interpretation (cf. 1:2, 15f.; 2:9), as does the connection of the stones with Zion (2:6). This verse, which ascribes the priestly function to the whole community, was of great theological-historical meaning, especially in the discussion of the universal priesthood of all believers (in contrast to a special class of priests). However, the point here is not the priestly status of each individual Christian but the status of the community (according to 2:9, giving witness to everyone).

2:6

What follows is a florilegium of Old Testament biblical passages that in various ways interpret the "stone" christologically:

One also finds a similar collocation in Luke 20:17f.; par.: Matthew 21:42, 44. The trigger for such an interpretation was possibly Daniel 2:34, 45, in which indeed in a vision of the world empires the stone is related to a divine intervention ("without any help from human hands"), which, together with the second vision in Daniel 7 (v.

[6] A spiritualized concept of offering is already hinted at in the Old Testament (cf. Ps 50[49]:14; 69[68]:31f.; 107[106]:22; 141[140]:2) and is also found in Qumran (1QS 9.3-5, prayer and a proper walk as a suitable offering; further 1QS 10.6; 4QFlor 3.6f.); here, it refers to the way of life (cf. R. Metzner, *Rezeption*, 180).

13, "as a son of man"), can be interpreted as referring to a messianic figure.[7] Further texts characterized by the catchword "stone," which were then similarly interpreted messianicly, were Isaiah 8:14 and 28:16 (Rom 9:32f.; cf. Luke 20:18; par.: Matt 21:44). Finally, the image from Psalm 118[117]:22[8] could also be invoked for the interpretation of Jesus' passion (Mark 12:10f. par.; Acts 4:11). The passages were then apparently brought together into a florilegium, in which by the transference of the "stone statements" to Jesus the "son" could also have been facilitated by a Hebrew wordplay between אבן (stone) and בן (son).[9]

The author of 1 Peter therefore transmits an early Christian tradition here. On the basis of the previously established relationship of Christians as "living stones" to Christ as the "living stone" he can with the christological statement now at the same time undertake the determination of the location of the community in the world. In doing so, he cites Isaiah 28:16, which passage is a word that can also be used for the community in Qumran (1QS 8.7f.). This word comes from an announcement of judgment that is directed against the priests and prophets of Jerusalem, who—as it says in Isaiah—have made a covenant with death and a contract with the realm of the dead (Isa 28:15, 18). It is difficult to determine the degree to which the author or the readers of 1 Peter are conscious of this context, which fits well with the previous theme of death/life. In any case, the biblical citation on the one hand confirms the statement about the election and value of the "living stone" Christ in verse 4 and on the other hand establishes a relationship to the addressees: The word, in the LXX version that is cited here,[10] underlines that the one who relies on Christ in a

[7] In Daniel, this still remains an image. The figure "as a human being" is as it were God's human alternative to the rule of the world empires personified in the beasts. Later, the son of man became a type of messianic figure; this titular sense is then in the New Testament also referred to Jesus (cf. the combination of Dan 7:13 and Ps 110[109] in Mark 14:62), presumably already by the historical Jesus himself (cf. G. Theißen/A. Merz, *Jesus*, 470–80). Such an interpretation is also found in the rabbinic literature (evidence in [Strack-] Billerbeck 1.877).

[8] Cf. J. Jeremias, "λίθος," 277ff.

[9] M. Black, "Use," 11ff.

[10] The meaning of the Hebrew text is uncertain. The form לא יחיש is generally translated with "who does not flee," but the hiphil of חוש ("hasten") would only here occur in the sense of "flee."

believing manner (πιστεύων) will not be put to shame (on belief cf. 1:5).

2:7-8

By means of an asymmetrical antithesis, the following verses again interpret the effect of the "stone" Christ on people. First, the catchwords πιστεύειν and ἔντιμος/τιμή are taken up again from the previous verse: For the believers, this stone that is valuable to God brings honor. This positive statement, however, only serves (through an introductory adversative δέ) to introduce the much more extensively discussed description of the negative effect of the stone on those who do not believe. This takes place through a combination of Psalm 118[117]:22 and Isaiah 8:14. In this combination Psalm 118[117]:22 serves above all as evidence for the rejection of the stone through the ἀπιστοῦντες. The positive aspect of "cornerstone" (cf. Mark 12:10 par.) is not explained again here; instead now in verse 8 by means of an allusion to Isaiah 8:14, the opposition is stressed, which opposition portrays this "living stone" Christ as "a stone of scandal and rock of offense" for those who do not believe. The Christian community, which is the "spiritual house" built out of "living stones," also participates in this fate of Christ. "Being rejected and crucified was not an episode in the career of Jesus that was put behind him by the Resurrection. He continues through history as the Rejected One, modeling the present status of his disciples."[11] This consequence is admittedly not yet explicitly stated here, but only first in 2:11f. with the renewed double reference to the foreignness of the Christians; instead, it is stressed that even this scandal of those who "do not obey the word" goes back in the end to an impenitence caused by God. That is the other side of the conviction that the elect know themselves to be called through God's mercy. If faith does not have its origin in the human will, then that must also be true for unbelief (cf. also 1 Thess 5:9). In our context, this statement—just as the two biblical citations have done—also stresses that the opposition of people against God does not mean a limit to God's power as well. It is also important that this predestinarian element (cf. also 4;17) that also was established previously (1:2, 20)

[11] Boring, 97.

is not the only thing that the author of 1 Peter has to say about the non-Christians. When it comes to social intercourse with the unbelieving, the Christians should not rejoice over their rejection, but rather do everything possible in order to win them (cf. 2:12; 3:1f., 15f.). In the end, there of course remains in such a word a hardness that is not to be softened.

Against this dark background the author of 1 Peter, in the conclusion of his first main part—that carries on and closes the discussion of 2:4f. with a resuming "but you"—lets the Christian fellowship light up as the place of salvation, using a density of statements about election that is unique in the New Testament.

2. The Foreigners as God's People 2:9-10

Literature on 1 Peter 2:9-10: **W. Pesch**, "Zu Texten des Neuen Testaments über das Priestertum der Getauften," in O. Böcher/K. Haacker (eds.), *Verborum Veritas* (*Festschrift* G. Stählin) (Wuppertal, 1970), 303–15, especially 306ff.; **P. Prigent**, "I Pierre 2,4-10," *RHPhR* 72 (1992), 53–60; **H. Schlier**, "Die Kirche nach dem 1. Petrusbrief," in J. Feiner/M. Löhrer (eds.), *Mysterium Salutis. Grundriss heilsgeschichtlicher Dogmatik, das Heilsgeschehen in der Gemeinde*, vol. IV/I (Einsiedeln, et al., 1972), 195–200; **E. Schüssler Fiorenza**, *Priester für Gott. Studien zum Herrschafts-und Priestermotiv in der Apokalypse* (NTA 7; Münster, 1972), 51–59; **R. Metzner**, *Die Rezeption des Matthäusevangeliums im 1. Petrusbrief. Studien zum traditionsgeschichtlichen und theologischen Einfluß des 1. Evangeliums auf den 1. Petrusbrief* (WUNT II/74; Tübingen, 1995), 176–81.

(9) But you [are] a chosen race, a royal priesthood, a holy nation, the people of [his] possession, in order that you proclaim the deeds of power bringing salvation of the one who has called you out of darkness into his wonderful light—(10) you who once were not a people, but now are the people of God, who were without mercy, but now have found mercy.[1]

In this statement that closes the first main part, the stylistic device of the nominal sentence, which underlines the ceremoniousness and the foundational nature of what is said, is used again in 1 Peter.

[1] Cf. E. Schwarz, *Identität*, 53–57, who shows that in the Old Testament the description "holy people," "elect people," and "people of possession" belong to the central statements that are the basis of identity.

However, this is interrupted through a final subordinate clause, which points out the obligation of the believers resulting from their new status.

2:9

This conclusion, which is introduced by ὑμεῖς δέ, expresses in a resumptive manner the new being of those who are called, whereby the author contrasts it to the previous existence through the opposition light-darkness (2:9) and also the twice-repeated "once/now" (2:10). With the plerophoric epithets of the Old Testament people of God (cf especially Exod 19:5f.), "one of the most dense constellations of ecclesiological imagery in the New Testament,"[2] God's history with his people is reclaimed for the Christian community, fostering their "selfconciousness as Israel."[3] At the same time, *the Christian community is also interpreted as a reference system totally on its own* against the pagan surroundings; *indeed, it is interpreted as a counter project rivaling the institutions of the world around them in its claims to validity*.[4] But this is the other side of what 1 Peter will then bring up again two verses later with the address to the "outsiders and foreigners."[5] The actual point is, however, neither the dif-

[2] Boring, 98.

[3] Michaels, 96.

[4] It is remarkable in this that the author of 1 Peter does not speak about the ἐκκλησία, but instead uses salvation-historical terminology. Perhaps this happens consciously, since for him this fellowship is precisely not something existing for itself, as is the meaning invested in the term ἐκκλησία (as the gathering of full citizens).

[5] A secondary introduction (cf. B. Altaner/A. Stuiber, *Patrologie*, 138) to the *Acts of John* (M. Bonnet, *Acta Ioannis*, 152), which however accurately reproduces the feelings against the Christians, shows this very well. It states in the indictment against John (allegedly brought by the Jews before the Caesar) that, with respect to the accused, the indictment is about a new and foreign people (καινὸν καὶ ξένον ἔθνος) that breaks with the traditions, is hostile to humanity, is lawless and revolutionary, and has acquired the foreign name "Christian" (*Acts John* 3). In the parallel tradition, the accusation is made more precise to the effect that the Christians have departed from the way of reverencing the gods that had been handed down by the fathers (ἐκ τῆς πατροπαραδότου θρησκείας), so that now a foreign name and a different people have arisen (ὥστε γενέσθαι ξένον ὄνομα καὶ ἔθνος ἕτερον). Here, one again finds all the motifs: turning away from the tradition of the fathers,

ferentiation from Israel nor that from society, but belongingness to God. That shows itself in that all the attributes of the people of God that are transferred to the Christian community[6] are connected in the closest way with God: *chosen* race, *royal priesthood*,[7] *holy* tribe, a people of God's *own possession*, people *of God*.

This is explicitly established by inclusion in God's sphere of salvation: "who has called you out of darkness into *his wonderful light*." The image of change from darkness into light is typical conversion language,[8] the call alludes to election; both are also already found in virtually verbally identical formulations in Judaism (*Jos. Asen*. 8.9; cf. Isa 42:16 LXX). Thus as darkness connotes ruin and death so light salvation and life.[9] Both together—the change from darkness to light produced through the word—together remind one of creation,[10] so that calling into the sphere of salvation and life appears as an act of new creation. Finally, this inclusion in the sphere of "light" contains the commission to witness to this God in the world (cf. also Matt 5:14-16; 1 Thess 5:4ff.; Eph 5:8ff.). The subject matter of this witness is God's ἀρεταί, as 1 Peter 2:9 in allusion to Isaiah 43:21 calls it. On account of the Hebrew equivalent תהלה in Isaiah 43:21, Bauer-Aland proposes the translation "praise."[11] This, however, is not within the range covered by the Greek term ἀρετή, which actually means "ability," "mastery," any good quality at all, then also moral qualities such as virtue,

---

dissociation, forming a people of one's own and, as a result, foreignness—now brought to expression by others.

[6] Something similar takes place in Qumran, in which the community understands itself as the true Israel to whom belongs the covenant of the fathers (cf. CD 8.17f.; 19.29ff.).

[7] This passage was the *dictum probans* of the Reformers for the priesthood of all believers. For the criticism of this from the Roman Catholic side cf. W. Pesch, "Priestertum."

[8] Cf. Acts 26:18; 1 Thess 5:4ff.; Eph 5:8ff.; *1 Clem*. 59:2; *Barn*. 14:5-7.

[9] Cf. John 1:9-11; 8:12; 1 Thess 5:4-10; Eph 5:8-14.

[10] Gen 1:3; cf. 2 Cor 4:6; καλέω is also encountered in the context of creation in Romans 4:17. *First Clement*, written a short time after 1 Peter, will explicitly refer this calling out of darkness into light to God as the creator of the universe (δημιουργὸς τῶν ἁπάντων), and gave hope in "the name of the one who is the original cause of all creation" (ἀρχεγόνον πάσης κτίσεως ὄνομα) as the goal of this calling (59.2f.).

[11] Bauer-Aland, 212f.

courage, magnanimity, philanthropy, and the like.[12] In the plural form that appears here and when related to God, the term can then also describe the (divine ability for) deeds of power and miracles,[13] whereby here the ethical aspect also belongs to the horizon of the word's associations.

2:10

The closing reference to God's mercy confirms this: this is a mercy through which those who were not previously God's people now become such. That statement is aimed at the situation of the addressees, who were for the most part from a pagan origin[14] and whose reception into the community of salvation was, right in the introduction to the letter, in 1:3, ascribed solely to God's great mercy. This statement is once again followed by an allusion to the Old Testament, in this case to Hosea 1:6, 9; 2:25, which was previously used by Paul to justify the calling of the Gentiles (Rom 9:25f.) and grants the statement additional authority. If one assumes that the author of 1 Peter thought his recipients capable of identifying biblical allusions as such—and only on the basis of this assumption is it meaningful, in my view, to compose a whole letter as a virtual mosaic of biblical citations and allusions—then one must assume that with this allusion 1 Peter also consciously alludes to the whole context of Hosea 1f. That context is about the judgment sign of a marriage with a prostitute (Hos 1) that is turned against an unfaithful people, which sign is then nevertheless outdone by God's love for his people (Hos 2). In 2:25, God finally holds as an "outcome": "I will . . . have mercy upon Lo-Ruhama [she who received no mercy] and will say to Lo-Ammi [not my people], 'You are my people,' and he will say, 'You are my God.' " First Peter 2:10 cites this passage. If exactly this remembrance of the passionate declaration of God's love to his unfaithful people closes the first main part of the letter, then it yet again underlines that everything that is said in the first main part is enclosed by the brackets of the divine mercy (1:3; 2:10).

[12] Cf. Liddell-Scott, 238.

[13] Liddell-Scott, 238, "later, of the gods, chiefly in pl., *glorious deeds, wonders, miracles*"; Adrados, 502, "sólo de los dioses 1 *capacidad de obrar milagros o prodigios . . . 2 milagro.*"

[14] Cf. 1:18; 4:3; see the Introduction above, pp. 42f.

3. Summary 1:3–2:10

The text of this chapter shows that Christianity with its claim to an exclusive commitment through which all other societal obligations are mediated de facto represented the establishment of a counter project to the existing society. If pagan society justified itself with reference to the traditional religion and customs of the ancestors,[1] if here πρεσβύτερον κρεῖττον was virtually the axiomatic assumption of religious and societal legitimation,[2] then Christianity lived from the expectation of God's renewal of the world and correspondingly stressed the breach with the past.[3] The author of 1 Peter underlines this in an absolutely provocative manner when he describes the traditions received from the forefathers as vain (1:18, ματαία ἀναστροφή) and the way of life based upon it as subject to death (1:24). Admittedly, one also finds references in 1 Peter (as in the whole New Testament) to the prophecies of the Old Testament (1 Pet 1:10-12), but this time of the prophets

[1] Cf. W. Schäfke, "Widerstand," 631, "Holding fast to *mos maiorum* [ἔθος, *consuetudo, disciplina*] is a striking trait of the Romans, but it is also found more or less developed in the whole temporal and spatial sphere of the ancient world. Religion and religious customs were included in the maintenance of tradition. The religious and political traditions of a society are therefore to be thought of as inseparably bound together. These ties also still characterized the first centuries after the birth of Christ."

[2] Plato already said that the ancients were "κρείττονες ἡμῶν καὶ ἐγγυτέρω θεῶν οἰκοῦντες" (Plat, *Phileb* 16c). This principle remained valid despite all the crises of received religion. Cicero repeated it when he justified the preservation of received religious rites by saying that "the ancient times were closest to the gods" (Cic., *DeLeg* 2.10.27). Thus he can also demand unconditional obedience towards the religion transmitted by the ancients (cf. Cic., *NatDeor* 3.2-6). Similarly, Porphyrius can formulate the principle, "This is the greatest fruit of piety: to honor God according to the customs of the fathers" (οὗτος γὰρ μέγιστος καρπὸς εὐσεβείας τιμᾶν τὸ θεῖον κατὰ τὰ πάτρια; Porphyr, *Marc* 18). On the whole, cf. P. Pilhofer, *Altersbeweis*.

[3] Cf. the summarizing presentation of W. Schäfke, "Widerstand," 630–48. The Jews had indeed demanded something similar from proselytes; the difference consisted in that Judaism understood itself as an ancient and honorable religion and thereby could offer a substitute *in puncto* of the venerability of ancientness. Exactly that was stressed in Alexandrian Judaism in that one presented the Torah as the most ancient original philosophy from which the Greeks had adopted (cf. the transmitted fragment of Aristobulus in Eus, *PraepEv* 13.12.1f.) or even stolen their philosophy (cf. Philo, *QG* 4.152).

is precisely not designated as the golden age that stands closest to God, but rather is viewed under the aspect of its lack as the time of expectation;[4] it is the time of preparation,[5] with which the stage that has now been reached contrasts as a time of fulfillment. The angels themselves, the heavenly beings, were not an exception to this (1:12 end). *The total weight of 1 Peter's discussion lies on the new, on the new beginning, rebirth*[6] *and the new life of hope that is connected with it*. Thereby, a clear contrast is marked in the whole self-understanding and understanding of reality. One could say in a somewhat stereotyped way that the contemporary world of the Christians was oriented on what had become; their present was legitimated by the past, while the Christian community related everything to God's future that in Christ already had broken in, which made the past appear as old and vain—whereby this new is again the totally original and is that which is already established by God's predestination before the creation of the world (cf. 1:20). This contrast of the interpretation of reality and the self-understanding that is founded upon it also constitutes a substantial moment of the theme of foreignness that is so important for the letter. This theme is now explicitly taken up again in the following verses and discussed to begin with in view of behavioral orientation.

III. Freedom and Obedience

Foreigners in the Society 2:11–5:11

The second main section is marked as a new entry by means of clear structural signals:

1. The recipients are addressed again, now as "beloved."

2. In the verb παρακαλῶ, the author uses the first person singular for the first time and at the same time sets the theme of what follows: it will be about paraenesis.

[4] Similarly also 1 Cor 10:11.

[5] 1:12 explicitly stresses that the prophets did not serve themselves by this, but served the Christians of the present.

[6] That extends to the image of the newborn infant that is used in 2:2 for believers and that clearly contradicts the ancient ideal image of the man in his ἀκμή (on the application of this image to proselytes cf. [Strack-]Billerbeck 3.763).

3. In two ways, reference is again made to the status of the Christians as foreigners.

If the first main part was about the self-understanding of the Christian community, then the second main part is about the relationship to the world, and that relationship is indeed both what concerns the active side of behavior in society and also what concerns the passive side of suffering from this society. Between 4:11 and 4:12, however, one finds a clear formal caesura that also correlates with a shift in accent in terms of content insofar as in the first section it is rather exhortation that stands in the foreground and in the second (4:12–5:11) more comfort. The following subsections—"Exhortation and Comfort" and "Comfort and Exhortation"—attempt to take this emphasis into account.

A. Exhortation and Comfort 2:11–4:11

1. Living as Foreigners 2:11-12

Literature on 1 Peter 2:11-12: **W. Brandt**, "Wandel als Zeugnis nach dem 1. Petrusbrief," in W. Foerster (ed.), *Verbum Dei manet in aeternum* (*Festschrift* Otto Schmitz) (Witten, 1953), 10–25; **M. de Jonge**, "Vreemdelingen en bijwoners. Enige opmerkingen naar aanleiding van 1 Petr 2:11 en verwante teksten," *NedThT* 11 (1956/57), 18–36; **E. Fascher**, "Fremder," *RAC*, vol. 8 (Stuttgart, 1972), 306–47; **R. Feldmeier**, *Die Christen als Fremde* (WUNT 64; Tübingen, 1992); **P. Gauthier**, "Meteques, Perieques et paroikoi: Bilan et points d'interrogation," in *l'Etranger dans le monde grec* (Nancy, 1987), 23–46; **H. Goldstein**, "Die politischen Paränesen in 1 Petr 2 und Röm 13," *BiLe* 14 (1973), 88–104; **P. Lampe**, "'Fremdsein' als urchristlicher Lebensaspekt," *Ref* 34 (1985), 58–62; **H. Schaefer**, "Paroikoi" in *PRE*, vol. 18/4 (Stuttgart, 1949), 1695–1707; **D. Senior**, "The Conduct of Christians in the World (2:11–3:12)," *RExp* 79 (1982), 427–38; **Ch. Wolff**, "Christ und Welt im 1. Petrusbrief," *ThLZ* 100 (1975), 333–42.

(11) Beloved, I exhort you as outsiders and foreigners to keep away from fleshly desires that wage war against the soul. (12) Live your way of life among the nations [Gentiles] well so that, in that in which they slander you as evil doers, they will come to see reason due to your good deeds and will praise God on the "day of visitation."

One of 1 Peter's stylistic peculiarities is the frequent use of participles; ἔχοντες stands here in verse 12 as in other places (2:18; 3:1, 7, 9 among others) without a direct connection to a finite verb. The imperatival meaning is clear from the context. According to Blass-Debrunner-Rehkopf (§468.2b n. 4), the participle stands "in line with other *nomina* (substantives and adjectives) that can also without a verb act in a popular, vigorous, slogan-like manner in place of a sentence." But it would also be worth considering if the general avoidance of forms of direct command also have something to do with the character of the writing that less dictates from above with apostolic authority than rather advises them from the perspective of participation in the fate of those addressees (cf. the author's inserting himself in 5:1 as "fellow elder and witness of the suffering of Christ") and wishes to stand beside them leading the way.[1]

2:11

The address ἀγαπητοί, a word rare in non-Christian Greek literature, should not be translated with "dear brothers," as do the (German) *Luther* translation and the *Einheitsübersetzung*, as well as the commentaries that follow them. It is not only that "dear brothers" excludes the "dear sisters," which is not grammatically compelling[2] nor justified by the context;[3] but above all that this translation (and "dear friends" of the NIV or the "dear brothers and sisters" of the NLV) does not convey the passivity contained in this address: the verbal adjective ἀγαπητός (cf. 4;12) does not only express (and does not primarily express) the connectedness of the Christians to one another but—as with Jesus, who in his being addressed as "son" by the father is always furnished with this

[1] Cf. also the critical remarks against the imperatival interpretation of participles in 1 Peter in Achtemeier, 117.

[2] Cf. Schwyzer II, 31, "Should masculine and feminine be designated together or if the distinction does not matter to the speaker, then the masculine appears . . .; thus especially in the plural. . . ."

[3] That the masculine ἀγαπητοί must be understood here as inclusive is shown by the sequel, for the foundational directives in 2:11f. that are aimed at everyone are made concrete in the three instructions on subordination, the last of which (3:1ff.) decidedly addresses women (whereby there again a masculine formulation—ὁ κρυπτὸς τῆς καρδίας ἄνθρωπος [3:4]—is explicitly referred to women). The address ἀγαπητοί therefore refers to the whole community.

attribute[4]—their *being* loved. Therefore, the previous discussion is summed up with this attribute, especially the election by God mentioned immediately previous (2:9) and his mercy and compassion as the foundation of the new community (2:10; cf. 1:3). The address ἀγαπητοί repeated again in 4:12 consequently states the address ἐκλεκτοί in the prescript (1:1) more precisely in that it stresses *God's* love as the basis of election.

"I exhort"—for the first time, the author of the letter personally makes himself evident. After the introductory part, which in a foundational way looked at God's action toward the believers, the author comes to speak about that which determines what follows: directions for how to act. However, one should observe that the English translation of παρακαλῶ with "I exhort" lopsidedly limits the horizon of associations of the Greek word to command. Παρακαλεῖν means significantly "to summon," "to exhort" and also "to encourage," "to speak comfort," "to comfort." What follows will offer both meanings: comfort and direction, summons and encouragement.

The connection of exhortation with the address as "outsiders and foreigners" is informative. The situation of being a foreigner also has, as was already noted in 1:17, an ethical dimension. Although the first main part developed from the self-designation "foreigners," the promise of salvation in the form of election and rebirth, the second part now constructs from that self-designation the duty that comes with it: to be different, to differentiate oneself is not only the accolade (conditioned by election) of the Christians, but also their duty. Here, this duty is formulated at first as a very general summons "to keep away from fleshly desires that wage war against the soul."

On the desires, see above Excursus 5: The Desires, pp. 102–5. In the Old Testamental tradition, "flesh" means first of all simply the whole human being, with respect to which, where the human being as "flesh" is there contrasted with the divine "spirit," the limitations and weakness of the human in contrast to God's power is being described. In Hellenistic Judaism, this can be sharpened to the understanding of σάρξ as a synonym for the mortality of the human being (cf. Wis 7:1). At first, no negative evaluation of flesh is yet connected with this. "Between flesh and spirit then there arises only

[4] So at the baptism Mark 1:11 par. and in the transfiguration Mark 9:7 par.; cf. also the allusion in the parable of the vineyard Mark 12:6 par.

difference, when the flesh forgets to trust in God who is the spirit. . . ."[5] In the New Testament as well, σάρξ designates at first only the earthly sphere in contrast to the heavenly.[6] This, however, then takes on a negative character to the extent that human beings base their identity on it and thereby comes under its influence. As a negative power on its own, as "unrighteous flesh" (בשׂר עוֹל), one meets it in the texts of the Qumran community (cf. 1QS 11.9), which, as Frey has made probable on the basis of recently edited texts, have further developed the pre-Essene wisdom tradition in which "flesh" is already "characterized by incapability of perception [of good and evil] and disobedience toward God" and thereby "the boundary of the field of meaning that is evidenced in the OT is clearly crossed."[7] This tradition may have (co-)influenced Paul,[8] because for him "flesh" can become a power of its own, even the subject of sin.[9]

In 1 Peter, σάρξ designates the limitation of human existence, especially as the sphere of suffering and transience (1:24f.; 3:18, 21; 4:1f.) without a direct affinity to sin being connected to it. Only our text comes near to the marked Pauline linguistic usage: the adjective σαρκικός—it otherwise only occurs in the New Testament six times in Paul—qualifies the ἐπιθυμία, which in 1 Peter is clearly a negative power (cf. 1:14; 4:2f.), more exactly as desires of the flesh. There arises a counterforce to rebirth as a life from hope (1:3, 13) in the form of an animal impulse that seizes the human will, which force through its promise of immediate satisfaction of needs grabs the person and so seeks to stop his or her relationship to God. Accordingly a power struggle arises in the believer. The military metaphor στρατεύεσθαι, "wage war," "go to war"—naturally with the goal of subjugation or conquest—starkly expresses this conflict between the old and the regenerate person. The form of the language—the fight of the desires against the soul—is influenced by Hellenism. But in terms of content, the author of 1 Peter differentiates himself from contemporary Stoic or Stoic-influenced moral philosophy in that the conflict does not consist of the tension between self-control and rule by something foreign

[5] E. Jacob, "ψυχή," 627.

[6] On this and what follows E. Schweizer, "σάρξ."

[7] J. Frey, "Antithese," 63.

[8] Cf. J. Frey, "Antithese," 67–73.

[9] Thus Paul can write in Galatians 5:17 that flesh struggles against the Spirit (and vice versa).

in which the subject has to maintain his freedom as self-rule *qua* reason in independence from all foreign rule *qua* sensuality.[10] It is much more about the protection of the relationality of existence, first and foremost the connection to God in which salvation is decided[11] and the integration into the community of God's house, people, race, and the like that results from this. The Diaspora synagogue has again been the likely mediator in the formulation of this thought: Philo above all repeatedly speaks about the fight in the soul against passion and self-indulgence,[12] but one also finds in other early Jewish writings the concept of conflict within a person caused by the desires,[13] as James 4:1 then also witnesses to in the New Testament. The clearly Hellenized anthropology in the concept of the soul[14] that already has been mentioned also shows itself in that these desires of the flesh do not, as Paul says, clamor against the (*divine*) Spirit,[15] but fight with the (*human*) soul as the anthropological correlate to the divine presence.This contrast of soul and fleshly desires reformulates the Pauline antithesis of Spirit and flesh as an anthropological dualism.[16]

2:12

The next verse makes it clear that this discussion is not only about "God and the soul," but those others "outside" are also always in

[10] Cf. Epict, *Diss* 4.1.175, "True freedom is namely not arrived at through the satisfaction of every wish, but through the extinction of the desires" (ἀνασκευῇ τῆς ἐπιθυμίας; see pp. 102ff.).

[11] Accordingly, the freedom of the believers consists in that they are, according to 2:16, "God's slaves" (see next on 2:16).

[12] Cf. Philo, *Ebr.* 111; *QG* 4.74; *Leg.* 2.106; *Opif.* 79–81; however, in Philo, it is about a πόλεμος κατὰ ψυχήν (Philo, *Opif.* 81), therefore a fight within the soul. That appears to link to the Middle Platonic teaching of the two souls (a θεία ψυχή and a ἄλογος ψυχή); cf. on this and on the conflict of the parts of the soul in general, H. Dörrie/M. Baltes, *Platonismus* 1, 403–6.

[13] Cf. *4 Macc.* 3:5; *Apoc. Mos.* 19:3; 25:4; 28:4.

[14] See Excursus 4: The Soul and Salvation of the Soul in 1 Peter, pp. 87–92.

[15] Cf. Gal 5:17, "ἡ γὰρ σὰρξ ἐπιθυμεῖ κατὰ τοῦ πνεύματος, τὸ δὲ πνεῦμα κατὰ τῆς σαρκός.

[16] Cf. E. Schweizer, "σάρξ," 145, "Formally this linguistic usage could depend on Paul, but in terms of content the passage is unequivocally Hellenisticly determined."

view, especially those who now slander the Christians and do them evil. With the expression "slander as evildoers," 1 Peter alludes to the hatred of Christians in the population, which accused that suspect group of every conceivable wickedness.[17] This prejudice should be refuted through exemplary behavior, and that to be sure is not only for the purpose of self defense. It is noteworthy how the author of 1 Peter uses the "Day of Visitation"—probably the Last Judgment is intended[18]—in this respect: He does not comfort them with divine retaliation and requital, the expectation of which could create a certain consolation for the oppressed. Admittedly he does hold firmly to judgment and he can also imply that this judgment especially affects unbelievers (cf. 4:18), but on the other hand, it is conspicuous that the theme of eschatological ruin as the counterpart to "salvation" and "life" is lacking in 1 Peter.[19] Instead of this, the author directs the interest of his addressees to the winning of others. To some degree boldly, but absolutely not without an instinct for its effect on the general public,[20] the offence is interpreted as an opportunity for recruitment and thereby the possibility is opened to transform the destructive pressure of suffering into an opportunity to actively take advantage of.

2. New Way of Life within the Society 2:13–4:6

Most of the following two chapters develop the task of the Christians' way of life within a society that confronts them with an attitude ranging from distrustful to hostile. It does this in two respects: First, subordination is commanded in view of relations with those of higher status upon whom the Christians are dependent—either the Christian community in its totality (upon the state authorities) or as members of a societal status group (as slaves upon their masters, as wives upon their husbands)—in order to minimize areas of friction. Then, directions follow about how

[17] Pliny (*Ep* 10.96) assumes as totally self-evident that outrages are connected with the name of Christians ("*flagitia cohaerentia nomini*"; Tac, *An* 15.44, "*quos per flagitia invisos vulgus Christianos appellabat*"); further examples are in the Introduction, page 1ff.

[18] This is called ἡ ἡμέρα τῆς ἐπισκοπῆς in Isaiah 10:3; cf. Sir 18:21[20]; Wis 3:7; Luke 19:44; *1 Clem.* 50:3.

[19] M. Reiser, "Eschatologie," 170f., has worked this out clearly and thereby also pointed out the markedly different handling of this theme in 2 Peter.

[20] Cf. R. Feldmeier, "Außenseiter," especially 174–76.

to deal with the actual hostility of the world around them—from the possibility of understanding and persuasion on the part of the others to differentiation.

(i) Subordination under Authority as Witness 2:13–3:12

This textual unit is often made into a reproach for 1 Peter. It is accused of falling away from the freeing message of Jesus; one sees in it the making of religion to an instrument for the stabilization of existing hierarchies. Balch sees here the liberation theology of Exodus and of the "early rural Palestinian Jesus movement" perverted into repression: "Pointedly phrased, whereas the commands in the Torah protect slaves, the NT exhortations are repressive, and this reflects the cultural change from the Mosaic story of salvation to Greek politics."[1] Even such a level-headed exegete as Eduard Schweizer believes one must detect here the beginning of the paganization of Christianity.[2]

Such evaluations have the disadvantage that they confront the testimony of a different epoch with the norms of the present—whether that may be to differentiate oneself from it as evidence of one's own progressiveness, or whether that may also be in order to use it reactionary in service of one's criticism of the present.[3] The prerequisite of an appropriate interpretation of these directions, however, is the appropriate consideration of its historical context both in view of the general legal relationships of the Roman Empire and in view of the special difficulties of a marginal group that was stigmatized. Further, one must observe how our letter treats the material that has come to it from tradition. The necessity of such contextualization implies for one that one cannot simply repeat such directions today (as is indeed already generally recognized with respect to slavery). But one will also distance themselves from the fashionable discrediting of any teaching about duty oriented on role and status, which was taken

[1] D. L. Balch, "Hellenization," 97. The research of J. Woyke, *Haustafeln*, also shows this same tendency to one-dimensional criticism.

[2] E. Schweizer, "Weltlichkeit," 407, 410.

[3] That is the case in Windisch, 62, who, with undeniable satisfaction, interprets this sequence of triple commands to subordination as, "a sign of the entirely patriarchal character of earliest Christianity that was not even remotely seeking reform, let alone revolution."

for granted not only by the pagan[4] contemporaries of 1 Peter, but also by the Jewish[5] and Christian.[6] One should do this in order to examine what these directives wished to and could accomplish for the social location of the Christian community within the existing power structures, including with respect to a responsible "worldliness" of the Christians.

Excursus 8: The Context of the Exhortation to Subordination

a) The social context: The first thing one should pay attention to is that all the exhortations through 1 Peter 2:12 are related in the first place to the situation of unjust suffering.[7] Thus already in the introduction to the instructions to subordination (2:12), the purpose of the proper lifestyle is justified by the fact that in this way one could meet the slander of the external world. Similar things are repeated in each of the three instructions. Verse 2:15 justifies the command of subordination to the authorities with the intention that through good deeds those verbally abusing them would be silenced. The slaves—especially exposed to hostility because of their conversion to Christianity and turning away from the religion of their masters that was connected with this[8]—should, according to 2:19f., only suffer because of injustice or because of their good deeds, which likewise may refer to suffering on account of their being Christian.[9] The following exhortations are directed

[4] Cf. Epict, *Diss* 2.14.8; 3.24; Sen, *Ep* 15.94.1.

[5] Cf. Philo, *Decal.* 165-167; Jos, *C. Ap.* 2.198–210.

[6] Cf. among other Col 3:18-4:1; Eph 5:22-6:1; further 1 Tim 2:8-15; 6:1f.; Tit 2:2-10; *1 Clem* 21:6-8; *Did.* 4:9-11.

[7] Cf. Knopf, 98f., "The diverse and in part rather different types of exhortation in the letter are held together in unity by the fact that the Gentile environment in which the Christians live is constantly in view, which environment intruded into, to a degree very deeply into, their personal lives . . . And the environment in which the Christians stood was as a whole . . . severely and hostilely disposed towards them. . . ."

[8] Cf. F. Bömer, *Untersuchungen*, 247ff.

[9] Brox, 133, believes any type of suffering of slaves is intended here to the degree that it was inflicted unjustly. This interpretation still makes sense of 2:19; but when in 2:20 the slaves' suffering is spoken of as ἀγαθοποιοῦντες, then it arguably is not compelling to see in this a causal connection between Christian behavior and suffering (Goppelt, 197), but it is nevertheless very likely, since that "doing right" is in 1 Peter virtually a synonym for a lifestyle as a Christian (cf. also John 5:29). One finds in Tertullian an instructive

especially to wives who are married to non-Christian husbands (3:1f.). Besides the slaves, it was especially women for which the possibility of membership on their own in the Christian community was attractive.[10] To the degree that their independent religious decision could be felt as a rejection of subordination and thereby as an attack on the household order they likewise had to reckon with the opposition of their husbands.[11] In both cases, an especially sensitive sphere was affected, for the house

---

complaint for the total context of this exhortation; in dealing with objections to Christians it says, "Well, then,what does it mean, when most people shut their eyes and run so blindfold into hatred of that name, that, even if they bear favourable testimony to a man, they throw in some detestation of the name? 'A good man,' they say, 'this Caius Seius, only that he is a Christian.' Then another says: 'I am surprised that that wise man, Lucius Titius, has suddenly become a Christian.' Nobody reflects whether Caius is good, and Lucius sensible, just because he is a Christian, or is a Christian because he is sensible and good. They praise what they know and blame what they don't know; and their knowledge they spoil with their ignorance; though it is fairer to prejudge what is hidden by what is manifest, than to condemn in advance what is manifest because of what is hidden. In other cases a person known before they had the name to have been vagabond, worthless, and wicked, they condemn and praise in one breath; in the blindness of hate they stumble into commendation. 'What a woman! how wanton, how frolicsome! What a young man! How wanton, how gallant! They have become Christians.' So the name follows the reformation as a fresh charge. Some men go further, bartering their own advantage against this hatred, content to suffer loss, provided they do not have at home what they hate. The wife is chaste now; but the husband has ceased to be jealous, and has turned her out. The son is now submissive; but the father, who used to bear with his ways, has disinherited him. The slave is faithful now; but the master, once so gentle, has banished him from his sight. As sure as a man is reformed by the name, he gives offence [*ut quisque hoc nomine emendatur, offendit*]." (Tert, *Apol* 3.1-4; English translation T. R. Glover). Even if with Tertullian one must also take into account apologetic simplification and overstatement (particularly in the moral contrast of previously and now), yet he would not have been able to write such things if they were without any foundation. It is instructive in that apparently alongside the fact of being a Christian as such, the different nature of the converts, which stemmed from their special ethos, was also found a source of irritation (cf. 1 Pet 4:3f.), that there was therefore a "suffering as one who does good"; cf. further U.-R. Kügler, *Paränese*, 172f.

[10] Cf. E. Ebel, *Attraktivität*, 218ff.

[11] Cf. D. L. Balch, *Wives*, 81ff. There, Balch presents extensive evidence; cf. further W. Schäfke, "Widerstand," 482f.

community, the οἶκος, was the nucleus of ancient society,[12] and the invasion of this order by Christianity was obviously especially resented; particularly the independent religious decisions of wives or slaves awoke suspicions of general insubordination and with this strengthened the existing aversion.[13] However, insofar as the house was of central meaning for early Christianity as a mission center and place of gathering, it was necessary not to produce offense here beyond the unavoidable degree. Accordingly, 1 Peter encourages the women (as earlier all Christians with respect to the authorities and slaves with respect to their masters) through an exemplary lifestyle and through conscious integration into and subordination to the existing power structures to resist the pressure and intimidation (3:6) by their environment that massively suspected and maligned them.[14] Likewise, the final exhortation

[12] Cf. J. H. Elliott, *Home*, 170–82.

[13] This is clearly reflected in the Pastoral Epistles where both the summons to the subordination of women (Titus 2:5) and of slaves (1 Tim 6:1) are justified by the argument that thereby the slandering of God's word and the teaching would be avoided (cf. also Titus 2:9f., where the same idea is formulated positively). D. Senior, "Conduct," 432, was not entirely wrong when he says precisely about the behavior of slaves and women that it was viewed by non-Christians as a barometer for "how compatible Christianity might be with Greco-Roman society."

[14] Apuleius' mocking story in "the Golden Ass" is instructive, in which story the archetype of a depraved woman is described. The recounting of countless faults and offenses culminates in that this epitome of depravity honored only one god—and thereby legitimated her offense: "That miller who acquired me for money," so Lucius, who had been transformed into an ass, recounts, "was otherwise a good and decidedly decent man, but he had obtained a wife, who was very evil and a shameful wife by a wide margin more than all others; he had to suffer so unbelievably day and night that, God knows, I often silently heaved a sigh on his behalf. Also, no vice was lacking in this bitch, but really all sins were flowing together in her being as in a sewer: imperious and foolish, prostituted and boozy, pigheaded and obstinate, greedy in disdainful taking, unrestrained in dissolute spending, no friend of propriety, an enemy of decency. *On top of this she despised and ridiculed the holy gods and instead of a firm faith made up as a confession a blasphemous imaginary concept of a single God* [*quem praedicaret unicum*]; in that she cited mischievous regulations, she bluffed everyone and deceived her poor husband, when she had already early in the morning surrendered to clear wine and incessant sexual offense." (Apul., *Met* 9.14; italics R. Feldmeier). The pointed reference of *deus unicus* only allows one to think of a Jewess or

(3:9) and the following passage (3:13ff.) reflect the situation of unjust accusation. Much more clearly than in the *Haustafeln* in Ephesians and Colossians the whole paraenesis in 1 Peter 2:11–3:9 is defined by the precarious societal position of the Christians and associated with the controlling theme of suffering.[15]

b) The context of the tradition: when one compares 1 Peter 2:11–3:9 with other New Testament *Haustafeln*,[16] it becomes clear that the author of 1 Peter uses a tradition that was widespread in early Christianity.[17] He takes up this tradition, however, in an independent form; he changes it and so give it a new orientation.

The distinctiveness begins right with the placement of the instructions: While in Ephesians and Colossians they are found at the end, where paraenesis traditionally has its place in early Christian letters influenced by Paul, *in 1 Peter* it is encountered *at the beginning* of the main part, therefore it stands *in the center of the work*.

It is further notable that here one's view is not directed on inner order but on the outward effect: it is about the missionary (2:12; 3:1f.) and apologetic (2:15; cf. 3:13ff.) dimension of Christian behavior. In contrast to the other *Haustafeln*, the paraenesis begins with the summons to subordination under Gentile authorities and the exhortations notably close with the—specially related to a situation of suffering—prohibition of revenge and with the summons to answer evil with blessing.[18] That is closely behavior on Pauline formulation (Rom 12:14, 17; cf. 1 Thess 5:15; 1 Cor 4:12); with respect to content; it also corresponds to Jesus' command that, parallel to the command of love of one's enemy, expects a new behavior toward a persecutor (Luke 6:28; Matt 5:44).[19]

---

a Christian, with respect to which the latter is the more liked since the final sentence appears to allude to the Lord's Supper.

[15] Cf. also on this E. Lohse, "Paränese," 73ff.; D. Hill, "Suffering," 181ff.

[16] One finds a beautiful overview in Selwyn, 430, which, however, needs to be read carefully, since it only places the agreements—isolated from their context—next to one another and so at first sight communicates the impression of a far greater agreement than the findings of the text support.

[17] Cf. the list in Selwyn, 423.

[18] 3:9; already mentioned in 2:23 in the example of Christ; cf. also 3:11, where, in a citation, Christians are advised to seek peace.

[19] First Peter's formulation is, as indicated, directly modeled on Paul—it can therefore not be decided whether 1 Peter consciously refers to the Jesus tradition here.

These basic differences also correspond to further deviations in individual characteristics. Thus the slaves are not—as in the other *Haustafeln*—exhorted in the last place, but as the first, in the process of which this exhortation to them is still furnished with the most extensive justification that connects their fate directly to that of Christ. In contrast to this, the exhortation to masters is totally lacking. Likewise the important exhortation for the "house," the exhortation to parents and children, is left out. The only paired exhortation of superiors and inferiors, which are typical of *Haustafeln*, found at all is only that of husband and wife, whereby also here the exhortation to the wives turns out disproportionately long and is justified in detail by a reference to the "holy women" (3:5).

All this shows that one is not dealing here with a "*Haustafel*" in the normal sense.[20] When one opens up the details of a text in its deviation from the norm, because there in particular it wishes to affect and does affect the recipients,[21] one has to guard oneself from the overinterpretation of the conventional passages, as this has repeatedly taken place precisely in the criticism of 1 Peter. It is not the order of the Christian house that stands in the foreground, but the upright "way of life among the people" (2:12), which means the question of the proper relationship with and behavior toward a hostile outside world and along with this the Christian commission in this world, that of "doing good" (ἀγαθοποιεῖν).[22] "Throughout, the emphasis is on mission, not on *sub*mission."[23] Thereby, it is precisely the socially weakest who step into the

[20] Cf. also M. Gielen, *Tradition*, 318. On the problem of this term as a designation of a *Gattung* see K. Berger, "Formgeschichte," 138f. Berger himself sees in 1 Peter in contrast to Ephesians and Colossians (Berger, 139) a not as advanced stage in the evolution of the paraenetic tradition. Since at least Colossians is probably older than 1 Peter, this is not very convincing.

[21] Cf. K. Berger, "Formgeschichte," 10.

[22] Goppelt, 163ff., had already worked this out. Goppelt speaks of a "Ständetafel"; in this he understands "Stand" (rank/status/class) in the sense of the Reformers: It "is the place assigned by God's sovereignty in the institutions of society, the 'role' that has been assigned" (Goppelt, 166). Correspondingly "to subordinate oneself [means] primarily that the person, who through their calling to faith has become 'foreign' with respect to society, nevertheless integrates themselves into that form of social life in which they are situated" (Goppelt, 177).

[23] Boring, 113.

middle here; those who are exposed to the greatest challenges stand closest to Christ or to the holy women and so become a paradigm for all Christians.[24] It explained for the first time to the slaves what it is about for all Christians: doing good (2:20; 3:11, 13, 16f.), renouncing revenge (2:23f.; 3:9), also being prepared for unjust suffering (2:19f.; 3:14, 16f.). Thus the apparently hopeless present can be understood as a chance of probation, indeed, still more as a place of salvation (2:19f.; 5:12).

(a) Subordination under the Government 2:13-17

Literature on 1 Peter 2:13-17: **E. Bammel**, "The Commands in I Peter II.17," *NTS* 11 (1964/65), 279–81; **M. Gielen**, *Tradition und Theologie neutestamentlicher Haustafelethik. Ein Beitrag zur Frage einer christlichen Auseinandersetzung mit gesellschaftlichen Normen* (BBB 75; Frankfurt, 1990); **H. Goldstein**, "Die politischen Paränesen in 1 Petr 2 und Röm 13," *BiLe* 14 (1973), 88–104; **J. Herzer**, *Petrus oder Paulus? Studien über das Verhältnis des ersten Petrusbriefes zur paulinischen Tradition* (WUNT 103; Tübingen, 1998), 227–44; **F. R. Prostmeier**, *Handlungsmodelle im ersten Petrusbrief* (FzB 63; Würzburg, 1990); W. Schrage, *Die Christen und der Staat nach dem Neuen Testament* (Gütersloh, 1971), 63–68; **F. Schröger**, "Ansätze zu den modernen Menschenrechtsforderungen im 1. Petrusbrief," in R. M. Hübner (ed.), *Der Dienst für den Menschen in Theologie und Verkündigung* (*Festschrift* A. Brems) (Regensburg, 1981), 179–91; **B. Schwank**, "Wie Freie—aber als Sklaven Gottes (1 Petr 2, 16). Das Verhältnis der Christen zur Staatsmacht nach dem ersten Petrusbrief," *EuA* 36 (1960), 5–12; **S. Snyder**, "1 Peter 2:17: A Reconsideration" (*Filologia Neotestamentaria* 4; Cordoba, 1991), 211–15; **B. W. Winter**, "The Public Honouring of Christian Benefactors. Romans 13.3-4 and 1 Peter 2.14-15," *JSNT* 34 (1988),

[24] F.-R. Prostmeier, *Handlungsmodelle*, 411, correctly establishes that the slaves are here "the model *par excellence*." "Their authentic life-situation—unconditional subordination and having to suffer despite fulfilling their duty and because of doing right—allows it to be demonstrated . . . for the Christian community what the 'Christ-pattern' means." Beyond this, H. Gülzow, *Christentum*, 71f., has drawn attention to the fact that here—in contrast to the whole tradition—slaves are addressed as being responsible for themselves. "This break with the schema of *Haustafeln* is totally un-Roman and also without parallel in the Stoa. The exhortation is aimed at a situation in which, for Christian slaves, the master and his household are always those who are to be won" (H. Gülzow, 72).

87–103; **J. Woyke**, *Die neutestamentlichen Haustafeln. Ein kritischer und konstruktiver Forschungsüberblick* (SBS 184; Stuttgart, 2000).

(13) Subordinate yourselves to each human institution[25] for the sake of the Lord, whether it be to the Caesar[26] as to the superior, (14) whether it be the governor as the one who is sent by him for the punishment of evil and the praise of good. (15) For thus the will of God is as doers of good to silence the ignorance of people who do not understand, (16) as free—and not as if you had your freedom as a cloak for badness, but as God's slaves. (17) Honor everyone, love the brothers and sisters,[27] fear God, honor Caesar.

2:13

In the light of the background of the criticism (just described) of 1 Peter's directions on subordination, the beginning is already noteworthy: the state or its rulers are characterized here as "human institutions." Now the religious dignity of the state and its representatives was indeed a crucial component of its legitimation that united the various groups and classes in the Empire through the impirial cult's "religion of loyalty."[28] In contrast to this, no religious dignity is conceded to the state here.[29] Also, in view of the closest parallel in the New Testament, in view of Romans 13:1-7,[30] it strikes one that the theological legitimation of the authorities in 1 Peter 2:13ff. happens in a far more restrained manner.[31] While

[25] On this translation of κτίσις cf. J. Herzer, Petrus, 229–31; the translation "each type of person" (W. Foerster, "κτίζω," 1034) is not persuasive.

[26] βασιλεύς (literally, "king") was also used for the Roman Caesar (cf. Jos, *B.J.* 5.563; John 19:15; Acts 17:7; Rev 17:9, 12; further evidence is in Bauer-Aland, 272, βασιλεύς §1.

[27] ἀδελφότης is the totality of the brothers (and sisters) in Christ (cf. *1 Clem.* 2:4).

[28] Especially Domitian, the Caesar under whom 1 Peter was most likely written, had promoted this to the extent that in the end, he had himself addressed and revered as "God and Lord" and built a temple in Ephesus with a colossal statue; on the probable connection of these events with the persecution of Christians cf. S. R. F. Price, *Rituals*, 197f.

[29] Cf. also the comment on 2:17.

[30] Whether 1 Peter knew this text or not is debated; cf. J. Herzer, *Petrus*, 227ff.

[31] Cf. W. Schrage, *Staat*, 66f., "The Caesar and the caesarian governors are

Paul bases his command of subordination on the fact that the state exercises its function of creating order as God's servant[32] with the result that "fear" is therefore due it (Rom 13:7; cf. 13:3f.) and resistance to the state is already resistance to God (13:2), 1 Peter is clearly more restrained here: The "servant of God" becomes the "human institution"; "fear" is decidedly commanded only toward God (2:17).

The justification of the summons fits with this: The rulers of the Roman Empire with the Caesar at the top are to be obeyed, but "for the sake of the Lord." With respect to this Lord, however, remarkably the point of reference is not one of a Lordship of Christ paralleling an earthly rule, but of his unjust suffering that is explained in 2:21ff. "Following his footsteps" (2:21) is necessary to do good even within societal power structures under which Christians suffer. To the degree that this obedience is based upon the reference to Christ it also thereby implicitly is limited. We know from other New Testament and early Christian texts that Christian obedience to the authorities was not unconditional, but that in the case of a conflict the superior connection to Christ as the "Lord" could also lead to the limitation of the claim of this or the other "lord."

In this sense, the apostles formulated the principle, "One must obey God more than people" (Acts 5:29; cf. 4:19) over the Jewish authorities who wanted to forbid them from further proclamation of Christ. As the Scilitan Martyrs were being pressured to participate in the Imperial cult, they praised God as *rex regum* and *imperator omnium gentium* (*ActScil* 6); therefore through political terminology, they made a provocative demarcation against the Caesar cult, which one of the martyrs then also expresses upfront before the interrogating proconsul: "*Ego imperium huius seculi non cognosco . . .*" (*ActScil* 6). The most radical is the Johannine Apocalypse, which forthrightly makes the Roman state into the henchman of evil (cf. especially Rev 17f.). In the middle of all the apparent ethic of subjection, a new and secular understanding of the state is already indicated here, and the world around them has perceived this quite accurately as a competing reference system that is not compatible with their self-understanding. Even if distorted, yet nevertheless this world around them has therefore

---

not *eo ipso* put in place by God, not of divine dignity, but are first of all simply creatures, and their authority is also that of creatures."

[32] Rom 13:4, διάκονος; Rom 13:6, λειτουργός.

from their perspective not totally incorrectly repeatedly suspected and accused Christianity of "revolt." For the Middle Platonic philosopher Celsus, whose Ἀληθὴς Λόγος presents the first comprehensive pagan dealing with the content of Christianity, the Christian principle, that one cannot serve two lords, is then also the "voice of rebellion" (φωνὴ στάσεως) through which the Christians "wall themselves off and break off" from all other people (Orig, *Cels* 8.2).

The author of 1 Peter does not go into the limits of obedience, for he desires above all to counsel his addressees to good behavior and obedience in order to prevent threatening conflict or defuse existing conflict. Perhaps also in contrast to a misunderstanding of Christian freedom (see next on 2:16), he praises above all the positive ordering function of the state that is directed by God (2:15).

2:14

The various organs of the government are legitimated through their function of ordering. This statement must be read against the background of the actuality that the Christians had in no way only had good experiences with the organs of government. Nevertheless, the author here holds fast to the foundationally good essence of the state and, in the next verse, bases obedience toward it directly on God's will. Now it may have also been a Christian strategy to address the state about its function as guarantor of justice even in those places where it did not meet up with this ideal.[33] But that alone does not explain 1 Peter 2:13ff.; as already in Romans 13:1-7, so also here, one sees what a high valuation one could—even in Christian circles—put on government order as a protected sphere of justice in that even in a place where one had problems with the representatives of this state one could show respect and obedience to the legal order of the state.

Thus, despite the repeatedly heightened tension (when seen as a whole), in early Christianity the radical stance of Revelation did not catch on, but the positive attitude toward the state evidenced in 1 Peter. Already in the letter of *Clemens Romanus* to Corinth that was

[33] In this sense, the Scilitan Martyrs repeatedly stressed at their hearing their exemplary fulfillment of moral and societal duties—including tax morality.

written a few years after 1 Peter[34] there is an allusion, indeed right at the beginning (1:1), to the "sudden and repeated disasters and tribulations that have come upon us"—probably under Domitian—and chapters 5f. make an explicit reference to the Neroian persecution of Christians, but at the same time the author requests obedience toward rulers (60:4), whose placing in office is ascribed to God (61:1f.). One also finds something similar in Justin Martyr, who assured the Caesar of Christian loyalty, although in the same breath he refers to persecutions (*Apol* 1.17.3f.), or in Athenagoras, who even prays for Rome's world domination (Athenag, *Suppl* 37).[35]

2:15

The "Gentile" rulers' ethical power of judgment should even be used as a chance to refute opponents—"ignorance" and "unreasonableness" are imputed to them, which in contrast to willful evil still allows for hope of improvement (cf. 1:14)—through the witness of the deed. Admittedly, this sentence does to a certain degree interrupt the discussion, not in order to add some "bad experience . . . in the persecution under Domitian,"[36] but to connect the command to subordination with the basic concern of the whole paraensis that was already formulated in 2:12 and is repeated in 3:1f., 16, i.e., to set the slanderers straight through an exemplary lifestyle. This strategy may not always have worked out, as the example of Pliny shows, who as governor some twenty years later had Christians executed, although he could not discover their supposed "outrages" (Plin, *Ep* 10.96.2) even through torture (Plin, *Ep* 10.96.8). However, one should also not simply assume from this that such an effort at understanding was always doomed to failure because one is only able to imagine the relationship of Christians to pagan society as full of tension. First Peter shows a far more differentiated picture. The explicit recourse to God's will with which this direction is introduced underlines yet again the duty of obedience.

[34] The letter is dated at the end of the reign of Domitian (81–96) or in the reign of Nerva (96–98); cf. J. A. Fischer, *Väter*, 19.

[35] Cf. further Theophil, *Autol* 1.11; Tert, *Apol* 30–33.

[36] Cf. K. Maly, "Staat," 275.

2:16

Subordination under the authority of the state was already presented in 2:13 as a consequence of the connection to the Lord and thereby an active decision. This is here now yet again stated more precisely by means of the insertion of the concept of freedom, which does not play a role for Paul in the context of Romans 13:1-7. First Peter stresses that recognition of the state is not a "knuckling under" to the superior force that contradicts Christian freedom; rather the freedom of the believers proves itself in that, in obedience to God,[37] it fits in with the state power structure as being in its essential nature a good order.[38] To what degree the warning about misinterpretation of Christian freedom that is immediately added was occasioned by a concrete problem[39] is difficult to judge. In any case, what the author of 1 Peter says here is an important contribution to the understanding of Christian freedom. This freedom is, as Paul had already stressed, the opposite of an uncommitted doing what one wishes: through freedom falsely understood the "flesh" in a person can build a "bridgehead," as the apostle says in a military metaphor, an ἀφορμή, from which it then seizes control of the whole person.[40] The author of 1 Peter expresses something similar with the more active picture of a disguise or camouflage when he speaks of such a false freedom as a

[37] Cf. Gerhard, 260, "*Estis quidem liberi, sed tamen servi DEO . . . Magistratui propter DEUM obedientes; non hominibus sed DEO servitis.*"

[38] However, as already noted, 1 Peter avoids any religious legitimation of this authority (cf. on the other hand, the massive stress on this legitimation in Rom 13:1f., 4, 6).

[39] It is unlikely that this situation was at all a political misunderstanding in the senses of a rebellion against the state—hardly conceivable for such an unimportant (in terms of numbers) fringe group. Rather, one should think about an ethical misunderstanding (cf. Gal 5:13; 1 Cor 8:9) that interpreted Christian freedom as separation from the world: "The freedom motif that one encounters in 2:16 and is connected to 2:17 points to a theologically based disinterest in worldly authorities; one considered oneself as a Christian to already be taken out of the world so that its societal-social structures were considered irrelevant for one's own behavior. First Peter corrects such a conception: Christians are in fact free from all inner-worldly compulsions; but they prove their freedom through fitting themselves in with the existing circumstances . . ." (Ch. Wolff, "Nachfolge," 428).

[40] Gal 5:13; thus people again fall back under the "yoke of slavery" from which Christ had freed them (5:1).

"cloak for badness,"[41] because a person denying all obligations is just not free, but falls under the control of his or her own greediness (cf. 1:14; 2:11). Freedom in the Christian sense is, by way of contrast, the other side of belonging to God, for people are not free by nature, but they are freed (cf. 1 Pet 1:18). Because of this, freedom is the result of commitment. In 1:14, the term for it was "obedient children"; now this crossing of commitment and independence that is specific to the Christian concept of freedom is pointedly put in a rhetorical nutshell through an oxymoron (provocative for the ancient world that was oriented on the ideal of the free man:[42] precisely "as God's slaves" the believers are "free."

One should also observe, however, that this picture of "slaves" does not stand in isolation here, but is completed and made more specific through all the other pictures of God and his community that have already been used up to this point and that show a very personal relationship. One should further consider that for a person conversant with the Old Testament/Jewish tradition not only oppression and exploitation were associated with the term δοῦλος. When a Paul—probably also in dependence upon the Old Testament tradition of עבד יהוה[43]—describes himself as "slave of Christ Jesus" (Rom 1:1; Phil 1:1; cf. 1 Cor 7:22; Gal 1:10; cf. also Jas 1:1), then he expresses by this his complete belongingness to Christ, which justifies his independence from all other things (cf. 1 Cor 7:29-31). Romans 6:18 formulates this pointedly: it is precisely in that they were made slaves of righteousness that Christians have been freed. Thereby, a freedom is established that does not contradict fitting in with the existing order (cf. 1 Cor 7:17-24). First Peter accordingly through the combination of freedom and slavery also stresses that Christian freedom consists of commitment to the "Lord."

[41] On the picture of a "cloak" for evil cf. also Menander's sentence about wealth; Menand, *Frgm.* 90, "πλοῦτος δὲ πολλῶν ἐπικάλυμμ' ἐστὶν κακῶν."

[42] Cf. K. H. Rengstorf, "δοῦλος," 264, "The Greek found their personal value in that one is free. Thereby right from the start Greek self-consciousness is completely differentiated from anything that falls under the term δουλεύειν . . ." (evidence for this from the classical period to the period of the Caesars, K. H. Rengstorf, 265–67).

[43] In the address to the God's servant, roughly translated as δοῦλός μου (Isa 49:3 LXX; cf. 49:5).

2:17

After this foundational excursus on freedom in verse 16, there follows a four-member concluding exhortation, the order of which is revealing. First, the members are commanded to encounter all people with respect. If one is clear about what, according to the letter's testimony, Christians suffered from "all people," then this exhortation impressively testifies to the basically open, indeed positive attitude toward the world around them that 1 Peter demands of his addressees (cf. 2:12).[44] After the attitude with respect to all people, there follows as a second command the attitude within the community; here 1 Peter repeats the obligation to love the brothers and sisters that was already expressed in the first main part as the direct consequence of rebirth by God as father. Third comes fear, which is shown toward God alone.[45] These three exhortations form a clear climax: The escalation from all people to the "brothers and sisters" to God corresponds to that from respect to love to fear (awe). The anticlimax in the fourth member is conspicuous: Caesar is to be honored. The author of 1 Peter thereby achieves two things: through a closing exhortation to honor Caesar a reference is once again made to the previous paraenesis about the government, and respect toward the authority of the state is confirmed as a "Christian duty." At the same time, the repetition of the verb τιμᾶν from the beginning of the series places the attitude toward Caesar on the same level with the attitude toward all people. This is a reduction with respect to the relationship to God (cf. by way of contrast, Rom 13:3, 7) that stresses that with all the recognition of the state order its claim of religious dignity is rejected.[46] That

[44] The exhortation is in the aorist, while the other three imperatives are present; on the possible interpretations of this difference in tenses cf. S. Snyder, "Reconsideration," who defends the old interpretation according to which the first member is the heading of what follows in the sense, "give everyone the honor due them, namely . . . ," whereby he references the three members back to 1:22 (love of the brothers and sisters), 1:17 (fear of God), and 2:13ff. But this neither takes into account the break in 2:11 nor explains the confusion between the first and second members by which fear of God receives a somewhat peculiar position between love of the brothers and sisters and respect of the government. It also appears questionable whether God can be so simply subsumed under a general πάντες.

[45] On the fear of God, see the discussion on 1:17.

[46] One also clearly finds this motif by the Scilitan Martyrs when, dur-

this is 1 Peter's purpose becomes even clearer when one compares the last two members with their probable *Vorlage* [pattern] Prov 24:21 LXX: φοβοῦ τὸν θεὸν, υἱέ, καὶ βασιλέα. While according to that instructive sentence of Proverbs, fear is to be shown equally toward God and the king, in 1 Peter this fear is explicitly limited to the relationship to God alone.

The connection of the self-designation δοῦλος Χριστοῦ with the attribute ἐλεύθερος in 2:16 had already shown that freedom and dependence do not contrast with one another antithetically, but that the connection with the "Lord" Christ above all constitutes freedom. The directions that now follow make this concrete with reference to slaves, whereby they probably profit from the new valuation of the term δοῦλος in 2:16. This new valuation shows itself here not least in the fact that slaves are directly addressed—which neither "in the Old Testament, the Jewish nor the Hellenistic paraenesis . . . was provided"[47]—and that they thereby also yet stand in the first place and through the paralleling of their fate with the passion of Christ become an example for all believers.

(b) Subordination and the Dignity of the Slaves 2:18-25

Literature on 1 Peter 2:18-25: **R. Deichgräber**, *Gotteshymnus und Christushymnus in der frühen Christenheit: Untersuchungen zu Form, Sprache und Stil der frühchristlichen Hymnen* (SUNT 5; Göttingen, 1967), 140–43; **H. Langkammer**, "Jes 53 und 1 Petr 2, 21-25. Zur christologischen Interpretation der Leidenstheologie von Jes 53," *BiLi* (1987), 90–98; **Th. P. Osborne**, "Guide Lines for Christian Suffering. A Source-Critical and Theological Study of 1 Peter 2,21-25," *Bib* 64 (1983), 381–408; **H. Patsch**, "Zum alttestamentlichen Hintergrund von Römer 4, 25 und I. Petrus 2, 24," *ZNW* 60 (1969), 273–79.

(18) You slaves, be subject to your masters in all fear, not to the kind and nice alone, but also the cranky. (19) For that is

---

ing their hearing before the proconsul, they refuse to make an offering to Caesar with the words, "*Nos non habemus alium quem timeamus nisi dominum Deum nostrum qui est in caelis*" (*ActScil* 8). Or, "*Honorem Caesari quasi Caesari; timorem autem Deo*" (*ActScil* 9).

[47] H. Gülzow, *Christentum*, 69. Cf. Boring, 117.

grace, when someone because of a conscience [tied] to God endures trouble in that he suffers unjustly. (20) For what type of honor is it, if you—beaten as a sinner—tolerate it? If, however, you—suffering as a doer of good—tolerate it, that is grace with God. (21) You were called to this very thing, for Christ has also suffered for us and left an example for you so that you might follow in his footsteps, (22) he who "had done no" sin "and in whose mouth no deception was found," (23) who did not reply with defamatory words when he was abused, did not threaten when he suffered, but left it to him who judges justly, (24) "who himself has born our sins" with his body on the tree, so that we, who have died to sin, live for righteousness, "through whose wounds you have become healthy." (25) For you were "as straying sheep," but you have now turned to the shepherd and bishop of your souls.

On the text: **19** Instead of συνείδησιν θεοῦ ("a conscience [tied] to God") C Ψ and the Syriac tradition read συνείδησιν ἀγαθήν ("good conscience"). This secondary reading (according to the witnesses) presents a simplifying adaptation of the text to 3:16. **21** Some witnesses, among them p[81] A and also some Latin, Syriac, and Sahidic manuscripts, read ὅτι χριστὸς ἔπαθεν/ἀπέθανεν ὑπὲρ ὑμῶν instead of ὅτι καὶ χριστὸς ἔπαθεν/ἀπέθανεν ὑπὲρ ὑμῶν, thus dropping a καί. By this, a reference to the suffering of Christ originally meant to be especially for the slaves has become a decontextualized confessional statement. **21** The variant ἀπέθανεν (in, among others, p[81] א Ψ and also in Cyril and Ambrosiaster) for ἔπαθεν is an adaptation to the confessional tradition of the church (Christ not only suffered but also died), but 1 Peter is above all about suffering (caused by societal exclusion); this also pertains to the slave-paraenesis, cf. 2:20. One can also locate a similar variant formation in 3:18. **21** One often finds ἡμῶν and ἡμῖν in the manuscripts for ὑμῶν and ὑμῖν. This variant also presents an adaptation to the form of speech of the confessional tradition and a decontextualization. Slaves are no longer addressed; rather, all Christians confess here that Christ has died for them. **23** Instead of δικαίως the Vulgate, Cyprian, and the Latin tradition of the Adumbrationes of *Clemens Alexandrinus* read ἀδίκως. Thereby Christ no longer—as in the main text—turns revenge over to God, but gives himself over to those who judge him unjustly, therefore probably Pilate.[48]

[48] Cf. Clemens, *Adumbrationes* (Latin; MPG 9.731), "*Tradebat autem judicanti se injuste: . . . Tradebat autem semetipsum secundum injustam legem judi-*

Verses 18-20 show anew a very unconventional grammar in that the main sentences are again nominal sentences. It is especially noticeable that the command to subordination that opens and dominates this paraenesis is formulated by means of a participle without a direct connection to a finite verb. Through the imperative ὑποτάγητε in 2:13 and also the four imperatives in 2:17, the imperatival meaning clearly appears here as well, but yet not as a direct form of command. Above (on 2:11f.), it was already contemplated that this could be a conscious abandonment of the authoritative form of command. That then would be interesting precisely if one considered that in contrast to all Christians, with whom 1 Peter 2:13 uses the direct imperative, now with slaves and then once again with women, two groups of people are addressed who were especially exposed to societal pressure and thereby to suffering, from whom is expected what for them was certainly an especially difficult subordination.

In verses 21-25, there is a remembrance of the Passion oriented on Isaiah 53. It was commonly assumed on the basis of stylistic,[49] content,[50] and tradition-historical[51] observations that in this section one is dealing with a hymn taken over from the tradition, which hymn 1 Peter adapts to his context.[52] This assumption is, however, not compelling, as Osborne, who has gone through the individual reconstruction attempts critically, has already shown.[53] Even the most important argument, the conspicuous change from the second person plural to the first and back again, can, to be sure, indicate the use of tradition; "nevertheless this shift may

---

cantibus, quia inutilis illis erat, utpote justus existens . . ." ("But he turned over to the one judging him unjustly . . . But he turned himself over to that one who judged according to an unjust justice, since he was useless to them on account of his being righteous [cf. Wis 2:12]").

[49] The change from the second person plural in v. 21 to first in v. 24, four New Testament and nine Petrine *hapax legomena*, and also the relative clauses in vv. 22, 23, 24.

[50] Mentioned is the content of 2:25, which goes beyond the topic or the irrelevance to a slave-paraenesis of the soteriology that is expressed in vv. 21b-24.

[51] Agreement with *Pol. Phil.* 8.1f.

[52] Windisch, 65; R. Bultmann, "Liedfragmente," 294f.; K. Wengst, *Formeln*, 83–86 among others.

[53] Th. P. Osborne, "Lines," 381–89.

be explained just as well by the reference to Isaiah 53."[54] Going beyond Osborne, Wolff[55] has again made one aware that the reference to Isaiah that is adduced for independence of the tradition is also found elsewhere in 1 Peter and that the argument from the *hapax legomena* is not so compelling: in the passage 5:1-4, which is uncontested with respect to its stemming from the author of 1 Peter, four New Testament and thirteen Petrine *hapax legomena* are found. Furthermore, the agreements with *Pol. Phil.* 8.1, which are brought forward as an argument for an independent hymn, can be explained, according to Wolff, by a knowledge of 1 Peter by Polycarp.[56]

2:18

The slaves, who, with some exceptions,[57] stood in the lowest place in the social hierarchy of ancient society, are of all Christians those who are the most at the mercy of the power and arbitrariness of others. In order to understand 1 Peter's directions, one should observe that the institution of slavery was to a great extent accepted as a self-evident fact in classical antiquity.

> It is true that in the time of the Principiate, due also to the drying up of the stream of slaves because of the decrease of new conquests, a more humane handling of slaves was put in place in the administration of justice; parallel to the good care of resources called for by economic reason, it was stressed by philosophy, especially by the Stoa, that the slave is just as much a fellow human being as the free person.[58] But the institution itself was not placed in question by this humanizing. The same forty-seventh letter of Seneca's

[54] Th. P. Osborne, 388.

[55] Ch. Wolff, "Nachfolge," 433.

[56] Elliott also comes to a similar conclusion in his excursus 543–50.

[57] G. Alföldy, *Sozialgeschichte*, 91f., points out as exceptions slaves that belonged to the *familia Caesaris*. A slave could also profit from a good master to the extent of a good education and a later release with the grant of citizenship (Alföldy, 118–25). Nevertheless, that does not change the fact that, seen as a whole, slaves formed the weakest part of ancient society.

[58] Cf. Sen, *Ep* 5.47.1, "'They are slaves!' No, rather people. 'They are slaves!' No, rather cohabitants in the house. 'They are slaves!' No, rather friends of low rank."; Sen, *Ep* 5.47.10, "Will you consider that the one who you call your slave has come from the same embryo, rejoices over the same heaven, in the same way breathes, in the same way lives, in the same way dies [as you]! You can view him in the same way as freeborn as he you as slave."

Epistulae morales that makes so nightmarishly visible and deplores the degradation and humiliation which slaves were to a great extent exposed to does not think about criticizing slavery itself; rather, the letter begins with praise for Lucilius, since he was on a friendly basis with his slaves. Even the participants in the slave rebellions admittedly fought for their personal freedom, but not for the abolition of slavery.[59] In ancient Judaism as well, slavery together with its results was in general[60] assumed and recognized.[61] Something similar is true for early Christianity. In the gospel tradition, the existing power structure can be made a problem (cf. Luke 12:37; 22:24-27), but slavery as such is never explicitly rejected. In contrast, it is taken for granted, e.g., in the parable of the servants. Likewise Paul can relativize slavery through reference to Christ, as also other societal conditions of human existence (cf. Gal 3:28), and also work toward an individual manumission (cf. Phlm 13f.) in places where he has influence, but he as well does not question the institution of slavery as such (cf. 1 Cor 7:22).

When slaves have joined the "corrupting superstition" (Tac, *An* 15.44.2) of the Christians against the will of their masters, then it could quickly lead to conflict. Therefore, 1 Peter stresses the necessity to remove the grounds for mistrust and accusation as much as possible through otherwise blameless behavior. Precisely obedient subordination, even with respect to "crooked" masters, seems to him suitable for this. In this the terms οἰκέται (house) slaves and δεσπόται are consciously used in order already to avoid on the conceptual level any parallelism of this relationship of dependency based on structural violence with the tie of the Christian δοῦλοι (2:16) to their κύριος (2:13).[62] Accordingly, in contrast to Ephesians 6:5, in which subordination to the κατὰ σάρκα κυρίοι is paralleled with subordination to Christ, here it is not the lordship of Christ that is stressed, but his—corresponding

[59] G. Alföldy, *Sozialgeschichte*, 66.

[60] There are only two fringe groups known who fundamentally rejected this institution: the first is the Essenes, according to the testimony of Josephus (*A.J.* 18.18–22) and Philo (*Prob.* 79), whereby this information is not confirmed by the writings from Qumran, if these then are Essene, and the other is the Therapeuts according to Philo (*Contempl.* 70).

[61] Josephus assumes the punishment of slaves who flee as an accepted matter of course (δίκαιον νενόμισται), even when these have fled unjust masters (*B.J.* 3.373).

[62] Cf. F.-R. Prostmeier, *Handlungsmodelle*, 408.

to the unjust suffering of the slaves—innocent suffering in the Passion. That is also not without meaning for the understanding of the disputed expression ἐν παντὶ φόβῳ.

The interpretation of φόβος here and in 3:2 with respect to the societally owed deference[63]—in the sense that the subordinated slave should freely take his place in respectful recognition of the difference in social rank—is indeed possible; however it does not take into account a quite considerable tension with the previous verse, where decidedly only God is entitled to this φόβος, in contrast to which Caesar and likewise all people receive only respect. When one has seen how carefully verse 17 is formulated in order to make this difference clear, then it is hardly conceivable that this "fear" to which even Caesar is not entitled now in 2:18 should be owed to masters and in 3:2 husbands, particularly since already in 1:17 the expression ἐν φόβῳ clearly refers to the fear of God. That also otherwise accords with the linguistic usage of 1 Peter, who views "fear" toward God positively while it is twice in what follows (3:6, 14) explicitly denied toward human beings. Therefore, it also here appears much more plausible to interpret φόβος as fear of God.[64]

The ἐν παντὶ φόβῳ is thereby not to be understood as the mode of subordination in the sense that through this attitude fear is, so to say, extended into the interior of the slave; rather the subordination is justified through responsibility toward God or Christ. Thereby, even in the strongest societal dependency the moment of inner independence is yet asserted: The slaves, despite all subordination to their "cranky" masters, are more than only possessions at their mercy. They are "beloved," they belong to God, and *his* reaction to the behavior of Christian slaves is crucial. That also accords with the justification in the first summons to subjection to the government, where the διὰ τὸν κύριον (2:13) indeed likewise justifies societal obedience with the superordinate loyalty to Christ[65] and thereby as an expression of Christian freedom (2:16).

[63] Cf. F-R. Prostmeier, 409f.; Brox, 131, 143; cf. also Wohlenberg, 74. As noted above, the reference to the parallel in Ephesians 6:5 is not persuasive, especially since there "fear before the earthly masters [is] only the consequence of awe towards Christ" (P. Pokorný, *Epheser*, 236).

[64] So also Goppelt, 193; Ch. Wolff, "Nachfolge," 430; Davids, 106.

[65] In 1 Peter, κύριος unequivocally designates Christ three times (1:3; 2:3; 3:15). In the two Old Testament citations in 1:25; 3:12, God is naturally

2:19

Verse 19 formulates one of 1 Peter's key sentences: "That is grace, when someone because of a conscience [commited] to God endures trouble in that he suffers unjustly," a sentence the meaning of which is repeated in the following verse. One should not describe it as "scandalous"[66] because slavery is, as shown, assumed as self-evident even by Christians.[67] Added to this comes the fact that Christians, as an excluded marginal group, not only were not in a position to change anything about the societal circumstances, but that such an attempt would have been a dangerous confirmation of the societal mistrust according to which the Christians formed a revolutionary community. Precisely indeed because of this danger, 1 Peter so decisively attempts to call for the social compatibility of Christians. Certainly, it is the weakest who pay the price here, but this does not take place without compensation. First, one should see that the letter does not in any way undertake to legitimate slavery. Quite the contrary, while a positive function as guarantor of order was stressed with respect to the government, here unjust suffering that affects (Christian) slaves is explicitly mentioned, and every effort is made to prove that precisely here, God's grace is present. Grace is otherwise in 1 Peter the epitome of that eschatological salvation that has been granted to the Christian.[68] This may also resonate in χάρις here, whereby, however, this "grace" (in marked contrast to the Pauline linguistic usage, but in agreement with other New Testament and early Christian writings)[69] is at the same time connected to a certain behavior, in this case to suffering on account of belonging to

---

originally intended, but it is not certain that 1 Peter also understands these in that manner, for in 3:15 the Isaiah 8:13 citation is also referred to Christ.

[66] Brox, 132, in view of the command in v. 18 and the justification in v. 19.

[67] See above pp. 168f. The "Christian" consists in that an eschatological and sociological perspective viewed the sexual differences and differences in social rank as irrelevant (cf. Gal 3:28), even more so as one expected the imminent end (cf. 1 Pet 4:7).

[68] Cf. 1:10, 13; 3:7; 4:10; 5:10, and above all yet again as the summary of the letter in 5:12.

[69] Cf. Luke 6:32, 33, 34; χάρις in 6:32 replaces μισθός in the parallel text Matt 5:46; even Luke 6:35 replaces χάρις, that has been previously used thrice with μισθός; similarly *Did.* 1:3 v.l.; *2 Clem* 13:4.

Christianity,[70] so that the moment of "merit" is also brought into play beside the divine favor. When participation in this salvation is explicitly granted here and in the following verse to those who as the weakest members are most defenselessly exposed to the arbitrariness and hostility of the world around them, when these then in verses 21ff. are even placed in an immediate relationship to the suffering Christ, then sociatally underprivileged slaves are revalued upward in the context of the Christian community.

2:20

The grant of grace is yet again repeated, introduced by the rhetorical question, "what type of honor" comes to one through punishment for one's offense. This reference to κλέος to be gained—a New Testament *hapax legomenon*[71]—underlines yet again the moment of merit that resonates in the term χάρις (cf. *1 Clem.* 54:3). Antithetically to this, 1 Peter specifies that only such suffering is "grace" that affects the "doer of good" and is not because of lapses for which he or she is to blame. The differentiation between guilty and innocent suffering—intensified here by means of direct address in diatribe style—will be repeated several more times in the further course of the letter (3:17; 4:15f.) in order to make clear that only that suffering that affects the believers because of their being Christians,[72] "due to righteousness" (3:14), "as a Christian" (4:16) and thereby "according to God's will" (4:19), is included in this grace. Through such an enduring of persecution—which can indeed be concluded on the basis of the corresponding formulations in 2:12 and 3:1f.—slaves who are so outwardly powerless can give a not insignificant contribution to the Christian mission.[73]

[70] Cf. also *2 En.* 51:3, "Every tiring and heavy yoke, if it comes upon you for the sake of the Lord, carry everything and remove it, and so you will find your reward on the Day of Judgment." (German translation Ch. Böttrich, *Henochbuch*).

[71] In the LXX, it is found only twice in Job and there in another meaning, that of "rumor" or "reputation" (Job 28:22; 30:8).

[72] Cf. the similar antithesis in 4:15f.

[73] For H. Gülzow, *Christentum*, 121, the bitter polemic of Celsus against the missionary activity of Christians of the lowest social rank (Orig., *Cels* 3.55) is a confirmation "that in the slaves the ancient church possessed one of the strongest weapons of its mission."

2:21

Through the expression "you were called to this very thing," the paraenesis is tied to a remembrance of the Passion in which Jesus' behavior in his Passion becomes a pattern for Christian life. The verb καλεῖν is used in 1 Peter for the integration into God's sphere of salvation.[74] That is also the case here, whereby just that salvation granted through the suffering of Christ is complemented by means of the thought of the example of Christ who with trust in God had endured the suffering and renounced retaliation and so became a norm of Christian behavior. But in doing this, the paraenetic actualization of the Passion of Christ remains enclosed by statements which, especially in dependence upon Isaiah 53, stress the salvific meaning of his substitutionary suffering that is dedicated to the addressees and thereby the uniqueness of his salvific act. The author of 1 Peter had already given the hermeneutical legitimation for this coupling of prophetic text and Passion in 1:10f. when he saw in the prophets the spirit of Christ at work, who testified beforehand to the suffering and glory of Christ.

The initial note of the remembrance of the Passion already makes reference to the substitutionary death of Jesus Christ, but formulates—a special effect of 1 Peter (cf. 3:18)—this confessional sentence as the *suffering* of Christ *for you*. This suffering is again an example that it is necessary to imitate in one's own life; ὑπογραμμός as *nomen proprium* designates the letters that a student traced.[75] The term then became a metaphor for a literary pattern (2 Macc 2:28), then also for the pattern of human behavior; ὑπογραμμός, then, means example.[76] Therefore, it is not in the strict sense about a following in suffering (the concept of discipleship is also lacking), but that Jesus' behavior supplies the model,

[74] According to 1:15, the believers are called to correspondence to God's holiness, according to 2:9 from darkness into light, according to 3:9 to blessing, and according to 5:10 to eternal blessedness. Only in 3:6 does a neutral use of the word appear.

[75] Cf. Bauer-Aland, 1681, "*die Vorlage* [German for "pattern"] to write over or trace over"; similarly Liddell-Scott, 1877, "pattern, model, outline"; H. Stephanus, *Thesaurus*, 305, "*Forma delineata, Praescriptum.*"

[76] Cf. *1 Clem.* 16:17 and *Pol. Phil.* 8:2, who likewise refer to the example (ὑπογραμμός) that Christ has given through his enduring his Passion; similarly *1 Clem.* 5:7 describes Paul as the "greatest example [μέγιστος ὑπογραμμός] of patience."

the "guidelines."[77] Thus 1 Peter connects Jesus' exemplariness with his giving of his life and in this way establishes a close interleaving of (founding) indicative and (that which is founded by it) imperative. *This interleaving of the soteriological singularity and ethical exemplarity of Christ's suffering is characteristic of 1 Peter.*[78] That is strengthened through the remembrance of the calling.

2:22-23

In verse 22, initially the sinlessness of Christ is emphasized (whereby ἁμαρτία speaks more to the aspect of offense against God, δόλος the offense between people). This stresses in an ethically pointed manner what was said metaphorically in 1:19, that Christ did not participate in the futile life-reality and precisely thus can free from it. Probably for the sake of correspondence to the redemption from sins in 2:24, 1 Peter has in the course of this replaced ἀνομία in Isaiah 53:9 with ἁμαρτία. However, Christology and ethics are also implicitly bound together, for the freeing through the sinless Christ and his example once again strengthens the summons in verses 19f. to doing good and avoidance of evil; but, above all, by means of the following verse 23 Jesus, who did not pay back abuse and blows with the same coin and thereby embodied the ethical goal of the whole paraenesis (cf. 3:9), is distinguished as an example of the renunciation of retaliation. This motif also reminds one of the song about God's servant (Isa 53:7), tangible above all in the Passion of Jesus in his silence toward the charges (Mark 14:61 par.; 15:5 par.; Luke 23:9). Such behavior could be understood in the context of ancient values by unfriendly interpretation as a weakness unworthy of the divine,[79] but one could also recognize in this—and thus 1 Peter wants it understood—exemplary moral strength.[80] The basis for this atti-

[77] Th. P. Osborne, "Lines," speaks of "guidelines."

[78] Cf. H. Manke, *Leiden*, 216ff.

[79] According to Celsus, Jesus had to give proof of his divinity precisely with such a punitive reaction toward whose who had mocked him, "Why, if not before, does he not at any rate now show forth something divine [θεῖόν τι] and deliver himself from this shame, and take his revenge on those who insult both him and his Father?"(Orig., *Cels* 2.35.—English translation H. Chadwick).

[80] The renunciation of retaliation toward hostile acts, which according to

tude of Jesus, however, is not the superiority to the world of the Cynic-Stoic imperturbability (*ataraxia*) or apathy (*apatheia*); it is rather based—in a good Jewish manner[81]—in trust in the God who establishes justice. This divine judgment is referred to anew with the specification added with the adversative "but left it to him who judges justly," whereby in contrast to 1:17, the point does not consist in the exhortation to the perpetrator, but in the comfort for the victim, comfort that this judge will also help the ones suffering unjustly to obtain justice for themselves in the end[82]—and they can therefore do without their own retaliation (cf. Rom 12:17-20).

2:24

Verse 24 combines further extracts from Isaiah 53 with its own statements about the Passion in order to interpret Jesus' death as forgiving sin by means of a reference back to Deutero-Isaiah's Servant of God. One should notice that sin is spoken about here (as also otherwise in 1 Peter) in the context of forgiveness. Talk about sin therefore is not aimed at yet further religiously discrediting the negative side of the person; rather, its point consists precisely in that the "sinner" is placed in relationship to the forgiving God; Jesus has "borne our sins with his body on the tree, so that we, who

---

Epictetus is a hallmark of the true Cynic (Epict, *Diss* 3.22.53f.), also makes itself concrete in silence with respect to abuse by an enemy: Thus Plutarch said that there is nothing more worthy and noble than imperturbability with respect to the enemy who abuses (τοῦ λοιδοροῦντος ἐχθροῦ τὴν ἡσυχίαν ἄγειν, Plut, *DeCap* 90D), and Marcus Aurelius Antoninus required from one who wants to "follow" him (Ἀντωνίνου μαθητής), among other things, that he not pay back like with like when receiving unjust criticism (. . . τοὺς ἀδίκως αὐτὸν μεμφομένους μὴ ἀντιμεμφόμενος, MAnt 6.30).

[81] Cf. *2 En.* 50:3f., ". . . when a danger comes upon you and a wound for the sake of the Lord—endure all that for the sake of the Lord. And, if you are able to requite a hundredfold, do not requite either the one near you or the one far away. For the Lord is the one who requites, [and] he will be a revenger for you on the day of the great judgment, so that you will not experience revenge by people here, but there from the Lord." In like manner *T. Benj.* 5.4, "For if anyone wantonly attacks a pious man, he repents, since the pious man shows mercy to the one who abused him, and maintains silence." (English translation H. C. Kee in J. H. Charlesworth [ed.], *Pseudepigrapha*, vol. 1).

[82] Cf. also 2 Macc 7:17, 19, 31, 35ff.; *4 Macc.* 10:11; *T. Gad* 6.7; Jos, *A.J.* 4.33, etc.; on this see Excursus 6: God as Judge,pp. 108–14.

have died to sin, live for righteousness," as it says here. Thereby he has opened up the possibility of a new life in which his followers are included. The antithetical contrasting of "died to sin" and "live for righteousness" reminds one of Paul's discussion in Romans 6;[83] 1 Peter to a certain degree here in dependence upon the Pauline message of justification reformulates that which he expressed in the first main part with rebirth (cf. Rom 6:4). However, just as 1 Peter has already connected the thought of atonement with that of example in verses 21-23, so verse 24 is also at the same time clearly ethically accentuated: "righteousness" in 1 Peter is less the freeing power of God (as in Paul) than the description of a certain behavior[84]—the Pauline singular "sin" (as an enslaving power) is transformed into the plural "sins" (as a synonym for human offenses).

2:25

Ecclesiology again builds the final chord of this excursus. The image of the straying sheep is taken from Isaiah 53:6, and the hopeless past of the addressees is characterized by it (cf. also 1:18; 2:9). Through the return to the "shepherd and bishop of souls," the believers are led out of this straying. The "foreigners in the dispersion" (1:1) are therefore those who *in truth have already returned home*. By "shepherd" Jesus, not God, is meant,[85] for precisely the image of a shepherd was applied to Christ in early Christian tradition[86] and also in 1 Peter 5:4. The double description "shepherd" and "overseer/bishop" expresses two things in relation to this: first the authority of Christ as "Lord" (1:3; 3:15; etc.) who is to be obeyed, but then also the care for the believers, a care which is perfected in sacrifice, in substitutionary suffering (2:21; 3:18).

[83] Cf. above all Romans 6:4, 11, 13, 18.

[84] 1 Pet 3:14; cf. 3:12, 18; 4:18; this aspect is, however, also not lacking in Romans 6 (cf. Rom 6:13).

[85] Against Brox, 139.

[86] John 10:11f.; Heb 13:20; Rev 7:17; cf. also Mark 14:27 par.; Matt 26:31; Luke 15:3-7; John 21:15ff.

(c) The Exhortation to Wives and Husbands 3:1-7

Literature on 1 Peter 3:1-7: **R. Deichgräber**, *Gotteshymnus und Christushymnus in der frühen Christenheit. Untersuchungen zu Form, Sprache und Stil der frühchristlichen Hymnen* (SUNT 5; Göttingen, 1967), 140–43; **H. Langkammer**, "Jes 53 und 1 Petr 2, 21-25. Zur christologischen Interpretation der Leidenstheologie von Jes 53," *BiLi* 60 (1987), 90–98; **Th. P. Osborne**, "Guide Lines for Christian Suffering: A Source-Critical and Theological Study of 1 Peter 2, 21–25," *Bib* 64 (1983), 381–408; **H. Patsch**, "Zum alttestamentlichen Hintergrund von Römer 4, 25 und I. Petrus 2, 24," *ZNW* 60 (1969), 273–79; **D. I. Sly**, "1 Peter 3:6b in the Light of Philo and Josephus," *JBL* 110 (1991), 126–29.

(3:1) Likewise you wives: be subject to your husbands so that—even if some do not believe the word—they will be won without a word through the lifestyle of their wives, (2) when they have observed your pure way of life defined by fear [of God], (3) whereby outward trappings should not count for you, that which consists of the braiding of hair, of wearing of gold or of clothing with garments, (4) but the hidden person of the heart in the imperishability of a gentle and quiet spirit, which is very precious to God. (5) For thus the holy women who hoped in God once adorned themselves, being subordinate to their husbands, (6) just as Sarah obeyed Abraham and called him lord, whose children you have become, you who do good and fear no intimidation. (7) Likewise, you husbands, live together sensibly with the females as the weaker gender,[87] show [the wives] honor, insofar as they after all are fellow-heirs of the grace of life, so that your prayers are not hindered.

On the text: **6** Instead of the aorist ὑπήκουσεν that was taken into the main text because of its better witnesses (among others p[81]א A C P 33 1739 and the majority text), some witnesses (among them B and Ψ) offer ὑπήκουεν. The imperfect probably underlines Sarah's

[87] The word σκεῦος means "equipment," "tool." In early Jewish and earliest Christian texts, it is then also used for the human body as the vessel of the Spirit (cf. Bauer-Aland, 1507). Since here it is about the woman's constitution through the body in contrast to the man's, the translation "gender" is used here.

continuing obedience, while the aorist refers it punctiliarly to the time of the address as lord.

3:1

The conversion of a wife to Christianity could also bring with it conflict with the non-Christian marriage partner,[88] who as a man determines which gods the family is to worship.[89] Subordination—placed by means of ὁμοίως in series with the previous directives—is recommended here as the way through the witness of a life (ἀναστροφή is again spoken about) alone not only to placate the marriage partner, but even to win him.[90] With the help of a play on words—those who do not believe "the word" should be won "without a word"—1 Peter orients himself on the (patriarchal) ideal of the wife who proves her worth through silence.[91] Here again, the closeness of 1 Peter to Hellenistic Judaism is apparent: this also had its place legitimated in the ancient society, chiefly through the fulfilling of the "good middle-class," that is, conservative, ethical values; the Jews presented themselves to a certain extent as the better Gentiles.[92] Exactly at the time of the New Testament, this tended to take place with respect to sexual morality.[93] The subordination of women, whose inferiority with respect to men is assumed, also belongs to this.

[88] Cf. Tert, *Ux* 1.2.

[89] Even Plutarch, who claims that women have all the virtues of men (cf. *Amat* 769 B–E), nevertheless states that the husband is the superior partner in the marriage (*PraecConiug* 142 C, E). Therefore, a wife must worship and acknowledge only the gods of her husband (*PraecConiug* 140D).

[90] Κερδαίνειν appears to be missions terminology (cf. 1 Cor 9:19-22).

[91] Cf. *1 Clem.* 21:7. Whether it can be concluded from the expression "without a word" that in principle women should not preach (1 Tim 2:11f.; cf. 1 Cor 14:33b-36) is questionable; the point is probably the wordless mission through those who as inferiors were not in the position to do the talking.

[92] This is very clearly already the case in the *Letter of Aristeas* (cf. R. Feldmeier, "Weise," 33).

[93] Cf. the Jewish self-presentation in *Aris. Ep.* 152, "The majority of other men defile themselves in their relationships, thereby committing a serious offence, and lands and whole cities take pride in it: they not only procure the males, they also defile mothers and daughters. We are quite separated from these practices" (English translation R. J. H. Shutt in J. H. Charlesworth [ed.], *Pseudepigrapha*, vol. 2).

Plato himself, who in contrast to the social status of women in his time pleaded for their equal treatment not only in education and in view of the duties assigned to them, but also right up to politics (Plat, *Polit* 451c–455e), since according to his persuasion "the natural talents are distributed in a similar way in both [that is, genders]" (*Polit*, 455d), could then yet conclude his astonishing plea in favor of the equal treatment of women with the summary, "But the woman is weaker than the man in everything" (*Polit*, 455e). Generally this societal subordination is legitimated through a religious-ethical devaluation of the female gender,[94] which also finds an echo in contemporary Judaism: thus Philo differentiates between the passive, clinging to matter, weak feminine and the active, "like the soul" (ψυχοειδής) and therefore meant for leadership masculine nature.[95] From this, it is explicable that the woman can also be made responsible for the fall in the first place: "From a woman came the beginning of guilt, and because of her we all die" (Sir 25:32[24]). This also finds its echo in early Christian literature (cf. 1 Tim 2:14). In pagan popular philosophy, this inferiority of woman can be yet additionally legitimated in that it is attributed to a complementary development of gender by means of the deity (τὸ θεῖον) (cf. Aristot, *Oec* 1.3f., 1343b–1344a);[96] Hellenistic Judaism accordingly took recourse in the creation order: "The women is in everything less than the man. She should therefore subordinate herself, not to her shame, but so that she be guided. For God has given power [κράτος] to the man."[97]

This is the context of 1 Peter's directions; even he can speak of women as the "weaker gender" (3:7). It is against the background of this (in principal unquestioned) societal context that it is then however also necessary to notice the special features of this text.

[94] Even Plato in the *Nomoi* expressed it astoundingly sharply with respect to the ethical inferiority of women: the female gender, so Plato, is πρὸς ἀρετὴν χεῖρων (Plat, *Leg* 6.781b).

[95] Philo, *QG* 3.3. Therefore, the fall narrative shows what happens when Adam listens to Eve, that is, when reason listens to sensory perception (Philo, *Leg*. 3.222f.).

[96] On the origin of the work cf. U. Victor, *Oikonomikos*, 167–75; Victor attributes the work to a student of Aristotle.

[97] Jos, *C. Ap.* 2.201; similarly *Aris. Ep.* 250f. already stress the necessity that the woman must be guided by the man; also the Fragment from Philo, *Hypothetica* 1, in Eus, *PraepEv* 8.7.3, passes off total subjection to the man as a biblical command.

3:2

The first thing to observe is that subordination is not commanded for its own sake but because through this an active role in mission is expected of the wives (as previously the slaves), and that is—this also connects the direction to the wives with that to the slaves—in the "winning" of people who are their social superiors, therefore more powerful. Also, because of the reasons given in the exegesis of 1:17 and 2:18, it is not appropriate to interpret the φόβος referred to here as awe before the husband, a point made clear again in 3:6; rather it describes godliness (i.e., fear of God) as the motivation of behavior, of "the way of life." That interpretation likewise fits better with the grounding of the instruction in God's esteem in verse 4 and especially with the virtually triumphant finale of the admonition to wives (see next on 3:6). As with slaves, conscious subordination is interpreted as an opportunity that presents itself to the weaker ones to convince non-Christian husbands through a "pure way of life determined by fear (of God)."

3:3

This is justified in the first place through contrast of outer beautification of the body through hairstyle, jewelry, and clothing *versus* the "hidden person of the heart," who distinguishes himself through a "gentle and quiet spirit" (v. 4). One can question whether the women 1 Peter addresses had golden chains and splendid clothing; that is not impossible for at least some,[98] but it could hardly have been the normal situation. Presumably we have less to do with an indication about the economic circumstances of the women addressed than with a topos (cf. also 1 Tim 2:9); the augmentation of attractiveness through cosmetics and jewelry can also be rejected in pagan ethics[99]—not least because of its affinity

[98] Cf. Act 17:12. According to Pliny, who reported about twenty years later on the Christians in the same area to which 1 Peter was sent, the Christians belong to every level of society (Plin, *Ep* 10.96.9, "*multi . . . omnis ordinis*").

[99] An example is the report in DiodS 12.21 about an enactment of the lawgiver Zaleukos: "Furthermore let her [that is the free woman] put on no gold jewelry or purple-hemmed garment unless she is a hetaera." Plutarch refers to the example of Lysander, who rejected jewelry for his daughters with the words that it would more easily disgrace them than beautify them (Plut, *PraecConiug* 141D), "καταισχυνεῖ . . . μᾶλλον ἢ κοσμήσει").

with prostitution.[100] Instead of this, an Epictetus or a Plutarch recommends to women the cultivation of their character and manner of life as the true ornamentation.[101] This topos is probably also at work here in the contrast between the outer (v. 3) and the hidden ornamentation of the heart (v. 4), whereby in the first part of the antithesis, it is less about jewelry as such as it is—the enumeration of the activities shows this—about occupation with the decoration of one's own body in order to make oneself attractive.[102]

3:4

In contrast to this, the Christian woman should direct her efforts toward another form of attractiveness conforming to the "hidden person of the heart" and its "gentle and quiet spirit."[103] Such is πολυτελές, extremely valuable to God. This special value of the "hidden person" is further underlined through the attribute of imperishability that refers to the "gentle and quiet spirit," which imperishability received a really outstanding role in the description of salvation.[104] As women live this faith visibly and emblematically through conscious subordination, they thereby do not confirm their gender determined inferiority, but evidence their special value to God.

3:5

Through the reference to the "holy women," 1 Peter adds yet a second justification, a salvation-historical one. Hope, which was already introduced in the first main part as the content of the new life,[105] already in the Old Testament determined the character of

[100] Cf. H. Herter, *Soziologie*, especially 89–94.

[101] Plut, *PraecConiug* 142B; Epict, *Ench* 40.

[102] Cf. Goppelt, 216, "The genitives circumscribing the activities depict the expenditure of work and time that this type of making oneself attractive requires. . . ."

[103] On πραύς as a desirable attitude to one another cf. Matt 5:5; Gal 6:1; together with ἡσύχιος the two are encountered as Christian virtues in early Christian literature (cf. *1 Clem.* 13:4; *Barn.* 19:4; *Did.* 3:7f.).

[104] 1:4, 23; cf. 1:18; see above Excursus 2: Imperishable, Undefiled, Unfading"—The Reception and Transformation of Metaphysical Attributes of God in 1 Peter, pp. 73–77.

[105] See above Excursus 1: Hope, pp. 65–70; cf. further 3:15.

those "holy women."[106] This is one of the few places in the New Testament where the women of the Old Testament are cited as independent examples. *As those who hoped in God they decked themselves out*, as is explained by means of the participle ὑποτασσόμεναι, *with subordination* to their husbands. The generalized reference to the "holy women" as biblical evidence for this thesis testifies to a selective perception of the text—the wives of patriarchs such as Rebecca absolutely went their own way.

3:6

That is also true for the explicitly named Sarah, for the scene from which the evidence for the address of Abraham as "lord" is taken, the promise of a son, Genesis 18:1-15 (18:12 in this passage), shows an "arch-mother" with unbelieving laughter who is presented as neither subordinate nor a specially good example of trust in God. Now [Strack-]Billerbeck 3.764 has already referred to a parallel from *Midrash Tanchuma* that in a very similar way praises Sarah's address of Abraham as "lord" as an expression of subjection (in contrast to Solomon's wives). First Peter may rely on such an exegetical tradition. The power of the argument here as there does not stem from the biblical text, "but from its 'patriarchal implications,' as they reflect in the submissive address 'my lord.'"[107] Nevertheless, one should be careful with the description "hostile to women,"[108] for whatever the reason may be for the subordinate rank of women in the ancient social order, which the author of 1 Peter as virtually all his contemporaries accepts as a given—one should observe that the interposition commanded by him in this place[109] is not based upon the inferiority of the female gender. Rather, subordination here is, just as with Christians in general and the slaves in particular, the other side of their commitment to God (1 Pet 2:16, 19; 3:5); it therefore belongs to the consciously implemented integration of the "foreigners" in the

[106] "The activity most characteristic of the women for our author was their continuing hope in God . . . it is that aspect of holiness the author wishes to emphasize." (Achtemeier, 215)

[107] M. Küchler, *Schweigen*, 70.

[108] M. Küchler, 114 and often.

[109] On the expression "weaker gender" in 3:7, see the comment on that verse.

existing structures of society. This—as already with the other two summons—is made more specific through the first coordinate participle as a "doing good." The second participle establishes that such wives whose behavior is motivated by the fear of God need not fear any human intimidation. Just like the "free" as "God's slaves" fear God (2:16) and therefore do not fear Caesar (2:17), so the God-fearing wives precisely through their "life in fear" become free from all fear of human or masculine intimidation (v. 6 end; cf. also 3:14).

3:7

As a relic of the *Haustafel* tradition with its paired members, the husbands are now also mentioned. In this verse, the women are described as "the weaker gender." Here, one sees perhaps most clearly 1 Peter's formation by his patriarchal context (see earlier on 3:1). One should nevertheless observe that this reference to female weakness does not prove the obligation of wives to subordination, as in the instances adduced in 3:1—this, rather, was positively justified in many respects in verses 3:1b-6—but the obligation of husbands to show wives the same deference that was already commanded toward all people and also toward Caesar in 2:17. The husbands are therefore instructed to live with their wives "according to knowledge" (κατὰ γνῶσιν). "In the Pauline tradition in which the author is embedded, such knowledge means concern for the weaker, more vulnerable members of the group (1 Cor 8:1-13)."[110] The "weakness" of women thereby does not accord men the privilege of superiority, but gives them a responsibility toward the weaker. Finally this is based upon the fact that with respect to eschatology—and that is the only measure that counts in view of the imminent end (cf. 4:7)—women as "fellow heirs of the grace of life" are put on an equal footing with men; as in Galatians 3:28 the societal hierarchies are therefore provisional and limited to this world that is passing away. *The* ὑπό *of the Haustafel is thus as it were beaten by the* σύν *of the eschatological promise.* The concluding clause also once again underlines this: "so that your prayers are not hindered"; what is meant is probably the joint prayer of husband and wife, which prayer does not tolerate disdain of the partner.

[110] Boring, 127.

"The point is clear: Men who transfer cultural notions about the superiority of men over women into the Christian community lose their ability to communicate with God."[111]

Thus, with respect to women, one does not find a revolutionary program in 1 Peter that seeks to make the societal relationships of the Roman Empire compatible with the standards of European or American society at the beginning of the twenty-first century. Whoever expects such and makes the disappointing of this expectation a reproach against 1 Peter betrays a problematic inability (not only from the historical point of view) to grant to another culture the right to set its own values and to seek first to understand these values before one passes judgment on them.[112] Especially in the case of 1 Peter, such an anachronistic distorted perspective also hinders one from noticing the soft tone with which this letter translates into the power structures of the existing society its impositions on male and female Christians (repeatedly newly formulated in each chapter) to encounter one another with love and humility (cf. 1:22; 2:17; 3:8f.; 4:8ff.; 5:5f.) and thereby, to the degree in which one has the possibility, also by all means seeks to reduce the potential for violence inherent in these structures. Something similar will show itself in the directions to the leaders in the community in 5:1ff.

(d) Closing Exhortation to All 3:8-12

Literature on 1 Peter 3:8-12: **W. Schenk**, *Der Segen im Neuen Testament. Eine begriffsanalytische Studie* (ThA 25; Berlin, 1967), 62–64.

(8) Finally, then, all be of one mind, sympathetic, loving the brothers and sisters, compassionate, humble. (9) Not repaying evil with evil or abuse with abuse; quite the contrary, blessing, for that is what you are called to, that you may inherit a blessing. (10) For whoever "wants to love life and see good days let them keep their tongue from evil and their lips from speaking deception. (11) They should turn from evil and do good; they should seek peace and pursue it. (12) For

[111] Achtemeier, 218.

[112] For a more extensive discussion, see Excursus 9: Subject and Responsible Citizen, pp. 189–91.

the eyes of the Lord [pay attention] to the righteous and his ears to their requests, but the face of the Lord [is directed] against those who do evil."

Again, one does not find an imperative in the admonitions of verses 8f. Verse 8 is a nominal sentence that describes the desired behavior in the form of five adjectives asyndetically listed next to one another; verse 9 uses two participles for the two types of behavior that are contrasted with one another, retaliation and blessing. Only in the dependent clause that justifies the rest and in its final explanation does one find finite verbs.

3:8

The introduction "finally, then" suggests a conclusion of the paraenesis. Since, however, yet further exhortations follow in the letter this expression is a type of intermediate summary, a first summarization that now again explicitly addresses "all." At the same time the section—especially through 9a—refers back to 2:12–3:7 and once again makes it clear that the directives about subordination did not have as a goal the hardening of societal hierarchies, but are about a behavior that by orienting on the suffering Christ's rejection of retaliation (2:21ff.) and the "holy women's" goodness (3:5f.) presents an alternative to the violence that is experienced. This is initially developed in verse 8 with respect to the inner relationships of the community; in the style of a virtue catalog via the five adjectives listed next to one another, (i.e., unanimity, sensitivity to one another, love, mercy, and humility), typical "biblical" virtues are commanded.[113] Love and humility are especially important for 1 Peter: Love for the brothers and sisters has already been repeatedly commanded as the basis of togetherness (1:22; 2:17) and also in what follows 1 Peter will not tire of inculcating this love in ever new words and expressions as the foundation of life together (cf. 4:7-11; 5:14). The other is ταπεινοφροσύνη, "humility." Such modesty—the antonym of ταπεινός is ὑπερήφανος in 5:5, "proud, arrogant"—is the conscious alternative to the power and force that define this reality and reveal themselves not least in the form of the hierarchal structures upon which Christians are

[113] A. Vögtle, *Lasterkataloge*, 188, "virtually unthinkable . . . on the ground of popular philosophy."

dependent and within which they—as shown in the examples of slaves and women—experience suffering. At the end of the letter where it is about the hierarchies within the Christian community, this ταπεινοφροσύνη is therefore stressed once again as the crucial attitude of Christians toward one another (5:5b) by means of which they have God on their side (5:5c); indeed it is virtually the condition of end time exaltation (5:6).[114]

3:9

If verse 8 profiles the Christian ethos in view of the community's inner relationships, then the following verse makes their outward relationships the subject of discussion. It is about the renunciation of retaliation in dealing with the "abuse" of the world around them. The renunciation of returning abuse picks up the example of Christ in 1 Peter 2:23; but the commands echo above all Jesus' instructions known from the Sermon on the Mount and Sermon on the Plain.[115] The renunciation of retaliation toward evil reminds one of the fifth antithesis of the Sermon on the Mount (Matt 5:38ff.), the answer of blessing of Luke 6:28a, whereby this Jesus tradition exists here in the form of the version that Paul transmitted: the rejection of retaliation of evil with evil is found in 1 Thessalonians 5:15 and Romans 12:17, the "answering" of abuse with blessing in 1 Corinthians 4:12 (cf. also Rom 12:14). This admonition gains its profile in the context of the previous dealing with unjust suffering: precisely there, where the Christians suffer violence and experience evil, they should break through the vicious circle of retaliation. The justification of this command by the position of the Christians as saved is, however, unusual: Since Christians are "called to this," "to inherit a blessing," a blessing should befall even their opponents in their encounter with them as blessing-bearers.[116]

3:10-12

This whole paraenetic block is closed by a relatively extensive Psalm citation, Psalm 34[33]:13-17, which is slightly altered by 1 Peter:

[114] See below Excursus 10: Humility/ταπεινοφροσύνη, pp. 239–41.
[115] Cf. on this, the research of R. Metzner, *Rezeption*, 75–89.
[116] Cf. U. Heckel, *Segen*, 186–190.

he adds an introductory γάρ (in place of the question τίς ἐστιν ἄνθρωπος ὁ θέλων) and so presents the citation as the basis of the paraenesis; at the same time within the citation then once again, the theological justification in Psalm 33:17 LXX, which asyndetically hung onto the rest of the citation, is in 1 Peter 3:12 explicitly related to the previous imperatives by means of a ὅτι. This scriptural word, in which beside a more or less verbal correspondence to the paraenesis[117] further aspects of it are also named (from "loving of life" to "pursuing peace"), not only authorizes the paraenesis, but also places it under a promise. For the word from the Psalm, which in its original context as wisdom coupled the promise of a good life to the condition of good behavior, becomes in the context of 1 Peter an eschatological promise, because the promise of life and of good days can in the context of 1 Peter only refer to eternal life with God.[118] Now, with the authority of the scripture, this is placed as the prospect for the behavior urged in 2:11–3:12.

(e) Summary 1 Peter 2:11–3:12

(a) Both in the three exhortations themselves (2:15, 20; 3:6) and also in their framework (2:12; 3:11), the content of Christian behavior is expressed as ἀγαθοποιεῖν. In that this behavior is based upon the renunciation of retaliation (2:23; 3:9) and following in suffering (2:21), it is about the opportunity of nonverbal (2:12; 3:1f.) witness to the unbelievers, which is given precisely in that place where Christians are outwardly powerless.[119] "Subordination" is thereby a conscious attitude with an apologetic and missionary purpose.

(b) Enduring unjust suffering is at the same time a badge of closeness to Christ. The paraenesis for the slaves shows this most clearly. A significant difference to the exhortations to the slaves in other letters consists in the fact that in 1 Peter the κύριος demanding obedience is not the basis for subordination,[120] but the suffering

[117] Turn from evil and every "ruse"; do good.

[118] Cf. the soteriologically filled expression of the "grace of life" in 3:7 and also generally the previous use of the concept of life (1:3, 23; 2:4f.).

[119] As H. Goldstein, "Paränesen," 97, 103f., established, subordination in 1 Peter is understood as a means by which obedience to God's will finds a visible and so also a missional-recruiting possibility of concretion.

[120] This happens most clearly in Ephesians 5:22-24 and Colossians 3:22-25, where the obedience of wives or slaves toward their husbands or lords is directly paralleled with and justified by obedience toward the "Lord Christ."

Christ (2:21ff.).[121] Accordingly, the existing hierarchy, even including its injustice,[122] is put up with, but not theologically legitimated.

(c) The instructions to subordination belong together with the exhortations to "humility" (3:8; 5:5b, 6; cf. 3:16), to which the eschatological promise is connected: "Thus humble yourselves under the power hand of God, so that he exalts you in his time . . ." (5:6).[123]

(d) Subordination aims at the conquest of evil by good (3:9; cf. 2:23) even when concrete experiences appear to show the opposite (cf. 4:3f.), and therefore final confirmation only takes place on the "Day of Visitation" (2:12).

This is in its way a thoroughly independent ethos. Admittedly, the author of 1 Peter shows himself to also be beholden to pagan values in the ethical content he advocates,[124] but he gives this content his own ethical orientation as defined by the Christian faith.[125]

[121] If one wishes to make conjectures about the person and social background of the author of 1 Peter just on the basis of the paraenesis for the slaves, then one should ask whether it was not more likely, on the basis of the exceptional response to the situation of the slaves and their absolutely unusual valuation, when in doubt an (educated) freed man should rather be conjectured than a slave owner, as D. L. Balch, "Hellenization," 95, alleges. Yet all this remains only a conjecture.

[122] This is indeed already intimated with the "cranky masters" in 2:18 and becomes explicitly stated in 2:19f., when the talk is about the slave's unjust suffering. "Thereby their suffering, which did not otherwise move their contemporaries at all, since slaves as possessions could not be done any injustice at all (cf. Aristot, *Eth. Nic.* 5.10.8), is brought into the closest connection with the center of Christian faith, the suffering of Christ." (Ch. Wolff, "Christ," 340).

[123] The numerous times the "revelation of Christ," to which the hope of an inversion of suffering into glory is joined (1:7, 13; 4:13), is stressed shows this clearly. On the relationship of the exhortation to subordination to the expectation of the reversal of circumstances cf. also K. Berger, *Formgeschichte*, 127.

[124] Cf. 2:14f., where it is indeed assumed that concerning that which is "good," a consensus is possible between Christians and pagans.

[125] In this context, it is also important to critically examine the difference (for Balch, fundamental) between the christological tradition that secures one's identity and the paraenesis that is allegedly less decisive for this identity. In doing this, one still need not reject Balch's thesis that such a separation and contrast of proclamation and law runs contrary to the whole Old

Excursus 9: Subject and Responsible Citizen

First Peter in no way considers a transformation of outward societal circumstances. For one, in the ancient world counter-concepts to the existing society were extremely uncommon anyway. Furthermore, Christians as a hated minority were certainly not in the position to make any proposals about this matter or to change anything in pagan society. In view of the deep mistrust with which they were met on the part of society and increasingly on the part of the officials, they would thereby have provoked their oppression and persecution all the more and perhaps the somewhat pushy (at least for today's reader) stress on subordination is also connected with the warding off of a misunderstanding of Christianity as a politically revolutionary movement,[126] which misunderstanding was promoted by the behavior of individual Christians.[127] In this situation, 1 Peter attempts to compensate for the departure from the societal norm contingent on the new religious orientation

Testament and New Testament self-understanding (and naturally also that of 1 Peter, for whom precisely the interlinking of promise and demand is characteristic). Here, Balch could nevertheless be correct insofar as, despite this self-understanding, the content of the respective ethic was adapted from the environment and contains absolutely nothing intrinsic. In this sense one should, then, interpret Balch's evidence that the material of the *Haustafeln* originated to a great extent in the Hellenistic-Roman sphere (whereby one should still add that a part of this material finds its origin in Hellenistic-Jewish sources). But one must now object against Balch's thesis that he does not go far enough with his concept of ethos with respect to 1 Peter's paraenesis when he only concentrates on the commands to subordination and sees as their highest goal the "domestic harmony between husband, wife, and slaves," as though 3:8f. were clearly the conclusion of the paraenesis (D. L. Balch, *Wives*, 88; cf. 109 and frequently). The stressing of harmony in 3:8 relates to the behavior of community members toward one another, but does not form the interpretive conclusion of the whole paraenesis. Rather, as stated, one finds this in 3:9.

[126] Cf. Acts 16:20f.; 17:6f.; 24:5, 12; cf. further Luke 23:2 and John 19:12, where in connection with Jesus' passion these charges do indeed ring out from both the Jewish and pagan sides.

[127] If Onesimus, as many exegetes assume, did actually flee to Paul, since he had run away from his master, the Letter to Philemon would thus show that the Christian message of the equality of all in Christ (cf. Gal 3:27f.) could be understood by slaves as a possibility of escape. In the same way, 1 Cor 7:13f. shows that Christian women wished to separate from their non-Christian husbands (cf. also Just, *Apol* 2.2).

through a "greater should" about fitting into the usual society hierarchies and so to minimize the area of friction. "Thus when the instructions . . . emphasize Christian responsibility to be subordinate, to respect the given order, to fit in, they cannot be properly understood except as in dialectical tension with the larger context identifying them as those who do not fit in and cannot."[128] Added to this is the fact that in 1 Peter, the expectation of the return of Christ still plays a role that should not be underestimated.[129] Whoever expects the end of this age of the world has hardly any purpose for the changing of the structures of this reality that is passing away;[130] these structures were rather assumed[131] as something given as a test,[132] and in the test it was necessary to prove oneself and to give testimony to God's future.[133] Therefore, the

[128] Boring, 111.

[129] Typically enough the reminder about this comes out clearly, especially toward the end of the document (4:7, 17f.; 5:6; perhaps also 5:8f.). Even if the imminent expectation no longer stands in the center for 1 Peter, it is, on the other hand, still not so unimportant as Brox, 201–4, believes.

[130] This is also something to take into account when one compares the New Testament statements about slavery with those in the Old Testament. The Old Testament laws—in contrast to the New Testament paraenesis—are constructed by a people who, for one, could give themselves their own laws, and that, for another, wished thereby to create its own longer-term reality.

[131] 1 Pet 2:13ff. shows clearly that 1 Peter accepts the order of the state simply as a worldly given (ἀνθρωπίνη κτίσις), which safeguards a necessary function of keeping order. He does not deal with it further—the (Roman) state is neither traced directly back to God (as in Rom 13:1ff.) nor is it a power hostile to God like the whore of Babylon in the Apocalypse, who is drunk with the blood of the saints (Rev 17:5f.; cf. also the attribution of worldly ruler to the devil in Luke 4:6b different from Matt). It is instead interested in the question how the Christians, who on the basis of their commitment to God (v. 13, διὰ τὸν κύριον; v. 16, ὡς θεοῦ δοῦλοι) are free (v. 16, ὡς ἐλεύθεροι) are to fit into this given reality and how they are to deal with it.

[132] Cf. 1 Pet 1:6; 4:12.

[133] D. Bonhoeffer has in view of 1 Cor 7:20-24 congenially interpreted this eschatologically conditioned paraenesis of early Christianity: "The truth of the matter is that the whole world has already been turned upside down by the work of Jesus Christ, which has brought a liberation for freeman and slave alike. A revolution would only obscure that divine New Order which Jesus Christ has established. It would also hinder and delay the disruption of the existing world order in the coming of the kingdom of God. It would be equally wrong to suppose that St. Paul imagines that the fulfilment of our

degree to which the criticism that is repeatedly expressed about these directions does justice to the self-understanding of that time is questionable, particularly because we perceive it one-sidedly against the background of the modern concept of freedom. "We hear the word (i.e., subordinate) automatically from its prefix. But in the New Testament, the tone lies first of all not on the prefix 'sub' but on the root 'order'."[134] The insights expressed earlier prepare one for a continuing consideration that 1 Peter admittedly assumed the present order as a given, but there where he had influence, namely in the Christian communities, he translated a Christian ethos in the form of mutual love and humility into the power structures of the preset society and thereby, to the degree that he had the possibility of doing it, also definitely sought to reduce the potential for violence inherent in these structures.

(ii) Hostility of the Environment as Challenge 3:13–4:6

The optimistic assurance of the Psalm provokes a critical query about the "harm" that the believers are presently suffering. The following section, 3:13ff., is about this. As a defense of the Christian life, this section can be assigned to the rhetorical genre *refutatio*.[135]

The whole argumentation-complex is a typical example of 1 Peter's style, which strings together one thought after another without a clear caesura.[136] So the three exhortations to subordination closed—introduced with a "but finally" (τὸ δὲ τέλος)—in 3:8f. with a type of summary. With γάρ a biblical justification was then connected to them, which justification promised a good life to the one who does good and seeks peace (3:10-12). By taking up the catchwords of doing good and evil, the situation of suffering—connected with καί—is now discussed as an objection to this promise, and directions

secular calling is itself the living of the Christian life. No, his real meaning is that to renounce rebellion and revolution is the most appropriate way of expressing our conviction that the Christian hope is not set on this world, but on Christ and his kingdom. And so let the slave remain a slave! It is not reform that the world needs, for it is already ripe for destruction. And so let the slave remain a slave! He enjoys a better promise." (D. Bonhoeffer, *The Cost of Discipleship*, 195).

[134] L. Goppelt, "Prinzipien," 289.

[135] K. M. Schmidt, *Mahnung*, 203.

[136] Cf. R. Feldmeier, *Fremde*, 134.

on dealing with the hostility are given (3:13-17) anew. To this discussion, which ends with the blessing of the one suffering unjustly, a christological justification is again added with ὅτι, a justification that has as its starting point the substitutionary suffering of Christ and widens itself into a foundational discussion about rescue, salvation, and baptism (3:18-22). In the process some things that were already discussed in 2:18ff. are here taken up once again and modified (cf. 3:13 with 2:20; 3:16 with 2:19; 3:17 with 2:20; 3:18ff. with 2:21ff.). Then 4:1 again refers back to the beginning point of the argumentation in 3:18-22, the suffering of Christ (3:18) (Χριστοῦ οὖν παθόντος σαρκί), in order to describe in 4:1-6 the different nature of the Christian way of life in contrast to the standards of the surrounding world. Even after this one still does not find a clear conclusion, for in 4:7-11 general exhortations follow once again, which exhortations are introduced by a reference to the imminent end, which the announcement of judgment in 4:5f. picks up. Only the concluding doxology of 4:11 and the new entry in 4:12 by means of a renewed address to the recipients mark a clear caesura.

(a) The Blessing of Those Who Suffer 3:13-17

Literature on 1 Peter 3:13-17: **F. Büchsel**, "'In Christus' bei Paulus," *ZNW* 42 (1949), 141–58; **A. Deissmann**, *Die neutestamentliche Formel "in Christo Jesu,"* Marburg, 1892; **J. Knox**, "Pliny and I Peter: A Note on I Peter 4:14-16 and 3:15," *JBL* 72 (1953), 187–89.

(13) And who can do you harm, if you are zealous for good? (14) Rather, even if you should suffer due to righteousness—blessed are you! "But do not fear their threats and do not be frightened." (15) "But sanctify the Lord" Christ in your hearts, being prepared at any time to respond to anyone who demands from you a justification about the hope that is in you, (16) yet with gentleness and fear [of God], and that with a good conscience, so that those who insult your good lifestyle in Christ will become ashamed through just that by which you are slandered. (17) For it is better that—if it may then be according to God's will—you suffer for good deeds than for evil deeds.

On the text: **16** For καταλαλεῖσθε, which is witnessed to by p[72] B Ψ and Clement of Alexandria, among others, some quite important witnesses such as ℵ A C P 33 the majority text and the Vetus Latina read καταλαλοῦσιν ὑμῶν ὡς κακοποιῶν. This *varia lectio* is to be explained as an adaptation to 1 Peter 2:12.

3:13

In 3:13ff., the assurance of verses 10-12 is followed by dealing with the actual situation that appears to belie this promise. "Who can harm you, if you are zealous for good?"—thus the introductory question, which is not totally unequivocal. Basically two possibilities are deliberated. One runs on the assumption that the verse in continuing and at the same time explaining of the words of the psalm wishes to say that all the Christians' suffering cannot really hurt them so long as they do good. What would then be meant would be that this suffering can not hurt the "hidden person of the heart" (3:4).[137] The advantage of this exegesis is that it can fit the verse without difficulty into the characteristic style of the letter. On the other hand, those who dispute this exegesis hold that κακόω is to be interpreted together with 3:9, 12 as concrete harm and that also in Acts it is "without exception used for 'persecute,' there corresponding to πάσχειν."[138] The last point, however, is not totally correct: in Acts 14:2, κακόω means "stir up to evil," or "anger." Also with the second interpretation, one must accept that 1 Peter formulates a theological principle in verse 13 that he immediately revokes in the following verse 14 to the degree that the possibility of unjust suffering is assumed there. Because the word κακόω can also describe harm to the inner person (cf. Philo, *Spec.* 3.99) the interpretation presented first is preferred here, which is also confirmed through Wisdom 3:1-4. The question introduced by τίς is thereby intended rhetorically and underlines the certainty that nothing at all is really able to harm the believers.[139]

The conditioning of the promise introduced by the conjunction ἐάν must not, however, be overlooked: The promise holds for those who stir themselves up for "good," put more pointedly, who become "zealots" for the good. Zeal with respect to God's

[137] Kelly, 139; Schenkle, 100; Bearer, 162; Knopf, 136f.; Brox, 157; Achtemeier, 230.

[138] Goppelt, 234; cf. Frankemölle, 57.

[139] Cf. the questions that are likewise introduced by τίς in Romans 8:33-35, which have the same function of a virtually triumphant assurance.

law belonged precisely to the self-understanding of contemporary Judaism, whether it be in the Pharisaic variant (cf. Phil 3:6; Rom 10:2), whether it be in the political, where the term used here, ζηλωταί, even became a self-designation of a revolutionary movement.[140] First Peter assumes this passionate effort for "good," which in a manner typical of 1 Peter encompasses both membership in the Christian community and also the "lifestyle" corresponding to it, as a condition of the promise.

3:14

The following verse repeats and strengthens the promise (and the demand that is contained within it) through the blessing of those who suffer "for the sake of righteousness." The slave-paraenesis had already prepared this thought in that it promised those who suffered as doers of good and remained steadfast in it that this is "grace with God." This is now here yet again strengthened by means of a blessing. This blessing of the suffering is a "fixed piece of tradition"[141] in early Christianity, but 1 Peter may here refer to the (redactional) eighth Beatitude of the Sermon on the Mount.[142] It is important that 1 Peter is responding to actual, existing suffering and stresses the dimension of grace in this situation. In this place, therefore, 1 Peter does not formulate a principle about the necessity of suffering for salvation. That is also confirmed by the potential optative (*optativus potentialis*) introduced by ἐι καί.[143] Just as in the first reference to suffering in 1:6, this is to be understood as a conditioning that makes a statement about a situation in which suffering does happen.

This promise is applied to the external situation through a citation taken from Isaiah 8:12: the "threatening" of those who cause the suffering should no longer frighten or shake the Christians.[144]

[140] Cf. on this, in general, the motif of zeal laid out by M. Hengel, *Die Zeloten*, 151–234.

[141] H. Millauer, *Leiden*, 146.

[142] Matt 5:10; cf. further Matt 5:11f.; Jas 1:12. On the dependence of 1 Peter on Matt 5:10 see R. Metzner, *Rezeption*, 7–33.

[143] The *potentialis* appears here without ἄν, cf. Blass-Debrunner-Rehkopf §385.2 (with n. 4).

[144] The negation is further strengthened in that φόβος from the same root is placed by the verb φοβέομαι as a direct object.

This promise makes the rhetorical question of verse 13 more precise and strengthens it at the same time by means of a reference to the prophecy from the Book of Isaiah that, as shown (see the Introduction) is the most meaningful reference text for 1 Peter.

3:15

The citation of Isaiah 8:12 is continued in verse 15 with Isaiah 8:13, whereby here, as also already previously (cf. 2:6, 8, 22ff.), it is interpreted christologically in that Christ is added to "Lord." He, the suffering and exalted one (and not God),[145] is here the Lord who rules over all powers (3:22). The verb ἁγιάζειν that is taken over from the LXX version of the Isaiah text is to be understood against the background of the discussion in 1 Peter 1:13-17 as a synonym for a lifestyle that accords with God. The "in your hearts" that is added to the biblical citation, making it more precise, should, just as in 1:22 and especially in 3:4 with the reference to the "inner person," serve to underline the sincerity and intensity[146] without implying a retreat into inwardness, as the sequel shows. Through their orientation on the Lord, through "sanctification," Christian existence becomes a pointer to Christ, and this missionary aspect of the Christian being is then also to be brought to bear "at any time" and toward "any one." This also implies the duty of "apology" toward those who demand from the Christian a "*logos*" (λόγος—basis, reason, answer, response, account).[147] This demand shows once more that for 1 Peter Christian existence is not realized in a sectarian separation from the surrounding world but in a readiness for dialogue.[148] The content of this *logos* that can and should be communicated is the "hope in you." Therefore, here again "hope" is the principle of the new life, that is, of the faith that, with reference to the fate of Jesus, is sure of its future

[145] In the Matt of Isa 8:13 is κύριος, יהוה צבאות.

[146] Cf. Brox, 159.

[147] Judaism also knows a similar duty to defend a controversial faith; cf. mAv 2.14a, "Be eagerly intent to learn what you have to say in answer to a free spirit [literally, Epicurean]."

[148] Goppelt, 236, "This linguistic clothing shows an openness for the Hellenistic world, even if Plato's *Apology* first comes within the horizon of Christian apologetics in the second century."

(see next on 3:18-22) and therefore in contrast to a doomed life without Christ takes shape as an attitude of hope.[149]

3:16

What follows gives directions about the style of this account: it should not be provocative but take place "with gentleness"; the manner and method of the information should therefore "once again bear in itself the signature of the Christian ethos."[150] Here as well the fear cannot—particularly after 3:14—be fear of people, but must refer to accountability before God.[151] The good conscience out of which the defense should take place refers, as the following shows, to the Christian lifestyle. A renewed reference is made to the slandering and abuse that are directed against this Christian way of life. These slanderers should be refuted through deeds, the "good manner of life." This way of living is good "in Christ." First Peter is the only New Testament writing apart from the Paulines to use this expression ἐν Χριστῷ, which appears 164 times in the *Corpus Paulinum* and with some likelihood was constructed by the apostle in dependence on the ἐν κυρίῳ of the LXX that he also took over (1 Cor 1:31; 2 Cor 10:17); but in any case it was theologically filled by him.[152] With this formula, Paul expresses that Christian existence is constituted anew through reference to Christ (cf. 1 Cor 1:30; Rom 6:11); whoever is "in Christ" is a new creation (2 Cor 5:17). Accordingly, 1 Peter 5:10 says that God "has called" the believers "in Christ Jesus to his

[149] See Excursus 1: Hope, 65–70.

[150] Brox, 161.

[151] On the fear of God, see above on 1:17; further 2:17, 18; 3:2.

[152] A. Deissmann in his relevant monograph comes to the conclusion that Paul is "the constructor of the formula, not in the sense as if he had for the first time connected ἐν with the personal singular, but thus, *that he created a totally new terminus technicus through the use of an already existing linguistic usage*" (A. Deissmann, *Formel*, 70). F. Büchsel is more cautious with respect to the origin, but he also establishes as the result of his research, "In that the ἐν K [i.e., the ἐν κυρίῳ of the LXX] etc. became an expression for Paul's faith in Christ, it won a meaning such as it had not remotely had before" (F. Büchsel, *Paulus*, 157). J. Herzer (*Petrus*, 84–106) assumes the construction of the expression ἐν Χριστῷ by Paul, but believes that this had become independent and then was also used by Christian circles "that are not tradition-historically dependent upon Paul" (105).

eternal glory." Here the "good lifestyle in Christ" describes the orientation of the Christian way of life on the example of Christ (cf. 2:21ff.; 3:17f.). The shaming of the slanderers could refer to eschatological shaming (cf. 2:12)m but a present interpretation as in 2:15 and 3:1f. is more likely.

3:17

The following sentence, that it would be better to suffer as doers of good than as evildoers, now expands to all Christians what was said to slaves in 2:20. This is formulated in the form of a saying that reminds one of an axiom of ancient ethics.[153] In the case that this allusion is purposeful, we have here the first example of that apologetic strategy that, for example, Justin or Origen later also follow in their apologies, which interprets the societal-religious exclusion ethically and places the discrediting and persecution of Christians into the context of the rejection of righteous men such as Socrates.[154] Thus their own stigmatization is to some degree made plausible from pagan conditions. The suffering is related to God's will, although in the form of a *potentialis* conditioned through ἐι, "if it should be God's will," which makes it clear that with this suffering as a doer of good one is dealing with just a possibility, not a necessity. With the expression "if God will," 1 Peter appears to take up a formula common in pagan Greek.[155]

(b) The Christological Reason 3:18-22

Literature on 1 Peter 3:18-22: **W. Bieder**, *Die Vorstellung von der Höllenfahrt Jesu Christi. Beitrag zur Entstehungsgeschichte der Vorstellung vom sog. Descensus ad inferos* (AThANT 19; Zürich, 1949); **R. Bultmann**, "Bekenntnis- und Liedfragmente im ersten Petrusbrief," in E. Dinkler (ed.), *Rudolf Bultmann, Exegetica. Aufsätze zur Erforschung des Neuen Testaments* (Tübingen, 1967), 285–97;

[153] The best-known parallel is the famous saying from *Gorgias*, in which the Platonic Socrates stresses in contrast to the Sophists that it would be worse to do injustice than to suffer injustice (Plat, *Gorg*, 508b).

[154] Cf. Just, *Apol* 5.3f.

[155] Goppelt, 239, note 42, refers to PsPlat, *Alc* 135d (ἐὰν θεὸς ἐθέλῃ) and Min, *Oct* 18.11, who can describe the expression *si deus dederit* together with similar pious expressions as the "natural language of the people."

W. J. Dalton, *Christ's Proclamation to the Spirits: A Study of 1 Peter 3:18–4:6* (AnBib 23; Rome, 1989); **K. Gschwind**, *Die Niederfahrt Christi in die Unterwelt. Ein Beitrag zur Exegese des Neuen Testaments und zur Geschichte des Taufsymbols* (NTA 2/3–5; Münster, 1911); **J. Jeremias**, "Zwischen Karfreitag und Ostern. Descensus und Ascensus in der Karfreitagstheologie des Neuen Testamentes," ZNW 42 (1949), 194–201; **O. Kuss**, "Zur paulinischen und nachpaulinischen Tauflehre im Neuen Testament (1952)," in O. Kuss, *Auslegung und Verkündigung*, vol. 1 (Regensburg, 1963), 121–50, especially 144–47; **R. E. Nixon**, "The Meaning of 'Baptism' in 1 Peter 3, 21," (StEv 4, TU 102; Berlin, 1968), 437–41; **A. Reichert**, *Eine urchristliche Praeparatio ad Martyrium, Studien zur Komposition, Traditionsgeschichte und Theologie des 1 Petr* (BET 22; Frankfurt et al., 1989), 208–47; **B. Reicke**, *The Disobedient Spirits and Christian Baptism. A Study of 1 Petr. III.19 and Its Context* (ASNU 13; Copenhagen, 1946); **F. Spitta**, *Christi Predigt an die Geister, 1 Petr. 3, 19ff. Ein Beitrag zur neutestamentlichen Theologie* (Göttingen, 1890); **A. Vögtle**, *Die Tugend- und Lasterkataloge im Neuen Testament. Exegetisch, religions- und formgeschichtlich untersucht* (NTA 16/4–5; Münster, 1936), 188–91.

With a substantiating "for" these exhortations with their positive interpretation of suffering for the sake of Christ are again connected back to the earliest Christian confession of Christ's suffering and death and also his resurrection and exaltation. This takes place in rhythmically shaped language. Many[156] therefore wish to see here a traditional song, whereby, however, the rather different attempts at reconstruction do not make such an assumption more plausible right from the start.[157] Beyond this, one does not see why an anonymous author must be postulated for such a text that—as will be shown—fits well into the intention of 1 Peter. A certain distance to the language and style of the context is connected with the tradition that is taken up here. One finds its individual elements scattered over the whole New Testament: the schema of humiliation/death–exaltation,[158] the formula of suffering/death ὑπέρ,[159] the access to God opened through Christ,[160] the Spirit as

[156] R. Bultmann, "Liedfragmente," 285ff.; M.-E. Boismard, *Hymnes*, 60ff.; K. Wengst, *Formeln*, 161ff. and others.

[157] For criticism cf. Goppelt, 240–42.

[158] Cf. 1 Tim 3:16; Phil 2:6-11.

[159] Mark 14:24 par.; John 10:15 and frequently, specifically as death for the unrighteous in Rom 5:6ff.; cf. Gal 2:20.

[160] Eph 3:12.

the power that makes alive,[161] the ascension,[162] the exaltation at the right hand of God,[163] and the subjugation of the powers,[164] to name only the most prominent elements.[165] The various confessional statements are recapitulated in a unique density. Thus 1 Peter represents an important stage on the way to the development of the earliest Christian dogma.[166] In this way with help of the earliest Christian confessions, 1 Peter authorizes his previous statement about the suffering of the Christians, whereby the change in style and diction makes this passage stand out rhetorically from its context. Incidentally, one also again sees here the sovereignty with which 1 Peter interweaves these various traditions into one self-contained passage of text.

(18) For Christ has also suffered for sins once, a righteous person for the unrighteous, so that he might bring you to God, put to death indeed in the flesh, but nevertheless made alive in the Spirit. (19) In which [Spirit][167] he has also preached to the spirits in prison, (20) who were once disobedient, when the patience of God waited in the days of Noah during the building of the ark, within which few, put exactly, eight souls, were saved through water. (21) Which [i.e., water] also now saves you in the antitype of baptism, not as the removal of dirt from the flesh, but as a request to God for a good conscience. [That takes place] on the basis of the resurrection of Jesus Christ, (22) who—gone up into heaven —is at God's right hand after angels and powers and authorities have been subjected to him.

[161] Rom 8:11; 1 Cor 15:44f.; 2 Cor 3:6; John 6:63.

[162] Luke 24:51; Acts 1:10.

[163] Mark 12:36 par.; Acts 2:33 and frequently.

[164] Phil 2:10; Eph 1:21; Heb 2:8.

[165] Cf. further the flood typology in Luke 17:26ff., baptism as purification (Titus 3:5; cf. Eph 5:26).

[166] See above Introduction, pp. 44f.

[167] The ἐν ᾧ is often (W. Bieder, *Höllenfahrt*, 106; E. Schweizer, "πνεῦμα," 446; Goppelt, 247; Brox, 170) understood simply as a conjunction (whereby, by which) as also elsewhere in 1 Peter (1:6; 4:4). But one should ask whether a relative sense is not nevertheless possible, particularly since the statement that Christ "in the Spirit" preached to the "spirits" in prison fits well with this (cf. A. Reichert, *Praeparatio*, 214–24).

On the text: **18** (a) On the leaving out of καί in some textual witnesses cf. the textual criticism on 2:21: in this place as well there is a confessional statement that was frequently detached from the context. (b) An abundance of variants exists on περί ἁμαρτιῶν ἔπαθεν, which virtually without exception offer ἀπέθανεν instead of ἔπαθεν. In fact, only B P the majority text and miniscule 81 witness to ἔπαθεν. It surprises few that the twenty-fifth edition of Nestle-Aland still holds περὶ ἁμαρτιῶν ἀπέθανεν to be original. The reading ἔπαθεν is nevertheless to be preferred as *lectio difficilior* on the basis of internal evidence, for "*died* for sins" is the familiar tradition, and it is easier to explain that 1 Peter was adapted to this than it was secondarily altered; to this come the further grounds that are related (1) to the context (only through πάσχειν does a reference forward from verse 17 ensue; likewise the double reference backward in 4:1 to the suffering of Christ—including redemption from sin—is only understandable if ἔπαθεν stands in 3:18) and (2) to the text itself (the specification "*once*" is not as meaningful with death; in verse 18d "put to death" is stressed, which would otherwise be a doubling). (c) When some witnesses read ἡμᾶς instead of ὑμᾶς it has the same reasons as in 2:21: the form of address does not fit with texts that are read as confessional formula. **19** (a) A few witnesses replace φυλακῇ with τῷ ᾅδῃ and thereby make it clearer that Christ has been in Hades. (b) Some textual witnesses have πνεύματι instead of πνεύμασι. In that case, Christ had not "preached to the spirits in prison" but has "preach in the Spirit to those in prison." **21** The replacement of ὑμᾶς with ἡμᾶς is an expression of the theological esteem for the statement about baptism that one meets in 3:21. Peter's communication applied to his addressees thus became a confessional statement. **22** Some witness of the Latin tradition add before the reference to the ascension of Christ (πορευθεὶς εἰς οὐρανόν) a reminiscence of Christ's fight in Hades: *deglutiens mortem ut vitae aeternae heredes efficeremur* ("swallowing up death so that we would be made heirs of eternal life"), cf. the coexistence of the descent into Hades and the ascent into heaven in the Apostles' Creed. On the formulation cf. 1 Corinthians 15:54: κατεπόθη ὁ θάνατος εἰς νῖκος. Further material on this variant is found in Wohlenberg, 119 (note 85 there). The back translation into Greek in the *Editio Critica Maior* of 1 Peter: καταβάλλων τὸν θάνατον, ἵνα ζωῆς αἰωνίου κληρονόμοι γενώμεθα does not tally with the tradition and is not comprehensible (why καταβάλλων ["throwing down"]?) (168).

3:18

The paragraph begins with the traditional interpretation of the Passion as the sacrifice of Christ's life for the forgiveness of sins, whereby, however, the familiar statement from Paul (cf. 1 Cor 15:3) and also the gospels (cf. Matt 26:28) is not initially related to the atoning death but to the suffering. Verse 18b defines this precisely as [the suffering] "of a righteous person for the unrighteous." This also contains tradition elements (cf. Rom 5:6-8) that have already occurred in another formulation in 1 Peter 2:22 and beyond this yet again underlines the "impeccability" of the sacrificial lamb who through his blood redeems us from the old life-context (cf. 1:19). The pointed emphasis on the contrast of "righteous" and "unrighteous" refers to the paraenetic context insofar as the previous verses have stressed that the promise is only valid for the suffering of the righteous. Verse 18c supplements the statement of 18a: Salvation consists in that Christ has now opened an access to God. Forgiveness of sin means therefore the removal of the separation from God (cf. Rom 5:1f.; 8:31ff.; Gal 5:4ff. and often elsewhere), as is explicitly stressed here. Insofar as immortal life is with God, this access to him opened by Christ implies the conquest of death (1 Cor 15:21ff.; Rom 5:12ff.). An antithetical *parallelismus membrorum* in this sense once again concisely recapitulates the Passion and resurrection with reference to Christ: "put to death indeed in the flesh, but nevertheless made alive in the Spirit." It makes it clear that Christ was handed over to death through his belonging to "flesh," but at the same time through his belonging to the (divine) Spirit[168] this death was conquered. The Spirit is also in Romans 1:3f. the power of God through which the Son of David, Jesus Christ, is singled out as God's Son by means of the resurrection. The verb ζῳοποιεῖν is also used in the

[168] Πνεύματι can be understood instrumentally here (cf. Rom 6:4; 1 Cor 6:14) or—more likely—as a dative of relationship. Elliott's (646f.) interpretation that, because of the parallel to σαρκί, πνεύματι should be understood as "with respect to [his] spirit," that is, anthropologically, is not persuasive. In the parallel in Rom 8:10 that Elliott brings up, it is unequivocally the divine Spirit and in no way "one's spirit (that lives)" (647) that dwells in the believers and creates life in the dead body (Rom 8:11).

Hellenistic-Jewish sphere for the creative power of God (*Jos. Asen.* 8.3, 9; 12.1; 20.7; 18 Benedictions). In Romans 4:17, it expresses the divine creative power, which, just as God caused being to emerge out of nothing, also makes the dead alive. Participation in the Spirit therefore brings about precisely in the sphere of death the conquest of the same; it "makes your mortal bodies alive" (Rom 8:9-11),[169] as this has already happened to Christ.

3:19–20a

The following passage of the text is difficult to interpret, because the author evidently assumes knowledge of traditions on the part of his addressees that are no longer accessible to us. It is neither unequivocal who those spirits are to whom Jesus preached nor what he has preached to them nor what is meant by "prison." The reference to the disobedience of the spirits "in the days of Noah" (3:20) is puzzling. Since the foundational work of Spitta,[170] the relationship of this statement to a tradition such as the one that is still preserved in the so-called Book of the Watcher-angels (*1 En.* 1–36) has been discussed,[171] *1 Enoch* being a document that played a not unimportant role in early Jewish[172] and early Christian[173] literature.

> The theme of the Book of the Watcher-angels is the fate of the fallen sons of God, which are described as ἄγγελοι in the Greek text of *1 Enoch*, but also—which in view of 1 Peter 3:19 is not unimportant—several times as πνεύματα (*1 En.* [gr.] 10.15; 13.6; 15.4, 6-8).[174] The patriarch is to go (in *1 En.* [gr.] 12.4; 13.3 and

[169] Rom 5:21 expresses it similarly: The Son also participates in the power of God to make the dead alive. John 6:63 then even places the flesh that is of no use at all in contrast to the Spirit that makes alive. In the great resurrection chapter 1 Corinthians 15, this ζῳοποιεῖν describes the effectiveness of God in creation (15:36) and in the resurrection (15:22), also here with a pointed Christological emphasis: while the first Adam was only "an enlivened soul," the "last Adam" (Christ) has become a "live-giving spirit" (15:45).

[170] F. Spitta, *Predigt*.

[171] On the interpretation of 1 Peter 3:19 as the Watcher-angels cf. B. Reicke, *Spirits*, 90f.; Selwyn, 326; Kelly, 156f.; Brox, 171ff.; Davids, 139–41; Achtemeier, 254–62.

[172] Cf. CD 2.18-21; 1QapGen[ar] 2.1, 16; *2 Bar* 56:12-15.

[173] In the New Testament, Jude 6:13; 2 Peter 2:4.

[174] The Greek remains of 1 Enoch are collected in M. Black, *Apocalypsis*.

15.2 a form of πορεύομαι is used in each case) to those whose disobedience was responsible for the Deluge and who are bound (*1 En.* [gr.] 10.4, 11; 14.5) or remain in a prison (δεσμωτήριον) (*1 En.* [gr.] 18.11–19.1; 10.13; 18.14; 21.10) and proclaim to them their definitive rejection (12.5). The petition for grace that he composes at their request (13.4-7) is rejected (14.4-7). Here one finds central motifs of the text—the "going" to the "spirits," the disobedience in the Deluge, the prison, and the visit of a person to them in order to communicate something to them. However, the meaning of this event remains unclear, "Either the sentence actually wants to say in a Christian context that the gospel was preached to the bound angels (whereby it remains open whether for repentance or for judgment) or Christ proclaimed his victory even to the remotest places of the cosmic scene, even [καί] to these 'spirits.' In my view, the matter cannot be decided. . . ."[175]

This interpretation of the text with respect to the fallen angels is, however, not compelling. The exegesis of the ancient church[176] already assumed that by these spirits the souls of the generation of the Deluge are meant and the Gospel of Peter that came into being about the middle of the second century assumes a preaching of Jesus before the dead. Such an understanding of πνεύματα as the souls of the dead is admittedly not common in the New Testament, but possible.[177] It also fits the Deluge narrative in a less forced manner, for the angels were indeed not first disobedient with respect to God's waiting patience in the days of Noah,[178]

[175] Brox, 175. On the whole complex cf. K. Gschwind, *Niederfahrt*, especially 97–144, who likewise refers it to the spirits; for the most part the proclamation of power over the fallen spirits is seen in this, as B. Reicke, *Spirits*, 133f. does, who sees at the same time in these spirits the power behind earthly authorities. W. J. Dalton, *Proclamation*, 200, also comes to a similar interpretation, "Christ, the new Enoch, has won, by His passion and resurrection, the definitive victory over these angelic powers of evil. The unbelieving world, allied with and instigated by these powers, shares their defeat and condemnation, a condemnation to be ratified at the last judgement."

[176] Cf. ClAl, *Strom* 6.6.44–46; Orig, *Princ* 2.5.3; Orig, *Cels* 2.43; Orig, *CommMatt* 132.

[177] Cf. Goppelt, 249, with reference to Heb 12:23; further Dan 3:86a LXX and *1 En.* 22.3-13; Luke 24:37, 39.

[178] On the motif of the patience of God before the Deluge cf. mAv 5.2a: "There are ten generations from Adam to Noah to make known how long-suffering God is, seeing that all the generations continued to provoke him

but already previously when they mingled with the daughters of human beings (cf. *1 En.* 7–9), but this does fit the human beings well; the 120 years of Genesis 6:3 could be understood as a limited period of grace.[179] Jubilees describes that not only the fallen angels (*Jub.* 5.6), but also the offspring of the angelic marriages[180] "[were] bound in the depths of the earth until the day of the great judgment" (*Jub.* 5.10). This otherworldly place of punishment of the πνεύματα τῶν ψυχῶν τῶν νεκρῶν (*1 En.* [gr.] 22.3; cf. 22.9) is described in *1 Enoch* 22 in direct connection with and correspondence to the δεσμωτήριον of the angels (*1 En.* [gr.] 21.10), whereby one especially notices the frequent use of the term πνεύ ματα for the souls of the dead (*1 En.* [gr.] 22.6f., 9, 11, 12, 13). This place of punishment of souls was then also explicitly designated a "prison" in early Christian literature.[181] When one adds to this that the verb κηρύσσειν elsewhere in the New Testament describes the proclamation of the Christian message of salvation,[182] while its use for a preaching of disaster would be unique, then this puzzling passage 3:19f. would be interpreted precisely in connection with the abruptly mentioned, but through the introductory γὰρ καί assumed to be known to the addressees, preaching of the gospel among the dead in 4:6, where a εὐαγγελίζεσθαι corresponding to κηρύσσειν makes life possible for the dead on the basis of God's Spirit. If this interpretation is true, then this passage could be understood as a conscious correction of the assumption of the definitive lostness of the generation of the Deluge, as for instance it is evidenced in the Jerusalem Talmud;[183] it would thereby stress

---

until he brought upon them the waters of the Flood" (English translation Ph. Blackman).

179 TPsJon on Gen 6:3; cf. Luke 17:26f.

180 Admittedly, these did not form the immediate generation of the Deluge, but they did probably produce the corruption of the earth that led directly to the Deluge (*Jub.* 5.1-4).

181 Cf. *2 Clem.* 6:8 (αἰχμαλωσία); *Herm.* 1.8 *Vis.* 1.1 (αἰχμαλωτισμός); *Herm.* 105.7 *Sim.* 9.28 (δεσμωτήριον).

182 "Through the proclamation the apprehension of God's power takes place" (G. Friedrich, "κῆρυξ," 703).

183 Cf. jSan fol. 29b, "The generation of the Deluge has no share in the resurrection." This definitive rejection is extensively justified in what follows (see G. A. Wewers, *Sanhedrin*, 287f.).

that even this archetype of depravity is siezed by the salvation taking place through the resurrection.[184]

Even this interpretation is laden with uncertainty; the context, however, continues to speak for it, into which context 1 Peter has added this motif that alone has no parallel in the early Christian confessions. It is hardly convincible that it is said about Christ—immediately following the praise of the saving deed of his death for the unrighteous and his resurrection because of his relationship to the Spirit of God—that he now (in exactly this Spirit!) goes to these spirits as a messenger of disaster and confirms their definitive damnation as proof of his triumph over all evil powers.[185] This applies even more because 1 Peter admittedly does intimate judgment on unbelievers but precisely never argues for their damnation, let alone make it a general theme.[186] One should further observe that Christ's descent is fashioned as a conscious counterpart to his ascension, as indeed also in the text the πορευθείς of the ascension into heaven in verse 22 corresponds to the πορευθείς of the descent in verse 19. As also elsewhere now and then in the earliest Christian confessions (cf. Phil 2:10; Eph 4:9f.; Rev 5:13) by this it is stressed that Christ's "seizure of power" does not only comprise heaven and earth, but even the underworld as the world of death and absence of God[187]—and so also reaches farther than the Christian proclamation.

Against this interpretation it is objected that the "descent into hell" cannot be meant because it could only have taken place before the resurrection, for which reason "the explanation of v. 19 given by the author in v. 20 . . . [is] in that case false."[188] This argumentation assumes for one that the event alluded to in v. 19 must have taken place after the resurrection mentioned at the end of v. 18, which is not compelling: the expression θανατωθεὶς μὲν σαρκί—ζῳοποιηθεὶς

[184] Cf. Goppelt, 250, "The saving effect of his suffering death reaches also to those people who do not come to a conscious encounter with Christ in this life, even to the most lost among them."

[185] Cf. Achtemeier, 245f.

[186] Against Elliott, 661f., who claims that the damnation of the angels of the Deluge tradition "would be consistent with the fate of the persistently disobedient, as described throughout 1 Peter."

[187] Cf. also Rom 14:9, where just as in 1 Pet 3:19 lordship over the dead and the living is the direct result of Christ's death and resurrection.

[188] R. Bultmann, "Liedfragmente," 288.

δὲ πνεύματι in v. 18 places the death and resurrection together in a formulaic manner; v. 19 connects by means of a reference to the Spirit expressed by the relative without there being a temporal arrangement that one can derive from this. It is just as thinkable that it is dealing with an addendum that had no place within the antithetically constructed confessional formula.[189] Furthermore, it is claimed that the placement of the "descent into hell" between the burial and resurrection (in the so-called *triduum mortis*), a placement known from the creed, is the only possibility for such, which claim is an anachronism. Even the normally repeated observation that Irenaeus did not refer to 1 Peter in his reference to Christ's "descent into hell" loses its convincingness upon closer examination: either Irenaeus simply assumes the "descent into hell" without any biblical reference (Iren, *Haer* 4.27.2) or he cites an apocryphal word of Jeremiah that is especially fitting for his explanation of the incident (Iren, *Haer* 4.22.1; *Epid* 78).

3:20b

The reference to the Deluge, especially the allusion to the ark, also lets, however, the theme of salvation sound: in the ark, eight "souls" were saved. This passage is normally produced as evidence that ψυχή is used in 1 Peter in the sense of "person," for here the statement can indeed only refer to the life of those protected from drowning through the ark. However, one should observe that this allusion to the Deluge narrative is consciously constructed as an "antitype"[190] to salvation through baptism exemplified in the following verse. But this makes it likely that also here the term ψυχή is used with deliberation: When it says about the eight ψυχαί: διεσώθησαν δι' ὕδατος, it can admittedly be translated "They were [saved] going through water," but one would yet rather expect an "out of the water." Now that δι' ὕδατος can also mean "through" or "by means of"[191] water and then in what follows water is also no longer spoken about as a means of death but—metaphorically (see v. 21)—about its purifying power. Furthermore the δι' ὕδατος

[189] A widespread tradition since Augustine even relates this statement to the preexistent Christ (cf. Elliott, 649f.).

[190] 1 Pet 3:21 also calls this ἀντίτυπος!

[191] διά with the genitive also means "through" in the sense of "by means of." With the more natural preposition ἐκ, this wordplay would not have been possible.

placed at the end of verse 20 corresponds to the δι' ἀναστάσεως Ἰησοῦ Χριστοῦ placed at the end of verse 21. Thereby verse 20 as the "counter-image" to baptism in verse 21 may allude to the "soul-salvation"[192] that takes place there.

3:21

As an antitype to the ark, baptism saves because in it one is also "saved" through water. This is further explained in an unconventional way. It is initially established negatively that baptism should not be envisaged as the bodily washing away of dirt. From this, the understanding of the controversial positive statement is then to be developed: the request to God for a good conscience. As a definition of baptism, which according to the earliest Christian conviction meant a change in lordship and thereby a foundational renewal of existence (cf. Rom 6) and also according to 1 Peter "saves" from disaster in correspondence to the ark, this definition of baptism as a request for a good conscience sounds somewhat colorless. Brox (178f.) will therefore see a self-commitment (ἐπερώτημα *stipulatio*, contractual agreement) expressed in the expression συνειδήσεως ἀγαθῆς ἐπερώτημα εἰς θεόν and translates "the promise of a firm commitment to God."[193] But that is questionable on a number of grounds. Purely philologically one discovers that ἐπερώτημα in the meaning supposed here, "contractual agreement," is first evidenced from the second century C.E.[194] Even if one may yet disregard this objection in view of the comparatively small number of examples passed down, still it is hardly explainable why in this case in 3:21 συνείδησις ἀγαθή can have a totally different meaning than it does five verses earlier, where it unequivocally has to do with a consciousness that the slander of others is false and Christian is not suffering as one who has done evil. Συνείδησις ἀγαθή can only mean "good conscience" here (cf. also 2:19). Finally, with an interpretation of the expression συνειδήσεως ἀγαθῆς ἐπερώτημα as "the promise of a firm commitment," the concluding reference to the resurrection

[192] διασώζεσθαι of the ψυχαί is perhaps not coincidentally reminiscent of the σωτηρία ψυχῶν in 1:9 (as a summary of the Christian offer of salvation).

[193] Brox, 164.

[194] Cf. Goppelt, 259.

(as the basis of salvation; cf. 1:3 end!) would hang there unconnected.[195] It is thereby concluded from this that συνείδησις ἀγαθή here as well means nothing other than "a good conscience." How then should the statement be understood?

With an interpretation, one should consistently proceed from the image of washing, which also already dominates in the negation: if baptism is not an external washing of the flesh, then this indeed demands in the parallel member (introduced by the adversative ἀλλά directly after this addition) that it then concerns another type of purification that does not just deal with the "dirt of the flesh" but the inside of the person, the conscience. That also fits the context. According to 3:18, Jesus' death and resurrection opened access to God—now "on the basis of the resurrection," which already in 1:3 was the basis of the new siring, a good conscience is requested, therefore the inner[196] purification of the person. The somewhat clumsy formulation of a "request to God for a good conscience" is explained by 1 Peter's concern, on the one hand, to hold firmly to the promise of God's grace that goes ahead of one, which shows itself here as effective in the "new creation of the whole person from his or her 'most inward part', his or her 'heart' "[197] that is requested from God, but, on the other hand, also to stress the obligation that is connected with it.[198] Apparently the image of a simple washing with respect to the conscience was for the author still something too easily misunderstood, particularly because he previously has demanded from the addressees a good conscience committed to God as a condition of his promise of grace (2:19; 3:16) and has thereby explicitly referred to their behavior, to the "doing good" (2:20) or "good way of life" (3:16). Here, therefore, the request (that also obligates the requester) to this God for a good conscience comes out of this.

[195] Which Brox himself establishes, Brox, 179.

[196] The comparable opposition in 3:3f. shows that such a contrast of unimportant outer and real inner is familiar to the author of 1 Peter. Also the salvation of the "soul," about which the previous verse speaks, fits this contrast with "flesh."

[197] H.-J. Eckstein, *Syneidesis*, 305 (with reference to the similar request for the "creation" of a pure heart in Psalm 51[50]:12). Similarly Hebrews 9:14 can say that Jesus' sacrifice of his life purifies the conscience.

[198] This tendency was indeed already observed previously in the letter (cf. 1:2; 1:13–2:3).

3:22

The *descensus ad inferos*, Christ's "descent into hell," is completed by his ascension (cf. Eph 4:9f.). The accomplishment of Christ's rule presents this, so to speak, dramatically, whereby the point of the two "trips" is connected with the contrasting assessments of the locations "above" and "below." If the descent to the spirits in prison signals that even the realm of guilt and death is not excluded from Christ's sphere of influence, then the ascension leads to enthronement at God's right hand;[199] the participation in the divine rule that is given through this is demonstrated by the subjugation of all powers under Christ.

The motif of exaltation to God's right hand (*sessio ad dexteram*) has numerous parallels in the New Testament just as that of the subjugation of the powers and authorities. In terms of content, one already finds the combination of the exaltation of the humiliated Christ and the subjugation of the powers in the hymn in Philippians (especially Phil 2:9-11). It is stressed in each gospel in its own way that precisely the one who suffered is also God's throne-companion: All power in heaven and on earth has been given to him (Matt 28:18), he is already exalted on the cross (John 3:14; 12:32ff.), and he ascends to heaven in order to endow his own with his Spirit (Luke 24:49-51; Acts 1:8ff.). Terminologically, the Deutero-Pauline Ephesians (1:20f.) stands closest to 1 Peter.[200] Tradition-historically Psalm 110[109]:1 has been the "godfather" for the formulation of these statements about exaltation. In this Psalm, the two motifs of exaltation to God's right hand and the subjection of hostile authorities are already connected: "YHWH spoke to my lord, 'Sit at my right hand until I make your enemies a footstool for your feet.' " This Psalm verse, whose importance for early Christian theology, even precisely for the development of Christology, cannot be estimated highly enough,[201] almost presented itself in the LXX version (εἶπεν ὁ κύριος τῷ κυρίῳ μου) for a christological interpretation of Father and Son (cf. Mark 12:35-37 par.; Acts 2:34f.) on account of the doubled κύριος; from the enemies came then the powers, frequently the anti-divine powers (cf.

[199] More exactly, as in v. 19 it speaks with an aorist participle about Christ's going—therefore also the translation "going into heaven."

[200] A further close parallel for the exaltation to God's right hand is Romans 8:34; there, the point of the exaltation is, however, Christ's intercession (his intercessory standing in for the believers with the Father).

[201] Cf. on this M. Hengel, "Inthronisation."

1 Cor 15:24). Whether the "powers and authorities" in 1 Peter 3:22 are also hostile must remain open—the connection with the "angels" suggests at least that one should not only think about hostile powers. A direct connection between the ascension and the sitting on God's right hand is found in the non-original ending of Mark (Mark 16:19; cf. also *Barn.* 15:9).[202]

In this whole paragraph, exaltation to God's right hand marks the counterpoint established by God to Christ's suffering and death. That makes clear—precisely as the suffering one, Christ is the one who in reality is already appointed as lord of the whole world. This entire excursus has an absolutely immediate meaning for the suffering Christians,[203] for in Christ, whose suffering they follow, even both of these have already become reality, the innocent suffering and death (3:18) that still yet characterize the existence of the followers, but also the exaltation to God's right hand (3:22) that will also be their future in participation in Christ's fate.[204] Baptism as salvation from disaster gives one a part in this.

The letter, of course, does not remain on the "heights" of God's right hand, but turns its view from there again back to Christ's suffering and together with this to the Christians' suffering.

(c) Being Different as Scandal 4:1-6

Literature on 1 Peter 4:1-6: **R. Bultmann**, "Bekenntnis-und Liedfragmente im ersten Petrusbrief," in E. Dinkler (ed.), Rudolf Bultmann, *Exegetica. Aufsätze zur Erforschung des Neuen Testaments* (Tübingen, 1967), 285–97; **W. J. Dalton**, *Christ's Proclamation to the Spirits: A Study of 1 Peter 3:18–4:6* (AnBib 23; Rome, 1989^2); **K. Gschwind**, *Die Niederfahrt Christi in die Unterwelt. Ein Beitrag zur Exegese des Neuen Testaments und zur Geschichte des Taufsymbols* (NTA 2/3–5; Münster, 1911); **J. Jeremias**, "Zwischen Karfreitag

[202] In *Barn.* 15:9, it is true that only the ascension is named; however, it is named in connection with the descent into hell.

[203] Against Brox, 164, "The contribution of these verses [i.e., 3:18-22] to the primary theme of the letter exhausts itself therefore in verse 18."

[204] Frequently, the connection of suffering and glory is stressed, which, as with Christ (cf. 1:11, 21), will also be the reality for the Christians who are connected to him through suffering (cf. 1:7; 4:13f.; 5:1, 10). Here it is redemption from (eternal) ruin.

und Ostern. Descensus und Ascensus in der Karfreitagstheologie des Neuen Testaments," *ZNW* 42 (1949), 194–201; **O. Kuss**, "Zur paulinischen und nachpaulinischen Tauflehre im Neuen Testament (1952)," in O. Kuss, *Auslegung und Verkündigung*, vol. 1 (Regensburg, 1963), 121–50, especially 144–47; **A. Reichert**, *Eine urchristliche Praeparatio ad Martyrium. Studien zur Komposition, Traditionsgeschichte und Theologie des 1. Petrusbriefes* (BET 22; Frankfurt et al., 1989), 208–47; **B. Reicke**, *The Disobedient Spirits and Christian Baptism. A Study of 1 Pet. III.19 and Its Context* (ASNU 13; Copenhagen, 1946); **F. Spitta**, *Christi Predigt an die Geister, 1 Petr. 3, 19ff. Ein Beitrag zur neutestamentlichen Theologie* (Göttingen, 1890); **A. Strobel**, "Macht Leiden von Sünde frei? Zur Problematik von 1 Petr 4,1f," *ThZ* 19 (1963), 412–25; **A. Vögtle**, *Die Tugend-und Lasterkataloge im Neuen Testament. Exegetisch, religions-und formgeschichtlich untersucht* (NTA 16/4–5; Münster, 1936), 188–91.

(4:1) Since Christ has now suffered in the flesh, also arm yourselves with the same cast of mind, for the one who has suffered in the flesh has put an end to sin, (2) so that you do not live your remaining time in the flesh anymore in accordance with human desires but in accordance with God's will. (3) For the past was sufficient to carry out the will of the Gentiles, when you spent your life in excesses, desires, drinking bouts, gluttony, boozing, and outrageous idol worship; (4) they are taken aback about the fact that you do not swim with them in the same stream of depravity and they disparage you. (5) They will give an account before the one who is prepared to judge the living and the dead. (6) For the gospel was also preached to the dead for this purpose, so that they admittedly are judged in the flesh just as human beings are, but they are to live through the Spirit just as God does.

On the text: **1** A number of variants exist for παθόντος σαρκί, which variants either bring in the concept of the atoning death in that ἀποθανόντος stands in the place of παθόντος (thus in ℵ*), cf. the formation of variants in 2:12 and 3:18, or alternatively they complete the concept of substitution in that ὑπὲρ ὑμῶν or ὑπὲρ ἡμῶν is added. The concept of substitution is not foreign to 1 Peter, cf. 2:21. When it comes to the concept of atoning death, noticeably only one witness supports it in this place, cf. the more widespread testimony to ἀποθνῄσκειν in 2:21 and 3:18.

4:1

By means of the catchwords "suffer" and "flesh," the paragraph goes back to the discussion in 3:18. If the meaning of Christ's suffering for salvation was featured there, then now—further supported through a resuming οὖν—it is about a cast of mind (ἔννοια) that corresponds to this Christ. The salvation that is allocated through Christ's suffering cannot simply be consumed but presses to take shape in the believer's implementation in life (cf. Gal 5:6b). In 1 Peter 2:21, this was expressed through the concept of imitation, *imitatio Christi*, now with a heightened linguistic emphasis it takes place through the command to "arm" (ὁπλίσασθε) oneself with the same cast of mind. Conflict and war metaphors are commonly used in the New Testament as a characteristic of Christian existence (cf. Rom 13:12; Eph 6:11-17). Remarkably, this metaphor is nevertheless not used against the world around them, which is experienced as hostile, which, at least linguistically, would perpetuate the retaliation:[205] The *miles Christianus*, armed with the cast of mind of Christ as the one who had suffered as the righteous for the unrighteous (1 Pet 3:18), fights against evil (cf. 1 Pet 5:8f.), but not against evil people. Here, as the following verses 4:3f. show, the arming serves the fight against the desires (cf. 2:11).

The statement that the one who suffers "has put an end to sin" is not very easy to understand. The talk about sin in the singular, which is unusual for 1 Peter, likely deals with a reformulation of the Pauline thought such as the apostle develops in Rom 6:1-11, as an example: through baptism the believers participate in Jesus' death and thus as those who have died become free from sin. As also elsewhere, 1 Peter replaces the reference to death with a reference to suffering, because the thought of participation in Christ's suffering as an expression of community with Christ plays for him a prominent role (cf. 2:19ff.; 3:13ff.; 4:13ff.; 5:1). The sentence therefore says, whoever suffers in following Christ and so arms himself with the same cast of mind as Christ, therefore remains connected to Christ and lives no longer in ways opposed to God's will. This one also participates in the sphere of salvation opened through Christ's suffering,[206] whereby the superordinate

[205] Against Brox, 191.

[206] On the general paralleling of statements about Christ and about the believers both in view of suffering as well as in view of its conquest cf. E. Schweizer, *Christologie*, 374–77.

imperative ὁπλίσασθε makes it clear that this participation at the same time demands the greatest effort on the believer's part.

4:2

What follows makes this explicit: The "remaining time in the flesh"—the formulation points to the limitedness of life and at the same time places this life within the horizon of God's eternality[207]—is now to be shaped in accordance with this release from sin. Thereby the believers are placed into the antagonism between two spheres of power, whose intentionality is underlined by means of the concept of willing that is used with each in its respective context: The one consists of "human desires,"[208] which are again in verse 3 specified as "the will [βούλημα] of the Gentiles"; the other is the "will [θέλημα] of God." Because of belonging to the suffering Christ and "arming" with his consciousness, it follows that the believers through turning away from "human desires" place themselves under God's will—and thus show themselves to be "obedient children" (1:14), as those who are truly free in their commitment to God (2:16).

4:3

The following verse deals yet further with the opposing power that has dominated "the past time," thus the earlier life of the believers. From "human desires" comes what is "the will of the Gentiles." Thus desire as a psychological counteracting force obtains now also a cultural-societal dimension and is at the same time yet more sharply contrasted with God's will. In terms of content, this is explicated through a vice catalogue, which in typical conversion language underlines the futility (cf. 1:18) and darkness (cf. 2:9) of the previous life. The "will of the Gentiles" is thereby characterized in a clichéd manner as unrestrained excess, which typically enough has its high point in idolatry. Such vice cata-

[207] The in itself superfluous defining of the "remaining time" as "in the flesh" may imply that there is also a life outside the flesh. The same implies 1 Peter 1:17, in which the perspective of divine judgment forms the basis of the call to live "the life of your being a foreigner" accordingly.

[208] Cf. Excursus 5: The Desires, pp. 102–5 and also the discussion on 2:11.

logues that polemically[209] connect idolatry and wild excesses are found yet more frequently in the New Testament.[210] They may be an inheritance from the Diaspora synagogue,[211] which had gladly interpreted its special place in the pagan world by means of its particular ethos.[212] The sphere of sexual morality and any influencing of people through lust and desire was apparently especially loved in this respect. Desire could indeed also be evaluated critically in pagan philosophy, especially in the Stoic tradition.[213] These critiques allowed Jews (then also Christians) to profile themselves as "better pagans" and thus to make their separation from pagan conditions reasonable.[214] Peter resolutely uses this chance to interpret in the sense of an ethical opposition the outsider position of Christians on the basis of their religious orientation and the tension that it produced with the surrounding world. Thereby the societal being different, the foreignness, receives an elite moment that can be positively integrated into the contested self-understanding and at the same time—as the frequently recurring admonitions in this context to do good and avoid evil show—motivate to a better way of life. This can then once again be used apologetically.

4:4

This strategy also determines what follows: The majority of non-Christian contemporaries would have subscribed to the fact that

[209] Presumably 1 Peter alludes to the (occasional) celebrations that then also always have a religious character.

[210] Cf. Gal 5:19-21; a list of direct parallels is found in Brox, 194.

[211] Cf. Sir 18:30–19:4, "Go not after your lusts, but keep your desires in check. If you satisfy your lustful appetites, they will make you the sport of your enemies. Have no joy in the pleasures of a moment which bring on poverty redoubled; Become not a glutton and a winebibber with nothing in your purse. Whoever does so grows no richer; whoever wastes the little he has will be stripped bare. Wine and women make the mind giddy, and the companion of prostitutes becomes reckless. He who lightly trusts in them has no sense, and he who strays after them sins against his own life. Rottenness and worms will possess him, for contumacious desire destroys its owner." (English translation P. W. Skehan).

[212] See above p. 178.

[213] How far this could go in the pagan sphere is shown by the rejection of sexual desire even within marriage in Musonius, *Diatribe* 12.

[214] See above Excursus 5: The Desires, pp. 102–5.

the Christian way of life "took aback" the surrounding world. Yet while non-Christians experienced Christian religiosity as a breach of the societal order and therefore viewed it with hostility, if they had not more or less offensively rejected it with suspicion and accusation,[215] for 1 Peter the commitment to God's will expresses itself in a foundationally new ethical orientation: Christians do not swim (literally, do not run) in the "stream of depravity." The hostility against the Christians is thus interpreted in the context of the contrast of virtue and vice, whereby the association of being without salvation also resonates in the word ἀσωτία (a negated derivative of σῴζω).[216]

4:5

Again there is a reference to the judgment—as in 2:23 above all in the sense of comfort, that God will not pass over without consequences the injustices that have been done to the Christians. The expression "to judge the living and the dead" sounds formulaic; there are corresponding formulas in the New Testament (2 Tim 4:1; cf. Acts 10:42) and in early Christian literature (*Barn.* 7:2; *Pol. Phil.* 2:1; *2 Clem.* 1:1), and it went verbally into the formulation of the Apostles' Creed.[217]

4:6

Occasioned by the catchword of the judgment of the living and the dead, 1 Peter comes back to Christ's preaching to the dead. This statement's reference to 3:19f. is, as seen earlier, often disputed;[218]

[215] The "disparage" here alludes to this; cf. Acts 13:45; 18:6.

[216] Cf. Goppelt, 274: It deals with "an attitude that compensates lack of meaning through excess, a way of life that, as the word says due to its root, is lacking salvation;" similarly W. Foerster, "ἄσωτος," 504: the word says that one "through their lifestyle ruins themselves." A vivid example is the use of the corresponding adverb ἀσώτως in the parable of the prodigal son, Luke 15:13.

[217] The infinitive construction that lies before one here, "to judge the living and the dead" is also found in 2 Tim 4:1, there, however, in the present infinitive; 1 Peter's formulation with the aorist infinitive is found verbally in the creeds; see above Introduction, p. 44.

[218] See above on 3:19; further Elliott, 730f.

the abrupt mention of a proclamation of the gospel before the dead is nevertheless explained in the most unforced manner if one relates the two passages to one another.[219] In that case also the remaining difficulties in this text solve themselves: the judgment of the dead that has happened once "in a human way" may refer to the punishment by death of the generation of the Deluge (κριθῶσι is aorist, while ζῶσι is present; the likewise aoristic εὐηγγελίσθη corresponds to the aoristic ἐκήρυξεν in 3:19). The contrast of σαρκί (as the sphere of mortality in which the judgment took place) and πνεύματι (as the sphere of activity of the divine power that makes alive), which directly refers to 3:18, also speaks for this connection. The verse with its surprising differentiation with reference to judgment would thereby be understood as an attempt to connect the statement about judgment in the previous verse, according to which God as judge punishes the unjust, with the statement of 3:19f., that through Christ salvation is offered even to the once disobedient generation of the Deluge. It must remain open to what degree this statement can be generalized in the sense that salvation is offered to all who have died without Christ; the aorist of εὐηγγελίσθη, however, speaks more[220] for a one-time action, which is what was spoken about in 3:19.

3. Exhortation to Love One Another 4:7-11

Literature on 1 Peter 4:7-11: **J. Reumann**, "'Stewards of God': Pre-Christian Religious Application of OIKONOMOS in Greek," *JBL* 77 (1958), 339–49; **J. N. D. White**, "Love that Covers Sins," *Exp* 1913–A (1913), 541–47.

(7) But the end of all things has come near. Now be level-headed and sober for prayer. (8) Above all hold stubbornly fast to love for one another, for "Love covers a multitude of sins." (9) [Be] hospitable to one another without grumbling, (10) each, just as he has received a gift of grace, employing

[219] So also B. Reicke, *Spirits*, 204–10; J. Jeremias, "Karfreitag," 196f.; Goppelt, 249f.

[220] The reference of νεκροί in v. 6 back to v. 5, where it speaks about a judgment of all the dead, could speak for the fact that all must indeed answer to the judge, but that through the same judge, salvation is offered to the dead at the same time.

it for mutual service as a good administrator of God's varied grace. (11) If one speaks, [then thus] as [if he speaks] God's words; if one serves, [then thus] as [if he acts] from the strength God grants, so that in everything God will be glorified through Jesus Christ, who has the glory and the power from eternity to eternity. Amen.

On the text: **8** Some witnesses (among them the majority text) have the future καλύψει instead of the present καλύπτει. Love's covering of sin is then not generally valid but takes place in the future, presumably at the final judgment. This is explainable as an adaptation to James 5:20.

The first section of the second main part closes with a series of exhortations. In this section, the relation to outsiders does not appear explicitly. The "two poles around which the discussion proceeds are the community's relation to God (4 times in 10-11) and their relation to each other (3 times in 8-10)."[1] Through the introductory reference to the end of all things that has come near and also the following series of directions for dealing with one another, the section is set off from the preceding one; more clear is the boundary at the end by means of the doxology and the "amen."

4:7

The explicit reference to the imminent end shows that the author of 1 Peter basically still holds firmly to the earliest Christian expectation of a speedy end to the world (cf. ἤγγικεν in Mark 1:15 par.; Jas 5:8), even if—from the theological location of Christians as "foreigners" in society to the command of integration in and subordination to the existing structures—his main theological interest concerns the shaping of the "remaining time in the flesh" (4:2), as it were, the "time between the times."[2] The following paraenesis is also determined by this, which paraenesis is initially profiled against the horizon of the common ancient ideal

[1] Boring, 148.

[2] A comparison with John's Apocalypse, which came into being about the same time, conspicuously demonstrates this. I cannot understand how one can say 1 Peter represents "the imminent expectation stressed in the same way as the Revelation of John" (Goppelt, 281).

of σωφροσύνη, of level-headedness and prudent self-control. In the context of the eschatological paraenesis, this corresponds to the prudence (praised in the eschatological parables) of the one who does not allow himself to be deceived by that which lies before his eyes about its provisional nature, but expects his lord (cf. Matt 24:45; 25:2, 4, 8, 9), whereby the replacement of φρόνιμος by σωφρονεῖν documents once again the enculturation of 1 Peter even in the sphere of ethics.[3] This is supplemented by the summons to soberness, which, just like the summons to vigilance, is characteristic of early Christian eschatological paraeneseis. It once again underlines the necessity of not allowing oneself to be deceived and led astray by that which exists, but of orienting oneself on God's coming rule.[4] Both, however, take place through prayer, the continual aligning of waiting and hoping on God (cf. Jas 5:7ff.).

4:8

After the long discussion of 2:11–4:6, which above all had as its theme Christian behavior toward the world around them, the author of 1 Peter *now comes to speak about the behavior of Christians among themselves.*[5] Thereby the command of mutual love—rhetorically further strengthened by an introductory "above all"—stands in the center. The central placement of the love command is common to Christians; the special stress on inner-communal love certainly also has to do with the pressure from without. Thus love to the "brothers and sisters" was already previously evoked as the epitome of the inner-communal ethos (1:22; 2:17); now it is for the first time discussed in detail. Thereby, immediately joined to this is that it should be practiced "persistently," that one must therefore work hard for its continued existence.

The importance of mutual love is further stressed through the statement that love covers the multitude of sins.[6] As the justifica-

[3] The verb σωφρονεῖν and its derivatives are typically found in the later writings of the New Testament, especially in the Pastoral Epistles; other than in Romans 12:3 and Acts 26:25, it is also found in Titus 2:2, 4-6, 12; 1 Tim 2:9, 15; 3:2; 2 Tim 1:7.

[4] 1 Thess 5:6, 8; see above on 1:13.

[5] Vv. 8, 10, εἰς ἑαυτούς; v. 9, εἰς ἀλλήλους.

[6] Usually this is understood as a citation of Proverbs 10:12, whereby, how-

tion of the summons to love the brothers and sisters, the sentence seems to say at first glance that through practicing love the person can compensate for his or her own offenses. If one took this sentence as a soteriological axiom, it would then stand in explicit contradiction to the other statements of the letter about Christ's reconciling work (cf. 2:24; 3:18). Now such fuzziness is not untypical for 1 Peter, and Goppelt rightly warns against pressing such a sentence.[7] Rather, in its ambivalence the sentence reminds one "about the cycle between the love that encounters us and the love that is given on by us, which love, according to the Jesus tradition, goes out from God (Mark 11:25; Matt 6:14f.; 18:35), which describes a correlation of personal relationships, not a settlement among accounts."[8] This fits with the author's general tendency: He does indeed hold firmly to the divine grant that goes before all human action—the metaphor of new siring/rebirth already shows that which has its equivalent in the address to the recipients as "beloved" in the beginning of both new sections in the second main part (2:11; 4:12). But, on the other hand, 1 Peter seizes—sometimes not totally without violence—each opportunity to stress the obligation that is created by it (cf. 1:2; 1:13–2:3; 4:1ff.). The other possibility to understand this verse is that the sins of the one loved are covered by the one who loves.[9]

4:9

The command of mutual love is supplemented in verse 9 by hospitality. This is a basic concretion of the love command in the whole New Testament tradition (cf. Rom 12:9-13; Heb 13:1f.). Christ himself is encountered in the foreigner (cf. Matt 25:35, 43). In the Pastoral Epistles, hospitality is an indication of the suitability of a bishop (1 Tim 3:2; Titus 1:8) or a widow (1 Tim 5:10) for church office. One reason why hospitality,[10] which was so highly valued in antiquity, played so great a role particularly in early Christianity is certainly that the reception of male and female missionaries or

---

ever, this (half) verse shows no agreement with the LXX version except the finite verb καλύπτει.

[7] Goppelt, 284.

[8] Goppelt, 285.

[9] Cf. Achtemeier, 295f; Boring, 150.

[10] Cf. G. Stählin, "ξένος," 16ff.

male and female messengers was decisive for the Christian mission and the contact of the communities among one another.[11] The possibility of the abuse of hospitality by spongers[12] will make it necessary a little later for the *Didache* to set up restrictive regulations (*Did.* 11:5f., 12; 12:5); that is not (yet) gone into here, but rather it is stressed that hospitality should take place "without grumbling," without sullenness or stinginess through which precisely the value of the donation to the guest is again ruined.

4:10

The unity of Christians is based on the fact that the various gifts of grace that the Christians have each received go back to the variegated "multicolored" grace of God. Only here does one find outside of the *Corpus Paulinum* an echo of the teaching about charismata,[13] whereby, however, in contrast to Paul not the gift but the duty stands in the foreground:[14] the Christians are therefore good administrators[15] of this grace exactly there where they serve one another in the "multicolored" variety of their charismas, that is, with their respective abilities—the variety of gifts accords with the variety of the challenges.[16] First Peter again takes over the central importance of service from the earliest Christian tradition where, precisely too in the context of power and hierarchy, it is an expression of the difference of God's rule: in Mark 10:42-45 par. and Luke 22:24-27 in a provocative antithesis to human striving for power Jesus himself defines his whole life as service and obligates his followers to it. Accordingly, Paul can stress that spiritual gifts are not an occasion for the promotion of one's public image, but are "services" (1 Cor 12:4f.; cf. Rom 12:6f.). That is

[11] Matt 10:11; Acts 16:15; 21:7, 18; 28:14; Rom 16:4, 23; 3 John 3, 7f.; *Did.*, 11.2, 4; cf. further on this D. Gorce, "Gastfreundschaft," 1105–7.

[12] This is satirically presented by Luc, *PergrMort* 11–13.

[13] Cf. above all, 1 Cor 12; further 1 Cor 7:7; Rom 12:6.

[14] See above on 2:20; J. Herzer, *Petrus*, 160–70, and Elliott, 757f. also stress the difference from the Pauline linguistic usage.

[15] On the religious metaphor of the "administrator" cf. 1 Cor 4:1 (Paul); Titus 1:7 (the bishop); *Ign. Pol.* 6.1 (the church); in the early Jewish sphere cf. *4 Bar.* 7:2 (Baruch). In contrast to Paul, the author of 1 Peter does not relate the term to the individual, but to the community.

[16] In 1 Peter 1:6, the attribute ποικίλος is used with πειρασμοί.

not unimportant in 1 Peter precisely in view of the questions of power within the Christian community. It is true that also in that community a hierarchy of precedence and subordination exists, but relationship through mutual service is primary.[17]

4:11

Of the "services," the variety of which is more or less seen in 1 Corinthians 12:8ff., 28ff., here only scantily "word" and "service" are named, probably proclamation[18] and charitable activities as pillars of the community (Acts 6:2f.; cf. Rom 12:7). That fits with the goal of this section: the variety of the charismas does not stand in the foreground but its linking back to God, who grants the power to serve, as is expressly emphasized. In the end, the unity of the community is based on this common linking back to God, which aims at God's glorification through the gifts of the individual members. Likewise, the catchword of the "glorification" of God reaches back again to the beginning of the section in 2:12, where this describes the desired outward effect of the Christian "way of life" on non-Christians. Beside the exemplary integration and subordination of Christians in the societal order, the community united in love through a common relationship to God is also a chance to testify to those outside about the faith. The whole is confirmed and brought to a conclusion with a doxology and "amen," which fits with an also clear new beginning in 4:12.

B. Comfort and Exhortation 4:12–5:11

1. Suffering as Fellowship with Christ 4:12-19

Literature on 1 Peter 4:12-19: **G. L. Borchert**, "The Conduct of Christians in the Face of the 'Fiery Ordeal'," *RExp* 79 (1982), 451–62;

[17] See below on 5:1ff. One should also observe that the whole community is described as an "administrator of the multicolored grace of God" and not just the bishop as in Titus 1:7. This designation joins the community together through the common task, but the οἰκονόμος θεοῦ in the Pastoral Epistle marks the special position of the office bearer.

[18] It seems forced when Elliot, 759, wishes to understand the "words of God" as "oracles," particularly since this meaning is also doubtful in the evidence that he cites for this interpretation, such as Rom 3:2 or Heb 5:12.

E. C. Colwell, "Popular Reactions against Christianity in the Roman Empire," in J. T. McNeill (ed.), *Environmental Factors in Christian History* (*Festschrift* for S. J. Case) (Washington, 1970 [1939]), 53–71; **J. L. Daniel**, "Anti-Semitism in the Hellenistic-Roman Period," *JBL* 98 (1979), 45–65; **J. Knox**, "Pliny and I Peter. A Note on I Peter 4, 14–16 and 3, 15," *JBL* 72 (1953), 187–89; **J. D. McCaughey**, "Three 'Persecution Documents' of the New Testament," *ABR* 17 (1969), 27–40; **M. Reiser**, "Die Eschatologie des 1. Petrusbriefs," in H.-J. Klauck (ed.), *Weltgericht und Weltvollendung. Zukunftsbilder im Neuen Testament* (QD 150; Freiburg et al., 1994), 164–81; **E. T. Sander**, ΠΥΡΩΣΙΣ *and the First Epistle of Peter 4:12* (Ph.D. Diss., Harvard University, 1967); **E. G. Selwyn**, "The Persecutions in I Peter," in BSNTS 1 (Oxford, 1950), 39–50; **W. C. van Unnik**, "The Teaching of Good Works," *NTS* 1 (1954/55), 92–110.

(12) Beloved, do not let yourselves be taken aback by the fiery ordeal that befalls you to test you as if something strange happened to you, (13) but—as you have fellowship with Christ's sufferings—rejoice, in order that you may also rejoice, shouting for joy, at the revelation of his glory. (14) When you are abused on account of Christ's name, [you are] blessed, for the Spirit of glory and of God rests on you. (15) May none among you suffer as a murderer or thief or evildoer or someone who gets involved in other people's business. (16) But if one [suffers] as a Christian, he should not be ashamed, but honor God with this name. (17) For the time has come that judgment begins starting with God's house. But if it [starts] first with us, what end will it come to for those who do not believe God's gospel? (18) And "if the righteous are hardly saved, where will the godless and sinner then be spotted?"(19) Therefore, those who suffer according to God's will should, through doing good, also commend their souls to him as to a faithful creator.

On the text: **14** There is an extensive formation of variants with respect to καὶ τὸ τοῦ θεοῦ. In essence, they are the result of an addition of καὶ τῆς δυνάμεως after τῆς δόξης, which presumably has taken place in dependence on liturgical linguistic usage (cf. the doxology of the Lord's Prayer). **14** At the end of the verse P Ψ, the majority text, the Clementine and Sixtine Vulgate, the Peshitta, the Bohairic translation, Tertullian, and possibly also Clement of Alexandria, among others, witness to the following addition: κατὰ μὲν αὐτοὺς βλασφημεῖται, κατὰ δὲ ὑμᾶς δοξάζεται ("[the Spirit] was reviled by them, but by you glorified"). Presumably those who revile Christians because of Christ's name are here being reproached with the sin against the Holy Spirit (cf. Mark 3:29; Luke 12:10).

After a clear break with doxology and amen in 4:11, there follows in 4:12—intensified through the address ἀγαπητοί[1]—a renewed turning to the addressees. That the recipients are again addressed as "beloved" underlines again the acceptance by God that goes before any of their own activity.[2] The paragraph 4:12-19 is tied closely with what goes before,[3] however it produces a change in perspective. The witness outward recedes (it is only mentioned in the δοξαζέτω of 4:16), and instead the principle discussion is about the issue of suffering, the crisis of faith produced by it, and its theological assessment: suffering is inherent in membership of the elect community and means testing (v. 12); in suffering, the eschatological glory already rests on the (therefore blessed) community; as the way of sharing Christ's suffering, it is a cause for joy, because thus they will also share his future glory (v. 13); suffering makes the Christians blessed (v. 14), it is a way of glorifying God (v. 16) and an anticipation of the final judgment that still awaits the others (vv. 17f). Thereby the previous statements of the letter about suffering are tied together and taken farther in order to take a position on this central problem of the letter with a thoroughness that has not yet been reached up to this point. Accordingly, the "temperature" changes.

[1] Cf. Frankemölle, 64, "The address is not primarily the signal of the opening of a new main part, but—rhetorically-pragmatically understood—a heightened turning to the audience, since the addressees need comfort and solidarity (5:9)."

[2] Cf. on this, the discussion on 2:11.

[3] That is already true, in view of the theme of suffering that already has been previously repeatedly spoken about (cf. 1:6, 8; 2:12, 15, 18ff.; 3:9, 13ff.; 4:4), for the concretization of this theme as abuse (cf. 2:12, 15; 3:16; 4:4), further for the contrasting of just and unjust suffering (2:20; 3:17), for suffering for the sake of one's faith commitment (2:19; 3:14), for suffering according to God's will (2:19; 3:14) and also for the interpretation of these events as purification and as πειρασμός (1:6f.). As in 3:14 the sufferers are called blessed, they should rejoice (1:6, 8), and this is justified as in 2:21ff. and 3:18 (cf. also 4:1) with the correspondence to Christ's suffering. The image of God's house is taken up from 2:5; the judgment on unbelievers is already intimated in 2:7f.

4:12

Suffering is now spoken about without any toning down as a "fiery ordeal," and the results from it are indicated, specifically when it is said they must not be "taken aback" by such suffering as if by it something "strange" happened to the Christians. Thereby, it is initially yet again put sharply that this one is dealing with a "testing/temptation." Here, the author first takes up, together with the traditional image of a "fiery ordeal,"[4] his interpretation given in 1:6f., where suffering in prophetic[5] and wisdom[6] tradition is compared with the melting of metal and interpreted as testing and the possibility of purification. The (twice underlined) "astonishment" over undeserved suffering shows, however, that the offence goes deeper. It is not clear to what the ἐν ὑμῖν with the πύρωσις relates: Usually, it is translated "among you"; the parallel to the expression of the "hope that is in you" in 3:15, where the ἐν ὑμῖν likewise stands between the article and substantive, could, however, also be thus understood that now an explicit reference is made to inner distress. In any case, the interpretation of suffering as testing no longer suffices. Further, profounder explanations therefore follow.

4:13

The first is a christological-eschatological explanation that at its core probably goes back to Paul (Phil 3:10f.; cf. 2 Cor 1:5-7; Rom 8:17). The author of 1 Peter develops this explanation in a three-part argument: (a) suffering because of following Christ is the consummation of one's attachment to the suffering Christ; (b) this fellowship with the suffering Christ establishes participation in his glory at his "revelation"—probably his Parousia is meant. Therefore, (c) the Christians can already rejoice now, and that is not just in spite of suffering, but—especially in anticipation of the jubilation of the end time—even because of suffering.[7]

[4] The metaphor of πύρωσις or the comparison with such can also be used for the "crucible" of suffering (Prov 27:21; *Did.* 16:5); cf. the use of the Hebrew equivalent in 1QS 1.17f.; 8.3f., 17f.; 1QH 8.16.

[5] Cf. Jer 9:6; Zech 13:9.

[6] Cf. Ps 66[65]:10; Prov 17:3; Sir 2:5; Wis 3:6, among others.

[7] Cf. Davids, 167: "This anticipated eschatological joy is a theme common to 1 Peter and James (Jas 1:2; 1 Pet 1:6)."

4:14

The following verse repeats this statement, justifies it, and outdoes it at the same time in that those who are abused for the sake of Christ are pronounced blessed. This abuse for the sake of Christ refers to societal discrimination in which "*odi[um] erga nomen Christianorum*"[8] quickly can escalate and suddenly change into a legal proceeding against the Christians; in the same way as suffering "as a Christian" (cited a little later), this "abuse" may indicate a situation such as what Pliny already witnesses to: there is, to be sure, yet no persecution of Christians organized by the state,[9] but membership in the Christian community as such—Pliny speaks about *nomen ipsum* (Plin, *Ep* 10.96.2)—can nevertheless in the case of a notification to the authorities be seen as sufficient basis for a legal proceeding against the Christians—and, in the case of refusing to apostatize, as *obstinatio* and therefore as a basis for the sentence of death (10.96.3).[10] The macarism—now 1 Peter appears to allude to the synoptic tradition[11] after the manner of the Pauline tradition in verse 13—is based on a citation of Isaiah 11:2: "For the Spirit of glory and of God rests on you" (4:14). The presence of this divine Spirit, who according to 3:18 had made alive Christ who was killed "in the flesh," is now promised to these suffering Christians, whereby this is made yet more specific through three redactional changes to the prophetic text:

(a) From the future ἀναπαύσεται witnessed to in all the LXX manuscripts known to us comes the present ἀναπαύεται; thereby the presence of the promised Spirit in suffering is stressed.

(b) Through the addition "on you" (ἐφ' ὑμᾶς), the messianic prophecy is related explicitly to the addressees.

(c) Through the supplement τῆς δόξης—particularly following the reference to the "revelation of his glory" in the previous

[8] Tert, *Apol* 1.4.

[9] Such things first took place from the middle of the third century.

[10] See Introduction, pp. 2ff.

[11] Cf. above all the Beatitude in Matthew 5:11 on the one who is abused for the sake of Christ; cf. further Mark 9:37, 39, 41; Luke 21:12. Goppelt, 298, "Again, as in 2:24f., similar statements are formulated first in a Pauline, then in a synoptic conceptualization"; on the influence of Matthew 5:11f. on 1 Pet 4:13f. cf. R. Metzner, *Rezeption*, 34–38.

verse—an explicit reference to the exaltation of Christ after his suffering is established.[12]

Thus the promise of the presence of God's Spirit is contrasted with the oppressive present experience of suffering, which Spirit for its part is a "pledge" of participation in the divine glory (2 Cor 1:22; cf. Rom 8:23). The Beatitude of those who are suffering is thus the positive counterpart to the introductory summons not to be taken aback about this suffering.

4:15

Once again (cf. 2:20; 3:13), 1 Peter feels compelled to specifically state that none of these promises hold good for a suffering that is earned through evil deeds. The chain of possible offenses (such as murderer, thief, or evildoer) is peculiar. What can the warning not to suffer as a murderer mean? One can consider whether 1 Peter takes up reproaches here "with which life was made difficult for the Christians in the form of defamation and slanderous accusations."[13] It remains unclear what can have been meant by the *hapax legomenon* ἀλλοτριεπίσκοπος.

The primary meaning of the word, which is not found in Greek literature before 1 Peter, appears to be "one who gets involved in other people's things."[14] A parallel in Epictetus (*Diss* 3.22.97) offers an initially enlightening explanation: the philosopher defends the Cynic against the reproach that he pays attention to other people's affairs (τὰ ἀλλότρια) when he observes (ἐπισκοπῇ) human practices. One can well understand the devaluation of "pagan practices" in vice catalogues such as 1 Peter 4:3 in this sense; such reproaches certainly did not contribute to the popularity of Christians, as 1 Peter 4:4 indirectly testifies and as we also know from anti-Christian polemic. However, against this explanation speaks, on the one hand, that 1 Peter would thereby put the criticism of pagan society that he himself represents in series with clearly criminal acts; on the other hand,

[12] As has been shown a number of times already, it is a characteristic of 1 Peter that he connects the concept of δόξα very closely with suffering: as with the suffering Christ (cf. 1:11; 2:21) also for his followers glory follows suffering (1:6f.; 4:13; 5:1, 10).

[13] Brox, 217.

[14] Cf. H. W. Beyer, "ἐπισκέπτομαι," 617–19.

the degree to which this criticism presents the existence of a criminal act analogous to the first members of the series is not apparent. Since, however, on the basis of being part of a series the last point likely is a criminal act, the translation "informer" or "fence" would be considered,[15] without this being able to be really persuasively established. In any case, the putting of the four members in series, beginning with murderer through thief then evildoer to that baffling ἀλλοτριεπίσκοπος seems to show "a descending order of gravity and specificity."[16]

4:16

Verse 16 formulates a positive equivalent: Whoever suffers because they are a Christian should not be ashamed of this. This is one of the oldest references to the designation "Christian"[17] and at the same time the oldest reference for the stigmatization and criminalization that was connected to this designation.[18] This societal exclusion and the legal uncertainty connected with it formed an offense that should not be underestimated (cf. Mark 4:17), which indeed already rings in the "astonishment" of 1 Peter 4:12 and is now alluded to again with the expression of "being ashamed"—an expression that one also finds in the words to followers in the gospels.[19] First Peter places over this the possibility of actively proving oneself precisely in suffering; the identification as a Christian should be simply grasped as a chance to glorify God "in this name."[20]

[15] So for example, Bauer-Aland, 78.

[16] Elliott, 783.

[17] According to Acts 11:26, the Christians were first so designated in Antioch; cf. also Acts 26:28; this foreign designation was very quickly taken over as a self-designation; cf. further outside of 1 Pet 4:16, *Did.* 12:5; *Ign. Eph.* 11.2; *Ign. Rom.* 3.2; *Ign. Pol.* 7.3; Tac, *An* 15.44; Suet, *Caes (Nero)* 16.2; Plin, *Ep* 10.96.1-3; Luc, *Alex* 25.38; Luc, *PergrMort* 11ff. According to E. Peterson, *Christianus*, the ending -ανος points to an origin in a Latin-speaking milieu and in Peterson's opinion goes back to Roman officials (cf. Peterson, especially 69–77).

[18] Cf. Plin, *Ep* 10.96.2; see Introduction, pp. 2ff..

[19] Mark 8:38 par.; Luke 9:26; cf. also the negation, Rom 1:16.

[20] Cf. 1 Pet 2:12; further, 4:11. The notion of glorifying God through one's own suffering is also found in ancient Judaism; the *terminus technicus* for martyrdom in rabbinic literature is *qiddush ha-shem*, "sanctify the name" (cf. on this J. W. van Henten/F. Avemarie, *Martyrdom*, 3.132).

4:17

The reference to judgment serves as a further argument. The absolute τὸ κρίμα can only refer to the final judgment, to which 1 Peter has already referred a number of times (1:17; 2:23; 4:5). In the previous passages this judgment came into view only as a future event, but it is now stressed that it is already beginning (ὁ καιρὸς τοῦ ἄρξασθαι) namely with God's house. Because this statement is related to the statements about suffering through the causal ὅτι, only the suffering that presently affects the Christians can be meant by that beginning judgment on God's house. The notion that judgment begins with God's own people is already found in Ezekiel 9:6 and Jeremiah 25[32]:29. Reiser,[21] it is true, points out correctly that in the prophetic texts, it is about a judgment of annihilation but in 1 Peter a judgment of purification, yet one cannot exclude that 1 Peter has nevertheless taken over this thought of the judgment's beginning at God's holy shrine from the biblical texts, particularly because this thought could be eschatologically sharpened in ancient Judaism in such a way that historical catastrophes could be interpreted as an anticipation of that judgment that still awaits the others; ". . . the Lord first judges Israel for the wrong she has commited, and he shall do the same for all nations."[22] It is intimated, but not discussed in detail, what can be concluded *a minore ad maius* about this judgment that still awaits those who as unbelievers have remained up until now spared from this "fiery ordeal"; it is even more important that the "strangeness" of suffering can be located in terms of salvation history.

4:18

This is justified by a citation from Proverbs 11:31, originally a wisdom sentence that concluded from the recompense on the righ-

[21] M. Reiser, *Eschatolgie*, 175.

[22] *T. Benj.* 10.8f; Engl. trans. H. C. Kee in J. Charlesworth (ed.), *Pseudepigrapha*, vol. 1; cf. *Pss. Sol.* 7 and 10; further *2 Bar.* 13:9-11, "Therefore he did not spare his own sons first, but he tormented them as those he hated, for they had sinned. Therefore they were chastened then so that it could be forgiven them. But now, you people and races, you have become guilty . . ." (English translation A. F. J. Klijn, in J. H. Charlesworth [ed.], *Pseudepigrapha*, vol. 1).

teous the so much greater recompense on the sinner and godless: "Behold, the righteous is paid back on earth, and how much more the godless and sinner!" In that ישלם ("it will be recompensed") is glossed by the Septuagint with μόλις σῴζεται and also supplemented with a ποῦ φανεῖται in the second member, the wisdom sentence can be interpreted as recompense in the final judgment as 1 Peter does here.

4:19

The paragraph is closed with the exhortation that those who suffer according to God's will should commend their souls to God. That is the promise of divine care, as he will yet again explicitly formulate in 5:7; here, however, he does it in a form that brings to mind Jesus' Passion (Luke 23:46; cf. 1 Pet2:23). God is more precisely described as "a faithful creator." This reference to the creation appears unexpectedly, and this even more so because the word "creator" (κτίστης) that is so common to us, which word originated in the language of early Hellenistic Judaism,[23] is only found in this place in the New Testament. If now here—following the judgment—the creation is referred to anew,[24] then this underlines God's superiority to the world, his salutary transcendence. It is not coincidental then that also yet again here the term "soul" is encountered, which term, as shown,[25] describes the human being vis-à-vis God and the addressee of his saving action.

The paragraph shows once again what is important for this document: *In view of the now unvarnished speaking about suffering and the temptations that are caused by it, 1 Peter interprets this present totally from God's future—and in fact from a future that has already dawned both in view of end-time salvation and also in view of final judgment.* Precisely in the negativity of the suffering that is happening the author of 1 Peter will open a positive dimension for his

[23] Cf. Sir 24:8; *Aris. Ep.* 16; 2 Macc 1:24; 7:23; *4 Macc.* 5:25; 11:5; Philo, *Spec.* 1.30 and frequently elsewhere.

[24] The creation was already spoken about in 1:20 in the context of the promise that God's plan of salvation for the creation was already established "before the founding of the world" and therefore also points beyond the emptiness and temporality of the creation.

[25] See above Excursus 4: Soul and Salvation of the Soul in 1 Peter, pp. 87–92.

addressees, as it were open up an experience with the experience, even joy in suffering. Thus the "foreigners" are confirmed as those newly sired by God as "reborn." But if now even this comfort is in a final step after all yet again provided with afterthought-like further description "through doing good" (cf. 2:20; 3:13; 4:15), this conditioning of the promise thus documents anew the other concern of the letter, to connect the promise of salvation in the closest way with the paraenesis.

2. Leadership and Service within the Community 5:1-5

Literature on 1 Peter 5:1-5a: **W. Nauck**, "Probleme des frühchristlichen Amtsverständnisses. I Ptr 5, 2 f," *ZNW* 48 (1957), 200–20.

(5:1) I exhort the elders among you now as a fellow-elder and witness of Christ's sufferings, in whose glory I am also a participant, which glory shall be revealed: (2) pasture God's flock that is given into your charge and watch over it, not because you are forced to, but voluntarily, according to how God does it, not for the sake of disgraceful profit, but willingly, (3) not in that you oppress those assigned to you, but in that you are an example to the flock. (4) Thus you will receive an imperishable crown of glory when the archetype of every office of shepherd[1] will appear. (5a) In the same way you younger ones submit to the elders. (5b) All of you, however, put on humility in your social intercourse with one another, for God "resists the arrogant, but gives grace to the humble."

On the text: **2** There are three short forms of ἐπισκοποῦντες μὴ ἀναγκαστῶς ἀλλὰ ἑκουσίως κατὰ θεόν (thus the text offered by Nestle-Aland[27] according to p^{72} A P Ψ and others; with minor variants also 33): 1. in ℵ* 323 and the Sahidic translation ἐπισκοποῦντες is lacking; 2. in the majority text κατὰ θεόν is lacking; 3. in B and Didymus of Alexandria both ἐπισκοποῦντες and κατὰ θεόν are lacking. Since ἐπισκοποῦντες is witnessed to neither by Vaticanus nor Sinaiticus, it is doubtful whether it belongs in the text (so also Nestle-Aland[25]).

In 5:1-5, the problem of authority within the community, the relationship of the leading "elders" to the members and the obedience

[1] On the basis for this translation, see below on v. 4.

of the "younger ones," is made the subject of a special discussion toward the end of the letter. In this, the "younger ones" are commanded to subordinate themselves to the "elders." This repetition of the catchword ὑποτάσσεσθαι that was already the central catchword for the paraenesis in 2:13–3:7 can easily deceive one into understanding this text only as a type of inner-community continuation of instruction in 2:13–3:7 about obedience and subordination and thus to read it as a further example of 1 Peter's repressive ethic.[2] Such an interpretation, however, does violence to this section and thereby to the whole of 1 Peter. It was indeed characteristic for the instruction in 2:13–3:7—formulated especially in view of the relationship to non-Christian superiors—that here the subordinate would always be spoken to first and that this subordination would be extensively justified theologically. The duties of the superordinate, on the other hand, would virtually not be discussed at all; only in the third instruction does one find—added with ὁμοίως—an afterthought exhortation to the men to considerate behavior (3:7). In view of the probation of Christian life in a hostile surrounding world, the accent of the instruction lay totally on the obedience of the subordinated, on conscious obedience "for the sake of the Lord" (2:13), so that Christian freedom proves itself precisely in this commitment (2:16). The exhortation in 5:1-5 is constructed in a contrasting manner; in its center stand the guidelines for the proper use of power. That should be noticed even more because precisely in the time of the second and third generation from the Pastoral Epistles to Ignatius one may observe the trend to compensate for the power vacuum and the varied turbulences[3] resulting from it (after the [natural or violent] death of the leading persons of the first generation) through the decided strengthening of the hierarchy and so to protect the unity

[2] That is rather typical for Balch's investigation, which never discusses anywhere the special features of this piece of text, but only cites it as a further example of the alleged ethic of subjection in 1 Peter; cf. D. L. Balch, *Wives*, 98: "'Be submissive' might be viewed as the superscript of the whole code (2:13, 18; 3:1, 5; cp. 5:5)."

[3] On the one hand, these turbulences concerned theological questions as can already be seen in the New Testament especially in the extremely sharp polemic against false teachers in Jude, in 2 Peter (2 Peter 2) and also in the letters of the Johannine Apocalypse (Rev 2f.); on the other hand, it concerned questions about the way of life and ethics (cf. Matt 7:15ff.; 24:11f.; 2 Tim 3:1-5).

of the church against centrifugal forces. In view of the open power struggle within the community in Corinth, *1 Clement* (only a little younger than 1 Peter) traces the church hierarchy back through the apostles and Christ directly to God (*1 Clem.* 42:1-5); besides this the office bearers were additionally legitimated through the concept of an apostolic succession (44:1f.). Accordingly, the letter demands, "subordinate yourselves to the elders/presbyters" (57:1) and adds to it as a principle, as it were, the command, "μάθετε ὑποτάσσεσθαι" ("learn to subordinate yourselves!") (57:2). This development was probably unavoidable; 1 Peter also takes part in it, however in contrast to the other early Christian writings with a noticeable sensibility for the dangers of power[4] and the necessity of a theological orientation for those who lead.

5:1

Yet again as in 2:11 a paragraph begins with παρακαλῶ. This as well is not a tone of command; with "fellow-elder," the author places himself on the same level as the "elders" he addresses, whereby he presumably constructed the term συμπρεσβύτερος himself.[5] Possibly the real author here falls out of his fiction of being the apostle and speaks as that which he is, as a Christian presbyter.[6] However it may be—he at any rate gives up the use of (which was possible in the authorship fiction) apostolic authority and puts himself on an equal footing with his addressees. "It is clear, then, that this is an inclusive term that, rather than stressing his authority, stresses his empathy with the elders in their task."[7] This can therefore be read as an example of "humility," which is the goal of the whole exhortation (5:5b; cf. 5:6). At the same time, the author lets one understand that he also holds a church office.[8]

[4] This sensibility also already shows itself in the slave-paraenesis; see above on 2:18ff.

[5] The author of 1 Peter loves the construction of such words with συν- (3:7; 5:13), which terms underline solidarity; cf. Elliott, 816, "The unique noun *sympresbyteros* . . . occurs nowhere else in Greek literature and represents another coinage by the author."

[6] On this title and its meaning in the Greco-Roman and Jewish world around them cf. R. A. Campbell, *Elders*.

[7] Davids, 176.

[8] P. Stuhlmacher, *Theologie*, 79.

In the second place, he claims that he himself is a witness of the Christ's sufferings. If one wishes to understand this in the sense of an eyewitness of the Passion, then one not only stands before the historical difficulty that Peter, according to the witness of all the gospels, was precisely not present at the Passion, but one also has to deal with the yet greater argumentative problem that the reason for his lack of being an eyewitness—the denial and flight of the disciple—is just not apt to strengthen his authority. A lot speaks for understanding μάρτυς here, not in the sense of the person being an eyewitness of the Passion, but as the person[9] who has "fellowship with Christ's suffering," (4:13) he is a witness by his participation in Christ's fate. As such Peter has authority—particularly if the letter as a pseudepigraphon (as it apparently is) looks back at the martyrdom of the apostle. Such an interpretation of μάρτυς would also fit better with the explication introducted with ὁ καί, according to which the witness of Christ's suffering is at the same time a "participant" in his future glory, for the connection between the suffering *which one suffers* in following and the glory *which is granted or promised as a consequence* is indeed explicitly established several times in the letter, both in relation to Christ himself (1:11, 21) and also in relation to his followers (4:14f.; cf. 2:19). The πρεσβύτεροι addressed should "pasture" God's flock; they are, therefore, people in leadership positions. As such they appear especially frequently in Acts.[10] In contrast to the Pastoral Epistles,[11] they are the only "office bearers" that are named explicitly in 1 Peter.[12] Their activity is, however, also described in 5:2 as ἐπισκοπεῖν, which points to the fact that the differentiation of offices only begins at this time.[13]

[9] Cf. H. Stratmann, "μάρτυς," 499, "a personal participation, namely in Christ's suffering"; similarly W. Michaelis, "πάσχω," 934; H. v. Campenhausen, *Idee*, 63–65; Brox, 229f.

[10] Acts 11:30; 14:23; 15:2, 4, 6, 22f.; 16:4; 20:17; 21:18.

[11] In 1 Tim 5:17-23, they are named besides bishops (3:1-7) and deacons (3:8-13). Just as the bishops (3:5), they have leadership functions, whereby in particular they take pains over "word and teaching" (5:17).

[12] One could at most ask whether the "shepherd" and "bishop" Christ (2:25) implicitly alludes to church offices.

[13] In Titus, bishops and presbyters still appear to fall into one category (cf. Titus 1:5 with 1:7); it is similar in Acts (cf. Acts 20:17 with 20:28).

5:2

The assurance of the unity of the sender with the elders he addresses in verse 1 forms the introduction to the summons to pasture God's flock. The image of pasturing as an ecclesiological metaphor is just as traditional as that of the flock.[14] The same is true for the motif of the shepherd (cf. Ps 23[22]). In 1 Peter, Christ has already been portrayed in 2:25 as the shepherd of souls, to whose example we are then also again referred in verse 4. But, before this, what it means to pasture God's flock is further defined through three antitheses: The first of these requires that this community leadership be carried out not because it is forced, but rather because it is done willingly. Apparently even then, the qualified people were not always those who were also prepared to take the office;[15] moreover, the holder of a leadership position may have been more exposed during measures against the Christians and thereby more endangered. The reference to the fact that such a willing carrying out of the office accords with God (κατὰ θεόν) sounds like an afterthought (and was probably therefore also left out of the majority text); but it may have originally belonged to the text and—in an allusion to the description of the community in the same verse as *God's* flock—it makes clear that it is God's business that one makes oneself available through service in the community.[16] The summons to take up a leading duty in this flock consequently receives increased emphasis through the double reference to God. In the second antithesis, the emphasis shifts to the possibility of the misuse of the office. Because the bearer of a leadership office in the community was evidently entitled to a

[14] In the Old Testament cf Jer 23:1ff.; Ezek 34:2ff.; Zech 11:16f.; Ps 79[78]:13; in Qumran CD 13.7-12 and 1QS 6.12, 20; the clearest parallel in the New Testament is the triple summons of the resurrected Jesus to Peter in John 21:15-17, βόσκε or ποίμαινε τὰ πρόβατά μου; cf. further Acts 20:28 or the application of the parable of the lost sheep (Matt 18:12-14) to the community situation. In the Old Testament, this image belongs to the concept of God's people (cf. Ch. Wolff, "Christ," 336).

[15] From a later time, the example of Augustine could be named, who initially took up his bishop's office in the Hippo Regius most unwillingly.

[16] Cf. U. Heckel, *Hirtenamt*, 53, "The genitive τοῦ θεοῦ points to God as the owner to whom the presbyters are responsible and on whose will they should orient themselves."

certain form of compensation,[17] there was always the danger that these offices would be taken on for the sake of material advantage and amenities,[18] a problem that the Pastoral Epistles (1 Tim 3:3, 8; Titus 1:7) and the *Didache* (15:1) also know and warn about. First Peter antithetically contrasts to this "disgraceful profit" the command that the motivation for taking on such an office should come from within.

5:3

Likewise, the third pair of contrasts also concerns the danger of the misuse of office, whereby it is now not about money, but about power. The leadership of a church community indeed also grants one power over others, as the following summons of the "younger ones" to subordination (5:5a) shows. The exercise of such power, however, is, according to 1 Peter, only justified when it is oriented on Christ. Through the use of the catchword κατακυριεύειν for the misuse of power, the formulation reminds one of a word of Jesus in the synoptics,[19] in which, with reference to his own sacrifice of his life interpreted as "service," Jesus, with respect to the relationship of Christians with one another, expressly rejects the usual form of ruling as subjugation and put serving in its place.[20] "Subjugation"[21] here is contrasted with leadership behavior that—itself influenced by Christ—now for its part seeks to influence the "flock" through the exemplariness of its own behavior (τύποι γινόμενοι τοῦ ποιμνίου) and so to lead. "This concept of leadership is common in the NT. Jesus often presented himself as an example (Matt 10:24-25; Mark 10:42-45; Luke 6:40; John

[17] Paul already assumes it as self-evident (1 Cor 9:9ff.; cf. also Matt 10:10 par.), even if the apostle himself often consciously gave up this right (cf. 2 Cor 11:8; Phil 4:10).

[18] Cf. the description in Lucian (*PergrMort* 11–13), according to which Peregrinus, who for a while joined the Christians and advanced to be a leading figure among them, made a very considerable income as a Christian "prophet, cult-leader, Master of the Synagogue."

[19] Mark 10:42 par.; the catchword κατακυριεύειν is found outside of Mark 10:42 par. Matt 20:25 only in Acts 19:16 and 1 Pet 5:3.

[20] The objective negation οὐχ that is used in Mark 10:43 underlines that this possibility is excluded.

[21] According to Bauer-Aland, 838, κατακυριεύειν means, "1. become master, overpower, subjugate, suppress . . . 2. be master, rule (brutally)."

13:16; 15:20). Paul could write, 'Walk according to the example you had in us' (Phil 3:17) and 'We gave an example to you so that you might imitate us' (2 Thess 3:9), or even 'Be imitators of me, as I am of Christ' (1 Cor 11:1; cf. Acts 20:35)."[22] The term κλῆρος (literally "lot, share"; from this our word "clergy") may, on the basis of the parallel to the ποίμνιον in verse 2, designate the part of the community assigned to each of the "elders."

5:4

The description of Christ as ἀρχιποιμήν (5:4) stresses the orientation of the community leadership on Christ. The word is found neither in the LXX nor the rest of the New Testament; the usual translation of ἀρχιποιμήν with "chief shepherd"[23] is admittedly possible,[24] but in this context 1 Peter stresses too one-sidedly the power characteristic and does not make it clear that the term ἀρχή (Latin *principium*) contains not only the thought of rulership but also and even in the first place that of an influencing/molding origin, therefore a normative moment. Christ as ἀρχιποιμήν is more than just the "chief" of all shepherds; as the "good shepherd," who offered himself for his sheep (1 Pet 2:21-25; John 10:11ff.; cf. 21:16; Heb 13:20), he is the epitome, "archetype" of every office of shepherd as of an alternative "serving" way of dealing with the power entrusted to one over other people.[25]

The promise of glory also holds true for such an administration of office oriented on the "archetype" Christ. The motif of δόξα as an expression for the award that will be granted to those at the Parousia who have followed Christ in suffering and therefore will be glorified as Christ himself (1:11, 21; 4:13) plays a decisive role in the whole letter (1:7; 4:13f.; 5:1, 10). Here it is strength-

[22] Davids, 181.

[23] Bauer-Aland, 226.

[24] The word is found only in 2 Kgs 3:4 S and in T. 12 Patr., Judg 8.1, there for the leading shepherd. That is possibly also the meaning of the title in a wood tablet from the period of the Caesars that was placed around the throat of a mummy for identification (cf. A. Deissmann, *Licht*, 77–79; Illustration 9f., p. 78).

[25] The discussion of the true shepherd in contrast to the "hired servant" in John 10:1-18 also says something similar; one also finds the shepherd motif in Heb 13:20 with a soteriological focusing.

ened through the metaphor of a garland or crown,[26] which alludes to a sport or military awards ceremony and is moreover anew reminiscent of the Pauline motif of Christian life as a fight,[27] perhaps not coincidentally precisely in the specially endangered sphere of power. The correspondence to a sport or military awards ceremony is, at the same time, surpassed in that the crown is described as "unfading." This also takes up a Pauline image (cf. 1 Cor 9:25), but at the same time establishes a relationship to the "unfading inheritance" in 1:4 and thus underlines with reference to the soteriology of the first main part that even a Christian's dealing with power is not simply a "worldly" affair, but—precisely because in dealing with God's "flock," it deals with God's people—also has an effect on salvation.

5:5a

Following this exhortation to the elders—introduced as in 3:7 with ὁμοίως—is the corresponding terse summons to the younger ones to subordination toward the "elders"(5:5a). Therefore, under the stated conditions there is also definitely a hierarchy in the Christian community. Who are these two groups? Because the πρεσβύτεροι in 5:1 were the office holders and the verses that lie between are about this office, a sudden change in meaning to those who are "elders" only because of their age is not persuasive. If, however, the "elders" are the community leaders, who, then, are the "younger ones?" Possibly this refers to a special group, whereby, then, one would think above all on the newly baptized.[28] But such an interpretation strikes one as forced: if up to now the passage is about the relationship of the πρεσβύτεροι to the whole "flock of God," why then should only the newly baptized be picked out when it comes to subordination? But if the exhortation concerns everyone who is not a community leader, why then the designation "younger ones"? A possible explanation could be that here in 1 Peter a piece of tradition has been taken over, which traditional piece commanded the subordination of the younger

[26] Cf. Jas 1:12; Rev 2:10; 3:11 and frequently; *T. Benj.* 4.1; *Ascen. Isa.* 7.22; 8.26 and frequently.

[27] Cf. especially 1 Cor 9:24f.; 2 Cor 10:3ff.; further Phil 3:14; 1 Thess 5:8; Rom 13:12; Eph 6:10-17; 1 Tim 6:12 and elsewhere.

[28] J. H. Elliott, *Ministry*, 379ff.; Elliott, 838, "recent convert."

to the elders and to which a special meaning was given through the contextual reference to the presbyters without one being able to identify the younger with a special group.[29] This is possibly favored through the fact that the designation "elder" was a designation of honor in antiquity and designated a preeminence not necessarily dependent upon biological age.[30] Thus the direction to the younger should be related complementarily to the rest of the Christians[31] who are to show special respect for their office holders and to obey them; one can also already read something similar in Paul (cf. 1 Thess 5:12f.; 1 Cor 16:16).

It is important, precisely here where the summons to subordination is now also taken into the sphere of the Christian community, to at the same time see the differences that were already mentioned: If in 2:18–3:7, the whole weight lay on the instruction to subordination, then the accent here lies clearly on the *direction about the proper exercise of the power entrusted to them and the warning against the misuse of authority*.[32] Therefore, for 1 Peter the "being different" of the Christian definitely expresses itself in an ethic that decidedly differentiates itself from the commonly practiced exercise of power; the use of power must let itself be evaluated by the standard that holds good in general for the relationship of Christians to one another. In 4:8-11, this was characterized as love and service; now—as already in 3:8—it is described as ταπεινοφροσύνη.

[29] So Brox, 234f.

[30] This is also true for the term πρεσβύτεροι as the designation for the lay aristocracy (besides the representatives of the high priestly families, the ἀρχιερεῖς) in the synoptic Passion narrative.

[31] Cf. Windisch, 79; Goppelt, 331. The parallel in *1 Clement*, which was composed a little later, is worth noting, where the turmoil in the Christian community was also condemned, among other things, as an uprising of the νέοι against the πρεσβύτεροι (3:3), and subordination to the πρεσβύτεροι (as office holders) is commanded (57:1).

[32] It also fits with this that the author of the letter, who in this exhortation alone refers to himself, does not call on his authority as an apostle (whatever may be held about the right to this) but speaks "as a fellow-elder and witness of Christ's suffering," that is, as one who is co-responsible and a fellow sufferer.

5:5b

The half verse 5b in the summons to all speaks twice of ταπεινοφροσύνη or ταπεινός in order to now characterize "humility" as the behavior that accords with God's will in dealing with power. Such ταπεινοφροσύνη, literally "a mind directed to low things," "self-moderation (with respect to needs)," "self-denigration," is an emotive word in a time in which the autonomy of the individual is the ideal. From this perspective, ταπεινοφροσύνη is quickly equated with crawling self-reduction, whether it be from religious compulsiveness, whether from hypocrisy, which in reality wishes the opposite, similar to what Nietzsche imputed to the Christian ethos: "Whoever humbles themselves wishes to be exalted."[33] Such an understanding does not do justice to the biblical image of humanity that consistently understands human beings from their commitment to God[34] and sees the existential recognition of this commitment as the human vocation, which vocation does not lessen human dignity but above all establishes it by means of the relationship to God.

Excursus 10: "Humility"/ταπεινοφροσύνη

One already finds criticism of the attitude of ταπεινοφροσύνη in antiquity. Thus the Stoic Epictetus condemns this as a submissive mentality that stems from a false orientation of being[35] and the Middle Platonist Plutarch had reproached the false relationship to God that is determined by fear (δεισιδαιμονία, Latin *superstitio*) in that it "degrades" people and "crushes" them and therefore was even worse than the indifference of godlessness.[36] A few decades later, this is one of the points about which Celsus directly attacks Christianity: ". . . the humble man humiliates

[33] Thus in a derisive correction of Jesus' words (F. Nietzsche, "Menschliches," 1.87, "Lucas 18, 14 verbessert").

[34] Cf. W. Zimmerli, *Menschenbild*, 16, "The Old Testament knows the human in their [*sic*] absolute original being only as the human called into being by the one God. It does not know anything about a human who can be understood apart from this God." Accordingly, "happiness [is] . . . the participation of the human in God's praise" (H. Spieckermann, *Kosmos*, 73).

[35] Epict, *Diss* 3.24.56.

[36] Plut, *Superst* 165B.

himself in a disgraceful and undignified manner, throwing himself headlong to the ground upon his knees, clothing himself in a beggar's rags, and heaping dust upon himself."[37] The assumption of this criticism is an image of humanity the ideal of which is self-improvement through outdoing the other, as was classically formulated in the Homeric saying, "to always be the best and surpassing all others."[38] It is true that inappropriate arrogance and human presumptuousness, for instance, toward the gods (ὕβρις, Latin *superbia*) was also censured, but the opposite extreme of self-deprecation was likewise regarded as unworthy of a free person and was scorned as groveling.

The theonomous image of humanity in the Bible, by way of contrast, does not see in bowing to God's power the self-degrading of the person; rather, this is the place that is assigned to the believer toward God, who resists arrogance but gives grace to the humble and exalts them through his "mighty hand," as the following explicitly stresses (5:5b, 6); as God's slaves Christians are actually free (2:16). Similarly in Mary's *Magnificat*, God is praised as the one who has scattered the proud in the intents of their hearts and overthrown the powerful from their thrones, but has exalted the low (ταπεινούς) (Luke 1:52)—whereby two things are intended by "high" and "low," the state but also the behavior, as the contrasting of the low to both the powerful and the "proud in their hearts' intention" shows. Thereby, it is a special point of the New Testament that the command of humility is based in Christ's self-degrading on our behalf, the Christ who described himself as πραῢς καὶ ταπεινὸς τῇ καρδίᾳ, as "gentle and humble in heart" (Matt 11:29). The Philippian hymn (Phil 2:6ff.) accordingly expresses the whole coming of Jesus Christ as self-abasement with the catchword ἐταπείνωσεν ἑαυτόν (Phil 2:8). Therefore, being a Christian concretizes itself for Paul in that one in his total behavior places himself under this new reality (Phil 2:5), which shows itself precisely in that one does not look on his or her own things, but on what serves the other (Phil 2:4). A little later (96 C.E.) *1 Clement* will describe in this sense the ideal picture of the

[37] Orig, *Cels* 6.15 (English translation H. Chadwick). According to Celsus, this is about a misunderstanding of Plato on the part of the Christians.

[38] Hom, *Il* 6.208; 11.784; on the meaning of this "agonistic life-ideal" (H.-I. Marrou, *Erziehung*, 26) for the image of humanity and education in the Hellenistic world cf. Marrou., 26f.

life of the Christian community by means of the programmatic renunciation of power: "Rather be subjugated than subjugate others";[39] precisely in view of the question of power, he describes humility as the epitome of behavior oriented on Christ himself: "For Christ belongs to the humble [ταπεινοφρονοῦντες], not to those who exalt themselves over his flock. The scepter of God's majesty, the Lord Jesus Christ, did not come in a self-glorifying and proud boasting, although he could have done so, but humble [ταπεινοφρονῶν] . . ." (*1 Clem.* 16:1f.). From there it is no longer far to the ideal of humility—not as servile submissiveness, but as *the response of the believers to God's turning toward them in his Son, which then on their part "becomes the content of dealings among people."*[40] Accordingly one finds the principle in the gospels, "Everyone who exalts themselves will be degraded, and whoever degrades themselves will be exalted" (Luke 14:11; 18:14; Matt 23:12), a principle that in Luke has its point in giving to those who have nothing with which to repay (Luke 14:13f.), in Matthew it is in the mutual service that is founded through Christ (Matt 23:11; cf. 20:25-28).

Instructions about humility in 1 Peter should be interpreted against this background: In 5bα, the previous regulation of power relationships is yet again surpassed through the command to all to put on humility in their relationship to one another as a slave puts on his loincloth,[41] therefore renouncing attempts to impress and attempts at intimidation, one is to prepare oneself for a service to the "brothers and sisters" oriented on Christ and thus to allow φιλαδελφία (1:22; cf. 2:17; 4:8ff.) to become reality. The graphic expression used for this in 1 Peter, "tie in a knot around you" (thus the imperative ἐγκομβώσασθε literally), underlines that such a lived alternative to "natural" self-assertion requires effort, work on one's self. Christian asceticism (above all in monasticism) has made this aspect of *humilitas* as a life attitude its own and thereby attempted to live an alternative concept to the societal power structures, even to a church reproducing these structures, which asceticism has placed hierarchal thinking more fundamentally in

[39] *1 Clem.* 2:1, ὑποτασσόμενοι μᾶλλον ἢ ὑποτάσσοντες.

[40] W. Grundmann, "ταπεινός κτλ.," 23.

[41] Grundmann, 24. A content parallel to this would be John 13:4 (cf. Luke 12:37).

question than any rebellion (which is itself captive to the paradigm of power).

The summons to mutual humility in 5bβ is justified by means of the reference to God, who resists arrogance, but gives grace to the humble. This underlines yet again that the *command of humility has its place in a relationship to God*, to the God who does not simply confirm hierarchy based upon the will to power and the ability of self-assertion, but can also according to his own standards thwart these. The author of 1 Peter refers to this power-critical aspect of the biblical God (cf. 1 Sam 2:4-8; *Aris. Ep.* 263; Luke 1:51-53) in the version of Proverbs 3:34 because thereby he can bring in the catchword "grace" (that has been important in the whole letter [cf. 1:10, 13; 3:7; 4:10; 5:10]) precisely also for the theological redefinition of the situation of suffering (cf. 2:19f.; 5:12). The following verses will then make explicit reference to the situation of suffering and at the same time make clear with the catchword "exaltation" what 1 Peter means in terms of content by this grace.

The transition shows yet again the peculiarity of this writing that has hardly any abrupt new departure of thought but favors connections and sliding transitions: It is true that the following paragraph 5:6-11—indicated through the resuming οὖν[42]—forms a concise *peroratio* in which the author of 1 Peter once again in a compressed manner summarizes and focuses the most important things.[43] But even this conclusion is directly connected with what precedes it by means of taking up the catchword of humiliation.

[42] Against Brox, 236, who connects vv. 6f. to what goes before.

[43] Cf. G. Ueding, *Einführung*, 220, "The peroration forms the concluding part of the speech or speech section and has a double purpose: on the one hand, it should summarize the facts and viewpoints of the speech in order to imprint them upon the memory of the listener, and, on the other hand, it should 'focus' the train of thought of the speech in 'well put sentences' in order by means of the emotional effect to totally win the listener for the point of view taken." This is true in the first instance for oral speech, but nevertheless does not remain limited to it. "In its function as the concluding part, the peroration was transferred to other written and oral rhetorical genre such as letters, documents, sermons, literary texts, essays" (I. Männlein-Robert, "Peroratio," 778).

3. Final Exhortation and Comfort 5:6-11

(i) The Closing Exhortation 5:6-9

(6) So now humble yourselves under the powerful hand of God so that he may exalt you in his time, (7) whereby you throw all your concerns on him, for you mean a lot to him. (8) Be sober, watch; your adversary the devil goes around like a roaring lion and seeks that he may devour someone. (9) Resist him firmly in faith and know that similar suffering comes upon your brothers and sisters in the world.

5:6

The catchword of self-abasement taken over from the previous verse is now picked up in another manner, and now it is no longer about the renunciation of oppression in interpersonal (more exactly, inner-community) intercourse but about humility toward God. Thereby—as the sequel in verses 7-9 shows—once again the hard-pressed situation of the believers is spoken to, which situation should be accepted from God's hand. When it is demanded that the believers should "humble" themselves under this hand, it is also about "submitting" oneself to that decreed by God. As a result, probably in a continuation of the statement about God's action in verse 5b, the "powerful hand" of God is expressly spoken about. First Peter (as does the whole biblical tradition) associates with God's power and control—explicitly praised in both doxologies (1 Pet 4:11; 5:11)—not subjugation but rescue;[1] *divine power [Macht] differentiates itself from human highhandedness [Eigenmacht] in that it is for the benefit of the powerless [Ohnmächtige].*[2] It does

[1] Cf. Davids, 186: "It was this 'hand' that delivered Israel from Egypt (e.g., Exod 3:19; 6:1; 13:3, 9, 14, 16; Deut 9:26, 29; 26:8; Jer 21:5; Ezek 20:33-34), and it was this hand that was behind his works in the NT (Luke 1:66; Acts 4:28, 30; 11:21; 13:11) . . . ." That those who suffer should entrust their souls to the "faithful creator" has already been spoken about in 1 Peter in 4:19.

[2] With this as well the author of 1 Peter takes up an aspect of the Old Testament picture of God. In that God turns the world's hierarchy that is fixed through force upside down, he becomes a refuge for those who are themselves weak and oppressed (cf. 1 Sam 2:3-8).

this in that, as stressed in the previous verse, it resists destructive human highhandedness; at the same time, it is a ground for hope for those presently humiliated, because God "in his own time"—probably at the Parousia—will exalt them.

5:7

This is also stressed by the continuation, which is already shown to be the explication of verse 6 by the participial construction. Subordination under God's "mighty hand" makes it possible to "throw off" every concern onto this God, as is dramatically stated, and so to "dispose" of one's own burden. One frequently finds this word of encouragement in the New Testament (cf. Matt 6:25-34; Phil 4:6); 1 Peter has masterfully compressed it into an aphorism—and this by taking up biblical language Psalm 55[54]:23, whereby the Psalm's promise is further strengthened by means of the reference to God's care that reminds one of Matthew 6:26, 28: μέλει περὶ ὑμῶν stresses that the believers are a heart's concern of this mighty God, that he cares about and for them.

5:8

In verses 5:8f., the hard-pressed situation of the believers is addressed yet more explicitly than in the previous verses. It is introduced with the double summons: "be sober" and "watch." One finds the metaphor of watching frequently in the New Testament,[3] that of soberness appears occasionally; the closest parallel to 1 Peter 5:8 is 1 Thessalonians 5:6, in which the summons to watch and be sober likewise stands in parallel. The meaning of the doubled summons is revealed from their opposite: Whoever is drunk or sleeps has lost reference to reality, cannot perceive threatening danger, and has forfeited the ability to judge

[3] The summons to watchfulness is found on the one hand in the eschatological parables (Mark 13:33-35 par.; Luke 12:37; 21:34-36; Rev 3:2f.), on the other in the distress of the Passion (Mark 14:38 par.) or of the end time (Rev 16:15). In Paul "to wake" has become a synonym for an orientation of life on God (1 Cor 16:13; cf. Col 4:2); whereby the eschatological aspect particularly explicitly resonates (1 Thess 5:6). Later "watchfulness" against false teachers is added (Acts 20:31).

with respect to phenomena; such a one takes the imaginary at face value, is easy to deceive, and therefore is also helpless and vulnerable. Just this is transferred to an attitude that allows itself to be so taken captive by the reality lying before its eyes that it loses God from view and therefore does not reckon with him anymore in the world, finally fading him out. Watching and being sober, by way of contrast, characterize an attitude that does not let itself be deterred by the apparent evidence of what lies before its eyes from seeing the present in the light of God's future and living accordingly.

This exhortation toward soberness and watchfulness is impressively justified through the reference to the deadly threat by the devil, who as the beast of prey *par excellence*, the hunting (under the protection of night and therefore not visible?) lion, who attacks and devours the inattentive. What one should observe is that here—and only here—the devil is spoken about in 1 Peter. That fits the concern of the *peroratio* to yet again imprint the most important things on the hearer/reader through heightened linguistic emphasis. The devil is absolutely the enemy of the believers; here he is even explicitly described as "your adversary" with a New Testament *hapax legomenon*.[4] On the other hand, one should observe that everything previously addressed with respect to evil, whether it be the hostility from outside or the threat inside (of the community or the individual), was concretely named as desire, sin, doing evil, cunning, hypocrisy, and the like, and thus did not need a reference to the personification of evil. Nor was the devil used to demonize the opponents; on the contrary, they are to be respected along with all people (2:17). This reserve toward the devil corresponds in essence to the evidence of the whole Bible, where the devil, in contrast to what one commonly associates with the devil,[5] does not serve as the explanation of evil *per se* through a single, counter-divine principle.

[4] ἀντίδικος is actually the opposing party in a lawsuit (cf. Matt 5:25 par.; Luke 12:58); here there is probably an allusion to the accuser in Job 1:6ff.; whereby it may already have widened the spectrum of meaning of ἀντίδικος to any adversary at all (cf. Bauer-Aland, 147). As a description for the devil, it only occurs here in biblical literature.

[5] Cf. on this R. Feldmeier, "Widersacher"; on the common conception of the devil as a type of evil anti-god cf. the iconographic testimony Feldmeier, 75f.; on the criticism of this Feldmeier, 62f.

Excursus 11: Devil/Satan

In the Old Testament, the devil/Satan hardly plays a part. *The majority and the most important writings* (Pentateuch, Psalms, Prophets[6]) *do not know about him*. One first encounters "Satan" in the framework story of Job (1:6-12; 2:1-7). There he is still a part of the divine court, so to speak a heavenly prosecutor, who, however, with his tempterlike questions and power over death and illness is already chiefly responsible for the dark sides of reality. That fostered his gradual removal from God's sphere of activity. In this respect, the first text in which the "Satan" is clearly encountered as an independent evil-acting figure is revealing. It is the narrative of David's census from the two different versions that have been handed down to us, an older in 2 Samuel 24:1, a younger in 1 Chronicles 21:1:

2 Samuel 24:1	1 Chronicles 21:1
Again the *anger* of the Lord was kindled against Israel, and he incited David against them, saying, "Go, count the people of Israel and Judah." (NRSV)	*Satan* stood up against Israel, and incited David to count the people of Israel. (NRSV)

In the later account of the narrative in the place of God, more exactly, his anger,[7] Satan enters as the cause of the census. One finds a similar process in Jubilees, in which God's attack on Moses (Exod 4:24) is replaced by an attack of Mastema (*Jub.* 48.2). Evidently, the later writings are making an effort to release God himself from the responsibility for evil. The creation of a concept of Satan was perhaps also promoted through the dualism of the Persian religion, which distinguishes between a good

[6] The single exception: Zech 3:1f.

[7] This is a distinction that does not totally identify this action with God.

and an evil god. In any case, in early Judaism a devil figure was established under a variety of names such as "Satan/Mastema," "Beelzebul," "Belial/Beliar," "Sammael," and soon, which figure one encounters in numerous writings as God's opponent—which in some Qumran writings goes as far as a proper dualism—who is of course put in place by God as creator (cf. 1QS 3.13-4.18) and so also eschatologically limited (cf. 1QS 4.18-26). Even in this extreme case, one therefore endeavored to subordinate to biblical monotheism the inherent tendency to dualism of the concept of the devil.

Through the temptation narrative at the beginning of the Synoptics, it is made clear that conflict with evil embodied in Satan determines Jesus' appearance right from the beginning (Mark 1:13; Matt 4:1-11; Luke 4:1-13). However, the devil plays only a subordinate role in the rest of the narrative. It is true that Jesus can occasionally make reference to Satan's activity (Mark 4:15; Matt 13:39; Luke 8:12; 10:18; 13:16; 22:31), but for the most part the destructive power is individually named as sin, sickness, possession, impenitence, and so on, without being referred to the form of an anti-divine opponent. The findings of the epistolary literature are similar: Without exception, they assume the existence of the devil/Satan, for the most part to warn about the endangering of believers (1 Cor 7:5; 2 Cor 2:11; 2 Thess 2:9; Eph 4:27; 1 Tim 3:6f.; Jas 4:7; 1 Pet 5:8), occasionally also to characterize the sphere outside the Christian community (1 Cor 5:5; 1 Tim 1:20; 5:15; 2 Tim 2:26), or generally to interpret hostile experiences of the community or of an individual (2 Cor 12:7; 1 Thess 2:18; 1 John 3:8-10). Yet also here the importance of the devil is a limited one. In Romans, for example, which has so much to say about the problem of sin and evil in the world, the single reference to Satan consists in the comforting assurance in the letter closing that "the God of peace will shortly crush Satan under your feet" (Rom 16:20; cf. Heb 2:14).

When one takes a closer look yet, something more attracts one's attention with respect to the devil/Satan: He has—in contrast to God—no personal name. The names that we know on the contrary characterize their bearer as a personification of a certain effect: Satan means "accuser," devil (διάβολος) "slanderer," Belial "malice" or "ruin," and the rabbinical Sammael is presumably to be translated by "poison principle."[8] Thus as the devil lacks a personal name,[9] he also lacks a history and individuality. Only speculation has spun a personal history for the devil out of Ezekiel 28:11-19, the judgment word over the King of Tyre.[10] Such prerequisites of a personal being one does not find in the Bible. As also seen in the demons lacking names, the naming of God's opponent with a designation of function indicates that this opponent *does not have a personality in the true sense, but is only a "functionary," a personification of a mode of operation of evil.*

This opponent concretely aims at *the destruction of the human being's relationship to the one God.* On the one hand, that can consist in that he, for instance, thwarts Paul's plans or also plagues him with sickness.[11] In contrast to the demons, he himself scarcely appears as a destructive spirit who destroys the relationship with the self; quite the contrary: he intensifies the person's relating to him or herself (through intimidation just as through enticement). Even when one cannot always totally unequivocally separate the action of the devil and that of demons from one another,[12] one can yet describe the difference between devils and demons as in effect that *the demons are after the destruction of the relationship to the self and the world while the devil is out to destroy the relationship to God.* Put another way, the possessed is no longer at home in him or herself, while the one seduced by the devil is only at home with him

not clear. please fix.

[8] The name is a combination of the Aramaic "*samma*" (poison) with the theophoric element *el*.

[9] Only Beelzebul is something like a proper name, namely the Aramaized form of the originally Philistine divinity Baal Zebul = "Lord of the heavenly dwelling." The name is transcribed by 2 Kgs 1:2, 6 S as Βεελζεβούβ = "Lord of the flies"—whether because of carelessness or on purpose one cannot say for certain; one occasionally encounters this in the New Testament as the devil-like "Lord of the demons" (Mark 3:22; Matt 12:24; Luke 11:15).

[10] Cf. Tert, *Marc* 2.10.

[11] 2 Cor 12:7; however in this case, it is typically enough only an angel of Satan.

[12] Luke 22:3 appears to imply a type of "possession" by the devil in the explanation of Judas' betrayal; cf. also the renarration of Gen 3 in the *Apoc. Mos.* 15-30, where the human being, who allows himself to be "inspired" by the devil, has also lost himself along with the relationship to God. However, even these types of "possession" are to be clearly differentiated from the pathological destruction of the relationship to one's self and the world that is caused by demons.

or herself. The self-relationship of the person that is essential for life and in no way reprehensible in itself thus becomes absolutized and displaces the relationship to God. Indeed, it seems the more the relationship to the one God becomes the basis for the orientation of being, the more clearly the action of the opposing power is also experienced. One can observe this very nicely in the temptation narrative at the beginning of Jesus' activity (Matt 4:1-11/Luke 4:1-13), the one NT story in which the devil appears as a person and speaks (to the extent that he claims worship for himself). His whole action is directed at only a single goal, to detach Jesus from his connection to God and to fixate him on himself. The devil wants a half-god, who is self-sufficient in his fullness of power (and precisely so serves him); he wants a son without a father, a Son of God without God.

In 1 Peter as well, the devil does not explain the origin of evil mythologically as a type of negative anti-God, but he "embodies" evil as a power having an effect on the personal center, which seeks to destroy the orientation of the believers on God. The reference to the devil thus stresses that a calculated will, a destructive energy, stands behind the Christians' afflictions, which will or energy is only here in the New Testament designated as the "adversary" of the believers.[13]

It is true that the lion belongs to the traditional metaphors for enemies,[14] however the comparison lion—Satan is only explicitly[15] found in the biblical writings in 1 Peter 5:8. The motif appears, however, to already be preformed in Judaism, as *Joseph and Aseneth* 12.9-11 shows, where the anti-divine power that persecutes the woman who prays is described as "ὁ λέων ὁ ἄγριος ὁ παλαιός" and at the same time as "the father of the gods of the Egyptians." In the context of 1 Peter, this metaphor for the devil gains its depth of focus through the contrast to the lamb Christ who is introduced in the beginning (1:18ff.): the lamb has given himself as an offering for others, but the lion is a beast of prey that, as is specially underlined, seeks to devour others, therefore lives from the lives of others; accordingly, the lion brings death to others for the sake of his own

[13] See p. 246 n. 5.

[14] The image stems from Ps 22:14; cf. further Ezek 22:25; 1QH 13.9, 13f., 18f. (there with reference to human adversaries).

[15] It is, at most, intimated in the "deliverance from the mouth of the lion" in 2 Tim 4:17.

> life, the lamb through his death brings others (eternal) life.[16] By means of the comparison of the devil with a lion going after prey, the destructive being of the anti-divine power is thereby also presented in contrast to the salvation-causing divine power.

The personification of the threat in the devil lends additional emphasis to the summons to watchfulness.[17] Thereby the endangerment of the Christians, which up to now has not yet been so clearly addressed (cf. 1:6f.), is underlined, a threat that one can only meet through a resolute orientation on God.

5:9

The following verse underlines this through the connection of resistance and faith;[18] however much of one's own effort is called for, the believers can nevertheless not withstand this conflict from their own strength but are dependent upon protection through God's power (cf. 1:5). This is even more true as "similar suffering comes upon your brothers and sisters in the world." With that statement, once again the universality of the threat is underlined. At the same time, this knowledge (εἰδότες) probably also provides the comfort that in this "strange" suffering something that is simply not "strange" happens (4:12), but something that is characteristic for the lives of Christians in the society—and this characteristic reaches beyond the circle of the addressees and extends to all brothers and sisters "in the [whole] world." The expression ἀδελφότης (a word that is found only in the New Testament in 1 Pet; cf. 2:17) that is used for the totality of Christians stresses their unity precisely in view of this suffering that affects all believers. The generalizing reference to a Christianity spread over the then-known world (ἡ ἐν τῷ κόσμῳ ἀδελφότης) shows for the historical background of 1 Peter that societal exclusion and oppression of Christians had already become the normal situation across the Empire; this is one of the most important arguments for the assumption of a later, pseudepigraphical authorship.

[16] Cf. R. Feldmeier, "Lamm."

[17] Cf. Brox, 237f., "Through the mythical image of the devil as a lion a new note of toughness and resistance (v. 9a) comes into the text, whereas up to now submission, gentleness, [and the like] were always advised."

[18] Faith was otherwise spoken about only in the first main part of the letter (1:5, 7, 9, 21).

(ii) Encouragement and Closing Doxology 5:10-11

(10) But the God of all grace, who has called you in Christ Jesus to his eternal glory, will, after you have suffered for a short time, put you to rights, make you firm, strengthen you, provide you with a foundation. (11) To him be the power in eternity. Amen.

On the text: **10** The Ἰησοῦ has been left out of ἐν Χριστῷ Ἰησοῦ by Vaticanus and Sinaiticus. The longer form is, however, as a whole better witnessed (among others p^{72} A 33). Also the fact that the letter closing (v. 14) was with some likelihood augmented with Ἰησοῦ speaks for an adaptation of this verse to verse 10 and with it for the long form in our text. **11** There is a rich variant construction on τὸ κράτος that is caused by the attempt to supplement τὸ κράτος with ἡ δόξα. In the background stands the formal language of doxologies, cf. the doxology of the Lord's Prayer.

5:10

The promise that is based in the "God of all grace" is strikingly contrasted (with the adversative "but") to the image of Satan as the roaring lion who seeks whom he may devour. It is true that grace and God are frequently connected, especially in Pauline and Lucan writings, but with the expression "God of all grace," which is unique in the New Testament, 1 Peter has as it were defined God as the origin of all grace, grace as the experiential divine answer—precisely in suffering—to oppression (5:5, 12; cf. 2:19f.). This is made more specific in the first instance through the participial expression "who has called you in Christ Jesus to eternal glory," which very briefly summarizes the basic theological assertions of the letter: the believers are called in Christ, that is, they belong to God's people, are born anew, and thus also participate in God's "eternal glory." The connection of suffering and glory characterized the whole letter (cf. especially 1:6f.; 4:13f.); in our verse, the weight lies on the comforting contrast of *brief* suffering and *eternal* glory. All this justifies the assertion of the main clause, the four verbs that have their nub in the transfer of power and stability by God: God himself (αὐτός) will keep his own on the right way, supporting and strengthening them. In the final verb θεμελιόω ("provide with a foundation"), reference is probably made to the metaphor of a "spiritual house" (1 Pet 2:5) or "God's house" (4:17). Thus the promise of divine protection in the face of suffering with which the letter began in 1:5f. also closes the letter.[19]

5:11

The letter body is closed by a doxology. As the letter body began with a eulogy, a thankful praise of God, so it also closes with worshipful praise; everything that was said in the work comes from the praise of God and leads to it. That contributes something not unimportant to the character of this work that is free from all maudlin sentimentality and bitterness despite all the assumed oppression, in which work, on the contrary, confidence, and joy dominate. The doxology itself is, in contrast to the somewhat fuller first one in 4:11, situationally focused: in the face of oppression by the devil, God's power is once more stressed, in contrast to the "brief suffering" God's eternality.

After the ceremonious conclusion of the doxology with "amen," the letter closing follows with the naming of Silvanus, a review of the intention of the writing and greetings. Together with the letter introduction 1:1f., it forms 1 Peter's letter framework.

IV. Letter Closing 5:12-14

Literature on 1 Peter 5:12-14: **C. H. Hunzinger**, "Babylon als Deckname für Rom und die Datierung des 1. Petrusbriefes," in H. Graf Reventlow (ed.), *Gottes Wort und Gottes Land* (*Festschrift* H. W. Hertzberg; Göttingen, 1965), 67–75.

(12) Through Silvanus, the faithful brother according to my conviction, I have written to you with a few [words] in order to exhort and to testify that just this is God's true grace: position yourselves within it! (13) The co-elect [Christian community] in Babylon and Marcus, my son, greet you. (14)

[19] G. Delling, "Existenz," 105, "God is the one working in the Christians from beginning to end, who on the basis of the Christ-event in the cross and resurrection creates and preserves new life through his word."

Greet one another with the kiss of love. Peace to you all who are in Christ.

On the text: **13** The minuscules 1611Z, 1890 and 2138 replace Βαβυλῶνι with Ῥώμῃ. This variant is based on the conviction that Babylon stands for Rome. **14** Instead of ἐν Χριστῷ (A B 33[vid] and others) א and others read ἐν Χριστῷ Ἰησοῦ. The external testimony supports the short form; the long form could be an adaptation to the expression in verse 10, particularly since formal additions are popular at the end of a work.

5:12

For the first time in the letter—if one ignores the information about the author in 1:1 and biblical figures such as Noah and Sarah—an individual name is given: Silvanus. This person may be identical with the Silas/Silvanus who, according to Acts 15:22, 27, 32, was an envoy of the earliest Jerusalem Christian community to Antioch and whom Paul then took as a companion on his missionary journey (Acts 15:40; cf. 17:10). This last information is confirmed by Paul himself: in 1 Thessalonians 1:1 the apostle names him as a coauthor of 1 Thessalonians; according to 2 Corinthians 1:19 he had even cofounded the Christian community in Corinth. Afterward, we lose trace of him. A rapprochement of Paul's coworker with Peter is not unthinkable,[1] especially since they probably knew each another from Jerusalem and were active in the Diaspora as Palestinian Jewish-Christian missionaries. This rapprochement could have taken place in Rome, either during the lifetime of Paul or—in the case that, because of his trial, Paul was already executed by the beginning of the 60s[2]—while Peter fell victim to the Neronian persecution in the year 64,[3] in the time between Paul's execution and Peter's martyrdom. This Silvanus might have belonged to the continuing Petrine circle. Besides

[1] Despite the tension between Paul and Peter resulting from the Antioch incident (Gal 2:11ff.), nothing points to a definitive rupture; the references by the apostle to the Gentiles to Peter—other than Galatians 2—are always respectful. If today the possibility of such a rapprochement is still viewed skeptically, then this may be the after-effect of the historical reconstruction of F. C. Baur, who wished to see the antagonist to the Pauline mission in Peter.

[2] Cf. E. Lohse, *Paulus*, 264f.

[3] Ch. Böttrich, *Petrus*, 211–20.

these historical questions, the naming of "brother Silvanus" by the "apostle Peter" testifies the amalgamation of Pauline and Petrine traditions in the Roman church.

The expression that the author has written "with a few words" sounds formulaic,[4] but it still does not seem implausible here in view of the undertaking in a relatively meager space to mobilize the most varied traditions (from the Old Testament through early Judaism, the Jesus tradition, and Pauline theology to pagan assumptions) in great linguistic density and to edit them so argumentatively that they all serve one goal: to interpret for the "foreigners" their situation of societal exclusion and defamation in such a way that this does not trouble them as an expression of being abandoned by God but, as a confirmation of God's fellowship, can even become a reason for joy. In this way, by perpetually new approaches, the "living hope" was made accessible to present experience. Just this is expressed here in retrospect by the author when he says he has written this letter "in order to exhort and testify that *just this*[5] is God's true grace: Position yourselves within it!"

5:13

By means of the term "co-elect"[6] in the closing greeting, it is made clear that election, which already was named alongside foreignness in 1:1 as an essential characteristic of Christians, is also the basis for the fellowship of the Christian communities with one another (cf. also 2:9). Two interpretive possibilities have been considered for the place designation "in Babylon"—after exclusion of the assumption that it refers to a real place with this name—a cryptogram for the *Imperium Romanum* or a symbol for the Christians' existence as foreigners, whereby, as shown earlier,[7] these two

[4] Cf. the similar expression in Heb 13:22, an unequally longer letter; further the corresponding assurance in 2 John 12; 3 John 13 and John 21:25 that one still could have written much more.

[5] Cf. Brox, 245f., "The demonstrative [i.e., with χάρις] refers to that which has been explained in the whole letter. The reader should understand this grace precisely as this 'logic' of faith, 'suffering'-existence and soteriology . . . Grace is the freeing possibility about which the letter constantly wanted to speak or to practice: to be able to hope under the present precarious conditions."

[6] On 1 Peter's preference for word connections formed with συν-, see 3:7 and 5:1.

[7] On this, see Introduction pp. 40f.

interpretations are not mutually exclusive. In that case, it would signal to the addressees in Asia Minor: the "co-elect" in Rome are also co-oppressed "foreigners in the dispersion." At the same time, the place designation Babylon, if it then refers to Rome, would also be meaningful in view of the history of early Christianity. In this case, 1 Peter would be the first writing of earliest Christianity that now treads in the opposite direction to the way of Christianity from east to west, which the mission had taken and also the first early Christian literature went (cf. Romans).[8] Here that network of an ἀδελφότης ἐν τῷ κόσμῳ (5:9), which allowed the early Christian communities to become a connected church empirewide in a relatively short time, becomes visible.

Besides the community, an additional name is given, the one who greets the Christians in Asia Minor: Mark. As with Silas/Silvanus, this persona may also be identical with the (John) Mark known from the Pauline circle (Acts 12:25; 13:5, 13), from whom it is true that Paul had, according to the testimony of Acts, separated,[9] but who later shows up again in the Pauline circle (Phlm 24; cf. Col 4:10), possibly during Paul's imprisonment in Rome (cf. 2 Tim 4:11). What connects John Mark with Peter is that he as well came from the earliest Christian community in Jerusalem (Acts 12:25) and that at least his mother seems to have known Peter well (Acts 12:12ff.). Therefore, it is quite possible that this Mark—as Silas/Silvanus after Paul's death in Rome?—had worked together with Peter for a while. The tradition that goes back to Papias (about 120), which sees in Mark the student and interpreter of Peter,[10] could also speak in favor of this; Papias, then, considers him also to be the author of the Gospel of Mark, which according to his statement, is based on Petrine tradition. The designation "my son" could—as the analogous designation τέκνον (in part with the possessive pronoun) in 1 Corinthians 4:17; Philemon 10; 1 Timothy 1:2, 18; 2 Timothy 1:2; 2:1 and Titus 1:4—refer to a teacher-student relationship.

[8] Cf. Goppelt, 353, "By means of the greeting in 5:13 our letter explicitly becomes the first Christian writing known to us that creates the arch of church contact from Rome to Asia Minor that would in the second century become the basis for the Catholic Church."

[9] Acts 15:37-39; John Mark followed Barnabas on his missionary trip to Cyprus.

[10] Transmitted in Eus, *HistEccl* 2.15; 3.39.15.

5:14

Before the closing wish of peace stands the final summons to greet one another with the "kiss of love." Paul also knows this tradition; several times at the end of his letters, using virtually the same words, he calls his addresses to greet one another with the "holy kiss" (Rom 16:16; 1 Cor 16:20; 2 Cor 13:12; 1 Thess 5:26). This kiss stresses the solidarity of the Christians with one another as a "brother-sister-hood."[11] Tradition-historically, it probably goes back to the kiss among relatives;[12] possibly the kiss also played a role as a sign of reconciliation (cf. Luke 15:20).[13] It was perhaps already practiced in the circle of Jesus' disciples as an expression of belonging to the *familia Dei* (cf. Mark 3:35 par.), which Judas' kiss could indicate (Mark 14:44 par.). As a sign of fellowship, it appears to be genuinely Christian, for such a tradition is not known from Judaism, and, in the pagan world, this expression of "brother-and-sisterly" solidarity among those not related to one another was not infrequently met with astonishment.[14] With his description of this sign as a "kiss of love," the author of 1 Peter underlines yet again the central meaning of mutual love for the Christian community precisely in view of external oppression.[15]

[11] In 1 Pet 2:17; in 5:9 one finds for this the word ἀδελφότης, which is not otherwise encountered in the New Testament.

[12] Evidence in G. Stählin, "φιλέω," 124.

[13] Cf. G. Stählin, "φιλέω," 121, 137f.

[14] This astonishment over the "brother-and-sisterly kiss of love" appears, for example, in the polemic of Caecilius in the *Octavius* of Minucius Felix: "They recognize one another by secret signs and distinguishing marks and already love each other [*amant mutuo*] virtually before they get to know each other. They indiscriminately perform with one another a type of ritual of lust; they call one another brother and sister so that the sexual offense that is customary with them even becomes incest through the use of such a holy word." (Min, *Oct* 9.2). Tertullian testifies indirectly to this astonishment, when he mentions among other things against the re-marriage of a Christian woman with a pagan that the pagan husband would hardly allow her, "*alicui fratrum ad osculum convenire*" (Tert, *Ux* 2.4).

[15] The summons to love the brothers and sisters is the only one that is repeated in each chapter of this letter (1:22; 2:17; 3:8; 4:8f.); on the shift of accent in comparison with the "holy kiss" in Paul cf. Goppelt, 354f.: "Yet again our letter emphasizes the horizontal where we find the vertical in Paul, that is, it stresses the concrete earthly form of the actualization of salvation."

The conclusion is formed by the peace greeting (cf. 1:2), which applies to all "in Christ." The Pauline expression ἐν Χριστῷ, which is found only three times in 1 Peter outside the *Corpus Paulinum*, here emphasizes that the believers are "Christians"[16] precisely in that as born anew they share in Christ and his fate; that means, as the letter has shown, they participate now in a way of life that accords with Christ and therewith also in his suffering (cf. 3:16) and in the future in his glory (cf. 5:10).

[16] As 4:16 shows, 1 Peter knew this designation already.

Bibliography

(Note: Bold type indicates the short title used in footnotes and other citations.)

1. Source

1.1. Bible

B. Aland et al. (eds.). *Nestle-Aland. Novum Testamentum Graece.* Stuttgart, 1993[27] (cited as: **Nestle-Aland**).

B. Aland et al. (eds.). *Novum Testamentum Graecum: Editio Critica Maior.* Institut für neutestamentliche Textforschung, IV/2: Die Petrusbriefe; Stuttgart, 2000 (cited as: **Editio Critica Maior**).

A. Rahlfs (ed.). *Septuaginta: Id est Vetus Testamentum graece iuxta LXX interpres, duo volumina in uno*; Stuttgart, 1979.

R. Weber (ed.). *Biblia sacra: Iuxta vulgatam versionem*; Stuttgart, 1994[4].

J. Ziegler (ed.). *Jeremias, Baruch, Threni, Epistula Jeremiae.* Göttinger Septuaginta 15; Göttingen, 1976[2].

1.2. Ancient Judaism

M. Adler. *Über die Flucht und das Finden.* In L. Cohn et al. (eds.), *Philo von Alexandria. Die Werke in deutscher Übersetzung*, vol. 6; Berlin, 1962[2] (Breslau, 1938[1]), 50–103.

M. Adler. *Über die Träume I–II*. In L. Cohn et al. (eds.), *Philo von Alexandria. Die Werke in deutscher Übersetzung*, vol. 6; Berlin, 1962[2] (Breslau, 1938[1]), 163–277.

M. Adler. *Über die Trunkenheit*. In L. Cohn et al. (eds.); *Philo von Alexandria. Die Werke in deutscher Übersetzung*, vol. 5; Berlin, 1962[2] (Breslau, 1929[1]), 1–76.

J. Becker. *Die* ***Testamente*** *der zwölf Patriachen*. JSHRZ III/1; Gütersloh, 1974.

K. Berger. *Das Buch der Jubiläen*. JSHRZ II/3; Gütersloh, 1981.

P. Bettiolo (ed.). *Ascensio Isaiae. Textus*. CChr.SA 7; Turnhout, 1995.

M. Black (ed.). ***Apocalypsis*** *Henochi Graece*. PVTG 3; Leiden, 1970, 1–44.

Ph. Blackman. *Mishnayot*. Vol. IV: *Order Nezikin;* Gateshead 1983[2].

K. Bormann. *Über das betrachtende Leben*. In L. Cohn et al. (eds.); *Philo von Alexandria. Die Werke in deutscher Übersetzung*, vol. 7; Berlin, 1964, 44–70.

K. Bormann. *Über die Freiheit des Tüchtigen*. In L. Cohn et al. (eds.); *Philo von Alexandria. Die Werke in deutscher Übersetzung*, vol. 7; Berlin, 1964, 1–43.

Ch. Böttrich. *Das slavische* ***Henochbuch***. JSHRZ V/7; Gütersloh, 1995.

S. P. Brock (ed.). *Testamentum Iobi*. PVTG 2; Leiden, 1967.

Ch. Burchard. ***Joseph und Aseneth***. JSHRZ II/4; Gütersloh, 1983.

Ch. Burchard (ed.). *Joseph und Aseneth. Kritisch herausgegeben, mit Unterstützung von* C. Burfeind *und* U.B. Fink. PVTG 5; Leiden/Boston, 2003.

J. H. Charlesworth (ed.). *The* ***Odes*** *of Solomon: The Syriac Texts*; Missoula, 1977.

J. H. Charlesworth (ed.). *The Old Testament* ***Pseudepigrapha*****, vol. 1**; Garden City/New York, 1983.

J. H. Charlesworth (ed.). *The Old Testament* ***Pseudepigrapha*****, vol. 2**; Garden City/New York, 1985.

J. Cohn. *Über Abraham*. In L. Cohn et al. (eds.), *Philo von Alexandria. Die Werke in deutscher Übersetzung*, vol. 1; Berlin 1962[2] (Breslau 1909[1]), 91–152.

J. Cohn. *Über die Frage: Wer ist der Erbe der göttlichen Dinge? und über die Teilung in Gleiches und Gegensätzliches*. In L. Cohn et al. (eds.). *Philo von Alexandria. Die Werke in deutscher Übersetzung*, vol. 5; Berlin, 1962[2] (Breslau, 1929[1]), 214–94.

J. Cohn. *Über die Weltschöpfung*. In L. Cohn et al. (eds.). *Philo von Alexandria. Die Werke in deutscher Übersetzung*, vol. 1; Berlin, 1962[2] (Breslau, 1909[1]), 23–89.

L. Cohn. *Über die Cherubim*. In L. Cohn et al. (eds.). *Philo von Alexandria. Die Werke in deutscher Übersetzung*, vol. 3; Berlin, 1962[2] (Breslau, 1919[1]), 167–205.

L. Cohn. *Über Joseph*. In L. Cohn et al. (eds.). *Philo von Alexandria. Die Werke in deutscher Übersetzung*, vol. 1; Berlin, 1962[2] (Breslau, 1909[1]), 153–213.

L. Cohn/P. Wendland (eds.). *Philonis Alexandrini Opera Quae Supersunt*, vol. 1: Edidit L. Cohn; Berlin, 1962 (1896) (cited as: **Cohn-Wendland I**).

L. Cohn/P. Wendland (eds.). *Philonis Alexandrini Opera Quae Supersunt*, vol. 2: Edidit P. Wendland; Berlin, 1962 (1897) (cited as: **Cohn-Wendland II**).

L. Cohn/P. Wendland (eds.). *Philonis Alexandrini Opera Quae Supersunt*, vol. 3: Edidit P. Wendland; Berlin 1962 (1898) (cited as: **Cohn-Wendland III**).

L. Cohn/P. Wendland (eds.). *Philonis Alexandrini Opera Quae Supersunt*, vol. 4: Edidit L. Cohn; Berlin, 1962 (1902) (cited as: **Cohn-Wendland IV**).

L. Cohn/P. Wendland (eds.). *Philonis Alexandrini Opera Quae Supersunt*, vol. 5: Edidit L. Cohn; Berlin, 1962 (1906) (cited as: **Cohn-Wendland V**).

L. Cohn/P. Wendland (eds.). *Philonis Alexandrini Opera Quae Supersunt*, vol. 6: Ediderunt L. Cohn et S. Reiter; Berlin, 1962 (1915) (cited as: **Cohn-Wendland VI**).

M. de Jonge (ed.). *The Testaments of the Twelve Patriarchs*. PVTG 1, 2; Leiden, 1978.

A. Díez Macho. *Neophyti 1, **Targum** Palestinense. Ms de la Biblioteca Vaticana*. Vol. 1. *Génesis*; Madrid/Barcelona, 1968.

J. Dochhorn. *Die **Apokalypse des Mose**. Text, Übersetzung, Kommentar*. TSAJ 106; Tübingen, 2005.

F. García Martínez (ed.). *The Dead Sea Scrolls. Study Edition*, vol. 1–2; Leiden, 2000.

J. Geffcken (ed.). *Die Oracula Sibyllina*. GCS 8; Leipzig, 1902.

M. Ginsburger (ed.). *Das **Fragmententargum** (Targum Jeruschalmi zum Pentateuch)*; Berlin, 1899.

M. Ginsburger (ed.). *Targum Jonathan Ben Uzziel*; Berlin, 1903 (cited as: **TPsJon**).

L. Goldschmidt. *Der Babylonische Talmud*. Vol. 1: *Berakhoth, Mišna Zeraim, Šabbath*; Berlin, 1929 (cited as: **Goldschmidt I**).

L. Goldschmidt. *Der Babylonische Talmud*. Vol. 8: *Baba Bathra, Synhedrin*, 1. Hälfte; Berlin, 1933 (cited as: **Goldschmidt VIII**).

L. Goldschmidt. *Der Babylonische Talmud*. Vol. 9: *Synhedrin, 2. Hälfte, Makkoth, Šebuoth, Edijoth, Aboda Zara, Aboth*; Horajoth; Berlin, 1934 (cited as: **Goldschmidt IX**).

R. Hayward. *The Targum of Jeremiah: Translated, with a Critical Introduction, Apparatus, and Notes*. The Aramaic Bible 12; Edinburgh, 1987.

I. Heinemann. *Über die Einzelgesetze*, Buch I–IV. In L. Cohn et al. (eds.). *Philo von Alexandria: Die Werke in deutscher Übersetzung*, vol. 2; Berlin, 1962^2 (Breslau, 1910^1), 1–312.

I. Heinemann. *Über die Landwirtschaft*. In L. Cohn et al. (eds.). *Philo von Alexandria: Die Werke in deutscher Übersetzung*, vol. 4; Berlin, 1962^2 (Breslau, 1923^1), 111–47.

I. Heinemann. *Über die Pflanzung Noahs*. In L. Cohn et al. (eds.). *Philo von Alexandria: Die Werke in deutscher Übersetzung*, vol. 4; Berlin, 1962^2 (Breslau, 1923^1), 147–87.

H. Hoffmann. *Das sogenannte hebräische Henochbuch*. BBB 58; Bonn, 1985^2.

S. Holm-Nielsen. *Die Psalmen Salomos*. JSHRZ IV/2; Gütersloh, 1977.

H.-J. Klauck. ***4. Makkabäerbuch***. JSHRZ III/6; Gütersloh, 1989.

A. F. J. Klijn. *Die syrische Baruch-Apokalypse*. JSHRZ V/2; Gütersloh, 1976.

F. W. Kohnke. *Gesandtschaft an Caligula*. In L. Cohn et al. (eds.). *Philo von Alexandria: Die Werke in deutscher Übersetzung*, vol. 7; Berlin, 1964, 166–266.

R. A. Kraft/A.-E. Purintun (eds.). *Paraleipomena Jeremiou*. SBL. PS 1; Missoula, 1972.

H. Leisegang. *Allegorische Erklärung des heiligen Gesetzbuches*, Buch I–III. In L. Cohn et al. (eds.; *Philo von Alexandria: Die Werke in deutscher Übersetzung*, vol. 3; Berlin, 1962[2] (Breslau, 1919[1]) 1–165.

H. Leisegang. *Über die Nachkommen Kains*. In L. Cohn et al. (eds.). *Philo von Alexandria: Die Werke in deutscher Übersetzung*, vol. 4; Berlin, 1962[2] (Breslau, 1923[1]), 1–53.

H. Leisegang. *Über die Nachstellungen, die das Schlechtere dem Besseren bereitet*. In L. Cohn et al. (eds.). *Philo von Alexandria: Die Werke in deutscher Übersetzung*, vol. 3; Berlin, 1962[2] (Breslau, 1919[1]), 265–331.

H. Leisegang. *Über die Opfer Abels und Kains*. In L. Cohn et al. (eds.). *Philo von Alexandria: Die Werke in deutscher Übersetzung*, vol. 3; Berlin, 1962[2] (Breslau, 1919[1]), 207–64.

H. Leisegang. *Über die Riesen*. In L. Cohn et al. (eds.). *Philo von Alexandria: Die Werke in deutscher Übersetzung*, vol. 4; Berlin, 1962[2] (Breslau, 1923[1]), 53–71.

H. Leisegang. *Über die Unveränderlichkeit Gottes*. In L. Cohn et al. (eds.). *Philo von Alexandria: Die Werke in deutscher Übersetzung*, vol. 4; Berlin, 1962[2] (Breslau, 1923[1]), 72–110.

H. Lewy. *Über das Zusammenleben um der Allgemeinbildung willen*. In L. Cohn et al. (eds.). *Philo von Alexandria: Die Werke in deutscher Übersetzung*, vol. 6; Berlin, 1962[2] (Breslau, 1938[1]), 1–49.

J. Maier. *Die Qumran-Essener: Die Texte vom Toten Meer*. Vol. 1: *Die Texte der Höhlen 1–3 und 5–11*; München/Basel, 1995 (cited as: **Maier I**).

J. Maier. *Die Qumran-Essener: Die Texte vom Toten Meer*. Vol. 2: *Die Texte der Höhle 4*; München/Basel, 1995 (cited as: **Maier II**).

R. Marcus. *Philo, Questions and Answers on Exodus: Translated from the Ancient Armenian Version of the Original Greek*. LCL 401; Cambridge, 2003 (1953).

R. Marcus: *Philo, Questions and Answers on Genesis: Translated from the Ancient Armenian Version of the Original Greek*. LCL 380; Cambridge, 1993 (1953).

K. Marti/G. Beer. ***Abot***, *Väter. Text, Übersetzung und Erklärung, nebst einem textkritischen Anhang*. Die Mischna IV/9; Gießen, 1927.

N. Meisner. *Aristeasbrief*. JSHRZ II/1; Gütersloh, 1973.

H. Merkel. *Sibyllinen*. JSHRZ V/8; Gütersloh, 1998.

J.-C. Picard (ed.). *Apocalypsis Baruchi graece*. PVTG 2; Leiden, 1967, 81–96.

R. Posner. Über Abrahams Wanderung. In L. Cohn et al. (eds.). *Philo von Alexandria: Die Werke in deutscher Übersetzung*, vol. 5; Berlin 1962[2] (Breslau 1929[1]), 152–213.

B. Solomonsen. *Seder Nezikin: Sanhedrin, Makkot, übersetzt und erklärt, mit Beiträgen von* K. H. Rengstorf. RT I/IV/3; Stuttgart et al., 1976.

G. Sauer. ***Jesus Sirach*** *(Ben Sira)*. JSHRZ III/5; Gütersloh, 1981.

B. Schaller. *Das Testament Hiobs*. JSHRZ III/3; Gütersloh, 1979.

B. Schaller. *Paralipomena Jeremiou*. JSHRZ I/8; Gütersloh, 1998.

J. Schreiner. *Das 4. Buch* ***Esra***. JSHRZ V/4; Gütersloh, 1981.

A. Sperber. *The Bible in Aramaic: Based on Old Manuscripts and Printed Texts*. Vol. 3: *The Latter Prophets According to Targum Jonahthan*; Leiden, 1962.

W. Staerk (ed.). *Altjüdische liturgische Gebete, ausgewählt und mit einer Einleitung herausgegeben*. KlT 58; Berlin, 1930[2].

E. Stein. *Über die Verwirrung der Sprachen*. In L. Cohn et al. (eds.). *Philo von Alexandria: Die Werke in deutscher Übersetzung*, vol. 5; Berlin, 1962[2] (Breslau, 1929[1]), 99–151.

W. Theiler. *Über die Namensänderung*. In L. Cohn et al. (eds.). *Philo von Alexandria: Die Werke in deutscher Übersetzung*, vol. 6; Berlin, 1962[2] (Breslau, 1938[1]), 104–162.

L. Treitel. *Über den Dekalog*. In L. Cohn et al. (eds.); *Philo von Alexandria. Die Werke in deutscher Übersetzung*, vol. 1; Berlin, 1962[2] (Breslau, 1909[1]); 367–409.

S. Uhlig. *Das Äthiopische Henochbuch*. JSHRZ V/6; Gütersloh, 1984.

R. Ulmer. *Maaserot, Zehnte, Maaser Sheni, Zweiter Zehnt*. ÜTY I/7; Tübingen, 1996.

G. A. Wewers. ***Sanhedrin***, *Gerichtshof*. ÜTY IV/4; Tübingen, 1981.

1.3. Greek and Roman Authors

M. v. Albrecht (ed.). *P. Ovidius Naso, Metamorphosen*. Lateinisch/ Deutsch; Stuttgart, 1994.

D. J. Allan. *Aristoteles, De caelo libri quattuor, recognovit brevique adnotatione critica instruxit*. SCBO; Oxford, 1955.

M. Baltes. "De Deo Socratis, Der Gott des Sokrates." In H.-G. Nesselrath et al. (eds.). *Apuleius, De Deo Socratis, Über den Gott des Sokrates: Eingeleitet, übersetzt und mit interpretierenden Essays versehen von M. Baltes, M.-L. Lakmann, J. M. Dillon, P. Donini, R. Häfner, L. Karfíková*. SAPERE 7; Darmstadt, 2004, 45–119.

E. Brandt/W. Ehlers (eds.). ***Apuleius***, *Der Goldene Esel, Metamorphosen: Lateinisch-deutsch, mit einer Einführung von N. Holzberg*; Düsseldorf/Zürich, 1998[5].

C. Büchner (ed.). *M. Tulli Ciceronis opera omnia quae exstant, Critico apparatu instructa: Consilio et auctoritate college Ciceronianis studiis provehendis*, vol. 19/2: *De legibus, Libri tres*; Milano, 1973.

H. Drexler. ***Polybios***, *Geschichte*, vol. 1. BAW. GR; Zürich/ Stuttgart, 1961.

O. Gigon/L. Straume-Zimmermann (eds.). *Marcus Tullius Cicero, Vom Wesen der Götter: Lateinisch-deutsch, herausgegeben, über-*

setzt und kommentiert. Sammlung Tusculum; Düsseldorf/Zürich, 1996.

H. Görgemanns (ed.). Plutarch, *Dialog über die Liebe: Amatorius. Eingeleitet, übersetzt und mit interpretierenden Essays versehen von H. Görgemanns, B. Feichtinger, F. Graf, W. Jeanrond und J. Opsomer*. SAPERE 10; Tübingen, 2006.

H. Görgemanns (ed.). Plutarch, *Drei religionsphilosophische Schriften, Über den Aberglauben, Über die späte Strafe der Gottheit, Über Isis uns Osiris: Griechisch-deutsch, übersetzt und herausgegeben, unter Mitarbeit von R. Feldmeier und J. Assmann*. Sammlung Tusculum; Düsseldorf/Zürich, 2003.

G. P. Goold. *Tertullian. Apology*. LCL 250; Cambridge Mass./London, 1931.

Ch. R. Haines (ed.). *The Communings with Himself of Marcus Aurelius Antoninus, Emperor of Rome, Together with His Speeches and Sayings*. LCL 58; London, 1961.

A. M. Harmon (ed.). *Lucian: With an English Translation*, vol. 4. LCL 162; Cambridge et al., 1999 (cited as: **Harmon I**).

A. M. Harmon (ed.). *Lucian: With an English Translation*, vol. 5. LCL 302; Cambridge et al., 2001 (cited as: **Harmon II**).

A. v. Harnack (ed.). *Porphyrus "Gegen die Christen." 15 Bücher, Zeugnisse, Fragmente und Referate*. APAW 1916, 1; Berlin, 1916.

E. Heller (ed.). *P. Cornelius Tacitus, Annalen. Lateinisch-deutsch, mit einer Einführung von M. Fuhrmann*. Sammlung Tusculum; Düsseldorf/Zürich, 1997^{3}.

H. J. Hillen (ed.). *Titus Livius, Römische Geschichte: Lateinisch und deutsch*. Sammlung Tusculum; Düsseldorf/Zürich, 1974.

J. Holzhausen. *Das Corpus Hermeticum Deutsch: Übersetzung, Darstellung und Kommentierung in drei Teilen*. Teil 1: *Die griechischen Traktate und der lateinische "Asclepius."* Clavis Pansophiae VII/1; Stuttgart-Bad Cannstatt, 1997.

C. Hubertus. *Plutarchus, Moralia*, vol. 5/3. BSGRT; Leipzig, 1960.

K. Hülser (ed.). *Platon. Sämtliche Werke, in zehn Bänden, Griechisch und Deutsch, nach der Übersetzung F. Schleiermachers, ergänzt durch Übersetzungen von F. Susemihl und anderen*, vol. 1–10; Frankfurt, 1991.

P. Jaerisch (ed.). *Xenophon, Erinnerungen an Sokrates: Griechisch-deutsch*. Sammlung Tusculum; München et al., 1987[4].

H. Kasten (ed.). *Gaius Plinius Caecilius Secundus, Briefe, Epistularum libri decem: Lateinisch-deutsch*. Sammlung Tusculum; Düsseldorf/Zürich, 1995[7].

H.-W. Krautz (ed.). *Epikur, Briefe, Sprüche, Werkfragmente. Griechisch-deutsch*; Stuttgart, 2000.

F. Loretto (ed.). *L. Annaeus Seneca, Epistulae Morales ad Lucilium, Briefe an Lucilius über Ethik, 5. Buch. Lateinisch-deutsch*; Stuttgart, 2001.

H. Martinet (ed.). *C.* ***Suetonius*** *Tranquillus, Die Kaiserviten, De Vita Caesarum, Berühmte Männer, De Viris Illustribus: Lateinisch-deutsch*. Sammlung Tusculum; Düsseldorf/Zürich, 2000[2].

W. Nachstädt et al. (eds.). *Plutarchus, Moralia*, vol. 2. BSGRT; Leipzig, 1971 (1935).

A. Nauck (ed.). *Porphyrii philosophi Platonici opuscula selecta*. BSGRT; Leipzig, 1886[2].

A. D. Nock. *Sallustius, Concerning the Gods and the Universe: Edited with Prolegomena and Translation*; Hildesheim, 1966 (Cambridge, 1926).

C. H. Oldfather (ed.). *Diodorus of Sicily, In Twelve Volumes*. Vol. 4: Books IX–XII, 40. LCL 375; Cambridge/London, 1961.

W. A. Oldfather (ed.). *Epictetus, The Discourses as Reported by Arrian, The Manual, and Fragments*, vols. 1–2. LCL; Cambridge/London, 1959–1961 (1925–1928).

W. R. Paton et al. (eds.). *Plutarchus, Moralia*, vol. 1. BSGRT; Leipzig, 1993[3] (cited as: **Paton I**).

W. R. Paton et al. (eds.). *Plutarchus, Moralia*, vol. 3. BSGRT; Leipzig, 2001 (1929) (cited as: **Paton II**).

A. C. Pearson (ed.). *Sophoclis fabulae: Recognovit brevique adnotatione critica instruxit*. SCBO; Oxford, 1961.

H. Rupé (ed.). *Homer, Ilias: Griechisch und deutsch, übertragen von H. Rupé, mit Urtext, Anhang und Registern*. Sammlung Tusculum; Düsseldorf/Zürich, 2001[11].

A. v. Schirnding. ***Hesiod***, *Theogonie, Werke, und Tage: Griechisch-deutsch, mit einer Einführung und einem Register von E. G. Schmidt*. Sammlung Tusculum; Düsseldorf/Zürich, 1997[2].

J. Schweighaeuser (ed.). *Epicteti dissertationes . . . Accedunt fragmenta, enchiridion* . . . BSGRT; Leipzig, 1898.

W. Sieveking/H. Gärtner (eds.). *Plutarchus, Pythici dialogi*. BSGRT; Leipzig, 1997[2].

A. Thierfelder (ed.). *Menandri opera quae supersunt*, vol. 2. BSGRT; Leipzig, 1953.

U. Victor. *(Aristoteles)*, ***Oikonomikos***: *Das erste Buch der Ökonomik-Handschriften, Text, Übersetzung, und Kommentar, und seine Beziehungen zur Ökonomikliteratur*. BKP 147; Königstein, 1983.

R. Woerner. ***Sophokles***, *Tragödien: Aus dem Griechischen übersetzt und mit einem Nachwort*; Darmstadt, 1960.

U. Wolf. *Aristoteles' "Nikomachische Ethik,"* Darmstadt, 2007[2].

D. Young. *Theognis: Post E. Diehl, Indicibus ad Theognidem adiectis*. BSGRT; Leipzig, 1961.

K. Ziegler (ed.). *Plutarchus, Vitae parallelae*, vol. 3/2. BSGRT; Leipzig, 2002[2].

1.4. Christian Sources

C. Becker (ed.). ***Tertullian***, *Apologeticum: Verteidigung des Christentums. Lateinisch und Deutsch*; München, 1984[3].

M. Bonnet (ed.). ***Acta Ioannis***. In R. A. Lipsius/M. Bonnet (eds.). *Acta Apostolorum Apocrypha* 2/1; Leipzig, 1898, 151–216.

J. G. Ph. Borleffs (ed.). *Tertullianus, De Corona*. In *Tertulliani opera 2: Opera montanistica*. CChr.SL 2; Turnhout, 1954, 1037–66.

J. G. Ph. Borleffs (ed.). *Tertullianus, De Resurrectione Mortuorum*. In *Tertulliani opera 2: Opera montanistica*. CChr.SL 2; Turnhout, 1954, 919–1012.

S. Brandt/G. v. Laubmann (eds.). *L. Caecilii qui inscriptus est De mortibus persecutorum liber vulgo Lactantio tributus, Lactantii opera omnia* 2, 2. CSEL 27, 2; Wien/Leipzig, 1893.

H. Chadwick. *Origen: Contra Celsum;* Cambridge, 1980 (cited as: **Cels**)

J. A. Cramer (ed.). *Catenae Graecorum Patrum in Novum Testamentum.* Vol. 8: ***Catena** in Epistolas Catholicas Accesserunt Oecumenii et Arethae Commentarii in Apocalypsin. Ad Fidem Codd. Mss*; Hildesheim, 1967 (Oxford 1840).

E. Dekkers (ed.). *Tertullianus, Ad Scapulam.* In *Tertulliani opera 2: opera montanistica.* CChr.SL 2; Turnhout, 1954, 1125–32.

E. Dekkers (ed.). *Tertullianus, Apologeticum.* In *Tertulliani opera 1: opera catholica.* CChr.SL 1; Turnhout, 1954, 77–172.

J. A. Fischer (ed.). *Die Apostolischen **Väter**. Eingeleitet, herausgegeben, übertragen und erläutert.* SUC 1; Darmstadt, 1998[10] (1993).

H. Görgemanns/H. Karpp (ed./trans.). *Origenes. Vier Bücher von den Principien.* TzF 24; Darmstadt, 1976.

E. J. Goodspeed (ed.). *Die ältesten Apologeten: Texte mit kurzen Einleitungen*; Göttingen, 1984 (1914).

E. Klostermann (ed.). *Origenes Matthäuserklärung.* Teil 1: *Die griechisch erhaltenen Tomoi.* GCS 40; Leipzig, 1935.

E. Klostermann (ed.). *Origenes Matthäuserklärung.* Teil 2: *Die lateinische Übersetzung der Commentariorum series.* GCS 38; Leipzig, 1933.

R. Knopf (ed.). *Ausgewählte Märtyrerakten: Neubearbeitung der Knopfschen Ausgabe von G. Krüger, mit einem Nachtrag von G. Ruhbach.* SQS NF 3; Tübingen, 1965[4].

P. Koetschau (ed.). *Buch 5–8 gegen Celsus, Die Schrift vom Gebet.* GCS 3; Leipzig, 1899.

P. Koetschau (ed.). *Die Schrift vom Martyrium, Buch 1–4 gegen Celsus.* GCS 2; Leipzig, 1899.

E. Kroymann (ed.). *Tertullianus, Ad Uxorem.* In *Tertulliani opera 1: Opera catholica.* CChr.SL 1; Turnhout, 1954, 371–94.

E. Kroymann (ed.). *Tertullianus, Adversus Marcionem.* In *Tertulliani opera 1: Opera catholica.* CChr.SL 1; Turnhout, 1954, 437–726.

B. Kytzler (ed.). *Minucius Felix, **Octavius**. Lateinisch-Deutsch*; Stuttgart, 1993[3].

M. Leutzsch. *Hirt des Hermas*. In U. H. J. Körtner/M. Leutzsch, *Papiasfragmente, Hirt des Hermas. Eingeleitet, herausgegeben, übertragen und erläutert*. SUC 3; Darmstadt: 1998, 105–510.

K. Mras (ed.). *Eusebius: Die Praeparatio evangelica*. GCS 8,1–2; Berlin, 1982–83[2].

J. C. Th. Otto. *Theophili episcopi Antiocheni ad Autolycum, libri tres: Ad optimos libros mss. nunc primum aut denuo collatos recensuit prolegomenis adnotatione critica et exegetica atque versione latina instruxit, indices adiecit*. CorpAp 8; Jena, 1861.

H. Rahner. *Die Märtyrerakten des zweiten Jahrhunderts*. Zeugen des Wortes 32; Freiburg, 1954[2] (1941[1]).

A. Rousseau (ed.). *Irénée de Lyon, Contre les hérésies, Livre 1*, vol. 1, 2. SC 264; Paris, 1979.

A. Rousseau (ed.). *Irénée de Lyon, Contre les hérésies, Livre 2*, vol. 2, 2. SC 294; Paris, 1982.

A. Rousseau (ed.). *Irénée de Lyon, Contre les hérésies, Livre 3*, vol. 3, 2. SC 211; Paris, 2002[2].

A. Rousseau (ed.). *Irénée de Lyon, Contre les hérésies, Livre 4*, vol. 4, 2. SC 100, 2; Paris, 1965.

A. Rousseau (ed.). *Irénée de Lyon, Contre les hérésies, Livre 5*, vol. 5, 2. SC 153; Paris, 1969.

A. Rousseau (ed.). *Irénée de Lyon, Démonstration de la prédication apostolique*. SC 406; Paris, 1995.

E. Schwartz/Th. Mommsen (eds.). *Eusebius: Die Kirchengeschichte*, Teil 1–3. GCS N. F. 6,1–3; Berlin, 1999[2].

O. Stählin (ed.). *Clemens Alexandrinus: Stromata Buch I–VI*. GCS 52; Berlin, 1985.

K. F. Urba/J. Zycha (eds.). *Sancti Augustini opera*. Vol. 8/1: *De peccatorum meritis et remissione et de baptismo parvulorum ad Marcellinum libri 3* . . . CSEL 60; Wien, 1913.

K. Wengst (ed.). *Didache (Apostellehre); Barnabasbrief, Zweiter Klemensbrief, Schrift an Diognet: Eingeleitet, herausgegeben, übertragen und erläutert*. SUC 2; Darmstadt, 1998 (1984).

2. Dictionaries and Lexica

F. R. **Adrados** (ed.). *Diccionario Griego-Español III*; Madrid, 1991.

W. Bauer. *Griechisch-deutsches Wörterbuch zu den Schriften des Neuen Testaments und der frühchristlichen Literatur. 6; völlig neu bearbeitete Auflage*. Edited by K. Aland und B. Aland.; Berlin/ New York, 1988[6] (cited as: **Bauer-Aland**).

F. Blass/A. Debrunner. *Grammatik des neutestamentlichen Griechisch*. Revised by F. Rehkopf; Göttingen, 2001[18] (cited as: **Blass-Debrunner-Rehkopf**).

M. **Jastrow**. *A Dictionary of the Targumim, the Talmud Babli and Yerushalmi, and the Midrashic Literature*; New York, 1992 (1903).

H. G. Liddell/R. Scott. *A Greek-English Lexicon*. Revised and Augmented throughout by *H. S. Jones*, with the Assistance of *R. McKenzie*, and with the Cooperation of Many Scholars, with a Revised Supplement; Oxford, 1996 (cited as: **Liddell-Scott**).

E. Schwyzer. *Griechische Grammatik: Auf der Grundlage von K. Brugmanns Griechischer Grammatik*. Vol. 2: *Syntax und syntaktische Stilistik*. Completed and edited by A. Debrunner; München, 1950 (cited as: **Schwyzer II**).

H. Stephanus. ***Thesaurus*** *Graecae Linguae IX, Nachdruck*; Graz, 1954.

3. Commentaries on 1 Peter

P. J. **Achtemeier**. *1 Peter*. Hermeneia; Minneapolis, 1996.

H. **Balz/W. Schrage**. *Die "Katholischen" Briefe: Die Briefe des Jakobus, Petrus, Johannes, und Judas*. NTD 10; Göttingen/ Zürich, 1993[4].

L. A. **Barbieri**. *First and Second Peter*. Everyman's Bible Commentary; Chicago, 2003 (1977).

F. W. **Beare**. *The First Epistle of Peter: The Greek Text with Introduction and Notes*; Oxford, 1970[3].

M. E. **Boring**. *1 Peter*. ANTC; Nashville, 1999.

N. **Brox**. *Der erste Petrusbrief*. EKK 21; Zürich/Neukirchen-Vluyn, 1993[4].

J. Calloud/F. Genuyt. *La Première Épître de Pierre: Analyse sémiotique*. LeDiv 109; Paris, 1982 (cited as **Calloud/Genuyt**).

P. H. **Davids**. *The First Epistle of Peter*. NICNT; Michigan, 1990.

J. H. **Elliott**. *1 Peter: A New Translation with Introduction and Commentary*; The Anchor Bible 37B; New York, 2000.

H. **Frankemölle**. *1. Petrusbrief, 2. Petrusbrief, Judasbrief*. NEB NT 18.20; Würzburg, 1987.

J. **Gerhard**. *Commentarius Super Priorem D. Petri Epistolam, in Quo Textus Declaratur, Quaestiones Dubiae Solvuntur, Observationes Erunntur & Loca Inspeciem Pugnantia Conciliantur: Cum Praefatione J. F. Mayeri, Zachariae Hertelii*; Hamburg und Leipzig, 1709[4].

L. **Goppelt**. *Der erste Petrusbrief*. KEK 12/1; Göttingen, 1978[8].

J. E. **Huther**. *Kritisch exegetisches Handbuch über den 1: Brief des Petrus, den Brief des Judas und den 2. Brief des Petrus*. KEK 12; Göttingen, 1877[4].

K. H. **Jobes**. *1 Peter*. ECNT; Grand Rapids, 2005.

J. N. D. **Kelly**. *A Commentary on the Epistles of Peter and of Jude*. Harper's New Testament Commentaries; New York/Evanston, 1969.

R. **Knopf**. *Die Briefe Petri und Judä*. KEK 12; Göttingen, 1912.

J. R. **Michaels**. *1 Peter*. WBC 49; Waco, 1988.

J. **Michl**. *Die katholischen Briefe*. RNT 8/2; Regensburg, 1968[2].

K. H. **Schelkle**. *Die Petrusbriefe, der Judasbrief*. HThK 13/2; Freiburg et al., 1980[5].

E. G. **Selwyn**. *The First Epistle of St. Peter: The Greek Text with Introduction, Notes, and Essays*; London, 1949.

C. **Spicq**. *Les Épitres de Saint Pierre*. Sources Bibliques; Paris 1966.

H. **Windisch**. *Die Katholischen Briefe*. Third, greatly revised edition by H. Preisker. HNT 15; Tübingen, 1951[3].

G. **Wohlenberg**. *Der erste und zweite Petrusbrief und der Judasbrief*. KNT 15; Leipzig, 1923[3].

4. Monographs, Articles, and Other Materials

F. H. Agnew. "1 Peter 1:2. An Alternative **Translation**." *CBQ* 45, (1983), 68–73.

K. Aland. "Der **Tod** des Petrus in Rom: Bemerkungen zu seiner Bestreitung durch Karl Heussi." In K. Aland, *Kirchengeschichtliche Entwürfe: Alte Kirche, Reformation, und Luthertum, Pietismus und Erweckungsbewegung*; Gütersloh, 1960, 35–104.

K. Aland. "Das **Verhältnis** von Kirche und Staat in der Frühzeit," ANRW II/23/1; Berlin/New York, 1979, 60–246.

G. Alföldy. *Römische* ***Sozialgeschichte.*** Wissenschaftliche Paperbacks. 8. Sozial- und Wirtschaftsgeschichte; Wiesbaden, 1984[3].

G. Alföldy. *The* ***Social History*** *of Rome.* Translated by D. Braund and F. Pollock; Baltimore, 1988.

B. Altaner/A. Stuiber. ***Patrologie***. *Leben. Schriften und Lehre der Kirchenväter*; Freiburg et al., 1978[8].

C. Andresen. *Logos und Nomos: Die* ***Polemik*** *des Kelsos wider das Christentum.* AKG 30; Berlin, 1955.

C. Andresen. "Zum **Formular** frühchristlicher Gemeindebriefe." ZNW 56 (1965), 233–259.

J. Annas. "**Plato**'s Myths of Judgement." Phron. 27 (1982), 119–143.

F. Back. "**Wiedergeburt** in der religiösen Welt der hellenistisch-römischen Zeit." In R. Feldmeier (ed.). *Wiedergeburt.* BThS 25; Göttingen, 2005, 45–74.

D. L. Balch. "**Hellenization**/Acculturation in 1 Peter." In C. H. Talbert (ed.). *Perspectives on First Peter.* NABPR SS 9; Macon, 1986, 79–101.

D. L. Balch. *Let* ***Wives*** *Be Submissive: The Domestic Code in I Peter.* SBL. MS 26; Atlanta, 1981.

H. Baltensweiler. *Die Ehe im Neuen Testament: Exegetische Untersuchungen über Ehe, Ehelosigkeit und Ehescheidung.* AThANT 52; Zürich, 1967, 243–249.

E. Bammel. "The Commands in I Peter II. 17." *NTS* 11 (1964/65), 279–81.

W. Bauer. ***Rechtgläubigkeit** und Ketzerei im ältesten Christentum. 2. durchgesehene Auflage mit einem Nachtrag herausgegeben von* G. Strecker. BHTh 10; Tübingen, 1964².

J. Behm. "προνοέω." ThWNT IV; Stuttgart et al., 1942, 1004–11.

J. A. Bengel. ***Gnomon** Novi Testamenti: In quo Exodus nativa verborum vi simplicitas, profunditas, concinuitas, salubritas sensuum coelestium indicatur*; Berlin, 1860 (1773³).

K. Berger. ***Formgeschichte** des Neuen Testaments*; Heidelberg, 1984.

K. Berger, "Hellenistische **Gattungen** im Neuen Testament." ANRW II/25/2; Berlin/New York, 1984, 1031–1432.

H. W. Beyer. "ἐπισκέπτομαι κτλ." ThWNT II; Stuttgart et al. 1935, 595–619, especially 617–19 (ἀλλοτριεπίσκοπος).

Th. Beza. *Iesu Christi Domini Nostri **Novum Testamentum**, sive Novum Foedus. Cuius Graeco Contextui Respondent Interpretationes Duae, Una Vetus, Altera Theodori Bezae. Eiusdem Th. Bezae Annotationes [. . .]*; Geneva, 1598⁴.

W. Bieder. *Die Vorstellung von der **Höllenfahrt** Jesu Christi. Beitrag zur Entstehungsgeschichte der Vorstellung vom sog. Descensus ad inferos*. AThANT 19; Zürich, 1949.

M. Black. "The Christological **Use** of the Old Testament in the New Testament." *NTS* 18 (1971–72), 1–14.

E. Bloch. *Das Prinzip **Hoffnung**. In fünf Teilen*. Vol. 1: *Kapitel* 1–37; Frankfurt, 1959.

O. Böcher. "Jüdische und christliche Diaspora im neutestamentlichen Zeitalter." *EvDia* 38 (1967), 147–76.

M.-E. Boismard. *Quatre **hymnes** baptismales dans la première Epître de Pierre*. LeDiv 30; Paris, 1961.

F. Bömer. ***Untersuchungen** über die Religion der Sklaven in Griechenland und Rom. Vierter Teil: Epilegomena*. Akademie der Wissenschaften und der Literatur. Abhandlungen der geistes- und sozialwissenschaftlichen Klasse 10; Mainz, 1963.

Ch. Böttrich. ***Petrus**. Fischer, Fels und Funktionär*. Biblische Gestalten 2; Leipzig, 2001.

D. Bonhoeffer. *The Cost of Discipleship*; London, 2001.

G. L. Borchert. "The Conduct of Christians in the Face of the 'Fiery Ordeal.'" *Review and Expositor* 79 (1982), 451–62.

W. Brandt. "Wandel als Zeugnis nach dem 1. Petrusbrief." In W. Foerster (ed.). *Verbum Dei manet in aeternum. Festschrift* O. Schmitz; Witten, 1953, 10–25.

N. Brox. "Der erste Petrusbrief in der literarischen **Tradition** des Urchristentums." *Kairos* NF 20 (1978), 182–92.

N. Brox. Falsche ***Verfasserangaben***: *Zur Erklärung der frühchristlichen Pseudepigraphie*. SBS 79; Stuttgart, 1975.

N. Brox. "Tendenz und Pseudepigraphie im ersten Petrusbrief." *Kairos* NF 20 (1978), 110–120.

H. Brunner. *Grundzüge der Altägyptischen* ***Religion***. Grundzüge 50; Darmstadt, 1983.

F. Büchsel. " λύω κτλ." ThWNT IV; Stuttgart et al., 1966 (1942), 337–59.

F. Büchsel. "'In Christus' bei **Paulus**." *ZNW* 42 (1949), 141–58.

R. Bultmann. "ἀγνοέω κτλ." ThWNT I; Stuttgart et al., 1957 (1933), 116–22.

R. Bultmann. "γινώσκω κτλ." ThWNT I; Stuttgart et al., 1957 (1933), 688–719.

R. Bultmann. "ἐλπίς κτλ." ThWNT II; Stuttgart et al., 1935, 515–20, 525–31.

R. Bultmann. "πιστεύω κτλ." ThWNT VI; Stuttgart et al., 1965 (1959), 197–230.

R. Bultmann. "Bekenntnis- und **Liedfragmente** im ersten Petrusbrief." In E. Dinkler (ed.). *Rudolf Bultmann, Exegetica: Aufsätze zur Erforschung des Neuen Testaments*; Tübingen, 1967, 285–97.

R. Bultmann. ***Theologie*** *des Neuen Testaments*; Tübingen, 1984[9].

J. Bunyan, *The Pilgrim's Progress*; London, 1678.

Ch. Burchard. *Der* ***Jakobusbrief***. HNT 15/1; Tübingen, 2000.

W. Burkert. *Antike* ***Mysterien***: *Funktionen und Gehalt*; München, 1994[3].

R. A. Campbell. *The* ***Elders***: *Seniority within Earliest Christianity*; Edinburgh, 1994.

H. v. Campenhausen. *Die **Idee** des Martyriums in der alten Kirche*; Göttingen, 1964[2].

M. A. Chevallier. "1 Pierre 1/1 à 2/10: Structure littéraire et conséquences exégétiques." *RHPhR* 51 (1971), 129–42.

M. A. Chevallier. "**Condition** et vocation des chrétiens en diaspora: Remarques exégétiques sur la 1re épître de Pierre." *RevSR* 48 (1974), 387–398.

S. Cipriani. "Lo 'spirito di Cristo' come 'spirito di profezia' in 1 Pt. 1,10–12." In G. Lorizio/V. Scippa (eds.). *Ecclesiae Sacramentum. Festschrift*. A. Marranzini; Neapel, 1986, 157–67.

M. Clévenot. "**Versuch** einer Lektüre des 1: Petrusbriefes." In T. Polednitschek (ed.). *Zur Rettung des Feuers*; Münster, 1980, 48–53.

E. C. Colwell. "Popular Reactions against Christianity in the Roman Empire." In J. T. McNeill (ed.). *Environmental Factors in Christian History. Festschrift* S. J. Case; Washington, 1970 (1939), 53–71.

H. J. B. Combrink. *The **Structure** of 1 Peter*. Neotestamentica 9. Essays on the General Epistles of the New Testament; Stellenbosch, 1975.

J. Coutts. "Ephesians I. 3-14 and I Peter I. 3-12." *NTS* 3 (1956–1957), 115–27.

A. Cowley (ed.). *Aramaic Papyri of the Fifth Century B.C.: Edited with Translations and Notes*; Oxford, 1923 (cited as: ***AP***).

W. J. Dalton. *Christ's **Proclamation** to the Spirits: A Study of 1 Peter 3:18–4:6*. AnBib 23; Rome, 1989[2].

W. Dalton. "The Church in 1 Peter." *Tantur Yearbook*; Jerusalem, 1981–1982, 79–91.

J. L. Daniel. "Anti-Semitism in the Hellenistic-Roman Period." *JBL* 98 (1979), 45–65.

J. Daniélou. ***Sacramentum** Futuri: Études sur les origines de la typologie biblique*. ETH; Paris, 1950.

G. Dautzenberg. "**Seele** IV. Neues Testament." TRE, vol. 30; Berlin/New York, 1999, 744–48.

G. Dautzenberg. "Σωτηρία ψυχῶν (1 Peter 1, 9)." *BZ* NF 8 (1964), 262–76.

R. Deichgräber. "**Benediktionen** II. Neues Testament." TRE, vol. 5; Berlin/New York, 1980, 562–64.

R. Deichgräber. *Gotteshymnus und Christushymnus in der frühen Christenheit: Untersuchungen zu Form, Sprache und Stil der frühchristlichen Hymnen*. SUNT 5; Göttingen, 1967, 140–43.

A. Deissmann. *Die neutestamentliche* ***Formel*** *"in Christo Jesu"*; Marburg, 1892.

A. Deissmann. ***Licht*** *vom Osten: Das Neue Testament und die neuentdeckten Texte der hellenistisch-römischen Welt*; Tübingen, 1923[4].

M. de Jonge. "Vreemdelingen en bijwoners: Enige opmerkingen naar aanleiding van 1 Petr 2:11 en verwante teksten." *NedThT* 11 (1956/57), 18–36.

G. Delling. "Der Bezug der christlichen **Existenz** auf das Heilshandeln Gottes nach dem ersten Petrusbrief." In H. D. Betz/L. Schottroff (eds.). *Neues Testament und christliche Existenz. Festschrift* H. Braun; Tübingen, 1973, 95–113.

G. Delling. *Die Taufe im Neuen Testament*; Berlin, 1963, 82–89.

A.-M. Denis/J.-C. Haelewyck. ***Introduction*** *à la littérature religieuse judéo-hellénistique I*; Turnhout, 2000.

W. Dittenberger. *Sylloge Inscriptionum Graecarum*, vol. 2; Hildesheim, 1960 (Leipzig, 1917[3]) (cited as: ***SIG***).

H. Dörrie/M. Baltes. *Die philosophische Lehre des* ***Platonismus****: Von der "Seele" als der Ursache aller sinnvollen Abläufe*. Der Platonismus in der Antike. Grundlagen, System, Entwicklung 6/**1**; Stuttgart-Bad Cannstatt, 2002.

H. Dörrie/M. Baltes. *Die philosophische Lehre des* ***Platonismus****: Von der "Seele" als der Ursache aller sinnvollen Abläufe*. Der Platonismus in der Antike. Grundlagen, System, Entwicklung 6/**2**; Stuttgart-Bad Cannstatt, 2002.

E. Ebel. *Die* ***Attraktivität*** *früher christlicher Gemeinden: Die Gemeinde von Korinth im Spiegel griechisch-römischer Vereine*. WUNT II/178; Tübingen, 2004.

H.-J. Eckstein. *Der Begriff* ***Syneidesis*** *bei Paulus: Eine neutestamentlich-exegetische Untersuchung zum "Gewissensbegriff."* WUNT II/10; Tübingen, 1983.

H.-J. Eckstein. ***Glaube****, der erwachsen wird*; Holzgerlingen, 2002[6].

H.-J. Eckstein. *Zur Wiederentdeckung der* ***Hoffnung****: Grundlagen des Glaubens*; Holzgerlingen, 2002.

U. E. Eisen. ***Women Officeholders*** *in Early Christianity: Epigraphical and literary studies.* Preface by G. Macy; translated by L. M. Maloney; Collegeville, 2000.

W. Elert. *Der Ausgang der altkirchlichen* ***Christologie****: Eine Untersuchung über Theodor von Pharan und seine Zeit als Einführung in die alte Dogmengeschichte, aus dem Nachlaß herausgegeben von W. Maurer und E. Bergsträßer*; Berlin, 1957.

J. H. Elliott. *A* ***Home*** *for the Homeless: A Sociological Exegesis of 1 Peter, Its Situation and Strategy*; London, 1981, 39ff.

J. H. Elliott. "**Ministry** and Church Order in the NT: A Traditio-Historical Analysis, 1 Peter 5,1-5 and plls." *CBQ* 32, 1970, 367–91.

M. Erler. "'**Sokrates**' Rolle im Hellenismus." In H. Kessler (ed.). *Sokrates: Nachfolge und Eigenwege.* Sokrates-Studien 5, Die Graue Reihe 31; Kusterdingen, 2001, 201–32.

M. Evang. "'Εκ καρδίας ἀλλήλους ἀγαπήσατε ἐκτενῶς: Zum **Verständnis** der Aufforderung und ihrer Begründungen in 1 Petr 1,22f." *ZNW* 80 (1989), 111–23.

E. Fascher. "Fremder." RAC, vol. 8; Stuttgart, 1972, 306–47.

R. Feldmeier. "Das **Lamm** und die Raubtiere: Tiermetaphorik und Machtkonzeptionen im Neuen Testament." In R. Gebauer/M. Meiser (eds.), *Die bleibende Gegenwart des Evangeliums. Festschrift* O. Merk. MATThSt 76; Marburg, 2003, 205–11.

R. Feldmeier. "**De Sera** Numinis Vindicta." In H. Görgemanns et al. (eds.). *Plutarch, Drei Religionsphilosophische Schriften: Über den Aberglauben; Über die späte Strafe der Gottheit; Über Isis und Osiris; Griechisch-deutsch, übersetzt und herausgegeben von H. Görgemanns unter Mitarbeit von R. Feldmeier und J. Assmann.* Sammlung Tusculum; Düsseldorf/Zürich, 2003, 318–39.

R. Feldmeier. "Die **Außenseiter** als Avantgarde. Gesellschaftliche Ausgrenzung als missionarische Chance nach dem 1. Petrusbrief." In P. W. van der Horst et al. (eds.). *Persuasion and Dissuasion in Early Christianity, Ancient Judaism, and Hellenism*. Contributions to Biblical Exegesis and Theology 33; Leuven et al., 2003, 161–78.

R. Feldmeier. *Die Christen als **Fremde**: Die Metapher der Fremde in der antiken Welt, im Urchristentum und im ersten Petrusbrief.* WUNT 64; Tübingen, 1992.

R. Feldmeier. "Die Darstellung des **Petrus** in den synoptischen Evangelien." In P. Stuhlmacher (ed.). *Das Evangelium und die Evangelien: Vorträge vom Tübinger Symposium 1982*. WUNT 28; Tübingen, 1983, 267–71.

R. Feldmeier. "Euer **Widersacher**, der Teufel: Frühchristliche Konzeptionalisierungen des Bösen am Beispiel des 1. Petrusbriefes." In W. H. Ritter/J. A. Schlumberger. *Das Böse in der Geschichte*. Bayreuther historische Kolloquien 16; Dettelbach, 2003, 61–76.

R. Feldmeier. "Nicht **Übermacht** noch Impotenz: Zum biblischen Ursprung des Allmachtsbekenntnisses." In W. H. Ritter et al. (eds.). *Der Allmächtige: Annäherungen an ein umstrittenes Gottesprädikat*. BTSP 13; Göttingen, 1997, 13–42.

R. Feldmeier. "**Paulus**." In Ch. Axt-Piscalar/J. Ringleben (eds.). *Denker des Christentums*; Tübingen, 2004, 1–22.

R. Feldmeier. "**Seelenheil**. Überlegungen zur Soteriologie und Anthropologie des 1: Petrusbriefes." In J. Schlosser (ed.). *The Catholic Epistles and the Tradition*. BEThL 176; Leuven, 2004, 291–306.

R. Feldmeier. "Θεὸς ζῳοποιῶν: Die paulinische Rede von der Unvergänglichkeit in ihrem religionsgeschichtlichen Kontext." In I. Dalferth et al. (eds.). *Denkwürdiges Geheimnis. Beiträge zur Gotteslehre. Festschrift* E. Jüngel; Tübingen, 2004, 77–91.

R. Feldmeier. "**Weise** hinter 'eisernen Mauern.' Tora und jüdisches Selbstverständnis zwischen Akkulturation und Absonderung im Aristeasbrief." In M. Hengel/A. M. Schwemer (eds.). *Die Septuaginta: Zwischen Judentum und Christentum*. WUNT 72; Tübingen, 1994, 20–37.

R. Feldmeier. "**Wiedergeburt** im 1. Petrusbrief." In R. Feldmeier (ed.). *Wiedergeburt*. BThS 25; Göttingen, 2005, 75–100.

P. R. Fink. "The **Use** and Significance of En Hoi in I Peter." *Grace Journal* 8 (1967), 33–39.

W. Foerster. "ἄσωτος κτλ." ThWNT I; Stuttgart et al., 1933, 504f.

W. Foerster. "κτίζω κτλ." ThWNT III; Stuttgart, 1957 (1938), 999–1034.

J. Frey. "Die paulinische **Antithese** von 'Fleisch' und 'Geist' und die palästinisch-jüdische Weisheitstradition." *ZNW* 90 (1999), 45–77.

G. Friedrich. "κῆρυξ κτλ." ThWNT III; Stuttgart et al., 1957 (1938), 682–717.

V. P. Furnish. "Elect **Sojourners** in Christ: An Approach to the Theology of I Peter." *Perkins Journal* 28 (1975), 1–11.

Th. W. Gaster. *The Dead Sea **Scriptures***; Garden City, 1976[3].

P. Gauthier. "Meteques, Perieques, et Paroikoi: Bilan et points d'interrogation." In R. Lonis (ed.). *l'étranger dans le monde grec*. Travaux et mémoires: Études anciennes 4; Nancy, 1988, 23–46.

H. Gese. "Die **Sühne**." In H. Gese, *Zur biblischen Theologie. Alttestamentliche Vorträge*; Tübingen, 1983[2], 85–106.

M. Gielen. "'Und führe uns nicht in **Versuchung**': Die 6. Vater-Unser Bitte, eine Anfechtung für das biblische Gottesbild?" *ZNW* 89 (1998), 201–16.

M. Gielen. ***Tradition** und Theologie neutestamentlicher Haustafelethik: Ein Beitrag zur Frage einer christlichen Auseinandersetzung mit gesellschaftlichen Normen*. BBB 75; Frankfurt, 1990.

H. Goldstein. "Die politischen **Paränesen** in 1 Petr 2 und Röm 13." *BiLe* 14 (1973), 88–104.

L. Goppelt. "**Prinzipien** neutestamentlicher Sozialethik nach dem I: Petrusbrief." In H. Baltensweiler/B. Reike, *Neues Testament und Geschichte. Historisches Geschehen und Deutung im Neuen Testament. Festschrift* O. Cullmann; Zürich/Tübingen, 1972, 285–96.

L. Goppelt. ***Theologie*** *des Neuen Testaments*. Vol. 2: *Vielfalt und Einheit des apostolischen Christuszeugnisses, herausgegeben von J. Roloff*; Göttingen, 1976.

D. Gorce. "**Gastfreundschaft** C. Christlich." RAC VIII; Stuttgart, 1972, 1103–23.

R. Grieshammer. *Das* ***Jenseitsgericht*** *in den Sargtexten*: Ägyptologische Abhandlungen 20; Wiesbaden, 1970.

K. Gschwind. *Die* ***Niederfahrt*** *Christi in die Unterwelt: Ein Beitrag zur Exegese des Neuen Testaments und zur Geschichte des Taufsymbols*. NTA 2/3–5; Münster, 1911.

H. Gülzow. ***Christentum*** *und Sklaverei in den ersten drei Jahrhunderten*. Nachwort G. Theißen. Hamburger Theologische Studien 16; Münster et al., 1999 (1969).

H. Gunkel. *Der erste Brief des* ***Petrus***. SNT 3; Göttingen, 1917[3], 248–92.

Ph. A. Harland. ***Associations***, *Synagoges, and Congregations: Claiming a Place in Ancient Mediterranean Society*; Minneapolis, 2003.

A. von Harnack. *Der Vorwurf des* ***Atheismus*** *in den ersten drei Jahrhunderten*. TU 28/4; Leipzig, 1905.

A. von Harnack. *Die* ***Chronologie*** *der altchristlichen Literatur bis Eusebius*. Vol. 1: *Die Chronologie der Literatur bis Irenäus. Nebst einleitenden Untersuchungen*. Geschichte der altchristlichen Literatur bis Eusebius 2, 1; Leipzig, 1897[2].

A. von Harnack. ***Marcion***, *Das Evangelium vom fremden Gott. Eine Monographie zur Geschichte der Grundlagen der katholischen Kirche*. TU 45; Leipzig, 1924[2].

U. Heckel. ***Hirtenamt*** *und Herrschaftskritik. Die urchristlichen Ämter aus johanneischer Sicht*. BTS 65; Neukirchen, 2004.

U. Heckel. *Der* ***Segen*** *im Neuen Testament, Begriff, Formeln, Gesten. Mit einem praktisch-theologischen Ausblick*. WUNT 150; Tübingen, 2002.

M. Hengel. *Die* ***Zeloten***. *Untersuchungen zur jüdischen Freiheitsbewegung in der Zeit von Herodes I. bis 70 n. Chr*. AGJU 1; Leiden/Köln, 1976[2].

M. Hengel. ***Judentum** und Hellenismus: Studien zu ihrer Begegnung unter besonderer Berücksichtigung Palästinas bis zur Mitte des 2. Jh.s v. Chr.* WUNT 10; Tübingen, 1988[3].

M. Hengel. *The "**Hellenization**" of Judaea in the First Century after Christ.* In Collaboration with Ch. Markschies; London/ Philadelphia, 1989.

M. Hengel. "'Setze dich zu meiner Rechten!' Die **Inthronisation** Christi zur Rechten Gottes und Psalm 110, 1." In M. Philonenko (ed.). *Le Trône de Dieu.* WUNT 69; Tübingen, 1993, 108–94.

J. W. van Henten/F. Avemarie. ***Martyrdom** and Noble Death. Selected Texts from Graeco-Roman, Jewish, and Christian Antiquity*; London/New York, 2002.

H. Herter. *Die **Soziologie** der antiken Prostitution im Lichte des heidnischen und christlichen Schrifttums.* JAC 3; Münster, 1960, 70–111.

J. Herzer. ***Petrus** oder Paulus? Studien über das Verhältnis des Ersten Petrusbriefes zur paulinischen Tradition.* WUNT 103; Tübingen, 1998.

J. Herzer. "Alttestamentliche **Prophetie** und die Verkündigung des Evangeliums. Beobachtungen zur Stellung und zur hermeneutischen Funktion von I Petr 1, 10-12." *BThZ* 14 (1997), 14–22.

D. Hill. "On **Suffering** and Baptism in I Peter." *NT* 18 (1976), 181–89.

E. Hornung. *Das **Totenbuch** der Ägypter. Eingeleitet, übersetzt und erläutert von E. Hornung.* Zürich/München, 1990 (1979).

P. W. van der Horst. "**Pseudo-Phocylides** and the New Testament." *ZNW* 69 (1978), 187–202.

C. H. Hunzinger. "**Babylon** als Deckname für Rom und die Datierung des 1. Petrusbriefes." In H. Graf Reventlow (ed.). *Gottes Wort und Gottes Land. Festschrift* H.-W. Hertzberg; Göttingen, 1965, 67–75.

E. Jacob. "ψυχή κτλ. B. Die Anthropologie des Alten Testaments." ThWNT IX; Stuttgart et al., 1973, 614–29.

B. Janowski. ***Sühne** als Heilsgeschehen. Traditions- und religionsgeschichtliche Studien zur Sühnetheologie der Priesterschrift*. WMANT 55; Neukirchen-Vluyn, 2000².

A. Jepsen. "בטח." ThWAT I; Stuttgart et al., 1973, 608–15.

J. Jeremias. "λίθος κτλ." ThWNT IV; Stuttgart et al., 1966 (1942), 272–83.

J. Jeremias. *Die **Abendmahlsworte** Jesu*; Göttingen, 1967⁴.

J. Jeremias. "Zwischen **Karfreitag** und Ostern. Descensus und Ascensus in der Karfreitagstheologie des Neuen Testamentes." *ZNW* 42 (1949), 194–201.

E. Jüngel. "Metaphorische **Wahrheit**. Erwägungen zur theologischen Relevanz der Metapher als Beitrag zur Hermeneutik einer narrativen Theologie." In P. Ricoeur/E. Jüngel. *Metapher: Zur Hermeneutik religiöser Sprache, mit einer Einführung von P. Gisel*. EvTh.S 1974; München, 1974, 71–122.

M. Kaser. *Das römische **Privatrecht** II. Die nachklassischen Entwicklungen*. HAW III/3/2; München, 1959.

H.-J. Klauck. "'**Pantheisten**, Polytheisten, Monotheisten'—eine Reflexion zur griechisch-römischen und biblischen Theologie." In H.-J. Klauck. *Religion und Gesellschaft im frühen Christentum. Neutestamentliche Studien*. WUNT 152; Tübingen, 2003, 3–53.

J. Knox. "Pliny and I Peter. A Note on I Peter 4, 14–16 and 3, 15." *JBL* 72 (1953), 187–89.

W. Kornfeld. "קדשׁ." ThWAT VI; Stuttgart et al., 1989, 1179–88.

M. Küchler. **Schweigen**, *Schmuck und Schleier: Drei neutestamentliche Vorschriften zur Verdrängung der Frauen auf dem Hintergrund einer frauenfeindlichen Exegese des Alten Testaments im antiken Judentum*. NTOA 1; Freiburg/Göttingen, 1986.

U. R. Kügler. *Die **Paränese** an die Sklaven als Modell urchristlicher Sozialethik*. Diss. theol; Erlangen, 1977.

W. G. Kümmel. ***Einleitung** in das Neue Testament*; Heidelberg, 1983²¹.

K. G. Kuhn. "πειρασμός, ἁμαρτία, σάρξ im Neuen Testament und die damit zusammenhängenden Vorstellungen." *ZThK* 49 (1952), 200–22.

O. Kuss. "Der Begriff des Gehorsams im Neuen Testament." *ThGl* 27 (1935), 695–702.

O. Kuss. "Zur paulinischen und nachpaulinischen Tauflehre im Neuen Testament (1952)." In O. Kuss., *Auslegung und Verkündigung*, vol. 1; Regensburg, 1963, 121–50.

J. Laaksonen. ***Jesus** und das Land. Das Gelobte Land in der Verkündigung Jesu*; Abo, 2002.

P. Lampe. "'Fremdsein' als urchristlicher Lebensaspekt." *Ref.* 34 (1985), 58–62.

H. Langkammer. "Jes 53 und 1 Petr 2, 21–25: Zur christologischen Interpretation der Leidenstheologie von Jes 53." *BiLi* 60 (1987), 90–98.

E. A. LaVerdiere. "A Grammatical **Ambiguity** in 1 Peter 1:23." CBQ 36 (1974), 89–94.

J. Leipold/W. Grundmann. ***Umwelt** des Urchristentums II. Texte zum neutestamentlichen Zeitalter*; Berlin, 1972.

H. Lietzmann. "**Petrus** römischer Märtyrer." In H. Leitzmann, *Kleine Schriften I. Studien zur spätantiken Religionsgeschichte*. TU 67; Berlin, 1958, 100–23.

A. Lindemann. *Der erste **Korintherbrief***. HNT 9/1; Tübingen, 2000.

E. Lohse. "**Paränese** und Kerygma im 1. Petrusbrief." *ZNW* 45 (1954), 68–89.

E. Lohse. ***Paulus**. Eine Biographie*; München, 1996.

H. E. Lona. *Der erste **Clemensbrief***. KAV 2; Göttingen, 1998.

M. Luther. *Werke*. Kritische Gesamt-ausgabe, Weimar 1883ff.

J. Maier. *Die **Texte** vom Toten Meer*. Vol. 2: *Anmerkungen*; München/Basel, 1960.

K. Maly. "Christ und **Staat** im Neuen Testament." In J. J. Degenhardt (ed.). *Die Freude an Gott, unsere Kraft. Festschrift* O. B. Knoch; Stuttgart, 1991, 271–77.

H. Manke. ***Leiden** und Herrlichkeit: Eine Studie zur Christologie des 1. Petrusbriefs*. Diss.; Münster, 1975.

I. Männlein-Robert. "**Peroratio**." In *Historisches Wörterbuch der Rhetorik* VI; Darmstadt 2003, 778–88.

J. R. Mantey. "On Causal **Eis Again**." *JBL* 70 (1951), 309–11.

J. R. Mantey. "The Causal Use of **Eis** in the New Testament." *JBL* 70 (1951), 45–48.

J. R. Mantey. "Unusual Meanings for Prepositions in the Greek New Testament." *Exp* 25 (1923), 453–60.

R. Marcus. "On Causal **Eis**." *JBL* 70 (1951), 129f.

R. Marcus. "The **Elusive** Causal **Eis**." *JBL* 71 (1952), 43f.

H.-I. Marrou. *Geschichte der **Erziehung** im Klassischen Altertum*. Edited by R. Harder, translated by Ch. Beumann; Freiburg/München, 1957.

T. Martin. "The Present **Indicative** in the Eschatological Statements of 1 Peter 1:6, 8." *JBL* 111 (1992), 307–12.

G. Mayer. *Die jüdische Frau in der hellenistisch-römischen Antike*; Stuttgart et al., 1987.

D. J. McCarthy. "The Symbolism of Blood and Sacrifice." *JBL* 88 (1969), 166–76.

D. J. McCarthy. "Further Notes on the Symbolism of Blood and Sacrifice." *JBL* 92 (1973), 205–10.

J. D. McCaughey. "Three 'Persecution Documents' of the New Testament." *ABR* 17 (1969), 27–40.

R. Metzner. *Die **Rezeption** des Matthäusevangeliums im 1. Petrusbrief: Studien zum traditionsgeschichtlichen und theologischen Einfluß des 1. Evangeliums auf den 1. Petrusbrief*. WUNT II/74; Tübingen, 1995.

W. Michaelis. "πάσχω κτλ." ThWNT V; Stuttgart et al., 1966 (1954), 903–39.

H. Millauer. ***Leiden** als Gnade. Eine traditionsgeschichtliche Untersuchung zur Leidenstheologie des ersten Petrusbriefes*. EHS.T 56; Bern/Frankfurt, 1976.

J. Molthagen. "'**Cognitionibus** de Christianis interfui numquam.' Das Nichtwissen des Plinius und die Anfänge der Christenprozesse." *ZThG* 9 (2004), 112–40.

J. Molthagen. "Die **Lage** der Christen im römischen Reich nach dem 1. Petrusbrief: Zum Problem einer domitianischen Verfolgung." *Historia* 44 (1995), 422–58.

H.-P. Müller. "קדש." THAT II; Stuttgart et al., 1984³, 589–609.

W. Nauck. "**Freude** im Leiden. Zum Problem einer urchristlichen Verfolgungstradition." *ZNW* 46 (1955), 68–80.

W. Nauck. "Probleme des frühchristlichen Amtsverständnisses. I Ptr 5, 2f." *ZNW* 48 (1957), 200–20.

F. Neugebauer. "Zur **Deutung** und Bedeutung des 1. Petrusbriefes." *NTS* 26 (1980), 61–86.

C. T. Newton. *The Collection of Ancient Greek* ***Inscriptions*** *in the British Museum*, vol. IV, 1. London, 1893.

K. Niederwimmer. "**Kirche** als Diaspora." In W. Pratscher/M. Öhler (eds.). *Kurt Niederwimmer, Quaestiones theologicae: Gesammelte Aufsätze*. BZNW 90; Berlin/New York, 1998, 102–12.

H. Niehr, "שפט." ThWAT VIII; Stuttgart et al., 1995, 408–28.

F. Nietzsche. "**Menschliches**, Allzumenschliches I und II." In G. Colli/M. Montinari (eds.), *Friedrich Nietzsche, Sämtliche Werke. Kritische Studienausgabe*, vol. 2; München et al., 1980.

R. E. Nixon. "The Meaning of 'Baptism' in 1 Peter 3, 21." StEv 4, TU 102; Berlin 1968, 437–41.

A. Oepke. "καλύπτω κτλ." ThWNT III; Stuttgart, 1957 (1938), 558–97.

Th. P. Osborne. "Guide **Lines** for Christian Suffering: A Source–Critical and Theological Study of 1 Peter 2, 21-25." *Bib.* 64 (1983), 381–408.

H. Patsch. "Zum alttestamentlichen Hintergrund von Römer 4, 25 und I. Petrus 2, 24." *ZNW* 60 (1969), 273–79.

R. Perdelwitz. *Die* ***Mysterienreligion*** *und das Problem des 1. Petrusbriefes: Ein literarischer und religionsgeschichtlicher Versuch*; Gießen, 1911.

W. Pesch. "Zu Texten des Neuen Testamentes über das **Priestertum** der Getauften." In O. Böcher/K. Haacker (eds.) *Verborum Veritas. Festschrift.* G. Stählin; Wuppertal, 1970, 303–15.

E. Peterson. "**Christianus**." In E. Peterson, *Frühkirche, Judentum und Gnosis: Studien und Untersuchungen*; Rom et al., 1959, 64–87.

P. Pilhofer. *Presbyteron Kreitton: Der **Altersbeweis** der jüdischen und christlichen Apologeten und seine Vorgeschichte*. WUNT II/39; Tübingen, 1990.

P. Pokorný. *Der Brief des Paulus an die **Epheser***. ThHK 10/2; Leipzig, 1992.

W. Popkes. *Der Brief des **Jakobus***. ThHK 14; Leipzig, 2001.

B. Porten/A. Yardeni (eds.). *Textbook of Aramaic Documents from Ancient Egypt: Edited and translated into Hebrew and English*. Vol. 1: *Letters, Appendix: Aramaic Letters from the Bible*. Texts and Studies for Students; Winona Lake, 1986 (cited as: ***TAD***).

S. R. F. Price. ***Rituals** and Power: The Roman Imperial Cult in Asia Minor*; Cambridge, 2002 (1986).

P. Prigent. "I Pierre 2, 4–10." *RHPhR* 72 (1992), 53–60.

O. Proksch. "ἅγιος κτλ." ThWNT I; Stuttgart et al., 1957 (1933), 87–97.

F. R. Prostmeier. ***Handlungsmodelle** im ersten Petrusbrief*. FzB 63; Würzburg, 1990.

L. Radermacher. "Der erste **Petrusbrief** und Silvanus. Mit einem Nachwort in eigener Sache." *ZNW* 25 (1926), 287–99.

B. M. Rebrik. ***Geologie** und Bergbau in der Antike*; Leipzig, 1987.

A. Reichert. *Eine urchristliche **Praeparatio** ad Martyrium: Studien zur Komposition, Traditionsgeschichte und Theologie des 1. Petrusbriefes*. BET 22; Frankfurt et al., 1989.

B. Reicke. *The Disobedient **Spirits** and Christian Baptism. A Study of 1 Pet. III.19 and Its Context*. ASNU 13; Kopenhagen, 1946.

M. Reiser. "Die **Eschatologie** des 1. Petrusbriefs." In H.-J. Klauck (ed.). *Weltgericht und Weltvollendung: Zukunftsbilder im Neuen Testament*. QD 150; Freiburg et al., 1994, 164–81.

K. H. Rengstorf. "ἀποστέλλω κτλ." ThWNT I; Stuttgart et al., 1957 (1933), 397–448.

K. H. Rengstorf. "δοῦλος κτλ." ThWNT II; Stuttgart et al., 1935, 264–83.

J. Reumann. "'Stewards of God': Pre-Christian Religious Application of OIKONOMOS in Greek." *JBL* 77 (1958), 339–49.

E. T. Sander. ΠΥΡΩΣΙΣ *and the First Epistle of Peter 4:12*. Ph.D. Diss.; Harvard University, 1967.

D. Sänger. "Überlegungen zum Stichwort 'Diaspora' im Neuen Testament." *EvDia* 52 (1982), 76–88.

H. Schaefer. "Paroikoi." PRE, vol. 18/4; Stuttgart, 1949, 1695–1707.

P. Schäfer. "**Benediktionen** I. Judentum." TRE, vol. 5; Berlin/New York, 1980, 560–62.

P. Schäfer. ***Rivalität** zwischen Engeln und Menschen: Untersuchungen zur rabbinischen Engelvorstellung*. SJ 8; Berlin/New York, 1975.

W. Schäfke. "Frühchristlicher **Widerstand**." ANRW II/23/1; Berlin/New York, 1979, 460–723.

W. Schenk. *Der Segen im Neuen Testament: Eine begriffsanalytische Studie*. ThA 25; Berlin, 1967, 62–64.

H.-M. Schenke/K. M. Fischer. ***Einleitung** in die Schriften des Neuen Testaments* I: *Die Briefe des Paulus und Schriften des Paulinismus*; Berlin, 1978.

H. Schlier. "Die Kirche nach dem 1. Petrusbrief." In J. Feiner/M. Löhrer, *Mysterium Salutis: Grundriss heilsgeschichtlicher Dogmatik, das Heilsgeschehen in der Gemeinde* IV/1; Einsiedeln et al., 1972, 195–200.

J. Schlosser. "Animadversiones. 1 Pierre 3, 5b–6." Bib. 64 (1983), 409f.

E. G. Schmidt. "**Einführung**." In *Hesiod, Theogonie Werke und Tage. Griechisch-deutsch, herausgegeben, und übersetzt von A. v. Schirnding, mit einer Einführung und einem Register von E. G. Schmidt*; Düsseldorf/Zürich, 1997^{2}, 149–211.

K. M. Schmidt. ***Mahnung** und Erinnerung im Maskenspiel: Epistolographie, Rhetorik und Narrativik der pseudepigraphen Petrusbriefe*. HBS 38; Freiburg et al., 2003.

U. Schnelle. "**Taufe** II. Neues Testament." TRE, vol. 32; Berlin/New York, 2001, 663–74.

W. Schrage. *Die Christen und der* ***Staat*** *nach dem Neuen Testament*; Gütersloh, 1971.

G. Schrenk. "ἐκλέγομαι." ThWNT IV; Stuttgart et al., 1966 (1942), 173–97.

F. Schröger. "Ansätze zu den modernen Menschenrechtsforderungen im 1. Petrusbrief." In R. M. Hübner (ed.). *Der Dienst für den Menschen in Theologie und Verkündigung. Festschrift* A. Brems; Regensburg, 1981, 179–91.

F. Schröger. "Die **Verfassung** der Gemeinde des ersten Petrusbriefes." In J. Hainz (ed.). *Kirche im Werden: Studien zum Thema Amt und Gemeinde im Neuen Testament*; München et al., 1976, 239–52.

E. Schüssler Fiorenza. "Priester für Gott. Studien zum Herrschafts- und Priestermotiv in der Apokalypse." NTA 7; Münster, 1972, 51–59.

B. Schwank. "Wie Freie, aber als Sklaven Gottes (1 Petr 2, 16). Das Verhältnis der Christen zur Staatsmacht nach dem ersten Petrusbrief." *EuA* 36 (1960), 5–12.

E. Schwarz. ***Identität*** *durch Abgrenzung. Abgrenzungsprozesse in Israel im 2. vorchristlichen Jahrhundert und ihre traditionsgeschichtlichen Voraussetzungen, zugleich ein Beitrag zur Erforschung des Jubiläenbuches*. EHS.T 162; Frankfurt/Bern, 1982.

E. Schweizer. "σάρξ κτλ." ThWNT VII; Stuttgart et al., 1966 (1964), 118–151.

E. Schweizer. "πνεῦμα, πνευματικός." ThWNT VI; Stuttgart et al., 1965 (1959), 387–453.

E. Schweizer. "Die **Weltlichkeit** des Neuen Testaments. Die Haustafeln." In H. Donner et al. (eds.). *Beiträge zur alttestamentlichen Theologie. Festschrift* W. Zimmerli; Göttingen, 1977, 397–413.

E. Schweizer. "Zur **Christologie** des Ersten Petrusbriefs." In C. Breytenbach/H. Paulsen (eds.). *Anfänge der Christologie. Festschrift* F. Hahn; Göttingen, 1991, 369–82.

E. G. Selwyn. "The Persecutions in I Peter." In BSNTS 1; Oxford, 1950, 39–50.

D. Senior. "The **Conduct** of Christians in the World (2:11–3:12)." *RExp* 79 (1982), 427–38.

K. Seybold. "**Gericht** Gottes I. Altes Testament." TRE, vol. 12; Berlin/New York, 1984, 460–66.

A. N. Sherwin-White. *The Letters of **Pliny**: A Historical and Social Commentary*; Oxford, 1998 (1966).

F. Siegert. *Drei hellenistisch-jüdische **Predigten**: Ps.-Philon, "Über Jonah," "Über Simson" und "Über die Gottesbezeichnung 'wohltätig verzehrendes Feuer.'"* Vol. 1: *Übersetzung aus dem Armenischen und sprachliche Erläuterungen*. WUNT 20; Tübingen, 1980.

F. Siegert. *Drei hellenistisch-jüdische **Predigten**. Ps.-Philon, "Über Jonah", "Über Jonah" (Fragment) und "Über Simson."* Vol. 2: *Kommentar nebst Beobachtungen zur hellenistischen Vorgeschichte der Bibelhermeneutik*. WUNT 61; Tübingen, 1992.

P. W. Skehan/A. A. di Lella. *The Wisdom of Ben Sira: A New Translation with Notes by* P. W. Skehan. *Introduction and commentary by* A. A. di Lella; New York, 1987.

D. I. Sly. "1 Peter 3:6b in the Light of Philo and Josephus." *JBL* 110 (1991), 126–29.

S. Snyder. "1 Peter 2:17: A **Reconsideration.**" Filologia Neotestamentaria 4; Cordoba, 1991, 211–15.

W. Soltau. "Die **Einheitlichkeit** des 1. Petrusbriefes." *ThStKr* 78 (1905), 302–15.

H. Spieckermann. "Der theologische **Kosmos** des Psalters." *BThZ* 21 (2004), 61–74.

H. Spieckermann. "Die **Liebeserklärung** Gottes. Entwurf einer Theologie des Alten Testaments." In H. Spieckermann, *Gottes Liebe zu Israel. Studien zur Theologie des Alten Testaments*. FAT 33; Tübingen, 2004, 197–223.

F. Spitta. *Christi **Predigt** an die Geister, 1 Petr. 3, 19ff. Ein Beitrag zur neutestamentlichen Theologie*; Göttingen, 1890.

G. Stählin. "ξένος κτλ." ThWNT V; Stuttgart et al., 1966 (1954), 1–36.

G. Stählin. "φιλέω κτλ." ThWNT IX; Stuttgart et al., 1973, 112–69.

E. Stauffer. ***Christus** und die Caesaren. Historische Skizzen*; Hamburg, 1960[5].

G. Stemberger. "**Seele** III. Judentum." TRE, vol. 30; Berlin/New York, 1999, 740–44.

H.-L. Strack/P. Billerbeck. *Kommentar zum Neuen Testament aus Talmud und Midrasch*. Vol. 1: *Das Evangelium nach Matthäus*; München, 1956[2] (1926[1]) (cited as: [**Strack-]Billerbeck I**).

H.-L. Strack/P. Billerbeck. *Kommentar zum Neuen Testament aus Talmud und Midrasch*. Vol. 2: *Das Evangelium nach Markus: Lukas und Johannes, und die Apostelgeschichte*; München, 1969[5] (1924[1]) (cited as: [**Strack-]Billerbeck II**).

H.-L. Strack/P. Billerbeck. *Kommentar zum Neuen Testament aus Talmud und Midrasch*. Vol. 3: *Die Briefe des Neuen Testaments und die Offenbarung Johannis*; München, 1965[4] (1926[1]) (cited as: [**Strack-]Billerbeck III**).

H. Strathmann. Art. "μάρτυς κτλ." ThWNT IV; Stuttgart et al., 1966 (1942), 477–520.

A. Strobel. "Macht Leiden von Sünde frei? Zur Problematik von 1. Petr 4, 1f." *ThZ* 19 (1963), 412–25.

F. A. Strobel. "Zum **Verständnis** von Matt XXV 1–13." *NT* 2 (1958), 199–227.

P. Stuhlmacher. *Biblische **Theologie** des Neuen Testaments*. Vol. 2: *Von der Paulusschule bis zur Johannesoffenbarung*; Göttingen, 1999.

C. H. Talbert. "Once Again: The **Plan** of 1 Peter." In C. H. Talbert (ed.). *Perspectives on First Peter*. NABPR SS 9; Macon, 1986, 141–51.

G. Theißen/A. Merz. *Der historische **Jesus**. Ein Lehrbuch*; Göttingen, 1997[2].

G. Ueding. ***Einführung** in die Rhetorik. Geschichte, Technik, Methode*; Stuttgart, 1976.

W. C. van Unnik. "**Christianity** according to I Peter." *ET* 68 (1956/57), 79–83.

W. C. van Unnik. *Das **Selbstverständnis** der jüdischen Diaspora in der hellenistisch-römischen Zeit: Aus dem Nachlaß herausgegeben* *und bearbeitet von P. W. van der Horst*. AGJU 17; Leiden, 1993.

W. C. van Unnik. "'Diaspora' en 'Kerk' in de eerste eeuwen van het Christendom." In W. H. Beekenkamp (ed.). *Ecclesia: Een bundel opstellen. Festschrift* J. N. B. van den Brink; Nijhoff, 1959, 33–45.

W. C. van Unnik. "The Critique of Paganism in 1 Peter 1:18." In E. E. Ellis/M. Wilcox (eds.). *Neotestamentica et Semitica. Festschrift*. M. Black; Edinburgh, 1969, 129–42.

W. C. van Unnik. "The Teaching of Good Works." *NTS* 1 (1954/55), 92–110.

Ph. Vielhauer. *Geschichte der urchristlichen Literatur:* ***Einleitung*** *in das Neue Testament, die Apokryphen, und die Apostolischen Väter*; Berlin/New York, 1985[4].

Ph. Vielhauer. ***Oikodome****: Das Bild vom Bau in der christlichen Literatur vom Neuen Testament bis Clemens Alexandrinus*. Diss. theol.; Heidelberg, 1939.

F. Vittinghoff. "'**Christianus** sum': Das 'Verbrechen' von Außenseitern der römischen Gesellschaft." Historia 33 (1984) 331–57 (Reprinted in F. Vittinghoff, *Civitas Romana: Stadt und politisch-soziale Integration im Imperium Romanum der Kaiserzeit*. Edited by W. Eck; Stuttgart, 1994, 322–47).

A. Vögtle. *Die Tugend- und* ***Lasterkataloge*** *im Neuen Testament: Exegetisch, religions- und formgeschichtlich untersucht*. NTA 16/4–5; Münster, 1936.

P. Volz. *Die* ***Eschatologie*** *der jüdischen Gemeinde im neutestamentlichen Zeitalter: Nach den Quellen der rabbinischen, apokalyptischen und apokryphen Literatur*; Hildesheim, 1966 (Tübingen, 1934).

G. Walser. "Flüchtlinge und Exil im klassischen Altertum, vor allem in griechischer Zeit." In A. Mercier (ed.). *Der Flüchtling in der Weltgeschichte: Ein ungelöstes Problem der Menschheit*; Bern et al., 1974, 67–93.

K. Wengst. *Christologische* ***Formeln*** *und Lieder des Urchristentums*. StNT 7; Gütersloh, 1972.

J. N. D. White. "Love That Covers Sins." *Exp*. 1913–A (1913), 541–47.

R. L. Wilken. *The Christians as the Romans Saw Them*; New Haven/ London, 1984.

B. W. Winter. "The Public Honouring of Christian Benefactors. Romans 13.3-4 and 1 Peter 2.14-15." *JSNT* 34 (1988), 87–103.

A. Wlosok. "Die **Rechtsgrundlagen** der Christenverfolgungen der ersten zwei Jahrhunderte." In R. Klein (ed.). *Das frühe Christentum im römischen Staat*. WdF 267; Darmstadt, 1982[2] (1971[1]), 275–301.

A. Wlosok. ***Rom** und die Christen: Zur Auseinandersetzung zwischen Christentum und römischem Staat*. Der altsprachliche Unterricht, Beiheft 1 zu Reihe XIII; Stuttgart, 1970.

Ch. Wolff. "**Christ** und Welt im 1. Petrusbrief." *ThLZ* 100 (1975), 333–42.

Ch. Wolff. "In der **Nachfolge** des leidenden Christus: Exegetische Überlegungen zur Sklavenparänese I Petr 2, 18–25." In Ch. Maier et al. (eds.). *Exegese vor Ort. Festschrift* P. Welten; Leipzig, 2001, 427–39.

J. Woyke. *Die neutestamentlichen **Haustafeln**: Ein kritischer und konstruktiver Forschungsüberblick*. SBS 184; Stuttgart, 2000.

K. Wyß. *Die **Milch** im Kultus der Griechen und Römer*. RVV XV/2; Gießen, 1914.

Th. Zahn. ***Einleitung** in das Neue Testament*, vol. 2. Sammlung Theologischer Lehrbücher; Leipzig, 1924[3].

W. Zimmerli. *Das **Menschenbild** des Alten Testaments*. TEH NF 14; München, 1949.

Scripture Index

1. Canonical Scriptures: Old and New Testament

4. Pseudo-Hellenistic Authors

5. Jewish-Hellenistic Authors

6. Qumran (Dead Sea Scrolls)

7. Rabbinic Writings

8. Apostolic Fathers

9. Apocrypha (NT)

10. Literature of the Ancient Church

11. Pagan Authors